A Moment of Danger

A Moment of Danger

CRITICAL STUDIES IN THE HISTORY OF U.S. COMMUNICATION SINCE WORLD WAR II

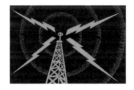

Edited by

Janice Peck & Inger L. Stole

MARQUETTE
UNIVERSITY

PRESS

DIEDERICH STUDIES IN MEDIA AND COMMUNICATION

NO. 2

BONNIE BRENNEN, SERIES EDITOR

© 2011 Marquette University Press
Milwaukee, Wisconsin 53201-3141
All rights reserved.
www.marquette.edu/mupress/

LIBRARY OF CONGRESS CATALOGING-IN-PUBLICATION DATA

A moment of danger : critical studies in the history of U.S. communication since
World War II / edited by Janice Peck & Inger L. Stole.
    p. cm. — (Diederich studies in media and communication ; no. 2)
Includes bibliographical references and index.
ISBN-13: 978-0-87462-034-4 (pbk. : alk. paper)
ISBN-10: 0-87462-034-1 (pbk. : alk. paper)
1. Communication—United States—History—20th century. 2. Mass media—
United States—History—20th century. 3. Mass media—Social aspects—United
States—History—20th century. I. Peck, Janice. II. Stole, Inger L.
P92.U5.M68 2011
302.23—dc23
                                                                    2011031461

♾The paper used in this publication meets the minimum requirements of the
American National Standard for Information Sciences—
Permanence of Paper for Printed Library Materials, ANSI Z39.48-1992.

MARQUETTE UNIVERSITY PRESS
MILWAUKEE

The Association of Jesuit University Presses

CONTENTS

ACKNOWLEDGEMENTS

We would like to thank first—and most—the contributors to this book for their patience with the process of putting together a collective project like this, their graciousness in responding to what may have seemed like our endless suggestions, requests and queries, the hard work they put into the research and writing found in these pages, and their commitment to the importance of connecting historical analysis and interpretation to contemporary social critique. We are also grateful to three University of Colorado graduate students—Brice Nixon, Rianne Subijanto, and, especially, Brooke Edge—who conscientiously, and with unfailing good cheer, assisted in the details of getting the manuscript ready for press, including tracking down citations, organizing files and copyediting chapters. We appreciate the University of Colorado's support of this project through an individual faculty growth grant. Thanks are also due to Bonnie Brennen, editor of the Diederich Studies in Communication and Media series, for her enthusiasm for this project from its inception, and to Andy Tallon, director of Marquette University Press, for his technical and editorial guidance and expertise. Finally, we want to acknowledge the contribution of graphic designer and editorial cartoonist Mark Hurwitt. The book's cover art and design are a reflection of Mark's collaborative spirit, aesthetic talent and political commitment.

Janice Peck
Inger L. Stole

CHAPTER I

INTRODUCTION

MOMENTS OF DANGER AND CHALLENGES TO THE "SELECTIVE TRADITION" IN U.S. COMMUNICATION HISTORY

Janice Peck

> To articulate the past historically does not mean to recognize it 'the way it really was.' It means to seize hold of a memory as it flashes up at a moment of danger. ... The danger affects both the content of the tradition and its receivers. The same threat hangs over both: that of becoming a tool of the ruling classes. In every era the attempt must be made anew to wrest tradition away from a conformism that is about to overpower it.
>
> —Walter Benjamin, Theses on the Philosophy of History, *Illuminations* (1968, 255)

INTRODUCING A COMPANION TO POST-1945 AMERICA, editors Jean-Christophe Agnew and Roy Rosenzweig point to a spectacular blossoming of historical research on post-World War II America (Agnew and Rosenzweig 2002). The study of communication history has enjoyed similar growth over the past two decades, becoming increasingly important in a wide range of fields from media studies to anthropology to literary studies, as scholars have come to recognize that media are "fundamental actors in the historical process and thus worthy of study in their own right" (Sparks 2007). This book contributes to both developments with a collection of critical studies that illustrate the central role media have played in American politics, economics, culture, and social life since the middle of the twentieth century. Specifically, the volume focuses on a period of U.S. history marked by a major political-economic shift that has been described as a passage from "long boom to long downturn" (Brenner 2006), from "Great Prosperity" to "Great Recession" (Reich 2010), and from "Keynesianism" to "neoliberalism" (Irvin 2008). The studies in this book situate specific moments of debate and struggle in U.S. media history within this larger political-economic sea change with the aim of shedding light on both developments.

Several critical works have confined the large-scale battles over and opposition to corporate media dominance in the U.S. to the first three decades of the twentieth century (e.g., McChesney 1993; Fones-Wolf 2006). It is certainly true that by the conclusion of World War II in 1945, commercial media interests in the U.S. had won some key regulatory battles as industry supporters looked toward the future with great optimism. From the late 1940s through the '50s, avenues of political and cultural dissent were ignored or actively suppressed in the context of Cold War foreign policy and domestic McCarthyism. The postwar economic boom, expansion of suburbia, proliferation of consumer goods, and introduction of television seemed to support assertions about the "end of ideology" and the dawn of a new age of political pluralism and cultural consensus (Bell 1960). However, as historian Robert Griffith reminds us, "If consensus did indeed characterize America's national culture in the 1950s it was perhaps to a degree we have not fully appreciated. It was perhaps a consensus manufactured by America's corporate leaders, packaged by the advertising industry, and merchandised through the channels of mass communication" (1983, 412).

Indeed, the long boom must be seen as both the basis of consensus and conformity in the 1950s and the wellspring of challenge and confrontation in the 1960s. Similarly, the "long downturn" has at once been attended by declarations that the "digital revolution" is ushering us into a world of "friction free capitalism" (Gates 1995) and triumphant liberal democracy (Fukuyama 1992), and by mass protests against neoliberal policies and campaigns against hyper-commercialization (Klein 2002) and corporate control of the means of communication (Lessig 2006; Foster and McChesney 2011).

It is within tensions like these that we might discover the seeds and catalysts of the "moments of danger" explored in the following chapters, which engage with instances from the mid-twentieth century to the present where the democratic promise of popular communication has collided with structural challenges inherent in a commercial media system. In the opening quote of this introduction, Walter Benjamin suggests that critical historical inquiry seeks to retrieve the meaning of the past—what he called "tradition"—from a "conformism" that ceaselessly threatens to "overpower it" (Benjamin 1968, 255). Cultural historian Raymond Williams was also attuned to struggles over the significance of the past and its relationship to the present. In particular, he paid keen attention to the process by which a "selective tradition" is "presented and usually successfully passed off as 'the tradition'" (1977, 115). Understood as "an intentionally selective version of a shaping past and a pre-shaped present," any selective tradition serves to ratify what is and to prescribe and limit the possibilities for what might be (ibid). This process is always dynamic and open-ended, however, because no selective tradition is ever total or final. As Williams observed, "forms of alternative or directly oppositional politics and culture exist as significant elements in the society" (113), exerting important pressures on what becomes the selective tradition in the first place and on how it evolves and changes through time.

As institutions located at the heart of social existence, the media are key players in this dynamic process of inclusion and exclusion, incorporation and resistance, and as such are prime sites and objects of critical historical examination. Through their role in the production, dissemination, and legitimization of a "selective tradition," media are also important targets for alternative and oppositional forces in society who strive to tell a different story about the past and to imagine a different social order in the future. Guided by Williams' perspective, this book examines key moments of media and cultural history in the period from World War II to the beginning of the twenty-first century with the goal of demonstrating the complex historical roots of our present media landscape, which is neither as natural nor as democratically derived as the media industries might have us believe.

The journey begins in the 1940s, as the "long boom" got underway. Emerging at the close of World War II and continuing through the early 1970s, the postwar boom was characterized by relatively "widely shared prosperity" (Reich 2010, 43) with high levels of economic growth and productivity, high employment, generous funding for public infrastructure and a social safety net, an energized labor force with a 35 percent unionization rate, and a progressive tax structure, all guided by Keynesian economic policy to steer the economy and cushion it from disruptive cycles of boom and bust. The first three chapters are set in the boom's early years, as citizens and workers challenged the economic structure, commercial priorities and institutional power of corporate media industries by taking on advertisers, broadcasters, and newspaper publishers. Inger L. Stole's "Politics as Patriotism: Advertising and Consumer Activism During World War II" (chapter 2) looks at how the advertising industry, having survived the powerful onslaught of an active consumers' movement in the 1930s, responded to wartime critics by creating the (War) Advertising Council, a group that did the industry's bidding and secured a prominent role for advertising in the postwar era.

Tensions between citizens and the broadcast industry are the focus of "The Revolt against Radio: Postwar Media Criticism and the Struggle for Broadcast Reform" (chapter 3), where Victor Pickard examines the backlash against commercial media by a broad sector of the American public. He explores the sources, range, and depth of grievances against the commercial radio system in the late '40s, assesses their impact and limitations, and considers the implications for contemporary media reform efforts. The rendezvous with the 1940s concludes with "'Our union is not for sale': The Postwar Struggle for Workplace Control in the American Newspaper Industry" (chapter 4) by James F. Tracy. In this first of several chapters in the book to address issues of labor and communication, the focus is on "the relationship between media workers and media institutions" seen through a confrontation between the International Typographers Union (ITU) and the American Newspaper Publishers Association (ANPA), and the latter's use of this labor/management conflict to advocate for the anti-labor Taft-Hartley Act. The chapter looks at how the publishers used their control of the press to shape public opinion on issues directly involving them—a perennial problem for those who challenge corporate media—and how the local labor community and independent media sought to counter that power with alternative representations of what was at stake in the strike.

Structural critiques of media institutions that were prominent in the 1940s had dissipated by the 1950s, as the potent combination of Cold War international relations and anti-communism at home narrowed the range of permitted political-economic critique. Struggles over and within media shifted to questions about who was fit to work in the culture industries and what they should be allowed to communicate.

Dinah Zeiger opens the volume's engagement with the period with
"'Things will never be the same around here': How *See It Now* Shaped
Television News Reporting" (chapter 5). Her study offers an alternative historical assessment of Edward R. Murrow's famous *See It Now*
program by focusing on the show's signature innovation in the form
of public affairs television—what Murrow called "the small story"—
which continues to dominate broadcast news narratives in the twenty-
first century. The "small story" responded to the prevailing social and
political conditions of postwar America, capitalized on TV's adaptation to the intimacies of family life, and marked the shift away from
collective responsibilities for social, economic, and political problems.
Carol A. Stabile's "'We can remember it for you wholesale': Lessons
from the Broadcast Blacklist" (chapter 6) approaches the Cold War
period from a different direction. Employing what she describes as a
"feminist recuperation," Stabile analyzes the lives and work of progressive women broadcast writers in the 1940s and 1950s and the orchestrated silencing of their voices during the blacklist era. The chapter
recovers examples of creative work in radio and television from the
period that reveal significant opposition to Cold War gender conservatism, exposing the misogyny implicit in the logic of the blacklist and
documenting these women's active resistance and challenge to the era's
narrow political and gender norms.

Edward Alwood continues the examination of the Cold War's impact on media content with "Foreign Correspondents, Passports and
McCarthyism" (chapter 7), looking at the implications of the U.S.
State Department's restrictions on travel by journalists during the Red
Scare of the late 1940s and 1950s. He shows how large commercial
media organizations, concerned about the effect on their bottom line,
refused to support and defend journalists targeted by anti-communism
campaigns. The final chapter to explore the '50s is Nathan Godfried's
"'Love That AFL-CIO': Organized Labor's Use of Television, 1950-
1970" (chapter 8), which looks at organized labor's early relationship
with the emerging medium of television. By situating unions' vision
of television in the context of Cold War and McCarthyism—which
facilitated and was used to help justify the purge of labor radicals that
took place during the AFL and CIO merger—Godfried explains why
labor activists held a rather pessimistic view of television as a site for
working-class challenges to the postwar political-economic order.

The next three chapters carry us through the 1960s into the mid 1970s, as the long boom approached its quarter century mark, the conformism of the '50s was receding into memory, and confrontation and challenge became increasingly common features of public and private life. In this context, structural critiques of media were back on the agenda, a trend reflected in the next set of essays, which deal with a campaign to create a public television system to offset the failings of commercial TV, a labor action against a powerful corporate newspaper chain, and the creation of an alternative news magazine in Chicago after the explosive 1968 Democratic National Convention. Laurie Ouellette tackles the subject of public broadcasting in "The Postwar 'TV Problem' and the Creation of Public Television in the U.S." (chapter 9). After extensive public criticism of commercial radio in the late 1940s, the U.S. commercial broadcasting system skated through the '50s with little structural scrutiny, thanks to broadcasters who had refined a strategy of casting the industry's critics as snobs who looked down on average Americans. Federal Communication Commission chair Newton Minow's 1961 "vast wasteland" critique of TV opened the door to calls for "better" television that gained support through the '60s and culminated in the creation of the Public Broadcasting System in 1969. In tracing this history, Ouellette shows how and why public television became an "oasis of the wasteland," instead of a popular democratic channel.

Bonnie Brennen's "Lockouts, Protests, and Scabs: A Critical Assessment of the *Los Angeles Herald Examiner* Strike" (chapter 10) returns to the issue of labor and corporate media—in this case with a focus on reporters and editors—with a study of the Los Angeles Newspaper Guild strike against the Hearst-owned *Herald Examiner*. The decade-long struggle (1967-77) between Guild members and publisher George R. Hearst illustrates news workers' strategies of resistance to media monopolization as well as the difficulties inherent in combating deep-pocketed corporate media, with their enormous advantage in shaping public opinion. In "The Reporters' Rebellion: The *Chicago Journalism Review*, 1968-1975" (chapter 11), Stephen Macek tells the story of a group of young Chicago reporters who, having witnessed the unprovoked police violence against anti-war demonstrators during the 1968 Democratic National Convention and the failure of the city's established newspapers to honestly cover the event, launched the *Chicago Journalism Review*—a monthly magazine whose goal was to "report on the news media and open up their internal processes to public scrutiny." Looking at how, in giving reporters more influence over editorial policy, the magazine ultimately helped effect changes in Chicago's establishment press, the chapter seeks to inform and inspire today's media workers and reform activists.

By the early 1970s, as the U.S. wrestled with mounting debt from the Vietnam War, competition from the recovered economies of Europe and Japan, and political challenges from Third World national liberation movements, the long boom was staggering to a halt. With the 1980 election of Ronald Reagan, a new political-economic model that would become known as neoliberalism was formulated as a response to those threats. That response entailed a restructuring of the economy—through de-industrialization, expansion of the service sector and shift of investment from goods to finance—and a revised role for government within the economy through tax cuts, de-regulation, privatization, and reduced spending on public infrastructure and social programs. This political-economic restructuring signaled the arrival of the long downturn, which continues to the present and which has brought a decline of organized labor, a return of dramatic financial crises and deeper recessions, the rise of a "two-tiered service economy" (low wage, low skill jobs vs. high wage, high tech careers), a dramatic upward redistribution of wealth, and increasingly inegalitarian society.

The U.S. media have not been immune to the sweeping political-economic changes wrought by neoliberalism, which economist Jeff Madrick (2002) has compared to a "social revolution." Since the 1980s, aided by deregulation policies that began under Reagan, continued under George H.W. Bush, and hit a high point under Bill Clinton with the 1996 Telecommunications Act, the trend toward media concentration, consolidation, and conglomeration has dramatically accelerated. At the same time, the ideal of public service within media—whether as an economic model or a professional principle—found itself increasingly under attack and in retreat (Tracey 1998; McChesney 1999). The next set of chapters leads us into the heart of the neoliberal order and its incorporation into media institutions, content, and practices. Beginning from the idea that a close examination of media texts and institutions can reveal the "defining characteristics, novelties, and conflicts" (Kellner 2003, 27) of the society in which they operate, Janice Peck's "Oprah Winfrey, Neoliberalism and the Politics of Race in the Late Twentieth Century America" (chapter

12) explores the idea that Winfrey, and with her, American society, have "transcended race"—and have thus vanquished racism and racial inequities. Situating Winfrey's ascent to cultural icon in the context of the bi-partisan embrace of neoliberalism and the rightward turn in politics over the last three decades, the chapter critically examines the redefinition of the "problem of race" that has enshrined the notion of the "underclass" and transformed issues of structural inequalities of class and race into individual moral failings and cultural pathologies.

In "Public Radio, *This American Life* and the Neoliberal Turn" (chapter 13), Jason Loviglio continues the exploration of the relationship of cultural forms and political-economic structural arrangements. In an analysis that situates *This American Life* within the last four decades of National Public Radio's history, Loviglio argues that the program has not only shaped the overall sound of public radio, but that it represents both the sound signature of neoliberalism and the preferred aesthetic of NPR's target audience—the professional managerial class. Deepa Kumar's "'Sticking it to the man': Neoliberalism, Corporate Media and Strategies of Resistance in the 21st Century" (chapter 14) approaches the intersection of neoliberalism, class and media from a different vantage point: the 1997 United Parcel Service strike in which the Teamsters union managed to gain public sympathy and support and thereby challenge and, for a time, destabilize the pro-corporate stance typically found in the commercial media. The chapter concludes by considering the implications of this case for the organized labor movement today in the context of the crisis of neoliberalism since the economic collapse of 2008.

The volume concludes with a pair of chapters that bring us to the present by engaging with the assumption that recent developments in communications technologies have created new avenues of individual expression, new means of critical communication, and new opportunities for resisting or transforming existing social arrangements and relations of power. In "Contesting Democratic Communications: The Case of Current TV" (chapter 15), James F. Hamilton interrogates the idea that user-generated content has ushered in a new age of public access and democratized media production. Instead, he proposes that such utopian claims need to be critically evaluated. Focusing on the cable-television and Internet company Current TV, Hamilton argues that the democratic potential of this and similar services always depends on how they deal, concretely, with the political-economic contradictions that made them possible in the first place. In the closing chapter, "Critical Media Literacy: Critiquing Corporate Media with Radical Production" (chapter 16), Bettina Fabos considers her experience teaching media production in the context of the development of a critical media awareness connected to the rise of new media from the 1990s to the present. The chapter proposes a pedagogical foundation for teaching critical media production to the digitally-immersed college student and suggests that such knowledge can be extended beyond the classroom, both to inform and transform media practices and to encourage and contribute to political awareness and action more broadly.

Historian Jean Cheneaux argues that history is "an active relationship to the past" in which the "past is present in every field of social experience" (Cheneaux 1978, 11). As this introduction is being written, efforts are mounting nationwide to further shrink government, eviscerate what's left of the public sector, neutralize the last significant sector of organized labor in the U.S., and undermine the remaining 25 percent of jobs that still provide a combination of pay and benefits that qualify them as "good jobs" (Schmitt 2007; Tavernise 2011). Public broadcasting—National Public Radio in particular—is under intense attack by a Republican-dominated Congress devoted to the idea that public service-based and publicly supported media are unnecessary when the market can better serve all of our communication needs (Jensen 2011). The Internet—once heralded as impervious to centralized control—is steadily being colonized by corporate interests (Foster and McChesney 2011). Public service journalism—and serious, high-end, labor intensive, and hence expensive, journalism in general—is being declared an endangered, if not dying, species. At the same time, throngs of citizens are filling the streets of Madison, Wisconsin and other cities around the U.S. to protest the assault on public sector employment and organized labor; alternative venues and sources of news and information are striving to counter the decontextualized infotainment favored by commercial media; and surveys demonstrating widespread dissatisfaction with and distrust of corporate media might be taken as signs of people's desire to be truly informed, rather than proof of their indifference toward knowledge (Public Accuracy Rating 2009; Dimiero 2011).

Walter Benjamin reminds us of the interdependence between historical and contemporary understanding: "For every image of the past that is not recognized by the present as one of its own concerns threatens to disappear irretrievably" (Benjamin 1968, 255). Rather than aiding us in that recognition, corporate media priorities and practices are more inclined toward narratives devoid of social and political context and historical grounding that prevent us from drawing a link between past and contemporary struggles against social and economic injustice. Every society, Cheneaux argues, experiences its past as both "*constraint and need*" in which "the past weighs on us and we strive to break its hold" (1978, 11). The contributors in this volume share Cheneaux's view of the dynamic relationship between past and present. United by a conviction that the study of media and communication must be situated within the whole of society, and a commitment to connecting historical analysis and interpretation to contemporary social critique, the works gathered here propose that delving into "moments of danger" in the history of communication and media provides a means by which to critically examine the intersection of American politics, economics, and culture over the past seven decades, and to help guide us in the present.

REFERENCES

Agnew, Jean-Christophe & Rosenzweig, Roy. 2002. *A Companion to Post-1945 America*. Malden, MA: Blackwell.

Bell, Daniel. 1960. *The End of Ideology*. Glencoe, IL: Free Press.

Benjamin, Walter. 1968. *Illuminations*. New York: Harcourt Brace Jovanovich.

Brenner, Robert. 2006. *The Economics of Global Turbulence*. London: Verso.

Cheneaux, Jean. 1978. *Pasts and Futures, or, What is History For?* London: Thames and Hudson.

Dimiero, Ben. 2011, January 19. "PPP: Public trust in Fox News is plummeting." *Mediamatters for America*. Accessed March 12, 2011. http://mediamatters.org/blog/201101190031.

Fones-Wolf, Elizabeth. 2006. *Waves of Opposition: Labor and the Struggle for Democratic Radio*. Champaign, IL: University of Illinois Press.

Foster, John Bellamy, and McChesney, Robert W. 2011, February. "The Internet's Unholy Marriage to Capitalism." *Monthly Review* 62 (No. 10). Accessed March 5, 2011. http://monthlyreview.org/110301foster-mcchesney.php.

Fukuyama, Francis. 1992. *The End of History and the Last Man*. New York: Free Press.

Gates, Bill. 1996. *The Road Ahead*. New York: Penguin Books.

Griffith, Robert. 1983. "The Selling of America: The Advertising Council and American Politics." *Business History Review*, LVII:1. 388-412.

Irvin, George. 2008. *Super Rich: The Rise of Inequality in Britain and the United States*. Cambridge: Polity Press.

Jensen, Elizabeth. 2011, February 27. "Public Broadcasting Faces New Threat in Federal Budget." *New York Times*. Accessed March 12, 2011. http://www.nytimes.com/2011/02/28/business/media/28cpb. html?scp=15&sq=national%20public%20radio&st=cse.

Kellner, Douglas. 2003. *Media Spectacle*. New York: Routledge.

Klein, Naomi. 2002. *No Logo*. London: Picador.

Lessig, Lawrence. 2006. *Code: and Other Laws of Cyberspace, Version 2.0*. New York: Basic Books.

Madrick, Jeffrey. 2002. *Why Economies Grow*. New York: Basic Books.

McChesney, Robert W. 1993. *Telecommunication, Mass Media and Democracy: The Battle for Control of U.S. Broadcasting, 1928-1935*. Oxford: Oxford University Press.

————. 1999. *Rich Media Poor Democracy*. Champaign, IL: University of Illinois Press.

"Press Accuracy Rating Hits Two Decade Low." 2009, September 15. Pew Research Center for the People and the Press. Accessed March 12, 2011. http://people-press.org/report/543/.

Reich, Robert. 2010. *Aftershock*. New York: Alfred A. Knopf.

"Save the Internet.com Coalition." N.d. http://www.savetheinternet.com/about. Accessed 3/1/2011.

Schmitt, John. 2005. *How Good Is the Economy at Creating Good Jobs?* Washington, DC: Center for Economic and Policy Research. Accessed August 28, 2007. http://www.cepr.net/documents/publications/labor_markets_2005_10.pdf.

Sparks, Colin. 2006. What is Media History? Call for Papers: *Westminster Papers in Communication and Culture*.

Tavernise, Sabrina. 2011, March 15. "Ohio Town Sees Public Job as Only Route to Middle Class." *New York Times*: p. A18, 22.

Tracey, Michael. 1998. *The Decline and Fall of Public Service Broadcasting*. Oxford: Oxford University Press.

Williams, Raymond. 1977. *Marxism and Literature*. Oxford: Oxford University Press.

CHAPTER 2

POLITICS AS PATRIOTISM

ADVERTISING & CONSUMER ACTIVISM
DURING WORLD WAR II

Inger L. Stole

ROM ITS HUMBLE START IN THE MID-NINETEENTH CEN-
TURY, national advertising has evolved into a massive enterprise. In 2007, the total amount spent on advertising in the
Unites States approached $280 billion with the average per-
son exposed to several thousands of commercial messages
every day. Ads now saturate every nook and cranny of our lived experiences, targeting individuals from the moment they are born. Our media system is drenched with advertisers hoping to further commercial-
ize the internet and turn the emerging social media into promotional
vehicles (McAllister 2010; Dwyer 2011; Linn 2004; McChesney and
Nichols 2010; McChesney 2004; Stole 2008; Thomas 2007).

Considering the premises of a democratic society, one might expect
this level of commercialization to rest on a strong public consensus and
that most Americans are happy with the status quo. This, however, is
not the case. Even studies conducted by the advertising industry find
a majority of the adult population objecting to the present advertising
and marketing levels, believing they are "out of control" (Elliot 2004).
More than half of the people polled in 2008 wanted to "eliminate all
advertising" and 72 percent found advertising "annoying" or "extremely
annoying," causing one business reporter to conclude that consumers
hated advertising (*Adweek* 2008).

Paralleling the increase in advertising has been a paradoxical decrease in legitimate discussion about advertising's exact function and
overall merit. Considering its status as a regulated industry, it is rather curious that advertising is never scrutinized and debated as other

major institutions are. And today, given the government's need for increased revenues, it is interesting that advertisers' right to write off promotional expenses as tax-deductible has not come under scrutiny. To the extent that advertising is analyzed, discussions tend to focus on its excesses (its ability to project a certain set of images and values) and not on its shortcomings and privileges. Although advertisers countenance certain forms of symbolic criticism of their methods, such as the "inappropriateness" or anticipated ill effects of a particular ad or campaign, they will rarely, if ever, encourage a dialogue about advertising's role in the economy or its power to influence cultural and social institutions.

Debates over advertising have not always been off-limits, however. During the 1930s, for example, the advertising industry was routinely challenged by consumer activists seeking federal regulation to restrict the dominant role of advertising in the United States. The decade witnessed the emergence of a surprisingly large and feisty consumer movement, led by the newly formed Consumers Union (CU), demanding systematic change and federal regulation of advertising in a manner that posed a threat to the corporate market system and its *modus operandi*. Unfortunately for consumer activists, the advertising industry launched a massive counter-attack which resulted in the business-friendly 1938 Wheeler-Lea Amendment to the Federal Trade Commission Act, a law that basically sanctioned industry practices while containing limited protection for the consuming public (McGovern 2006; Stole 2006; Cohen 2003; Glickman 2001, 2009).

Still, the most important battle over the role of advertising in the nation's political economy took place during World War II when a set of conditions indicated a lesser need for advertising, a fact that consumer advocates and other critics of advertising were quick to point out. The situation approached a real crisis for the advertising industry, particularly because it did not want to appear uncooperative in a time of national need. Fighting for its political life, the advertising industry created a public relations organization called the (War) Advertising Council (Fox 1975; Lykins 2003; Stole 2006; Henthorn 2006).

Supported by individual advertisers, advertising agencies, and the many media interests that depended on advertising for their survival, the council was to assist the government with its promotional needs. Implicitly, however, the council aimed at winning war-time concessions for advertising, currying beneficial relations with Washington officials, and elevating the public's view of advertising. This chapter discusses the planning and strategizing behind the Advertising Council and the industry's success in evading critics. Both were important parts of the ultimate goal of securing a political environment that was friendly to advertising in the postwar era and even beyond.

ADVERTISING AND THE WAR ECONOMY

For at least two years before the attack on Pearl Harbor in December 1941, war-related production required an increasing and disproportionate share of the nation's labor and raw materials. Production for the consumer market was constrained as a result, and concerns about inflation led the government to consider price controls. Advertisers worried that encouraging people to consume during a period when raw materials and consumer products were scarce and almost no new products were being launched might lend credence to the argument that advertising was wasteful, if not downright unpatriotic. The creation of two new government agencies for defense-related purposes, the Office of Product Management (OPM) and the Office of Price Administration and Civilian Supply (OPA), caused additional uneasiness. It soon turned out, however, that the business-friendly OPM posed few challenges, but that the OPA, which was created to control the civilian consumption of resources needed for defense, included top officials that members of the advertising community considered hostile to advertising because they viewed it as an impediment to efficient resource allocation during wartime. In the late summer of 1941, OPA director Leon Henderson confirmed the industry's suspicions by suggesting that manufacturers could offset the rising costs of raw materials and transportation due to war conditions by cutting their advertising expenditures. The industry was up in arms. "Rather suddenly it has dawned upon the advertising realm that Uncle Sam is doing a job of sniping at their business, which now looms as coordinated effort dictated from inner New Deal councils," stated the trade journal *Broadcasting*, wondering how a government that was "crowded to the eyebrows with war and defense activity" could find time to "attack" advertising (Fox 1975, 39; *Broadcasting* 1941).

By late 1940, the federal government's need for new revenues to finance national defense had become urgent; it was looking to raise an additional $3.5 billion (*Advertising & Selling* 1941; for a treatment of the advertising industry's fight against taxation during the war, see

Leff 1991; *Advertising Age* 1941a). The law that allowed businesses to deduct advertising expenditures from their income taxes had existed without interruption since World War I, and had spurred spending on advertising to far greater levels than would have been the case had it been taxed as an unnecessary business expense, as profit. Now, several politicians, including Senator Harry S. Truman (D-MO), suggested an end to tax-deductibility for business promotions, at least during the defense and possible war period, when, because of raw material shortages, limited products were available for the consumer market. If companies wanted to advertise, argued these politicians, they should pay for it out of their own pockets, and not (in effect) charge it to the financially strapped government as a tax-deductible expense (Barnouw 1968; Lasser 1940).

Naturally, the advertising industry viewed the situation differently, as did the nation's largest businesses and manufacturers. They approached the tax debate with two contrasting responses. In its public statements, the industry was cautious, if somewhat pedantic, not wishing to give the impression that its position could be construed as unpatriotic. It made its case by pointing to advertising's social utility, arguing that American manufacturers would be performing a far more patriotic function if their money were invested in advertising than if those funds were paid directly to the government in the form of taxes. Advertising, because it flowed through a series of taxable channels— advertising agencies, printing houses, lithographers, paper manufacturers, and the mass media—in fact boosted the government's tax revenues. Moreover, advertising contributed to increased production and higher employment, which ultimately translated into a broader tax base for the government (*Advertising Age* 1940a, 1940b; *Advertising & Selling* 1940a, 1940b).

If anything, the industry argued, the uncertain times had elevated the importance of advertising because it could guide consumers toward goods that did not compete with defense production for supplies and raw materials. As such, it was a necessary tool in the fight to prevent inflation. Advertising could increase business activity and employment and contribute to a healthy economy, the argument went, and would provide increased tax revenues that could be used to support defense expenditures. Taken all together, this new rationale for advertising sounded both plausible and upbeat (Hughes 1941;

Stevens 1941; Nichols 1941; *Advertising Age* 1941b; *Industrial Marketing* 1941).

THE (WAR) ADVERTISING COUNCIL

Getting on the good side of government was the highest priority for the advertising industry, especially with some key members of the Roosevelt administration appearing unsympathetic to their cause as the war was approaching. "Grave concerns about advertising and what may happen to the business which is largely dependent upon it is manifesting itself in many quarters," warned the president of the Association of National Advertisers (ANA), Paul West. He encouraged the industry to rethink its lobbying and PR strategies (Thomas 1952, n.p.).

In November 1941, a few weeks before the Japanese attack on Pearl Harbor, representatives for the advertising industry convened with sympathetic high-ranking members of the administration to discuss the new economic situation. The meeting produced the outlines of an industry-wide program to elevate perceptions of advertising and to educate people on its usefulness. Then, before the plan could be put into action, the United States found itself in the middle of a war. Within days of the fateful attack on Pearl Harbor, and to the advertising industry's surprise, Donald M. Nelson, then director of priorities in the government's OPA, approached the advertising community to request promotional assistance in spreading information about the upcoming home-front efforts (Bethune 1968).

From the industry's perspective, this was a heaven-sent opportunity to showcase the useful and patriotic sides of advertising and to improve its public image. Advertisers quickly envisioned themselves as builders of the nation's morale—all in a generous and selfless spirit, acting "primarily as a public information service." Expressing hope that the government would decide to "make full use of advertising in all its forms to accelerate accomplishment," the trade publication *Advertising Age* promised that advertisers were "ready and willing to do their share in behalf of the national war effort through promotion of defense bonds and stamps and other government activities in their advertisements and on their radio programs." A handful of key advertisers, ad agencies, and media representatives, moving at a breakneck pace in the weeks after the Pearl Harbor attack, formed the Advertising Council in January 1942 (*Advertising Age* 1941c, 1941d, 1941e, 1942f; Bethune 1968).

The creation of the council was not the first instance of industry cooperation with the government. During World War I, advertisers had constituted an important part of the Committee on Public Information and used the industry's resources to publicize the propaganda efforts of Woodrow Wilson's administration. However, whereas during World War I the government had been in charge of domestic war campaigns, World War II introduced the advertising industry as more of an equal partner, with the power to determine the merits of campaigns proposed by the government (Jackall and Hirota 1995). Washington and the industry were working in tandem as never before. Controlled by the industry, the Advertising Council became a quasi-governmental organization during the war. By 1943, it had changed its name to the War Advertising Council in an effort to better reflect its mission (Stole 2001).

The first step for government agencies in need of promotional assistance was to contact the Bureau of Campaigns, an agency created under the domestic branch of the Office of War Information (OWI). Once government approval had been obtained, the Advertising Council stepped in. If the council's board of directors agreed to the proposed campaign, they assigned to it one or more of the more than four hundred advertising agencies that had volunteered their services. The assigned agency then had the task of developing campaign plans in cooperation with a project director from the Advertising Council's paid staff and the government department that had requested the council's help. Preliminary plans, usually copy suggestions, layouts, and miscellaneous material, were developed and submitted to the board of the Advertising Council. Individual advertisers were then asked to incorporate the campaign material into their regular product advertising. As one advertising practitioner later explained, "The government is the client, OWI is the advertising department and the War Advertising Council is the advertising agency" (*Advertising Age* 1942b, 1942f; Jones 1976; Consumers Union 1943).

As 1942 came to an end, the council was actively involved in several major government campaigns. One large project addressed the food situation. The promotional material explained the government's agricultural goals and problems associated with farm labor shortages. Another campaign informed the public on nutrition-related issues, including the importance of starting "victory gardens" for the individual household table. A conservation campaign promoted the importance of carpooling, tire preservation, economical automobile driving, and conservation of gasoline (tires and gasoline, of course, were rationed), and a campaign under the U.S. Treasury Department's sponsorship urged everyone to invest at least 10 percent of their earnings in war bonds and stamps (*Broadcasting* 1942d). The food industries sponsored a national nutrition campaign under the slogan "U.S. Needs Us Strong. Eat Nutritional Food." In this manner, advertisers could combine their sales objectives with Council promotions. Typical was a Kraft cheese promotion where half of the two-page advertisement displayed a government nutrition table and the other half showed Kraft cheese in appetizing, nutrition-wise servings (*Advertising & Selling* 1942).

The working relationships between the Advertising Council and influential Washington officials facilitated familiarity and mutual respect. It was not long, for example, before President Roosevelt was praising the industry for its valuable assistance and "splendid spirit of cooperation," promising that advertising would have a "worthwhile and patriotic place in the nation's total war effort" (Stole 2001, n.p.). Other government agencies, including the Bureau of Foreign and Domestic Commerce, shared this sentiment and proclaimed that advertising was "indispensable to the functioning of free enterprise and the creation of a high standard of living" (*Advertising Age* 1942c; Larrabee 1942; see also *Advertising Age* 1942d).

Madison Avenue was particularly fortunate to have a strong supporter in treasury secretary Henry Morgenthau, Jr., who was one of the first government officials to seek help from the Advertising Council. By 1942, the Treasury Department was relying almost entirely on the council's help in promoting war bonds and stamps to the American public. The sale of these securities allowed the government to borrow money for the war effort from its citizens, relieving some of the pressure for new tax revenues. The importance of this connection was not lost on the Advertising Council, which addressed the bond promotion with great urgency. It designed an elaborate campaign plan and instructed individual advertisers to incorporate the war bond pleas into their product advertising. The Treasury came to realize that a new tax law prohibiting or severely restricting advertisers' ability to deduct advertising expenses from their income taxes would mean the end to much of their cooperation. The result would be far fewer venues for the Treasury's campaign.

This might have been a decisive factor behind the Treasury Department's final decision to side with advertisers in the debate over whether advertising should remain a tax-deductible business expense. The issue had a final hearing in 1942, after Congress had washed its hands of the matter. Morgenthau, emerging as a driving force, stated that his department and the Bureau of Internal Revenue (predecessor to the Internal Revenue Service) fully appreciated the importance of advertising to the national economy, and that reasonable and normal advertising would remain a deductible business expense. "The test of whether expenditures for advertising are deductible," he stated, "is whether they are ordinary and necessary and bear a reasonable relationship to the business activities in which the enterprise is engaged." Institutional advertising in reasonable amounts and goodwill advertising calculated to influence the buying habits of the public would still qualify for tax deductions (*Broadcasting* 1942c; Advertising Council 1943–44).[1] Advertising met these criteria so long as it was not carried to an "unreasonable extent" and did not constitute an obvious attempt to avoid tax payments. ANA president West was quick to congratulate the Treasury on "a fine understanding of the true functions of advertising and its place in business" (*Broadcasting* 1942b, 1942c; Printers' Ink 1942a; *Consumers Union Reports* 1943; for a celebratory trade-press account of Morgenthau's decision, see *Advertising Age* 1942a).

Partly because of the Advertising Council's work, Washington's view of advertising turned increasingly positive. Morgenthau remained one of Madison Avenue's most steadfast supporters throughout the war, routinely praising the industry for its patriotic contributions (Morgenthau 1943; *Advertising Age* 1943c; see also Consumers Union n.d.). This was where the council came to serve in yet another useful capacity; beyond paying off in the battle over tax-deductibility and polishing its public image, the working relationship between Madison Avenue and the government had created a collegial atmosphere and had helped to elevate the perception of advertising in the corridors of

---

1   Rather than tax advertising, the Treasury Department sought revenues from other sources. Part of the government's solution was to increase the tax paid by private citizens. This option, which many found grossly unfair, is well discussed in Leff 1991.

Washington (Stole 2001). It had finally been legitimated as a central and nonnegotiable institution and a mainstay of the political economy.

THE RETURN OF THE CONSUMER MOVEMENT

During the 1930s, a rapidly growing consumer movement had represented the advertising industry's greatest threat. The passage of the business-friendly Wheeler-Lea Act in 1938 had exhausted some of the critics' momentum. But for the consumer movement's most committed core, the war economy raised new and troubling questions about advertising's role and economic function. Leading the fight was Consumers Union and its president, Colston E. Warne, a prominent professor of economics at Amherst College who was determined to use the war conditions to press CU's case against advertising as a wasteful institution, antithetical to consumer and public interests. As powerful and sophisticated as the advertising industry was as a lobbying force, the consumer movement was weak and ineffectual, even bordering on inept. Its strength was in the power of its ideas, and the belief that those ideas would resonate with the vast majority of Americans if they were exposed to them—a concern the advertising industry had as well.

Warne was an outspoken critic of the Treasury Department's decision to allow advertising as a tax-deductible expense for business. Speaking to the seventh annual meeting of CU in 1943, he stressed the absurdity not only of allowing advertisers to waste raw materials in order to stimulate consumption when the opposite was desirable, but of giving them tax benefits to boot. Instead of providing advertisers with a break, he suggested an excise tax on advertising for the duration of the war and called on the OPA and individual advertising associations to discourage advertising of scarce goods and to scrutinize price ceilings to make sure that prices did not contain allowances for unnecessary advertising. He called for the public's help in protesting wasteful advertising (Morse 1993; *Consumers Union Reports* 1943).

In early 1943, Warne organized a group of more than two hundred educators from major U.S. colleges and universities in an effort to draw attention to the problematic use of wartime advertising. In a letter to Secretary Morgenthau, Director of Economic Stabilization James M. Byrnes, Chairman of the War Production Board Donald Nelson, and OPA head Leon Henderson, the group pilloried advertisers who exploited the war for personal gain. They particularly objected to some manufacturers' tendency to wrap their copy in patriotism for the sole purpose of selling consumer products and preserving their brand names for the postwar era (*Printers' Ink* 1943a). They acknowledged that advertising played an important part in the government's information campaign, and for this reason they did not advocate a ban on such practices. They asked, however, that the promotions be paid for directly by the government rather than associated with the private trade names of commercial companies. They also demanded that manufacturers' right to deduct advertising as a business-related expense be limited to promotional expenses in connection with their actual current output. This, they argued, would prevent the federal government, or rather the average taxpayer, from having to subsidize corporate America's public relations programs. (For a list of those who signed the letter, see *Printers' Ink* 1943b, 1943d; *Advertising & Selling* 1943a. Private citizens expressed similar concerns; see Tierney 1943.)

This may have been too fine a point when what was seen by the public and, especially, government officials was basically a lot of free advertising for government information campaigns, but for Warne and CU, this was not a theoretical or purely moral concern. Toward the end of 1943, the paper shortage grew worse, and consumer advocates were outraged when a Department of Commerce report showed that advertising in all media was 60 percent higher than it had been before the war (*Bread & Butter* 1943a, 1944). Much of the paper was being used to advertise products that not only added little to the war effort but, because they were in short supply, might actually increase the threat of inflation. For example, no fewer than 470 of the 576 columns in the November 28, 1943 issue of the *New York Sunday Times* were devoted to ads for handbags, compacts, gloves, lamps, ties, oriental rugs, mink coats, and expensive perfume. A few days later, and in spite of the fact that scotch and rye were practically unobtainable in the city at the time, the *New York Times* carried eleven liquor ads. As early as 1942, Warne had accused advertisers of largely disregarding the ongoing war effort and had proposed that they and the many publications they supported begin "tapering off advertising volume and expressing their patriotism with an appropriate silence in print accompanied by participation in useful war activity" (*Bread & Butter* 1943b; Warne 1942).

Warne also spoke widely on the subject although, ironically, much of the press coverage he received came in disparaging reports in the advertising trade press. He argued that in wartime, more than ever, advertisers should give people straightforward information about the utility of their products instead of focusing on their prestige, glamour, and useless attributes. According to his assessment, more than two-thirds of all commercial advertisers seemed to be ignoring the fact that America was fighting a war. Instead of converting to wartime needs, they were sticking to the same "buy now, bargain, stock-up appeals" they had always used. Given this fact, Warne confessed bewilderment about the advertising industry's claim that its contributions to the war effort were of such spectacular quality (*Advertising Age* 1942e, 1943a).

The advertising industry was not amused. *Business Week* went so far as to characterize Warne's proposals as a "design for socialization." "The really vital reason why every business should continue and if practicable increase its advertising during the war," it argued, "is to help preserve the framework of the American economy. That is what we are fighting for—at least, what most of us are fighting for. But the collectivists have other war aims." Opponents maintained that neither Warne nor the educators supporting him were qualified to speak with authority on the subject of advertising. George Burton Hotchkiss, a professor of marketing at New York University, attacked the group's arguments, arguing that they were based on a series of false assumptions. He lambasted Warne and his co-signers for being "pathetically grotesque" in their denunciation of advertising, and for not giving it sufficient credit for its patriotic contribution to the war effort. "The main question," he concluded in reframing the issue, "is whether the Government can do a better job of advertising than is being done by private concerns" (*Business Week* 1943a; Hotchkiss 1943).

The American Federation of Advertisers assured the advertising community that Warne's accusations were more reflective of CU's view than of educators in general (*Advertising Age* 1943b; see also Griffin 1943). Fearing a possible spread of such radical ideas, however, the federation decided to pour renewed energy and resources into educating the public about the functions of advertising in a war economy: "The emotionally prejudiced cannot be educated, but we can inform a large part of the general public so as to counteract the influence of irresponsible statements and appeals," the advertising organization stated (*New York Times* 1943a).

Some of the highly defensive attitude was traceable to the industry's insecurity about its chances in pulling through the war in a successful manner. Individual advertisers' inability to envision the overall plan and long term public relations benefits from cooperating with the Advertising Council was a constant worry among advertising leaders. Although there was consensus on strategic and tactical matters at the highest levels of the industry, individual businesses tended to be primarily concerned with their own near-term profitability. There was great incentive for advertisers to take care of themselves and let others carry the ball for the industry to satisfy the public and politicians, to be the proverbial "free rider." Although all advertisers were allowed to deduct their advertising expenses from their taxable income, half of them, according to one study, avoided any mention of the war whatsoever and stuck to regular product advertising. And only one-third of that group adhered to the guidelines prepared by the Advertising Council. The rest decided to design their war-related copy on their own or to leave out war-related references entirely. Even advertisers who chose to cooperate with the council demonstrated different levels of commitment to the cause. Only a few devoted their entire advertising copy to the war effort. Most simply tacked on a line about buying war bonds or the importance of planting victory gardens, and despite promising to provide facts and information to guide consumers, few actually did so (Fox 1975, 33; Morgenthau 1943; Warthon 1944). These actions could potentially detract from the council's objective and long term goals for the industry, a fact that industry defenders themselves were quick to point out. "Advertising's many outstanding contributions to the war effort are in danger of being nullified by the tasteless, unintelligent efforts of a few advertisers," warned the editor of the advertising-friendly trade journal *Printer's Ink*. "The bright glow" of advertising's achievements is being "dulled by the methods of a comparatively small group of unimaginative, unpatriotic men." He complained that some advertisers showed "a bull-headed cynicism utterly out of keeping with the times" by continuing to use "themes and tricks that were unpleasant enough in pre-war days" but downright outrageous during a war. "Others," he continued, "try to climb [on] the war-time bandwagon by using a war theme for products that are only remotely, if at all, related to our Victory effort. A few are still so unimaginative as to think that the public will believe that without their products the war might well be lost. To all these may be added the advertisers who insipidly congratulate themselves because they are doing no more and no less than what any other patriotic citizen should be doing. Advertising is running a grave risk of having the public turn on all because of the faults of a few" (Larrabee 1943). Not surprisingly, unlike consumer advocates in constant search for publicity, the Advertising Council was in no way eager to start a public debate over these issues.

THE CRUCIAL ROLE OF THE PRESS

Unlike the advertising industry which had ample opportunities to reach the public, media access was a central problem for the consumer movement. The movement's political project was in essence to generate popular support for the progressive New Dealers in power, to give them some leverage to pursue regulation of advertising against a powerful industry with broad support in the business sector. The hope was to reach that 59 percent of the population who favored increased regulation of advertising, as the advertising industry's own research concluded in 1940. CU, the main consumer organization, was relatively small and had few resources. With a wartime circulation of around 55,000, its *Consumer Reports* reached a limited audience; its war-time publication *Bread & Butter* attracted even fewer readers (Gallup 1940; Cohen 2003, 131). Thus it needed to generate coverage—ideally at least neutral, if not sympathetic—of the issue in the news media. Given that the nation was at war, it was arguably harder to make advertising regulation an issue than it otherwise would have been. That said, news reports on the subject were virtually nonexistent, and what few there were did not do a particularly good job of explaining the issues at stake. The problem was compounded by the lavish coverage that the advertising industry received, and people themselves were inundated with advertising promoting the industry's patriotic contributions to the war effort. This all but sealed the doom of the advertising reform proposals during the war.

Such press coverage was no surprise then, nor should it be in retrospect. The consumer movement had never had a friend in the commercial mass media, especially when it came to the topic of advertising. Most of its efforts, including its attempt to regulate advertising on the federal level during the 1930s, had not been given fair treatment in the mainstream press (Stole 2006). There existed little doubt about the reason for this: nearly all of the news media depended upon advertising for the lion's share of their revenues and profits. Journalists and editors were hardly encouraged to pursue stories critical to an industry of which the news media were, in effect, a key part. Whatever benefits the newly emerging professional journalism may have offered with respect to protecting editorial content from the influence of media owners and advertisers, they did not extend to providing for ample and balanced coverage of advertising policy debates in this period.

Radio was a regulated industry and adhered to different rules. Unlike print media, broadcasters received valuable monopoly licenses to scarce channels from the government at no charge. In exchange, they were expected to serve the public interest and provide a balanced presentation of the important issues of the day (McChesney 1993). Decisions as to what constituted an "important issue" were a matter of ongoing interpretation, and commercial broadcasters rarely deemed the consumer movement to fall in this category.

So while advertising was frequently praised on commercial radio—where advertisers actually produced most of the entertainment programming—the consumer movement only rarely was deemed to be in the public interest. One such occasion was when the Columbia Broadcasting System (CBS) allowed Colston Warne a thirteen-minute slot in December 1941 to "balance" an interview with the research director of the McCann-Erickson advertising agency, Dr. L. D. H. Weld. Unbeknownst to the listening audience, however, Warne was censored from mentioning specific advertisers (and likely CBS sponsors) who were involved in stipulations and cease-and-desist orders of the FTC. He nevertheless managed to make a case for his "10-point indictment of current advertising." The industry trade press shouted hosannas about CBS's willingness to provide Warne with this opportunity and offered it as "proof" of the industry's tolerance of opposing views. CBS did not invite Warne back, however, and there is no evidence that he received similar invitations from any other commercial broadcasters (*Broadcasting* 1942a; *Sales Management* 1942).

This lack of public exposure continued to be a great frustration for consumer advocates. Thus they were quite excited a few months later in 1942 when Warne was invited to debate Lee Brantly, the advertising director of the conservative Crowell-Collier Publishing Company—a firm with a long history of undermining consumer activism—about the merits of wartime advertising (Stole 2006, chap. 5). Sponsored by the American Economic Foundation, a weekly column called "Wake Up, America" was published in some four hundred newspapers, typically reaching six million readers. Opening the debate, Brantly argued for the importance of advertising during wartime. He stated that not only did advertising educate people about the war effort, but it also built morale and helped preserve the mechanisms of the American economy for the postwar era. "Talk of employing ads to build morale is sheer nonsense," countered Warne. "Hitler will never be defeated by whiskey ads, toothpaste ads, or even by noisy, patriotic affirmations of companies with nothing to sell. Manpower and materials are needed for total war, not for disguising advertising ballyhoo." Wartime advertising, according to Warne, was just an excuse for profit-laden companies to perpetuate their brand names while dodging excess profits taxes because the war had made it possible to sell most products "without a nickel's worth of advertising." Responding to Warne's attacks and his claim that advertising wasted valuable resources such as paper, chemicals, and transportation, Brantly contended that advertising was as essential to the war effort as "planes, tanks, and ships." This did not sit well with Warne. "Just turn our pond-heavy Sunday papers loose on Hitler," he taunted. "He will run before the pulchritudinous females, armed with cosmetics and girdles. Beat Hitler with three color ads saying 'forget-me-not.' Or, better still; loosen our pontifical radio announcers to do battle for company and country. Forget the cannon. Bring on the advertisers!" To the dismay of the consumer movement, only a handful of the newspapers that regularly carried "Wake Up, America" elected to publish the debate (*Consumers Union Reports* 1942a, 1942b).

Given the more or less one-sided portrayal of the issue of wartime advertising in the media, it should come as no surprise that the advertising industry could point to a series of polls that supported its conduct. A survey by the ANA on "Public Sentiment toward Wartime Advertising" in the summer of 1943, for example, concluded that 63 percent of the respondents thought that advertising had done a good job of explaining how rationing worked. Eighty-two percent praised advertising's job in selling war bonds, and 55 percent thought that advertising had done well in delineating America's objectives during the war. Eighty-four percent viewed advertising as an important contribution to the war effort. According to the ANA, the responses demonstrated "growing confidence in advertising for promoting the war effort" among the public (*Business Week* 1943b; *Printers' Ink* 1942b, 1943e; *Business Week* 1942). Most Americans, it seems safe to say, did not know that there was any alternative.

CONCLUSION

As World War II came to an end in 1945, the advertising industry found itself in an enviable position. Through its wartime services to the government, the Advertising Council had fulfilled an important public relations function for the industry. Its immediate objective had been to secure advertisers' right to advertise throughout the war, despite major shortages that logically suggested that advertising might stimulate demand, spur inflation, and prove counterproductive to the war effort. An important secondary goal had been that of securing the status of advertising as a tax-deductible business expense by defending its privileged wartime position, claiming that it was playing an indispensable patriotic role. Its unstated but overarching goal was to have the American public internalize a view of the advertising industry as a democratic institution that had been instrumental in winning the fight against the Axis Powers. The purpose of the Advertising Council, as Frank W. Fox argues, was to promote "the ad behind the ad," that is, to use advertising to sell not only products but also the institution of advertising itself, as well as the corporate system behind the products (Fox 1975, chap. 5).

During the 1,307 days of war, the Council had encouraged Americans to purchase more than 800 million war bonds and to plant 50 million victory gardens, as well as raising several million dollars for the Red Cross and the National War Fund Drives. It had also fought inflation, recruited military personnel, spread information about a wide variety of salvage campaigns, and enlisted workers for industrial warplants. All in all, the (War) Advertising Council had been involved in more than 150 different home-front campaigns and, by its own estimate, had contributed more than $1 billion in time, space, and talent toward the war effort (Young 1945).

Largely as a result of the council's relentless work, the advertising industry enjoyed improved relations with the public as the war faded from view. By war's end it had become almost self-evident in advertising circles that the benefits of its operation were such that the Advertising Council needed to be reconstituted as a permanent organization, and with an expanded mandate. By seeming to set its own self-interests aside for the common good, the industry hoped to expand upon the public relations gains it had achieved during the war. No longer directly affiliated with the government, the postwar council was free to chart its own course. Whereas its wartime campaigns had asked people to plant vegetables and purchase war bonds to express their patriotism, its postwar campaigns redefined the meaning of this noble sentiment. Patriotism was now pegged to the unconditional acceptance of "free enterprise," emphasizing the positive aspects of consumer capitalism while embracing vague and uncontroversial liberal values (Griffith 1983; McGinnis 1992; Lykins 2003). Efforts to position the advertising industry as a self-effacing pillar of society continue to this day, with long-running campaigns to raise funds for the United Negro College Fund, and to prevent crime, drunk driving, and domestic violence (Ad Council 2011).

Although the relationship between business, industry, and government leaders grew increasingly close after the war (Mills, 1956), it did not mean that advertising was no longer controversial. The postwar decades were rife with satire and criticism of the asininity of advertising, ranging from novels and films like *The Hucksters* and satire such as *Mad Magazine*, to exposés like Vance Packard's *The Hidden Persuaders*. What had changed, however, was the nature of the debate. While advertising could be lampooned, and specific ads or advertising practices criticized, its institutional role had become off-limits for fundamental debate. The caliber of criticism that had been routine before WWII was pushed to the distant margins of acceptable commentary. And whereas the war experience had provided clear evidence of the crucial role that commercial news media played in shaping journalism to promote their commercial interests at the expense of the public interest, this tendency intensified with increased advertising influence over the communications industries in the decades that followed. The ultimate triumph for the advertising industry in World War II was the enduring success in keeping advertising off-limits to fundamental debate in the years and decades to follow (Griffith 1983).

REFERENCES

Ad Council. 2011. "Historical Campaigns." Accessed on January 3, 2011 from http://www.adcouncil.org/default.aspx?id=61.

Advertising Age. 1940a. "More Advertising Will Take Sting Out of New Taxes." July 1, 23.

———. 1940b. "500 Advertisers Would Be Curbed under the Voorhis Bill." December 16, 48.

———. 1941a. "Sales Tax Gains Favor as Aid in Meeting Expenses." April 21, 6.

———. 1941b. "Looking Ahead to Peace." April 28, 12.

———. 1941c. "Advertising Council Serves to Coordinate War Activities." December 15, 24.

———. 1941d. "War Comes to America." December 15, 12.

———. 1941e. "Advertising for Uncle Sam." December 22, 12.

———. 1942a. "Morgenthau Clears the Air." June 8, 12.

———. 1942b. "260 Ad Agencies Volunteer Services for War Effort." June 15, 8.

———. 1942c. "President Roosevelt's Message." June 29, 12.

———. 1942d. "Anti-Advertising Fears Allayed by Government Steps." July 13, 1.

———. 1942e. "Consumer Union Has 'Victory Plan,'—at $4 a Year." August 31, 4.

———. 1942f. "Advertising Council Serves to Coordinate War Activities." December 21, 24.

———. 1943a. "Educator and Adman Debate Wartime Ad Ban." March 15, 38.

———. 1943b. "Finds Advertising Inseparable from Free Economy." March 22, 1.

———. 1943c. "Morgenthau to Address ANA War Conference." November 15, 36.

———. 1945a. "Grade Labeling Hurts Consumers, NPA Says." March 12, 1–2.

Advertising & Selling. 1940a. "Is It Patriotic to Save Taxes by Advertising?" November, 34.

———. 1940b. "A Statement by the Editors on Advertising and the New Tax Law." December, 29.

———. 1941. "Will Heavy Defense Taxes Cut Down Consumer Sales?" June, 17–18.

———. 1942. "The U.S. Nutrition Project." July, 17-18.

———. 1943a. "The Critic's Showdown." February, 114–15.

Advertising Council. 1943–44. "Excerpt from Renegotiation Manual." Ad Council Papers, Record Group 13/2/305, Box 4, Folder: Government Contracts 1943–1944. University of Illinois Archives, Urbana.

AdWeek. 2008. "You Can't Avoid Ad Avoidance." September 8, 16.

Barnouw, Erik. 1968. *A History of Broadcasting in the United States*. Vol. 2: *The Golden Web*. New York: Oxford University Press.

Bethune, Jack Malcolm. 1968. "A History of the Advertising Council, 1942–1967." M.A. thesis, University of Texas at Austin.

Bread & Butter. 1943a. "It Pays to Advertise." October 9, 3.

———. 1943b. "Advertising and Waste." December 11, 3.

———. 1944. "Wasting Paper and Money." April 8, 2.

Broadcasting. 1941. "Advertising under Fire." August 25, 34.

———. 1942a. "Advertising Flaws Outlined on CBS." January 5, 17.

———. 1942b. "Advertising Tax Status Draws Morgenthau, Henderson Views." June 1, 51.

———. 1942c. "Tax Rule Explains Advertising Status." August 31, 52.

———. 1942d. "Advertisers Mustered for War Campaign," November 16, 10.

Business Week. 1942. "Advertisers' War Effort." November 21, 92.

———. 1943a. "Design for Socialization." January 23, 79.

———. 1943b. "Advertising at Work." June 19, 96.

Cohen, Lizabeth. 2003. *A Consumer's Republic: The Politics of Mass Consumption in Postwar America*. New York: Vintage Press.

Consumers Union of U.S., 1943. "Meeting of Advertising Agencies Called by OWI and War Food Administration to Launch 'Food Fights for Freedom' Campaign." August 24. Colston Warne Papers, Box 63, Folder 1. Consumers Union Archives, Yonkers, N.Y.

———. n.d. "How Government Recognizes the Information Industry as an Essential Part of Our Free Enterprise System and a Powerful Force for Good in Wartime." Colston Warne Papers, Box 62, Folder 1. Consumers Union Archives, Yonkers, N.Y.

Consumers Union Reports. 1942a. "Advertising and the Public Interest." September, 227.

———. 1942b. "Our Mistake." October, 255.

———. 1943. "Wartime Advertising." July, 193.

Dwyer, Tim. 2011. "Net worth: Popular Social Networks as Colossal Marketing Machines." In *Propaganda and Public Persuasion in Liberal Democracies*, G. Sussman ed. New York: Peter Lang.

Elliot, Stuart. 2004. "A Study of Consumer Attitudes Reveals the Depth of the Challenge that the Agencies Face." *New York Times*, April 14, C8.

Fox, Frank W. 1975. *Madison Avenue Goes to War*. Provo, Utah: Brigham Young University Press.

Gallup, G. 1940. "An Analysis of the 'Study of Consumer Agitation.'" February 9. National Broadcasting Corporation Papers, Box 76, Folder 11. Wisconsin Center Historical Archives, State Historical Society of Wisconsin, Madison.

Glickman, Lawrence B. 2001. "The Strike in the Temple of Consumption: Consumer Activism and Twentieth-Century American Culture." *Journal of American History* 88 (June): 99–128.

———. 2009. *Buying Power: A History of Consumer Activism in America*. Chicago: University of Chicago Press.

Griffin, C. E. 1943. "A Dean Answers the Professors." *Advertising & Selling*, April, 34.

Griffith, Robert. 1983. "The Selling of America: The Advertising Council and American Politics, 1942–1960." *Business History Review* 57 (Autumn): 388.

Henthorn, Cynthia Lee. 2006. *From Submarines to Suburbs: Selling a Better America, 1939–1959*. Athens: Ohio University Press.

Hotchkiss, George Burton. 1943. "A Professor (*Who Didn't Sign*) Replies." *Printers' Ink*, February 19, 52, 54.

Hughes, Lawrence M. 1941. "Many Firms Launch Advertising Now to Build Tomorrow's Sales." *Sales Management*, November 1, 37.

Industrial Marketing. 1941. "You May Be out of a Job." September, 77.

Jackall, Robert, and Janice M. Hirota. 1995. "America's First Propaganda Ministry: The Committee on Public Information." In *Propaganda*, edited by Robert Jackall, 137–73. New York: NYU Press.

Jones, David Lloyd. 1976. *The U.S. Office of War Information and American Public Opinion during World War II*. State University of New York at Binghamton. Ph.D. dissertation,

Larrabee, C. B. 1942. "A Thing of Peace, Advertising Is Now Geared to Winning the War." *Printers' Ink*, July 10, 28.

———. 1943. "*A Challenge* to the Decent and Patriotic Elements in Advertising." *Printers' Ink*, April 23, 13.

Lasser, J. K. 1940. "Advertising and the New Tax Law." *Advertising & Selling*, November, 29.

Leff, Mark H. 1991. "The Politics of Sacrifice on the American Home Front in World War II." *Journal of American History* 77 (March): 1296–1318.

Linn, Susan. 2004. *Consuming Kids*.: *The Hostile Takeover of Childhood*. New York: New Press.

Lykins, Daniel L. 2003. *From Total War to Total Diplomacy: The Advertising Council and the Construction of the Cold War Consensus*. Westport CT: Praeger.

McAllister, Matt. 2010. "But Wait—There's More: Advertising, the Recession and the Future of Commercial Culture." *Popular Communication* (8) 3, 189-193.

McChesney, Robert W. 1993. *Telecommunications, Mass Media, and Democracy: The Battle for the Control of U.S. Broadcasting, 1928–1935*. New York: Oxford University Press.

McChesney, Robert W. 2004. *The Problem of the Media: U.S. Communication Politics in the Twenty-First Century*. New York: Monthly Review Press.

McChesney, Robert W. and John Nichols. 2010. *The Death and Life of American Journalism: The Media Revolution that Will Begin the World Again*. New York: Nation Books.

McGovern, Charles F. 2006. *Sold American: Consumption and Citizenship, 1890–1945*. Chapel Hill: University of North Carolina Press.

McGinnis, John Vianney. 1991. *The Advertising Council and the Cold War*. Syracuse University: Ph.D. dissertation, chapters 3-4.

Mills, C. Wright. 1956. *The Power Elite*. New York: Oxford University Press.

Morgenthau, Henry, Jr. 1943. "The Job Has Just Begun." *Advertising & Selling*, December, 60.

Morse, Richard L. D. 1993. *The Consumer Movement: Lectures by Colston E. Warne*. Manhattan, Kans.: Family Economics Trust.

New York Times. 1943a. "Advertising News and Notes." January 22, 34.

Nichols, G. A. 1941. "AAAA Sharpens Tools for Huge Defense Task." *Printers' Ink*, May 9, 25–26.

Printers' Ink. 1942a. "Advertising Expense and Corporate Income Tax Returns." September 4, 19.

———. 1942b. "Advertisers Take Stock of Themselves at A.N.A. Meeting." November 20, 16.

———. 1943a. "Text of Open Letter Urging Limitation of War-time Advertising." January 1, 16.

———. 1943b. "Now for the Names …" January 8, 52–53.

————. 1943d. "Gentlemen! Gentlemen! Professor Warne Has the Floor." January 29, 20.

————. 1943e. "ANA Finds Public Appreciates War Advertising." June 11, 24.

Sales Management. 1942. "CBS Gives Consumers Union Free Time to Attack Advertising." January 15, 47–48.

Stevens, Henry M. 1941. "New Horizons Now." *Printers' Ink*, December 19, 51–52.

Stole, Inger L. 2001. "The Salesmanship of Sacrifice: The Advertising Industry's Use of Public Relations during the Second World War." *Advertising and Society Review* 2. http:/muse.jhu.edu/journals/asr/v002/2.2stole.html.

————. 2006. *Advertising on Trial: Consumer Activism and Corporate Public Relations in the 1930s.* Urbana: University of Illinois Press.

————. 2008 "Philanthropy as Public Relations: A Critical Perspective on Cause Marketing." *International Journal of Communication*, Vol. 2, ijoc.org.

Thomas, Harold B. 1952. *The Background and Beginning of the Advertising Council.* Ad Council Papers, Record Group 13/2/203, Box 13, Folder: Background and Beginning of the Advertising Council (1952). University of Illinois Archives, Urbana.

Thomas, Susan Gregory. 2007. *Buy, Baby Buy: How Consumer Culture Manipulates Parents and Harms Young Minds.* New York: Houghton Mifflin Company.

Tierney, C. L. 1943. Letter to Franklin D. Roosevelt. January 17. Franklin D. Roosevelt Papers, The President's Official Files, Box 196, Folder: Advertising 1943. Franklin D. Roosevelt Library, Hyde Park, N.Y.

Warne, Colston E. 1942. "Advertising vs Aluminum." *Consumers Union Reports*, June, 167.

Warthon, Don. 1944. "The Story Back of the War Ads." *Advertising & Selling*, June, 146.

Young, James W. 1945. "1307 days." September 4, Ad Council papers, Record Group13/2/305, Box 6, Folder: War Advertising Council News Releases. University of Illinois Archives, Urbana.

CHAPTER 3

THE REVOLT AGAINST RADIO

POSTWAR MEDIA CRITICISM &
THE STRUGGLE FOR BROADCAST REFORM

Victor Pickard

FOLLOWING WORLD WAR II, THE UNITED STATES WIT-
NESSED a period of transition and transformation rivaled
by few others in its history.[1] This watershed moment saw
major institutions open up to reformist impulses, with both
national and geopolitical power relations in flux. Media
magnate Henry Luce dubbed it "The American Century" as the U.S.
emerged as a global leader, a status soon defined and legitimated by
the Cold War with the Soviet Union. It is easy to forget, however, that
a fleeting window of opportunity appeared before Cold War imperatives and red-scare hysteria firmly took hold—a moment when the
country was not yet in the thrall of far-right politics, and some still
believed New Deal aspirations could be further realized. This hope
was particularly true for the new medium of broadcasting, which saw
a wide array of constituencies organize against its corporate consolidation to advocate for a more democratic system.

The commercial broadcasting system in the 1940s was founded on
the 1934 Communications Act, which sanctioned commercial broadcasting at the expense of other alternatives (McChesney, 1993). Most
broadcasters viewed their primary role as that of selling receivers and
airtime to individual advertisers who would then use their rented
time-slot to develop programs and promote their product. Hence,
programs like "soap operas," the term given to radio serials after World

---

1   This chapter draws from Victor Pickard, "Media Democracy Deferred:
The Postwar Settlement for U.S. Communications, 1945-1949," Ph.D.
Dissertation, University of Illinois, Urbana-Champaign, 2008, 69-133.

War II, were "sponsored" by specific companies, giving them free reign to air numerous commercials. Despite relatively little documentation in existing scholarship, much evidence suggests that many listeners found this arrangement objectionable. The following chapter fleshes out the major strands of radio criticism aimed at commercial radio's excesses that peaked in the postwar years and drove a short-lived but vibrant broadcast reform movement. In so doing, it casts into stark relief both the contingencies of our current commercial media system, as well as promises for future reform.

This period in U.S. media history is a largely forgotten one. Although revisions are on the rise (e.g., Fones-Wolf, 2006), most official accounts depict Americans as largely satisfied with their radio by the 1940s (e.g., Baughman, 1992), and the conventional view sees this period as radio's "Golden Age." Recovering significant dissent and resistance underscores the crucial fact that the development of the American commercial media system was neither natural nor inevitable, but rather the direct result of suppressing many voices that agitated for granting a new medium its full democratic potential.

THE POSTWAR UPRISING
AGAINST COMMERCIAL RADIO

The years 1945-48 saw media criticism gather critical mass, providing the driving narratives for a vibrant media reform movement. Although a critical strain of intellectual commentary toward radio had existed since the early 1930s from the likes of James Rorty and Ring Lardner (Lenthall, 2002), a leap occurred in the 1940s in the vehemence and sheer number of critical voices. This criticism took shape across grassroots social movements, commentary from varied newspapers and opinion journals, as well as hundreds of letters from average listeners to editors, broadcasters, and the FCC. Dissident intellectuals provided further coherence by extending this critique into trenchant polemics embraced by social movement groups (Ernst, 1946; Siepmann, 1946; Konecky, 1946). Activists organized "listening councils" and letter-writing campaigns in communities across America. Popular criticism reached its greatest expression in left-leaning opinion magazines like *Harpers*, *New Republic*, *The Nation*, and *The Atlantic*, but also appeared in less likely places: general interest journals and specialized publications as diverse as the *Antioch Review*, the *Saturday Review of Literature*, and the *American Mercury*, as well as business journals like *Fortune* and *Business Week*, mainstream journals like *Reader's Digest* and *Time*, and trade journals like *Variety* and *Tide*. Moreover, this critique also manifested in popular culture in the form of novels and films, including the bestselling book and film "The Hucksters." In a year-end review, the *Times* reported, "The year of 1946 found radio subjected to more obverse and insistent criticism than the industry had experienced in the whole of its previous twenty-five years ..." (Gould, 1946). *Fortune* described this outpouring in 1946 as "The revolt against radio" (1947).

One historian of this period describes the uproar as "the first significant and widespread public debate in American history focused on the nexus of advertising, broadcasting, and the public interest" (Socolow, 283). This debate reflected a deep-seated disgust with commercial radio and spanned both radical and mainstream discourses, giving rise to policy reform efforts such as the FCC "Blue Book," which aimed to curb "excessive advertising" and mandate "public service responsibilities" (Pickard, 2011). One commentator marked the moment by claiming, "Criticism of radio is not new, but in 1946, as the industry enters its third decade richer, more powerful and more excruciatingly vulgar and meaningless than ever before, impatience has reached a higher peak of articulate disgust" (Young, 1946). By 1946, criticism seemed to have reached a pivotal threshold. An irate listener summarized the onslaught against broadcasters:

> "The Hucksters," the FCC's so-called "Blue Book," The N.Y. "PM's" campaign, Crosby, Gould et al critics, discussion on ABC's "Town Meeting" ... the adverse editorials and your own listeners' letters, has put your industry-spokesmen ... on the defensive, apologetically insisting that radio *does* operate *in the public interest*.

The listener asserted that "purely business considerations" create an "obviously intolerable limitation ... that definitely prevents American Radio becoming the *effective* instrument of *democracy* that our new national position of world leadership and the many other crucial postwar conditions *now* make imperative" (Miller, 1947).

Also in 1946, the *New York Times Magazine* ran a long article by the *Public Opinion Quarterly* editor lambasting broadcasters' "binge of commercialism." Encouraging listeners "to make their pressure felt" by forming "listeners' councils," the article concluded that "The program which advertisers believe will sell goods has become the god of the industry," resulting in "an extraordinary preponderance of mass entertainment ... especially during the good listening hours." Such low-quality programming, ignored the desires of "minority groups" like "farmers, labor union people, women; lovers not only of fine music but of serious drama and literature, listeners interested in science, in problems of health and social betterment, in international affairs, in the great issues before Congress" (Free, 1946). Others concurred. A Scripps Howard columnist argued that the effects of such commercialism rendered all radio "corny, strident, boresome, florid, inane, repetitive, irritating, offensive, moronic, adolescent, or nauseating" (Quoted in Fones-Wolf, 126-127). "Nobody can be found today who will deny that the radio commercial in its present form is the most offensive breach of good taste the Nation has ever seen," added a columnist writing for the adless newspaper PM (quoted in Konecky, 10).

Despite earlier excitement about this new medium, the sense that radio had failed was palpable. Near the 40th anniversary of his invention of the audion tube, Lee de Forest, considered "the father of radio," wrote a scathing letter to the NAB:

> What have you gentlemen done with my child? He was conceived as a potent instrumentality for culture, fine music, the uplifting of America's mass intelligence. You have debased the child... You have made him a laughing stock of intelligence... The occasional fine program is periodically smeared with impudent insistence to buy or try... Soap opera without end or sense floods each household daily. Murder mysteries rule the waves by night, and children are rendered psychopathic by your bedtime stories. This child of mine has been resolutely kept to the average intelligence of 13 years... as though you and your sponsors believe the majority of listeners have only moron minds. Nay, the curse of your commercials has grown consistently more cursed, year by year (Time, 1947).

Such powerful indictments against commercial radio in the 1940s were launched by a diverse range of voices. The staggering number of news articles, books, and activist pamphlets that burst forth in the postwar 1940s is difficult to synthesize, but media criticism fell generally into four categories: structural, ideological, commercial and racial critiques.[2] Understanding the nature of this criticism is to not only

---

2   Although space limitations preclude its discussion here, the racial critique is discussed in Victor Pickard (forthcoming), "'The Air Belongs to the People': The Rise and Fall of a Postwar Radio Reform Movement."

glimpse the intellectual arsenal of the 1940s media reform movement; it reminds us of a rich critical tradition that connects contemporary crises and opportunities with past conflicts. Correcting historical amnesia about forgotten struggles against the American commercial media system recovers resistance and corrects the historical record. It also sets the stage for remaking the system today.

STRUCTURAL CRITIQUE

Echoed across a broad canvas of journal articles and books, the structural critique saw commercial broadcasting as excessively profit-driven, monopolistic, and advertiser-controlled. Much of this criticism suggested that without immediate structural reform, American broadcasting's potential would be squandered. A piece in the *Antioch Review* phrased it dramatically: "These next few years of physical development are crucial for the salvation of broadcasting's soul." The article declared, "Only by facing realities and contemplating our vanishing freedoms can we be armed for the impending battle of the air" (Timber, 1946). Similarly, a two-part series published in the periodical *Forum* addressed the question "Why Broadcasting Has Failed." The four main failures of broadcasting in serving the public interest, according to the article, were low quality of entertainment; excessive commercialism and advertising; lack of local talent; and lack of public service programs. "To understand why," the article suggested, "one must understand something about the broadcasting business, which is a get-rich-quick-stay-rich-easy business." The article stressed that many listeners were unaware that broadcasting, as public property, was amenable to reform——"That the kilocycles on which stations broadcast are not the private preserve of those lucky few who got there first …" (Knepper, 1948, 7-8).

Broadcasters' lack of public service was a recurring theme: "The national advertisers whose broadcasts consume very nearly all the precious evening time of the principal networks are probably unfamiliar with [public interest] provisions… Their basic concern is to increase the sale of the breakfast foods, drugs, soaps and cigarettes they manufacture by extolling the virtues of their products in the course of broadcasts designed to attract mass audiences" (Ibid.). This critique dovetailed with growing concern that broadcast media were culpable in the public's misunderstandings of key issues. A much-discussed 1944 article in the *Times* by Hadley Cantril found that a shocking percentage of people were ill-informed about important foreign and domestic policy issues (1944, 9). "If we do not provide criteria of public service," cautioned a *New Republic* writer, "it is doubtful whether such yard-sticks will be established with respect to FM, television and facsimile broadcasting, the commercial application of which is bound to increase rapidly in the postwar period." This would be disastrous for democracy, because "Without such safeguards, these new and revolutionary methods of radio communication will do little more than compete with the comic strip and motion picture for the leisure time of a listening public already overwhelmed by a plethora of light entertainment." And, the article forewarned, "such a public cannot be expected to develop as an informed and thinking citizenry, without which a truly democratic government cannot survive" (Smith, 1944, 13).

IDEOLOGICAL CRITIQUE

Radio had reached a kind of ideological equilibrium during the war, in which progressive views were given unprecedented access to the airwaves. The *New Republic* went so far as to run an article in early 1945 titled "Is Radio Going Liberal?" (Corwin & Reitman). Indeed, FDR used broadcasting as his personal amplifier and Democrats, as the party in power, overall fared well in radio representations. One prominent radio researcher, after finding an imbalance, called for an "equal time" provision between Democrats and Republicans, though not for members of smaller parties like Communists and Socialists because "It is generally agreed that ours is a two-party system" (Kaltenborn, 1946).

As the 1940s progressed, however, ideological imbalance became a frequent lament among liberals. As early as November 1943 an *Atlantic Monthly* news analyst wrote that a premium on audience appeal "in turn puts a premium on sensationalism," and leads to a de facto conservative slant in broadcasting. "The serious news broadcaster ... finds himself under pressure from two quarters. On the one hand, he is tempted to play up the widest possible audience; on the other, he is tempted to slant his interpretation the way he thinks his sponsor might like it to go." Considering the trend of vanishing liberal viewpoints, he observed, "In recent months we have seen ... sponsors snap up the news programs with a conservative slant as they never snapped up the programs with a liberal slant." When a sponsor buys a news show, "he will tend, nine times out of ten, to prefer the kind of analyst who at least does no violence to the National Association of Manufacturers."

Noting the political economic landscape shifting away from the New Deal to the "big wartime profits of American industry," he suggested that not only were the sponsors "exerting more indirect pressure" but that the public and news broadcasters were "responding to that pressure." Commentators who reflect the "New Deal line," he maintained, "now find they get into trouble with their sponsors" (Howe, 1943).

The speed with which a purge of liberal, labor-friendly voices from radio occurred was stunning. A 1945 survey conducted by *Variety* indicated a relative balance between liberal and conservative commentators. However, this quickly changed in 1946–47. By one count, the four major radio networks eliminated two dozen left-leaning commentators in less than a two-year span (Barnouw, 1968, 241; *Broadcasting*, 1946, 22). The casualty list included liberal luminaries like William Shirer, Don Hollenbeck, Raymond Swing, John Vandercook, Don Goddard, Frank Kingdon, Robert St. John, and former NYC mayor Fiorello La Guardia. R.C. Davis's letter to the FCC was one of many decrying

> a very obvious trend among the big broadcasting companies to systematically suppress any and all information of domestic and foreign affairs that does not fit the strait-jacket on the thinking of the boards of directors of the advertisers. The latest——and probably not the last——victim of this crusade to kill free information is William Shirer, a commentator who believed that news is a public trust, not an advertiser's puff (1947).

The letter concluded: "We the people own the [airwaves] ... they are not the private preserve of huge corporations currently abusing their leased property." Similarly, noting how "pressure to 'tone down' news which is sympathetic to organized labor and to Russia has increased rapidly in the last few months," a *New Republic* article struck an alarmist note: "To protect our minds and their pocketbooks, networks are dropping liberal commentators from coast to coast." (Oliver, 1947, 12). Fones-Wolf writes that by early 1948, analysts like Edward R. Murrow and Eric Sevareid were barred by CBS from interpreting the news, and "the network airways had a decidedly conservative cast." Other than ABC's Elmer Davis, the "only commentators heard more than once a week on network prime time were the conservatives H.V. Kaltenborn, Earl Godwin, Fulton Lewis Jr., Henry J. Taylor, and Gabriel Heatter" (133).

An article in the *New Republic* titled "Thought Control—American Style" captured what many progressives were feeling by 1947: American broadcasting was increasingly hostile to not only liberal ideas but intelligent discourse in general as broadcasters replaced informative programming with cheaply-produced entertainment. Citing cases where outspoken liberals were dropped even when sponsors lined up to buy their airtime, the article claimed that "most removals" were decided "by the networks themselves," not the sponsors. Some observers saw "a concerted reactionary drive behind the purge of liberals from the air." Others saw at work "chiefly a wave of irresponsibility in the radio industry" that was interrupted only by wartime exigencies, afterward returning to "old-time commercialism of the most blatant sort." According to the article, "Whatever the main cause may be, the result adds up to the same thing, namely the increasing refusal of the networks to give adequate room to anything but stand-pat interpretation of the news" (Oliver, 13).

This purge did not go unnoticed by the public, media, and Congress, but the reactionary tide against all things left-of-center proved to be devastating for radio's liberals. Cold War imperatives provided cover for right-wing forces to drive progressives from the air. As a result, few issues suffered as much as labor. The *CIO News* referred to commercial radio as "moneyed masters" who let loose "their mechanized hounds of the press and radio ... after the American working people and their unions." (Quoted in Fones-Wolf, 2006b). One radical pamphleteer argued that "Big Business interests—the monopoly corporations, the old-system standard (AM) broadcasting giants, and the big-money publishers and newspaper owners ... have taken FM from labor and the people..." (Konecky, 1-2). One of many letters to the FCC expressed frustration with radio's anti-labor slant: "It is regrettable that a means of disseminating knowledge such as the radio should be utilized so exclusively for sheer advertising and propaganda purposes ..." The letter pleaded, "Let labor and capital both be heard equally. Only in this way can the uninformed public gain fair knowledge of the issues it must vote for and decide on" (Nations, 1946).

COMMERCIAL CRITIQUE

Focusing primarily on content, the commercial critique of radio held that American broadcasting typically provided low-quality, homogenized, unintelligent programming. Many critics discerned an underlying pattern: cheaply produced programming crafted to just barely pass the lowest quality threshold and still be acceptable to large audiences. Broadcasters typically employed established names instead of developing new creative talent. This held true especially with soap operas and other widely syndicated programs, giving rise to questions of indecency, loss of local programming, and homogenization. The most passionate indictment by far was aimed at excessive commercialism in the form of invasive on-air advertising, particularly the widely reviled "singing commercials" and "plug-uglies."

Poor Programming Quality

A recurring media critique focused on poor programming quality. For example, an article by the culture critic Gilbert Seldes lamented how societal imaginations of "the mass" were driven by "repetitive gestures on the producing end and passive enjoyment for the consumer." Given the commercial imperative of reaching the largest audience possible, Seldes argued that broadcasters' "first principle" was "Radio ought *never* to serve any interest except that of the mass" to the detriment of an "intellectual minority." The sole exceptions had been the "sustaining programs" provided when radio gave in to a "variety of pressures," proving that "society is not a monolithic mass: it is … pluralistic." "Where there is no mass," Seldes claimed, "there is no danger of a master." But broadcasters abandoned pluralism in favor of a more "established zone of interest." Thus, broadcasts of symphonies and powerful documentaries were becoming relics of the past. Seldes, urged broadcasters to consider America's pluralism, a richly diverse composite of "many large groups, many small ones, and individuals belonging to several major and several minor groups at the same time." He argued that "The purpose of entertainment is to make people listen to the commercial; when entertainment has reduced the listener to a passive, noncritical state, the announcer moves in with his clubs or machine guns or soothing syrup and finishes the job." Our "great entertainment industries," he warned, "are creating before our eyes a cultural *proletariat*: the intellectually disinherited, the emotional homeless, whose function is only to answer the telephone and say what program they are listening to." He concluded, "No matter what is said about program content, the commercial is sacred—it's the sponsor's private property" (1948).

Similarly, Lewis Gannett, book critic of the *New York Herald Tribune*, wrote in the *Atlantic* a "meditation" on the "hopelessly diseased state of the American radio public." After spending six months overseas, where he listened to the "sedate programs of the BBC," he returned to American broadcasting, and his "ears were horrified" to hear "enough laxative advertising to convince a visitor to this country … that the chief wartime occupation of the USA was performed in its W.C.'s." Gannett gathered that "we were a nation of sufferers from acid stomach, chronic headaches, inadequate elimination, and general physical incompetence." Indeed, "The only way to escape the constant oleaginous chatter on these topics," Gannett reckoned, "was to turn off the radio altogether." He pondered if, upon military personnel's return to the U.S., they would not be "plumb disgusted with radio commercials" (1945a). The outpouring of supportive letters caused Gannett to wonder, "Perhaps the radio commercials didn't express the basic metabolism of America after all." He urged that "if more of us stood up and shouted what we feel as we hear, night after night, the shoddy nastinesses of everyday radio commercials, the industry would listen" (1945b, 117).

The *New Republic* also linked poor program quality with structural characteristics of commercial broadcasting: "The radio has become increasingly a device to sell foods by any means fair or foul while the question of usefulness to the public is more and more neglected …" Thus, "As a result the amount of time available for non-commercial sustaining programs is down almost to the vanishing point; … either cancelled entirely or relegated to bad time when they have practically no listening audience …" The article concluded, the U.S. is "almost the only great nation on earth which permits the homes of its citizens to be invaded by vulgar and often false claims of private individuals and corporations seeking to make money" (1945).

These sentiments also registered in more mainstream media. The popular radio host Fred Allen presented an irreverent burlesque of commercial radio on his show, which gained major print media attention. "There was no mistaking the tune. With apologies to Gilbert & Sullivan, Fred Allen, radio's comic Pooh-bah, this week joined the growing ranks of the industry's flagellants with a withering burlesque: *The Radio Mikado…*," *Time* magazine reported in an article that opened with one of Allen's songs: "'You want to know who we are, We're the hucksters of radio … We're vice presidents and clerks, Confidentially, we're all jerks ….'" (1946).[3]

---

3   See also Alan Havig, "Critic From Within: Fred Allen Views Radio," *The Journal of Popular Culture* 12, no. 2 (1978), 328–340.

It was not just large papers and political weeklies that leveled bold media criticism in the mid 1940s. The *Evening Bulletin*, in Providence, Rhode Island, editorialized that "It is no compliment either to the American intelligence or to its character that these radio voices indulge in such unmitigated tripe, with the excuse (we hope) that this is what the people want ...." It asked: "Why do the radio people do these things? Can it be that as a nation we are as bad and as moronic as they would make us out to be? Are we the fantastic fools and they the stern and hard-headed realists? Are they really reflecting the mores of this great nation...?" (1944). A torrent of letters sent to the FCC, Congress, and radio networks reflected many of these criticisms. After breaking down the time allocated to commercials and vapid commentary of a typical broadcast, a concerned listener wrote: "Do not delude yourself, Mr. Reece, the American listening public is not getting what it wants on the radio—it is, on the contrary, taking unbelievable amounts of mental punishment which it is apparently powerless to prevent" (Ruff, 1946).

Disgust with Soap Operas

Many critics singled out daytime programming as the nadir of commercial logic. An exposé appeared in the March 1946 issue of *Fortune* with a devastating portrayal of the quintessential daytime program: the soap opera. With the caption "Manufactured at low cost, it pleases advertisers and flatters women," the article noted that "about 20 million women listen each day to the more than forty soap operas on the air." While "apologists" refer to them as "daytime serials or serial dramas," others "speak of them as soap operas, soapers, washboard weepers, and cliffhangers." And while defenders see soap operas as "good storytelling," critics reply that "at best it is tedious bilge and at worst it is stark, revolting morbidity." "The soap opera's foes usually end by denying that it is what the housewife wants," the article observed. "She wants something better, they say, and listens to soap opera only because she has been conditioned by years of trash."

Soap operas' benefits for advertisers were two-fold. First, they were "habit-forming" because "women would come back to the radio day after day to see what would happen." Second, they were "economical" because "money could be saved on talent" given that soap operas were "a fraction of the cost of a musical program having comparable appeal." Noting that soap operas were actually "an advertising agency production," the article described how "the agency acts as general manager or producer, and gets 15 percent of the gross cost for its work" by purchasing "a serial as a 'package' from a writer or, more commonly, hires the writer, actors, organist, director, and announcer, and supervises the whole affair." Thus, a network's role could be limited to approving scripts and keeping one person in the control room. "The serial story itself," the article observed, "is mere bait to persuade the housewife to listen to the commercial announcement." These commercials typically ran over three minutes within 15-minute daytime programs, often receiving more attention and resources than the programs themselves, "delivered by well-paid announcers, men at once chatty and orotund, confidential and pontifical, sweet and portentous." The article observed, "A few commercials are even purposely irritating because of an advertising theory that certain kinds of exacerbation have sales value" (Ibid.).

Examining formulaic plot constructions, the *Fortune* article emphasized how broadcasters did not simply give people what they wanted: "working people almost never appear," and if politicians are introduced as characters, "their political views are foggy, if stated at all." Women are typically presented in these dramas as virtuous, subservient to men but commanding a "homely wisdom" that men depend on. The article cited data suggesting that women did not love soap operas but "only listen because they can find nothing better to listen to." [4] Based on content analyses of daytime programming across all networks, the article concluded that "the level of day-time radio is abysmally low, primarily because advertisers aim at the lowest common denominator." Noting that "radio has profited hugely by using the people's air," it conceded that "improvements must in all probability be made without altering the structure of American radio." [5] The article concluded: "Something ought to be done about this excessively shabby art, but not much is likely to be done very quickly unless the people insist—or

4   The article cited Department of Agriculture findings that half of all rural women listened to serials, but only a quarter liked them. Another quarter disliked them intensely, and the remaining half had no strong opinion. ABC in 1943 found that 36% of women surveyed thought there were too many serials. Even among serial listeners, 28% thought there were too many.

5   It proposed creating a public fund like those available to the board of education to pay for musical and educational programs sponsored by local boards.

the networks belatedly recall—that the air belongs to the people and ought to be used for their benefit" (Ibid.).

Echoing this critique were numerous complaints to the FCC about daytime radio fare, including its disservice to women. One self-described "house wife" wrote to Commissioner Durr that after illness left her bedridden and subjected to daytime programs whose quality was "abysmally low," she was compelled to campaign for better radio. She urged Durr, "Please keep up the fight. If it means government control better that than [advertiser] control" (Ragsdale, 1946). In addition to soap operas, a nursing magazine editor was upset about the lack of children's fare. Noting how "awful" she and other housewives found soap operas, she asked "Why isn't there anything available for the two to five year olds, especially in the morning hours? The youngsters aren't buyers, but their mothers are. And how grateful we'd be if some of the soap opera time would go into programs for our youngsters!" She continued, "not only is the great bulk of women capable of absorbing better stuff than they're getting, but that they would welcome programs that would enable them to grasp world affairs better—and thus hold their own in the family dinner discussions" (Geister, 1946).[6]

Disgust with Advertising

Many critics feared advertising's effects on radio content. Noting that most radio advertising came from a select group of agencies connected to automobiles, drugs and cosmetics, processed food, and tobacco, media critic Morris Ernst lambasted advertisers' undue influence, citing NBC president Niles Trammel's infamous remarks before Congress in December 1943: "The argument is now advanced that business control of broadcasting operations has nothing to do with program control. This is to forget that 'He who controls the pocketbook controls the man.' Business control means complete control and there is no use arguing to the contrary" (159-160). Jack Gould, the *Times* radio critic, wrote of similar consequences. "The fact remains," Gould contended, "that the whole course of network broadcasting in recent years has drifted more and more toward control by the advertiser rather than by the chains themselves." "As a result," Gould argued, "the emphasis has been primarily on the commercially 'safe' and 'selling' aspect of radio's

---

6   See also Jennifer Wang, "The Case of the Radio-active Housewife: Relocating Radio in the Age of Television," *Radio reader: Essays in the Cultural History of Radio,"* 343-366.

function. Since the advertiser understandably is primarily concerned with putting over an idea or a product, he is most wont to devote undue thought to the concurrent problems of over-all sound programming and taste." Gould argued that advertisers' control over media degrades everyone involved—from media producers to the audience. He concluded that such conditions would remain until "the networks reassert their own independence and decide to call the tune rather than dance to another's." Gould suggested that although the "broadcaster often has argued that it is not his function to 'reform' the public taste … it certainly is the broadcaster's responsibility not to lower it" (1945).

Other data from this period bear out the widespread disgust felt toward advertising. The Committee on Consumer Relations in Advertising reported that nearly 75 percent of people polled felt that radio advertising was worse than any other type (Knepper, 9). *Variety* magazine noted that commercial interests had begun to aggressively air political message points, including the "telephone hour" show having "taken up the cudgels against pending legislation for expansion of rural telephone service" (1945a). An article in the *Saturday Review* noted that "[Radio's] endless bombardment of the nation's ear—with stimuli whose chief aim is to sell the goods and occasionally the ideas of sponsors—takes seemingly little thought of public responsibility" (Wecter, 1946). That radio was selling ideas as well as goods draws attention to sponsors' promotion of an ideology as well as products—an ideology that privileged private enterprise over the public good.[7]

Opposition to "Singing Commercials" and "Plug-Uglies"

In 1942 a *Reader's Digest* article titled "Radio's Plug-Uglies" presented its 7 million recipients with embarrassing transcripts from typical radio advertisements about bodily functions and hygiene products. The article apparently tapped into a wellspring of anger, eliciting 80,000 letters from listeners disgusted with various forms of advertising (Siepmann, 33). In response to the growing offensiveness of these "plug-uglies" (a phrase referring to a political gang or group of thugs), a group of fed-up NYC listeners formed the Plug Shrinkers Club to campaign for the cessation of these offensive commercials (Reader's Digest, 1942). Marjorie Kelly described the phenomenon in the *Washington Post* in 1943

---

7   Fones-Wolf and others demonstrate how business interests waged an all-out public relations war to elevate their ideology to the level of a guiding national narrative.

as "Those 'terrible commercials'" that "continue to be a favorite American gripe." Kelly wrote, "Despite the anguished howls of thousands of listeners, the earnest attempts of forward-looking broadcasters to keep commercials inoffensive, and the efforts of advertising agencies to sell sponsors on the idea that short, listenable commercials can be effective, a vast number of plug-uglies remain on the air, infuriating the public and undermining respect for American radio." Listeners responded with comments like "'They're too long, they're repetitious, they're silly and an insult to our intelligence.'" Also annoying were the "cowcatchers," the designation for preceding plugs for a sponsor's minor products before a radio program, and "hitchhikers," which referred to a plug for a second product by the shows' sponsor after promoting the featured product. Media reformer and scholar Charles Siepmann noted that such "new language has had to be invented to keep apace with [advertisers'] enterprising innovations" (1946, 135-136).

Beginning in January 1945, the *St. Louis Post-Dispatch* garnered much national attention for a months-long campaign in a series of editorials and articles advocating for an end to interruptive plug-uglies and other offensive radio commercials. One article likened the campaign to "earlier crusades to keep the public domain from being cluttered by the excesses of American publicity" when "a painted sign recommending 'St. Jacob's Oil' on the rocks at Niagara Falls in 1860 led the New York legislature to pass the first law restricting outdoor advertising" (Wecter, 1946). On February 17, 1945, under the title "Radio Chains Don't Want Reform," the *Post-Dispatch* informed readers of the big four networks' advertising policies in a report that spanned several columns: "The *Post-Dispatch* editorial campaign against radio's commercial 'plug-uglies' in newscasts advised the networks … [to eliminate] interrupting plugs and objectionable sponsorship in news broadcasts." These included "remedies for kidney trouble, body odors, hangovers and the like.…" As to "Middle commercials" that "interrupt recitation or comment on the news in dead center to permit an effusive description of the sponsor's product," the networks see "nothing reprehensible in the practice." "A related nuisance," the *Post-Dispatch* continued, "is the 'self-announcer' newscaster who springs from a news report to commercial blurb, frequently tricking the listener's attention." Despite minor improvements, "the practice of using the same voice for news and commercial persists" (1945b).

The *Post-Dispatch* campaign gained wide national attention and led to some concrete outcomes.[8] Nonetheless, although some individual stations voluntarily complied, the networks largely ignored the campaigns, despite endorsements from print media like the *Times* and the *New Republic*—and even the pro-industry *Broadcasting*. Responding to a *Times* article that urged networks "to put aside the indiscretions of youth," the *Post-Dispatch* opined, "The truth is that the networks ought long ago to have reached maturity. Their income now is higher than ever, and they can well afford to reject news commercials which annoy the public" (1945c).

Eighteen days after first launching the campaign, the *Post-Dispatch* reported widespread support from leading radio newscasters who detested the "hideous" practice of interrupting newscasts, especially when reporting on important issues such as war-related news. The article claimed support from FCC Commissioner Wakefield as well as leading advertisers, with du Pont's advertising director quoted as saying "I am sure something must be done by the industry or will be done for it." Implying governmental intervention, the article stated that "Broadcasters should remember the White-Wheeler bill; they criticized it angrily enough when it appeared in the Senate Interstate Commerce Committee last spring. This measure would have forbidden *all* advertising in newscasts. The bill is dormant but not dead" (1945a).

The *Times*'s Jack Gould joined the growing chorus, describing the *Post-Dispatch* campaign as "an editorial campaign against two of the most prevalent evils in connection with the presentation of news on the radio. They are the interruption of news broadcasts with a commercial spiel and the sponsorship of such programs by 'objectionable advertisers.'" Gould wrote that the *Post-Dispatch* believed "the public is entitled to hear its news, particularly war news which may vitally involve loved ones, without being forced to listen to a plug for a product." According to Gould, the public's reaction to the *Post-Dispatch*'s "thesis" had been "immediate and virtually 100 percent favorable." He wrote that "Listeners, commentators and a few of the more thoughtful advertisers have voiced their full support," but industry had done

---

8   Announcing an end to all middle commercials, one station manager informed the *Post-Dispatch*'s editor that the editorials raised awareness of plug-uglies. "You are to be congratulated .... Radio stations certainly have been derelict in not improving newscasts..." Paul Bartlett, *Post-Dispatch*, February 20th, 1945.

little more than "finger-pointing," although some had "professed to be uneasy about" the state of their industry (1945).

General manager Ralph Smith of the ad agency Duane Jones, which was airing over 2,000 weekly commercials, defended radio advertising in the *Times* (Time, 1945). Without a trace of irony, Smith explained the class politics behind commercials: "Persons who complain about commercials are as a rule disgustingly healthy or so strongly fortified financially that grocery bills are no problem." According to Smith, "commercials are not written for such as these. Commercials are written as a form of service to persons who hope to cut budgets or find new methods and products of personal value." Smith claimed that except for the "critical minority who are either professional or amateur objectors," people enjoy commercials and benefit immensely from information contained within them. "People listen to radio commercials by choice, regardless of where they are placed in the program," he claimed. Implying that a handful of killjoys were trying to prevent average listeners who "love to look at the ads in the papers and hear the ads on the radio" from enjoying their simple pleasures, Smith ended with an appeal to American principles: "Freedom of speech is one of the Four Freedoms Americans are fighting for!" (1945). Few people were convinced. An article in *Time* magazine mocked "Adman Smith's" efforts: "just take a moment and look around your home for the various items that have made your life easier, happier. ... Dozens and dozens of these things, you'll find, were recommended to you over your radio. ... So today, let's tip our hats to radio's forgotten man—the radio advertiser" (1945).

Harlow Shapley channeled the public's disgust toward plug-uglies and singing commercials in a Harvard address that excoriated broadcasters for their "propaganda against government regulation" and for employing the "totally false use of a trite slogan—freedom of speech ... to ask the government not to try to protect us." Instead, broadcasters should worry less about government control and "worry about the much more dangerous control by national advertisers and by a few advertising agencies." Shapley exhorted his fellow intellectuals and scientists to oppose the vast resources of the advertisers and their allies across various powerful industries with "a budget of good will towards American culture in the post war world. You may even help to preserve higher standards for FM," especially from "that current vulgar inanity—the singing commercial" (1944a).

Shapley's critique resonated widely. A *Times* editorial opined: "Life in America does threaten to become pretty sad if something is not done soon about those commercial jingles which drive Professor Shapley crazy with millions of others." Responding to the firestorm, NBC president Niles Trammel offered Shapley an opportunity to express his "reactions to certain phases of the broadcasting enterprise." Shapley happily complied by describing a recent experience of "listening with immense appreciation" to the composer Toscanini and the "superb NBC orchestra" as if "communicants in a majestic ethereal cathedral":

> And then suddenly ... a revolting, leering vulgarian defecated in the altar before us all, desecrating the cathedral, destroying the ecstasy of the communicants, defaming the symphony and the artists... Before we could defend ourselves, a squalling, dissonant, hasty singing commercial burst in on the mood. The impostor used the same medium of music used by the high priest Toscanini. The vast audience would have been quite willing at that time to hear General Motors tell of further concert plans, or even tell with dignity suitable to the occasion about the products of General Motors. ... But what we got was a hideous jingle about soap; and we could not protect ourselves. The great art had been prostituted in the interests of immediate cash return to the broadcasting industry and its commercial patron (1944b).

Shapley widely distributed copies of his letter, including to NBC advisory board members. Building upon the "record of the fight of the timid public against the bold advertising monopolies," he forwarded his exchanges with industry representatives to FCC Commissioner Durr (1944c). Durr commended Shapley's "one-man crusade" but reminded him of advertising's larger systemic problems that exceeded one particularly annoying quality. Nonetheless, he welcomed that "Listeners are ... beginning to ask embarrassing questions" and felt "hopeful" that public pressure could eventually achieve "a pretty good system of broadcasting" (1944). That same week, *Business Week* reported "Radio listeners may take hope that the epidemic of singing commercial which began with the Pepsi-Cola's 'Nickel, nickel, nickel, nickel'... is finally running its course" (1944).

MEDIA REFORM DEFERRED

Alas, even if commercial radio may have eventually relented on some of its more egregious practices, radio ads did not disappear. While "plug uglies" may no longer terrorize the airwaves, even the most casual listener today will note that crass commercialism remains undeterred. Some anecdotal evidence suggests that broadcasters were somewhat chastened by postwar media reform efforts (Ehrlich, 2008); however, by and large, commercial radio emerged from the 1940s further inoculated against structural interventions.

What went wrong? Despite having the potential to connect with a critical mass of support, popular media criticism often failed to make the crucial move from the "symptomatic" (discussing the excesses of commercial radio) to the "structural" (discussing its underlying causes). Part of this trend can be attributed to the purge of those activists and critics most prone to such structural criticism; namely, radical leftists who were mercilessly redbaited within cultural industries as well as many social movements. In addition to fueling the communist hysteria that discredited progressive state regulation and helped demobilize reform movements, mass media institutions themselves often helped tamp down criticism of commercial radio by failing to cover it. Morris Ernst noted, "The greatest single asset of the networks in their drive for continued monopoly of thought lies in the ignorance of the public ... perpetuated by the failure of the networks to allow any debate or discussion [on media ownership and advertising]" (159-160).

In this context, progressive policy initiatives like the FCC's Blue Book were negated or deeply compromised (Pickard, 2010). With the spectacular defeat of progressive regulation, commentary on the state of radio continued to be noticeably anguished. However, as attention increasingly shifted to television, and many of the more strident progressive and radical voices were red-baited and blacklisted into silence, much of the more hard-hitting postwar radio criticism dissipated. Nonetheless, this criticism provides a window into the depth and breadth of opposition against commercial radio during its presumably "golden age." Indeed, that its failings were the subject of primetime radio burlesques and the focus of print media—ranging from small-town newspapers to national dailies and political weeklies—should call into question received notions about commercial radio's popularity and acceptance. Varying intensities of media criticism have continued to the present day, driving media reform activism like the microradio movement as well as recent campaigns for a new public media system.

What this history also shows us is that alternative visions of a public service-oriented media system were deferred for another, more opportune moment. The American broadcasting system we have inherited today could only emerge by ignoring the discontent toward commercial radio of significant swathes of the listening public. While scholars are beginning to recognize this pivotal moment, more research is needed. As we recover this history, we call into question the very legitimacy of the current media system. Critical historical work that denaturalizes commercial media by showing how its ascent resulted from subverting the public interest is a first crucial step toward reforming this system.

BIBLIOGRAPHY[9]

Barnouw, Erik. 1968. *The Golden Web: A History of Broadcasting in the United States*. New York: Oxford University Press.

Broadcasting, 1946. "'Crusade' against liberals seen by three left-wing groups." 31, 26 (December 30), 22.

Baughman, James 1992. *The Republic of Mass Culture: Journalism, Filmmaking, and Broadcasting in America since 1941*. Baltimore, MA: John Hopkins.

Business Week. 1944. December 2.

Cantril, Hadley 1944. "What We Don't Know Is Likely to Hurt Us" *New York Times*, May 14.

Corwin, Emil & Alan Reitman, 1945. "Is Radio Going Liberal?," *New Republic*, February 12, 218-220.

Davis, R.C. 1947. Letter to the FCC, April 22.FCC papers. Office of Exec. Director, Gen Correspondence 1947-56, Box 53.

Durr, Clifford. 1944. Letter to Shapley, December 7, DP, Box 30, Folder 2.

Ehrlich, Matthew. 2008."Radio Utopia: Promoting Public Interest in a 1940s Radio Documentary." *Journalism Studies*, 9, 6, 859–873.

Ernst, Morris. 1946. *First Freedom*, New York: Macmillan.

Evening Bulletin. 1944. June 27.

Fortune. 1946. "Soap Opera," 33, 1 (March), 119-129.

———. 1947. "The Revolt Against Radio," 35, 102 (March).

Fones-Wolf, Elizabeth. 2006a. *Waves of Opposition: Labor, Business, and the Struggle for Democratic Radio*. Urbana: University of Illinois Press.

---

9 "DP" refers to the Clifford Durr collection located in the state archives in Alabama, Montgomery.

————. 2006b. "Defending Listeners' Rights: Labour and Media Reform in Postwar America," *Canadian Journal of Communication* 31, 3, 499–518.

Free, Lloyd. 1946, "What Can Be Done to Improve Radio?," *New York Times Magazine*, August 25- 9, 50, 52.

Gannett, Lewis. 1945a. "Feeling Tired?," *The Atlantic* (August) 115–117.

————. 1945b. *This Week Magazine*, February 28.

Geister, Janet.1946. Letter to Cliffor Durr, June 30, DP, Box 30, Folder 6.

Gould, Jack. 1945. "Plug-Uglies," *New York Times*.

————. 1946. "Backward Glance," *New York Times*, December 29, 9.

Howe, Quincy. 1943. "Policing the Commentator: A News Analysis," *Atlantic Monthly*, November.

Kaltenborn, Rolf. 1946. "Is Radio Politically Impartial?" *The American Mercury* LXII, 270 (June), 665-669.

Kelly, Marjorie. 1943. *Washington Post*, October 31.

Knepper, Max. "Why Broadcasting Has Failed" *Forum* CIX, 1 (January 1948) 7-10.

————. "Why Broadcasting Has Failed—II." *Forum* CIX, 2 (February 1948): 79-82.

Konecky, Eugene. 1946. *Monopoly Steals FM From the People.*

Lenthall, Bruce. 2002. "Critical Reception: Public intellectuals decry Depression-era radio, mass culture, and modern America," *Radio Reader*, 343-366.

McChesney, Robert, 1993. *Telecommunications, Mass Media & Democracy: The Battle for the Control of U.S. Broadcasting, 1928-1935.* New York: Oxford University Press.

Miller, Fred. 1947. Letter to MBS, Jan 20, DP, Box 31, Folder 2.

Nations, C. 1946, Jan. 6. FCC Papers. Office of Exec. Director, Gen Correspondence 1927-46, Box 60, National Archives.

New Republic, 1945. February 26.

Oliver, Bryce, 1947. "Thought Control—American Style," *New Republic*, January 13, 13.

Pickard, Victor. 2010. "Reopening the Postwar Settlement for U.S. Media: The Origins and Implications of the Social Contract between Media, the State, and the Polity." *Communication, Culture & Critique* 3, 2, 170-189.

————. 2011. "The Battle of the FCC Blue Book: Determining the Role of Broadcast Media in a Democratic Society, 1945-1949," *Media, Culture & Society* 33, 2, 171–191.

————. (Forthcoming). "'The Air Belongs to the People': The Rise and Fall of a Postwar Radio Reform Movement"

Ragsdale, Belle. 1946. Letter to Durr. June 27. DP, Box 30, Folder 6.

Reader's Digest, 1942. "Radio's Plug-Uglies" August.

Ruff, A.S. 1946. Letter to Congressman B. Carroll Reece, May 18, DP, Box 30, Folder 6.

Seldes, Gilbert. 1948. "How Dense is the Mass?" *Atlantic Monthly*. 182, 5 (Nov): 23-27.

Shapley, Harlow. 1944a. National Wartime Conference Address, NYC, June 2.

————. 1944b. Letter to Trammel, August 29, DP, Box 30, Folder 1.

————. 1944c. Letter to Durr, Sept. 9, and Nov. 24, DP, Box 30, Folder 2.

Siepmann, Charles. 1946. *Radio's Second Chance* (Boston: Little, Brown & Co).

Smith, Ralph. 1945. "An Agency Speaks," *New York Times*, March 11.

Smith, Bernard. 1944. "The People's Stake in Radio," *New Republic*, July 13.

Socolow, Michael. 2002. "Questioning Advertising's Influence Over American Radio: The Blue Book Controversy of 1945-1947." *Journal of Radio Studies* 9: 292-302.

St. Louis Post-Dispatch, 1945a. "The Revolt against Radio Plug Uglies," February 5.

————. 1945b. "Radio Chains Don't Want Reform," February 17.

————. 1945c. "Networks Trail the Parade," February 20.

Timberg, Eleanor. 1946. "The Mythology of Broadcasting," *Antioch Review*, 354-355.

Time. 1945. "Plug for Plugs," March 19.

————. 1946. A Bah! from the Pooh-bah," Oct. 21, 66.

————. 1947. "Radio: Debased Child," Feb. 10.

Variety. 1945a. July 25.

————. 1945b. September 5.

Wecter, Dixon. 1946. "The Public Domain of the Air," *The Saturday Review of Literature*, IXIX, 20, May 18, 5.

Young, Vernon 1946. "The Big Noise of the Hucksters," *Arizona Quarterly*, 5-12.

CHAPTER 4

"OUR UNION IS NOT FOR SALE"

THE POSTWAR STRUGGLE FOR WORKPLACE
CONTROL IN THE AMERICAN NEWSPAPER INDUSTRY

James F. Tracy

I N 1947 A HANDFUL OF THE INDUSTRY'S MAJOR NEWSPAPER
OWNERS moved to challenge blue-collar newsworkers in an
effort to set an industry-wide precedent on workplace rights,
employing the federal Taft-Hartley Act to do so. How the
event was represented to the public became a critical factor for
both labor and management. Similar to the practices of commercial
American mass media today, where work-related phenomena are either overlooked or misrepresented, most of the news outlets reporting
on this event routinely distorted their coverage and commentary. This
was compounded by the fact that the workers were struggling against
some of the country's most powerful newspaper publishers.

Newspaper strikes have usually been described through the eyes of
the publishers (Folkerts and Teeter 1998, 481; Smiley 1984, 228-236;
Wendt 1979, 680-682;). Yet when one examines the strike from the
perspectives of the newsworkers an entirely different story unfolds.
This chapter takes the less orthodox approach of relying primarily on
documents generated by the independent media outlets that were controlled or favorable toward the striking workers and their supporters.
These are contrasted with the interpretation of events in the Chicago
press. Although at the time the labor union movement in Chicago and
throughout the United States was at its height, public opinion toward
workers was still to a large degree shaped by the commercial press.
The striking workers thus fought an uphill struggle for public support
against an avalanche of propaganda. From the strike's start the Chicago labor community and independent media outlets overwhelmingly

resolved to support Chicago's printers against a powerful propaganda campaign waged by Chicago's newspapers.

THE "TYPOS" AND THEIR UNION CULTURE

In the 1940s, workers employed in the commercial newspaper industry were represented by one of several national labor unions. These unions were distinguished by workers' specific roles in the production process—journalists, typographers, press operators, deliverers, and so on. The International Typographical Union (ITU) represented "printers" (typographers, or "typos")—printing room staff that set, cast, and proofread metal type—and it was the oldest union in the newspaper and book publishing industries. Though comparatively much smaller to unions in other industries, the ITU was also among the most powerful unions of its size in the U.S., with "the most complete control of job conditions of any union in the world" (Lipset, Trow and Coleman 1956, 24; Perlman and Taft 1955, 51).

The ITU's strength derived mainly from its "closed shop" workplace policy. In contrast to an "open shop," where union membership was not a prerequisite to employment, union and non-union members worked alongside each other, and management in turn exercised much more power, the closed shop required that all printing room workers be union members. In turn, the union handled various responsibilities that employers usually control today, such as proper training, overall workplace conditions, seniority, and even the place where a printer worked. Maintenance of the printers' closed shop relied on union members' individual and collective technical expertise—which publishers' came to rely on—and strict adherence to ITU "union laws." These laws, which constituted the union's accomplishments over many decades of bargaining with employers, stipulated conditions of employment, professional autonomy, and workplace control (McKercher and Mosco 2008; McKercher 2002; Taft 1978; Perlman and Taft 1955; Lipset, Trow and Coleman 1956; Porter 1954; Champney 1948). Overall, the union imbued the relationship between worker and employee with special significance because power and responsibility were shared through a contract bargained anew every few years.

Timeline to Chicago Strike

Because precedents established in the laws strengthened the union, they became a persistent target of the publishers when bargaining new contracts. Since the 1890s, organized American newspaper publishers, represented by regional publisher organizations and the American Newspaper Publishers Association (ANPA), had pursued the union to open the laws to arbitration during contract negotiations. ITU officials countered that this could dilute the laws, and thus the union.

Overall, strikes between printers and publishers rarely took place, as most bargaining over contracts resolved disagreements. Several exceptions to this transpired in the years leading up to the Chicago ITU strike. In early 1945 the ITU proposed a contract clause between its local chapters and newspapers formally requiring that publishers recognize the laws (Brown 1945, 20; Taylor 1945, 137). Several exceptions to this transpired in the years leading up to the Chicago ITU strike. Newspaper publishers, represented by the ANPA, stood opposed, realizing that it would only fortify the printers' already impressive workplace control. In response, ITU union chapters struck several newspapers in cities throughout the U.S. that summer (*New York Times* 1945, 9). By fall of 1945 ITU chapters won recognition of the union's laws and significant pay increases at dozens of newspapers across North America (Tracy 2008; *Editor and Publisher* 1945, 8; *Business Week* 1945a, 98; *Business Week* 1945b, 103-104;).

The majority of the larger newspapers could easily afford to pay their workers higher salaries. Yet publishers increasingly saw better pay for their employees as cutting into the bottom line. Throughout the late 1940s, newspapers experienced record profits from increasing advertising revenues. Publishers moved to bolster these profit margins by challenging their unionized workers for concessions. To put their workforce in its place once and for all, ANPA officials and commercial printing interests actively supported and participated in the creation of the federal anti-labor Taft-Hartley Act. The combination of Taft-Hartley and a redesigned National Labor Relations Board (NLRB), the federal body charged with enforcing the new law, was used by the newspaper industry to undermine the ITU and the power of other newspaper unions. The 22-month-long Chicago strike was seen as crucial by the newspaper publishing industry because publishers reasoned that if the ITU could be defeated in Chicago, Taft-Hartley could be used against the printers' union and its less-powerful counterparts at papers throughout the country.

Expanding Profits, Squeezed Workers

The political economic backdrop to the newspaper industry's postwar labor management struggle involved substantial profit accumulation alongside modest gains for newsworkers. By the end of 1946 average hourly pay grew by ten percent, but this increase was quickly eaten up by inflation (Fleisher 1948, 10). The U.S. Department of Labor reported that between June 1946 and December 1947 retail food prices increased by an average of 39 percent, clothing prices were up 21 percent, and rent hikes averaged 6 percent. At the same time corporate profits totaled $12.5 billion in 1946—an adjusted-for-inflation increase of one quarter over the previous annual record of $8.4 billion set in 1929. In 1947 another record $16.9 billion was taken in (CIO News 1948a, 7; Fleisher 1948, 10).

Not surprisingly, the newspaper industry made record profits from advertising in 1947 and 1948, especially for newspapers with over 100,000 in circulation. Between 1946 and 1947 the industry's profits increased by 37.8 percent—far higher than any other advertising venue (Friedman 1949, 24). In 1947 newspapers as a whole took in close to 35 percent of the nearly $4.3 billion spent by advertisers, or $1.475 billion. In 1948 $1.75 billion was taken in (*Economist* Intelligence Unit 1949, 66). Readers were likewise paying almost three million dollars per day to purchase newspapers in 1947, an increase of over one-third of the amount spent five years earlier.

As a result of these developments, larger newspapers became necessary to accommodate more print and display advertising. Thus the publishers' paramount concern involved securing more expansive and dependable sources of newsprint. In the postwar era newsprint manufacturers in Canada, the United States, and Newfoundland produced close to 75 percent of newsprint, with Canadian plants accounting for almost 60 percent, the U.S. 11 percent and Newfoundland around 5 percent. Yet U.S. newspapers accounted for 62 percent of global consumption, and by the late 1940s the overall global demand for newsprint was outstripping supply. Many of the large-circulation ANPA-member papers and chains had long-standing agreements with a handful of dominant newsprint manufacturers that made the market for newsprint more and more uncompetitive, with smaller publishers typically left to purchase newsprint on the spot market (Friedman 1949, 22-24). New York's nine dailies, for example, consumed 545,000 tons of paper annually, versus 5,000 tons used in one year by the city's combined labor, religious, fraternal, ethnic, and African-American papers (*CIO News* 1947a, 5).

The situation was made worse through elimination of price controls in mid-1946. The Office of Price Administration (OPA) dispensed newsprint to publications large and small on a parity basis determined from pre-war consumption figures (United States Senate 1947, 37). In an effort to influence the newsprint market in their favor, newspaper publishers petitioned to relax price controls. "Early action by OPA," the ANPA declared, "is most desirable and each day of delay by OPA in promulgating an order increasing the newsprint price increases hazards that might effect the steady flow of newsprint to the United States newspapers" (*New York Times* 1946a, 35). When price controls were abandoned a few months later, the largest U.S. publishers scrambled to forge contracts. "They also tried to boom circulation held down in many cases during the war because of newsprint controls," a special Congressional committee concluded. The major dailies and chain papers "put the pressure on mills to give them more paper, and to guarantee them future service. The mills in many cases complied, cutting off jobbers and small consumers whom they considered less reliable, less desirable customers" (United States Senate 1947, 37).

The publishers' zeal to corner the newsprint market and boost profits was not reflected in better pay and benefits for the workers. In fact, newsworkers pointed to the industry's expenditures for newsprint versus what it was willing to pay labor. The union representing newspaper reporters, the American Newspaper Guild, for example, asserted that U.S. daily newspapers "paid an unnecessary $50,000,000 to the Canadian newsprint trust" in 1948 alone. "How can the publishers say they cannot afford higher wages, or a decent retirement plan for employes," the Guild asked, "when they do nothing collectively to break this gouge by the newsprint monopoly?" (*Guild Reporter* 1948a, 8) The major newspaper publishers might also have petitioned for a reinstatement of price controls to rein in the inflationary conditions affecting newsprint and a host of other goods proffered through print advertising. Instead, they turned to challenging the compensation and workplace autonomy of their skilled workers.

Taft-Hartley's Challenge to Printers' Union Control

Formally known as the Labor-Management Relations Act, the "Taft-Hartley Act" constituted a distinct reversal of the legal and legislative gains the labor union movement had established in the 1935 Labor Relations Act, or "Wagner Act," a cornerstone of the Franklin Roosevelt Administration's New Deal reforms package. The Wagner Act essentially extended to all workers the right to free association and the ability to form unions for representation without the fear of employer reprisal. This legislation also required employers to recognize unions and bargain with them "in good faith," setting the stage for a surge in unionism throughout the U.S. in the late 1930s through the 1940s. Employer violations of the law were met with stiff penalties. In addition, the NLRB was established to mediate labor management relations and enforce the Wagner Act. Many within the business community complained that labor was unfairly favored under the new law, and in 1947 Taft-Hartley was enacted by a coalition of Congressional Republicans and conservative southern Democrats over President Harry Truman's veto (Millis and Brown 1950).

Taft-Hartley curtailed the practices of labor unions on a number of fronts, and Republican legislators led by Senator Robert Taft, the law's co-sponsor, more than doubled the NLRB's budget to enforce the new law (*CIO News* 1947b, 7). Under Taft-Hartley, the NLRB also became subject to the oversight of a powerful new general counsel position (Gross 1995). Taft-Hartley posed a tremendous threat to the ITU by outlawing the closed shop and making the printers' immediate workplace supervisor, the shop foreman, part of management. "The whole structure of rule and practice which prevails in a union composing room is based on the closed shop, and it centers around a union foreman," the ITU observed. By making the foreman part of management the union's workplace power was severely curtailed. Another provision of Taft-Hartley "tailored especially for the I.T.U.," was the prohibition against strikes to prevent an employer from outsourcing composing room work to non-union print shops for completion. ITU President Woodruff Randolph predicted "the destruction of the I.T.U." if such provisions were accepted without a fight (*Typographical Journal* 1949, 88).

There is a strong likelihood that Taft-Hartley's authors targeted the ITU because it was an especially powerful union; if it could be broken many other lesser unions would fall by the wayside. The ANPA and the Printing Industry of America (PIA), the employer group representing commercial print shops, were instrumental in crafting and implementing the new legislation with an eye toward the ITU. The Senate's legal advisors on Taft-Hartley included Thomas Shroyer and Gerald Reilly (*Business Week* 1947, 18). A Washington D.C.-based attorney, Reilly's clients included the PIA; under the direction of Senator Taft, Reilly wrote an early draft of the Taft-Hartley bill for the Senate Labor Committee (*Federation News* 1949a, 11). Shroyer was lead counsel of the Joint Committee on Labor-Management Relations who wrote Taft-Hartley's final draft. Alongside Taft, Shroyer pushed the NLRB's newly-appointed chief legal counsel Robert Denham and his staff to target unionized workers of prominent employers. Speaking before the PIA conference in September 1947, Shroyer "congratulated the participants because so many of their suggestions had been incorporated into the act, and assured them that the ITU would not 'escape responsibility under the new law'" (Gross 1995, 37). Not surprisingly, the editorial pages of newspapers across the U.S. hailed Taft-Hartley as appropriate legislation to rein in labor unions' achievements and surging membership under the Wagner Act

SHOWDOWN BETWEEN CHICAGO PUBLISHERS & THE TYPOS

The ANPA designated Chicago as the battle ground for challenging the ITU with the new law. The city was ANPA headquarters, and the industry reasoned that Chicago's major newspapers could collectively withstand a long confrontation with the printers. Newspaper publishers Robert McCormick (*Chicago Tribune*), William Randolph Hearst (*Herald-American*) John Knight (*Chicago Daily News*), and Marshall Field (*Sun* and *Times*, consolidated in early 1948), comprised the Chicago Newspaper Publishers Association (CNPA) along with the Journal of Commerce, *Chicago Defender* (African-American weekly), and the *Hammond* (Indiana) *Times*.   Anticipating the expiration of their contract in the fall of 1947, the Chicago ITU Local Chapter 16 officers submitted a new contract proposal to CNPA that summer which included a wage increase of 15 percent, which would boost a typical printers' weekly salary of $91.00 to about $106.00 (Larkin 1947, 133; *Guild Reporter* 1947a, 1). At a meeting on August 13, nine days before Taft-Hartley became law, CNPA requested the union sign a set of preconditions conforming to Taft-Hartley before any discussion of the printers' proposals. The preconditions included, for example, that union members work alongside non-union employees and handle printed matter processed in non-union shops—activities considered anathema to union laws and practice (Larkin 1947, 133). "They knew that we would not agree to these changes," one printer noted, "for they would take away from us working conditions that we had gained [through bargaining] over the period of ninety-six years."[1]

Since the CNPA persisted in refusing to discuss the printers' contract proposals, ITU national headquarters officials directed printers in Chicago and elsewhere to post "conditions of employment" in the workplace and proceed without a contract (*New York Times* 1947a, 9). This "no-contract policy" (*Editor and Publisher* 1947a, 10), union officials believed, could safeguard against various interpretations of Taft-Hartley the union would be bound to if it formally entered into contracts (*Editor and Publisher* 1947b, 10). Newspaper publishers across the U.S. accepted this policy in every city but Chicago, and many entered into contracts amenable to both the ITU and the ANPA. Indeed, the ANPA filed a formal complaint with the NLRB against the ITU for resisting the CNPA's preconditions (*Los Angeles Times* 1947, 9). Chicago publishers then prepared for a showdown, fitting their plants with technology for continued publication in the event of a strike (*Guild Reporter* 1947a, 1).

Negotiations ensued throughout the fall with little progress. The printers overwhelmingly supported a "no contract" policy,[2] yet Chicago publishers would accept the policy only if the union withdrew its wage demand. Five consecutive meetings took place in early November, yet the publishers still refused to negotiate wages. On November 15 the union's negotiating committee walked out in frustration.[3] On November 23 the printers ratified a new wage proposal that the publishers

---

1 "Collective Bargaining," *Meet the Union Printers*, script, WCFL, February 25, 1948, Box 86, Folder 1, Chicago Typographical Union Number 16 Papers, Chicago Historical Society [hereafter CTU Papers].

2 John J. Pilch, "President's Report," *The Reporter*, November, 1947, Box 36, Folder 2, CTU Papers.

3 Ibid.

again refused to negotiate. The following day the union voted by a ratio of almost forty to one to strike (*New York Times* 1947b, 1).[4]

Informed of the strike while traveling abroad, *Tribune* publisher McCormick replied, "Good. I hope it lasts a long time" (Wendt 1979, 680). As the strike began the publishers set out to skew public opinion through coverage likely intended to discredit and isolate the printers from other labor unions and the greater Chicago community. The propaganda effort was especially challenging for newspaper owners because the papers' makeshift printing process was not compatible with an editorial and production regimen so reliant on the typographers' mechanical and intellectual skill. We turn now to an examination of how the first several months of the strike played out by looking at coverage of the strike in the newspapers being struck, and contrasting this with stories from the labor press. In the first several months of the standoff the Chicago publishers unleashed a multi-faceted propaganda campaign that seriously distorted events and issues surrounding the strike. The printers, on the other hand, resorted to Chicago's independent labor media to relate a far more nuanced, detailed set of accounts that often contradicted the Chicago papers' version.

CONFRONTING THE PUBLISHERS' PROPAGANDA CAMPAIGN

Exaggerated and prominent coverage of strikes in the commercial news media during the mid-to-late 1940s cast labor unions in a negative light and contrasted sharply with close-to-nonexistent coverage of far more common (yet much less sensational) union and workplace politics (*CIO News* 1947c, 6). This was especially the case with newspaper strikes. National news outlets likewise routinely presented distorted and confusing accounts of the strike. "[T]he minute we, or any other union, are provoked into walking out on strike," one Chicago union official observed, there are "banner headlines!...front page news stories...editorials...they throw everything at us but the kitchen sink. And that's been particularly true in this strike, because the employers involved are the newspaper publishers themselves."[5]

---

4 "Strike Review," *Meet the Union Printers*, script, WCFL, October 11, 1948, Box 86, Folder 1, CTU Papers.

5 "George Bante," *Meet the Union Printers*, script, WCFL, December 19, 1947, Box 84, Folder 5, CTU Papers.

The Chicago strike likewise occurred before a backdrop of broadly positive coverage of Taft-Hartley appearing in mainstream outlets. One study of 220 articles appearing between April 1947 and January 1948 in widely-circulated news and opinion journals found an overwhelming majority neutral or in favor of the law, and less than 10 percent opposed. The labor-oriented and progressive publications where critiques of Taft-Hartley appeared reached only a slim cross-section of the American public. "The viewpoints of organized labor, presented in positive terms," the analysis concluded, "did not appear in any of the major periodicals of wide circulation. On the other hand, the viewpoints of management and related groups that favored the Act appeared frequently in these periodicals" (Ash 1948, 271).

When Chicago's printers sought a public platform to share their accounts of the strike they found that most media outlets in the city were controlled by or associated with Chicago's major newspaper publishers (Godfried 1997, 245). "Anti-union forces have been flagrantly misrepresenting the position of No. 16 in this controversy," ITU Local 16's president pointed out. "More ems of type have been set, more press impressions have been made in describing this strike to the American people, than have been used for any other strike in American history, including those strikes where a hundred times as many employees were involved. And at least 99% of the accounts have been deliberately falsified to confuse the public and alienate from our cause the support of those who have everything to win if they understand and support our position, everything to lose if they misunderstand and abandon our position."[6] Yet throughout the strike the Chicago Federation of Labor's radio station, WCFL, allowed the union to host a fifteen-minute program six nights per week (Godfried 1997, 245-246). This, combined with the printers' monthly strike publication, *The Picket*, and the Chicago Federation of Labor's *Federation News*, were all important conduits to counter the commercial press' propaganda (*Typographical Journal* 1948, 109).

The Chicago newspapers' reportage and editorials throughout the first weeks of the strike sought to downplay the issue of wages and instead stressed the publishers' strict adherence to the law. ""The union's policy is based upon its opposition to the Taft-Hartley Act," Knight's *Chicago Daily News* pointed out in bold print a few days before the

6   John Pilch to Leslie G. Cutler, June 15, 1948, Box 36, Folder 4, CTU Papers.

Fig. 1. Cartoon by Bernard Seaman. "Go Ahead—I'm Listening," *The Guild Reporter*, December 26, 1947, p. 1. Courtesy of *The Guild Reporter* / American Newspaper Guild.

strike. "The law outlaws the closed shop, which the union now has and is seeking to preserve" (*Chicago Daily News* 1947a, 6). The *Chicago Tribune* (1947a, 1) likewise argued how its 95 years of harmonious relations with the ITU "has been interrupted because the union now wishes us to proceed on the theory that the Taft-Hartley law is not the law of the land." Along similar lines, the *Chicago Daily News* declared how the ITU, "alone among the major labor organizations of the country, has adopted the policy of not signing contracts with employers." The paper continued, "At all times, the publishers have been willing to discuss the higher rate of pay for the printers, within the framework of a contract" (*Chicago Daily News* 1947b, 1).

The commentary overlooked how many U.S. newspaper owners feared that striking printers would have also curtailed their record-setting profits. Indeed, a majority accepted the ITU's no con-tract policy, including the *Cincinnati Times Star*, owned by Senator Taft.[7] Further, Hearst, Knight, Ridder, and McCormick's newspapers in thirteen other U.S. cities had already forged agreements with ITU chapters.[8] Overall, six months following Taft-Hartley's enactment ITU locals throughout the U.S. signed contracts establishing higher wages at 347 newspapers and 304 commercial print shops (*Guild Reporter* 1947a, 1; Rosemont 1948, 9).[9]

At December meetings held between union officials and publish-ers' representatives convened by Chicago Mayor Martin Kennelly, the publishers were asked why they were unable to negotiate with Local 16 when hundreds of newspapers in other cities were giving raises to printers without signed contracts (*Business Week* 1948, 98; *Chicago Daily News* 1947c, 16; *Chicago Daily News* 1947d, 6). The CNPA's representative responded: "Chicago was selected for the battleground because conditions were more favorable to the newspapers owners here than in any other American city."[10] The publishers' bargainers un-abashedly remarked to union negotiators "that this city was chosen as the battleground because [the publishers] believe they can win here on account of their solidarity locally. They do not conceal their ultimate purpose of establishing the same unbearable conditions in other cities where their chains operate if the scab experiment is successful here" (Rosemont 1948, 109; Eubanks 1947, 2).[11] ("Scab" or "scab labor" are slang terms for one or more individuals hired to replace workers out on strike.) John Knight divulged how the ANPA's Taft-Hartley campaign against the ITU would have been more far-reaching had many publishers not broken ranks. "This unprincipled circumvention and evasion of the law has been practiced by some of the most gallant

---

7   "Eleventh Anniversary," *Meet the Union Printers*, script, WCFL, Novem-ber 9, 1948, Box 86, Folder 1, CTU Number 16 Papers.

8   Chicago Typographical Union No. 16, "Why Doesn't the Chicago Her-ald-American Tell You..." (leaflet), n.d., Box 36, Folder 1, CTU Number 16 Papers.

9   "Questions and Answers," *Meet the Union Printers*, script, WCFL, March 9, 1948, Box 84, Folder 6, CTU Papers.

10   "Strike Review," *Meet the Union Printers*, script, WCFL, October 11, 1948, Box 86, Folder 1, CTU Papers.

11   Pilch to ITU Chapters, n.d. (June 1948?), Box 36, Folder 4, CTU Papers.

scotch-and-soda warriors ever to assemble at an American Newspaper Publishers' convention. Bold words spoken at the Waldorf were soon forgotten, however, when these daring knights of the cash register ran into trouble back home. Then they took to the tall timbers the moment the first shot was fired (*Guild Reporter* 1948b, 1)."[12]

The Chicago papers also played up the alleged technological ease and superiority of photoengraving. "Having demonstrated they could print a newspaper without the help of ITU members," historians Harry Kelber and Carl Schlesinger (Kelber and Schlesinger 1967, 40) explain, the Chicago "publishers began a campaign of psychological warfare aimed at demoralizing striking printers by forecasting revolutionary technological improvements which would make the journeyman printer obsolete." For example, just after the strike began the *Tribune* reported, "The daily news [*sic*] appeared yesterday with an edition of 34 pages, containing interesting pictures, advertisements, and features, as well as news and their production has been produced with the help of varitype, a relatively new development of the grafic [*sic*] arts" (*Chicago Tribune* 1947b, 4). Through photoengraving, the paper asserted, "it will be possible to present adequate coverage of local, national, and foreign news as well as comics, columns, and other features in the news issues, daily and Sunday [*sic*]" (Ibid. 4). Teenagers from Chicago's art schools were hired to assist with the new production process, and some of the papers ensured the young workers' loyalty through cash raffles, daily bonuses, and free meals (*Guild Reporter* 1947b, 2).[13] One day after the strike commenced the *Tribune* devoted a full half-page to photos of picketing printers, rows of idled linotype machines, and editorial staff assembling page layouts for printing via photoengraving (*Chicago Tribune* 1947c, 24).

"Chicago's photo-engraved newspapers are being so well received by the public," the *Daily News*' Knight editorialized, "that sweeping changes in typography are in prospect when the printers' strike is eventually settled." Limited technological progress, Knight argued, was largely due to the craft unions' unfounded protectiveness of their members' jobs. "The Chicago experiment, born out of necessity, may chart the way toward better newspapers by discovering new methods

12 "Eleventh Anniversary," *Meet the Union Printers*, script, WCFL, November 9, 1948, Box 86, Folder 1, CTU Papers.

13 "Maxwell Pyle," *Meet the Union Printers*, script, WCFL, February 18, 1948, Box 84, Folder 6, CTU Papers.

to replace the cumbersome and inefficient practices of the past" (Knight 1947, 6).

In reality, publication through photoengraving was both inefficient and more expensive than the normal printing process. Text was produced on a special typewriter that automatically justified type. Each page layout was photographed and a zinc engraving was made from the photo. The engraving was then routered to remove excess metal and a mat impression was cast for the press.[14]

Labor newspapers labeled Chicago's new broadsheets "newsless" and "ersatz" newspapers (*Guild Reporter* 1947c, 3; *CIO News* 1947c, 7). Unlike the more mechanically versatile "hot-type" process, where type could be quickly and accurately manipulated for corrections and inclusion of late news, photo-engraving took up to six times longer and errors usually went uncorrected. This had an appreciable effect on the very form and content of the newspaper. Further, with photoengraving more space was required because the letters needed to be larger for legibility (*Guild Reporter* 1947c, 3; *CIO News* 1947c, 7). As a result newspapers carried less news, and national and international news tended to crowd out local reportage that took more time to produce. Often if a news event occurred after 10 p.m. it would not make it into the newspaper until the following afternoon, if at all. Thus, newspapers that owned radio outlets like the *Tribune* referred readers to their broadcasts for late-breaking news.

Newspapers were hard-hit by advertising losses because of advertisers and readers' dislike of photoengraving. After the strike began ad rates were reduced and management required their advertising salesmen put in seventy-two-hour weeks to cater to angry advertisers (*Guild Reporter* 1947c, 3; *Guild Reporter* 1948c, 2). Classified advertisers were required to take out ads for a minimum of three days since they were so expensive to photoengrave. One analysis estimated a 50 percent net loss in classified content when comparing a *Tribune* photoengraved Sunday classified section to an edition produced one year earlier through regular methods (*Federation News* 1947, 1).

The papers' flawed graphics were accompanied by frequently outdated or inaccurate content. Because of the high cost of addressing mistakes, factual or typographical errors went uncorrected until the next day's paper. As a result, people were being directed to non-existent

---

14 "Your Chicago Daily News Keeps Right on Publishing! Here's How" (brochure), Box 36, Folder 1, CTU Papers.

funerals, or to ones that had already taken place. Movie-goers similarly went to theatres to find the film they wanted to see was not playing, and smaller theatre owners that couldn't afford to take out display ads relied on two-to-three line listings that were sometimes botched.[15]

With advertisers and audiences dismayed, the demand for Chicago newspapers decreased significantly, yet an approximate figure was difficult to assess. By late December the papers used various means to obscure declining circulation figures. For example, the *Tribune* turned to annual averages versus monthly, pressmen noted repeated press runs in each printing plant, and delivery drivers saw high rates of returned papers. Even with enticements for new and existing subscribers the *Tribune's* daily circulation decreased by an estimated 100,000 (*Guild Reporter* 1948c, 2; *Federation News* 1948a, 8). As the strike wore on, papers ignored subscriber cancellations and unloaded thousands of newspapers on out-of-town distributors (*Federation News* 1948b, 1).

Commercial press coverage also drew readers' attention to a purported disunity in newsworker ranks by highlighting how other unions routinely crossed the printers' picket lines, giving the impression that printers lacked their fellow workers' support. Actually, the ITU received wide support within the labor community because it was perceived as probably the only union with enough organization and resources to withstand a lengthy strike (Rosemont 1948b, 182). Moreover, the newspapers failed to explain how Taft-Hartley outlawed "sympathy strikes"—those carried out in support of another union already on strike.

By February 1948 Chicago's typos had received $85,471 in contributions from across the country (*Guild Reporter* 1948d, 2; *Guild Reporter* 1948e, 7). "Even outside the graphic arts industry," the printers noted, "there is growing realization of the crucial significance of the strike, and this realization has been expressed in check, resolutions, editorials, public statements and in every conceivable form" (Rosemont 1948, 182). Chicago area unions provided food and winter coats to the picketing printers, while officials of labor federations throughout Illinois issued statements in support of the strike (*Guild Reporter* 1947d, 2). "The fight of the ITU against the Taft-Hartley act, the [NLRB] and its union busting general counsel is the fight of the entire labor movement,"

---

15 "Maxwell Pyle," CTU Papers.

the Congress of Industrial Organizations (CIO) declared.[16] ITU locals
throughout the U.S. and Canada also committed five percent of their
pay toward a strike fund.

Support among Chicago's civic groups and clergy was also substantial. Chicago community clergy spoke regularly at Number 16's
daily strike meetings[17] and conducted a study on the strike's causes. In
their report they "urg[ed] that the publishers make a wage offer" and
called on Congress to amend Taft-Hartley (*Guild Reporter* 1948d, 2;
Webber 1948, 3; *CIO News* 1948b, 5). The Chicago printers initiated a telephone survey to gauge Chicago area residents' support of the
standoff; 72 percent expressed approval of the strike, 9 percent disapproved, and 19 percent were undecided (*Guild Reporter* 1948e, 7).

Finally, across the U.S. a long series of NLRB complaints and court
injunctions were thrown up against the ITU for purported violations
of Taft-Hartley. This culminated in a far-reaching plea by Denham
for a court injunction against Chicago's printers. The injunction "asks
that the ITU officers be restrained from everything the publishers'
aides claim we are doing that they do not like," such as working under posted conditions of employment and insisting on union foremen
(*Federation News* 1948c, 3). Legal experts assessed the request as "the
most drastic decree against a union in the history of American labor"
(*Guild Reporter* 1948g, 1).

In February, ITU attorneys asked the court to dismiss the injunction because Denham was not invested with injunction-seeking power (*Federation News* 1948d, 1). The judge denied the motion and on
March 27 granted Denham's request. To avoid charges of contempt, a
formal understanding was achieved that if any unintended violation
of the decree took place the union would be allowed to address any
alleged violations.

FIGHTING THE PUBLISHERS'
BACK-TO-WORK MOVEMENT

Armed with an injunction, the CNPA made its first complete wage
proposal since October 1946 — $6 per week. The offer called for "the

---

16   "Attack on No. 16: Blow by Blow," *The Picket*, August 1948, Box 36,
     Folder 2, CTU Papers.

17   "Labor Editor," *Meet the Union Printers*, script, WCFL, February 18,
     1948, Box 84, Folder 5, CTU Papers.

entire elimination of the General Laws of the ITU."[18] The wage increase was especially modest in light of both Chicago's high cost of living and raises offered printers in other locales. Further, the proposal sought to undermine ITU gains achieved over several decades of bargaining. The following month the CNPA made a "final" proposal of $9, requesting an immediate vote by the printers. The agreement, however, had to be approved by ITU officials, who rejected it for not acknowledging union laws. Thereafter, the papers criticized the ITU for not allowing the printers to promptly vote on the offer, but failed to point out how the publishers' offer would have essentially put an end to the union (*Chicago Tribune* 1948a, B4).

The publishers then introduced a "back-to-work" program that included a propaganda campaign intended to depict the printers as unreasonable for not voting on the offer (*Chicago Tribune* 1948b, B9). A full-page advertisement was carried in the *Daily News, Tribune, Herald-American, Sun-Times,* and *Journal of Commerce* announcing that printers would be able to return with the $9 weekly raise and full seniority rights, but must do so by a deadline of June 7 or non-union replacements would be hired.[19] A tabloid-style publication, "The Chicago Story," was also distributed anonymously to newspaper publishers throughout the U.S. and Canada in an attempt to isolate Chicago's typos from their supporters and the broader public. "The only way our enemies could beat us would be to create distrust and suspicion in our own ranks and thus divide the membership," the Chicago printers declared in a statement (*Federation News* 1948e, 2).

Fearing the publishers' propaganda offensive, Local 16's officers issued a communiqué to the Chicago community and ITU chapters nationally. "We urge your chapel to disregard vicious falsehoods which our enemies may circulate in your city to the effect that we are seeking to violate the Taft-Hartley act." The printers explained how their union was working within the parameters of the agreement following the March court injunction while fighting for a better contract. "The Chicago newspapers did offer us a wage increase after eight months of negotiation and after four months of strike, and they increased this offer after another month, but for this wage increase they demand

---

18   "Summary of Week's Activities," *Meet the Union Printers,* script, WCFL, October 14, 1948, Box 85, Folder 2, CTU Papers.

19   John J. Pilch and George N. Bante to ITU Chapters, n.d., Box 36, Folder 4, CTU Papers.

that we sell out our union and every sister local of the ITU. This we will never do. Our union is not for sale. Repeat: Our union is not for sale"(*Federation News* 1948e, 2). Number 16 also dispatched one of its officials on a tour of ITU locals in cities throughout the country to more fully explain its position.[20]

Letters and telegrams were sent to Hearst and Knight from ITU chapters at Hearst and Knight-owned papers across the country, informing the publishers that attempts to replace union labor with strikebreakers in Chicago would be considered an action against union printers everywhere. "You are the same man [in Chicago] that you are here, in Akron and in Detroit, and printers are the same, by cross section the world over," printers at the Knight-owned *Miami Herald* declared.[21] Chicago's typos likewise broadcast their message via WCFL.[22] In July, Local 16's membership voted 1,011 to 90 to turn down the offer (*Federation News* 1948f, 3).

After securing a two-year contract with the Chicago photo engravers' union for pay increases and reductions in hours (*Federation News* 1948g, 1), CNPA publishers appeared more determined than ever to break the strike. In late July, Knight and representatives of McCormick and Hearst traveled to Washington DC for a special consultation with Senator Taft. At Taft's request, NLRB attorneys overseeing injunctions were present (Kaiser 1948, 9). The publishers contended that the ITU was violating the injunction and requested that Taft pressure the NLRB to pursue a contempt of court action (Loftus 1948, 6). Taft saw the Chicago strike as a proving ground for his legislation. According to one NLRB counsel who was present, "Taft repeated in substance that he had called us because he wanted us to know that he was keenly interested in effective enforcement of the statute and that in his view ... the Typographical union case was the most important proceeding that had arisen under the new act" (*Guild Reporter* 1948h, 1).

---

20   Report of Peter Larkin Covering Trip to Seattle and Tacoma, Wash., San Francisco, Oakland and Los Angeles, Calif., San Antonio Dallas and Denison, Tex., Tulsa, Okla., and Return to Chicago, Illinois, June 5-17, incl. Box 36, Folder 3, CTU Papers.

21   Carl W. Barton to Chicago Typographical Union, June 4, 1948, Box 36, Folder 3, CTU Papers.

22   "This is the Proposition," *Meet the Union Printers*, script, WCFL, June 9, 1948, Box 85, Folder 4, CTU Papers.

Holding their union convention when the story broke, ITU officials called on President Truman to launch an investigation into Taft's meeting with the publishers (Kaiser 1948, 9, 36). Responding by telegram, Truman asserted that he found the charges "'shocking,' ... promising that 'it will be investigated thoroughly and immediately.'" The investigation confirmed the meeting, leading Truman to condemn Taft for 'entirely improper' conduct of attempting 'to put the heat on one of the Executive Departments'" (Kaiser 1948, 36). Nevertheless, the NLRB continued to press for contempt hearings. Of the twenty-nine instances of contempt, the judge upheld only five. In the end the court did not find any violation of the injunction, and the strike ensued until September 1949, largely because the ITU was allowed to continue distribution of strike benefits.[23]

When the ITU voted its continued support of Randolph's presidency at its 1949 convention, Chicago publishers concluded that the union could not be broken and moved for compromise (*Guild Reporter* 1949, 1). At the 135th bargaining session on September 14 a new contract was forged that included a ten percent, or roughly $10, weekly salary increase, in addition to guarantees of "maximum union security" allowed under Taft-Hartley (*Federation News* 1949b, 1). In the early afternoon of September 18, hundreds of Number 16's members "jammed every seat...sat around the stage, stood in the aisles and clung to the rafters high in the balcony" to hear the contract offer. As the union president "slowly read the provisions of the contract proposal ... there was complete silence as the printers followed his clause-by-clause analysis of the document" (*Federation News* 1949c, 1). While the $10.00 raise wasn't adequate, the membership was asked whether it wanted to endure several more months of struggle for a better offer. With less than ninety minutes of balloting the vote was 1,287 to 279 to accept the offer and end the strike. "We won," said a printer on the *Herald-American*, "not only to protect my job, but we showed just how vicious the Taft-Hartley Act really is" (*Federation News* 1949c, 2).

Even though the wage settlement was a setback, the contract reinforced and protected the union's shopfloor autonomy in five important respects. First, and most importantly, acknowledgment of the ITU General Laws was included. Second, the union secured control over operation of new automatic teletypesetting equipment. Third,

---

23 "President's Report," *Meet the Union Printers*, script, WCFL, October 14, 1948, Box 86, Folder 1, CTU Papers.

printers would not be required to handle printing matter made by non-union labor. Fourth, Local 16's stance on seniority was retained, making seniority the sole determinant in workforce reductions and re-employment. And finally, the shop foreman remained within the union (*Guild Reporter* 1949, 1).

Following the Chicago strike the ITU maintained its workplace control despite Taft-Hartley by requiring that employers either accept the closed shop or be subject to sanctions. This position was written into union law in 1950 (Lipset, Trow and Coleman 1956, 25). Over the next few decades, however, the ITU was reduced to a shadow of its former self much less through legal challenges than the industry's economic consolidation, adoption of "cold type," and increased automation and computerization of the production process. The union's attempt to address management's increased use of technology by re-training workers was in the end unsuccessful (Kelber and Schlesinger 1967, 65-93; Zimbalist 1979, 107-109).

In the late 1940s, only 20 percent of newspapers were owned by large national corporations. Yet fast-forwarding fifty years, we find the proportion had climbed to eighty-percent. Conversely, between 1961 and 1976 ITU membership decreased by one-third, from 94,500 to 66,000. In 1986 the ITU was absorbed into the 600,000-member Communication Workers of America (CWA). "By the time the [CWA] took it into its fold, the ITU was largely a spent force" (McKercher 2002, 70, 80-81, 190).

Examination of the printers' struggle against the prerogatives of newspaper owners reveals a great deal about the underlying dynamics of these economic processes, particularly in terms of the relationship between workers, management, and the broader public sphere at a time when organized labor was at its height in political and economic power. Even with such power and the union's ability to organize, labor unions as strong as the ITU were typically outflanked in terms of media and communication. Labor's broader fight against Taft-Hartley, crystallized in this specific episode, did not gain sufficient traction because of the absence of a more powerful national voice capable of competing with commercial media outlets (Fones-Wolf 2006).

REFERENCES

Ash, Phillip. 1948. The periodical press and the Taft-Hartley Act. *The Public Opinion Quarterly* 12: 266-271.

Brown, Elmer. 1945. Publishers plan war on I.T.U. rules. *Typographical Journal*, January: 20.

Business Week, 1945a, December 29. "I. T. U. Strategy," 98.

———. 1945b, August 25. "I. T. U. Wins Test," 103-104.

———. 1947, June 28. "A New Deal for America's Employers," 18.

———. 1948, December 11. "'Taft-Hartley strike' Enters Second Year," *Business Week*, 98.

Champney, Freeman. 1948. "Taft-Hartley and the Printers," *Antioch Review* (Spring): 49-62.

Chicago Daily News. 1947a, November 20. "Printers Offer Deal to End Deadlock."

———. 1947b, November 25. "A Statement to Our Readers on the Strike."

———. 1947c, December 26. "Progress Indicated in Typo Peace Talks."

———. 1947d, December 29. "Striking Printers Called Guinea Pigs."

Chicago Tribune. 1947a, November 22. "After 95 Years."

———. 1947b, November 26. "Today's Tribune Produced with New Typing Process."

———. 1947c, November 26. "Tribune Publishes Despite Printers' Strike."

———. 1948a, May 20. "Nothing More to Offer ITU, Publishers Say."

———. 1948b, June 4. "Randolph Bars Vote on Pact, Printers Say."

Chicago Typographical Union Number 16 Papers, Chicago Historical Society, Chicago, Illinois.

CIO News. 1947a, February 10. "Corner on the Newsprint Market Threatens Free Press," 5.

———. 1947b, July 21. "NRLB's Funds to Be Doubled," 7.

———. 1947c, August 11. "Strike News Overplayed," 6.

———. 1947d, December 22. "Newspapers Without News," 7.

———. 1948a, January 19. "Prices Surely *Are* Worth Paper They're Printed On," 7.

———. 1948b, January 19. "Union Shop Votes Make Charges of Labor Coercion of U.S. workers Look Ridiculous."

———. 1948c, January 19. "General Counsel Appeals Trial Examiner's Ruling."

Economist Intelligence Unit. 1949. *The problem of newsprint and other printing paper.* Paris: UNESCO.

Editor and Publisher, 1945a, July 21. "WLB Stops ITU Contracts, Puts All in Dispute File," 8.

———. 1947a, July 19. "No Closed Shop—No Work, Randolph Tells Printers," 10.

———. 1947b, October 25. "ITU's Life Is at Stake, Randolph Argues in Test," 7.

Eubanks, Sam. 1947. "Printers Gird for Bitter Fight as Publishers Turn to T-H Law to Smash ITU," *Guild Reporter*, December 12.

Federation News. 1947, December 13. "Chicago Dailies Hard Hit by the Printers Walkout on Wage Issue."

———. 1948a, January 17. "Typo Union No. 16 Chicago Strike Shows No Sign of Weakness."

———. 1948b, May 1. "Chicago Daily Newspaper War Continues Stronger Than Ever."

———. 1948c, January 31. "ITU Life Sought by a Nation-wide Injunction of the NLRB."

———. 1948d, February 21. "ITU Injunction Case Adjourned."

———. 1948e, July 10. "Job Shops Sign Up With Printers."

———. 1948f, May 22. "Chicago Printers Strike Tale Told."

———. 1948g, July 17. "Proceedings of Chicago Federation of Labor Meeting."

———. 1948h, August 7. "Photo Engravers New Agreement Sets An Example."

———. 1949a, February 19. "T-H Brain Trust, Who They Are and Their Public & Private Business."

———. 1949b, September 17. "Typos Win $10 Weekly Raise After Long Strike."

———. 1949c, September 24. "All Chicago Newspapers Now Union Made as Typos Get Raise, Security in Pact."

Fleisher, H. C. 1948. "GOP and Truman Fight for Glory," *CIO News*, January 19, 10.

Folkerts, Jean and Dwight L. Teeter, Jr. 1998. *Voices of a Nation: A History of Mass Media in the United States*. Boston: Allyn and Bacon.

Fones-Wolf, Elizabeth. *Waves of Opposition: Labor and the Struggle for Democratic Radio*. Urbana IL: University of Illinois Press, 2006.

Friedman, Clara H. 1949. *The Newsprint Problem: Ten Questions and Answers*. New York: American Newspaper Guild.

Godfried, Nathan. 1997. *WCFL: Chicago's Voice of Labor, 1926-78*. Urbana IL: University of Illinois Press.

Gross, James A. 1995. *Broken Promise: The Subversion of U.S. Labor Relations Policy, 1947-1994*. Philadelphia: Temple University Press.

Guild Reporter. 1947a, November 28. "One paper closed as ANPA and printers lock in showdown battle."

———. 1947b, December 26. "Chicago Publishers Still Play it Straight, But it's Fantasy," *Guild Reporter*.

———. 1947c, December 12. "Chicago's Newsless Newspapers."

———. 1947d. December 12. "No Break in Chicago ITU Walkout," 2.

———. 1948a, October 22. "Break Newsprint Price Gouge, Publishers Told."

———. 1948b, February 27. "John S. Knight Lambastes Publishers, Hinting Broken Pact in Fight on ITU."

———. 1948c, January 23. "Circulation Off, Ad Rates Cut in Chicago Strike."

———. 1948d, January 23. "Printers Gain Wide Support."

———. 1948e, February 27. "Chicago Printers Win New Support Via Phone Drive."

———. 1948f, January 27. "Typos Nearer Showdown in NLRB Proceedings."

———. 1948g, January 23. "Denham Seeks Drastic Injunction Against ITU."

———. 1948h, September 24. "ITU is Battling New T-H Union-Busting Maneuver."

———. 1949, September 23. "Typos at Work in Chicago at Strike Ends."

Kaiser, Henry. 1948. Taft Cracks the Whip: Before the I.T.U. He Orders N.L.R.B. Men," *American Federationist*, October: 9.

Kelber, Henry and Carl Schlesinger. 1967. *Union Printers and Controlled Automation*. New York: Free Press.

Knight, J. S. 1947. "Strike Spurs Advances in Newspaper Typography," *Chicago Daily News*, December 6, 6.

Larkin, Peter. 1947. "News and Comments from Local Unions: Chicago Ill. 16," *Typographical Journal*, August.

Lipset, Seymour Martin, Martin A. Trow, and James S. Coleman. 1956. *Union Democracy: The Internal Politics of the International Typographical Union*. Glencoe, IL: Free Press.

Loftus, Joseph A. 1948. "Taft Would Hold ITU for Contempt," *New York Times*, August 14.

Los Angeles Times, 1947a, February 18. "Florida Papers Upheld in Replacing Strikers."

———. 1947b, October 8. "Typographical Union Accused by Publishers."

McKercher, Catherine. 2002. *Newsworkers Unite: Labor, Convergence, and North American Newspapers*. Lanham, MD: Rowman and Littlefield.

Millis, Harry A. and Emily Clark Brown, 1950. *From the Wagner Act to Taft-Hartley: A Study of National Labor Policy and Labor Relations*. Chicago: University of Chicago Press.

New York Times, 1945, July 11. "3 Newspapers Suspend," 9.

———. 1946, August 2. "Quick OPA Rise Urged by ANPA in Newsprint," 35.

———. 1947a, September 27. "Publishers' Talks with Printers Fail," 9.

––– . 1947b, November 25. "Chicago Printers Go on Strike After Preparing Early Editions," 1.

Porter, Arthur R. 1954. *Job Property Rights: A Study of the Job Controls of the International Typographical Union*. New York: King's Crown Press.

Rosemont, Henry. 1948a. "News and Comments from Local Unions: Chicago Ill., 16," *Typographical Journal*, February: 9.

———. 1948b. "News and Comments from Local Unions: Chicago Ill., 16," *Typographical Journal*, March: 182.

Smiley, Nixon. 1984. *Knights of the Fourth Estate: The Story of the Miami Herald*. Banyan Books.

Taft, Phillip. 1978. "The Limits of Labor Unity: The Chicago Newspaper Strike of 1912," *Labor History* 19: 100-129.

Taylor, Larry. 1945. "A.N.P.A Opposition to I. T. U. Laws Continues," *Typographical Journal*, February, 137.

Tracy, James F. 2008. "Strikebusting in St. Petersburg: Nelson Poynter's Postwar Assault on Union Printers," *American Journalism* 25: 37-63.

Typographical Journal. 1948. "On the Air" (boxed announcement), February.

Typographical Journal. 1949. "Randolph Warns Guild T-H-L Used to Fullest Only in Newspaper Industry," August.

United States Senate Special Committee to Study Problems of American Small Business. 1947. *Survival of a Free, Competitive Press / The Small Newspaper: Democracy's Grass Roots.* Washington DC: US Government Printing Office.

Webber, Charles C. 1948, January 26. "Clergy, Labor Blast T-H," *CIO News.*

Wendt, Lloyd. 1979. *Chicago Tribune: The Rise of a Great American Newspaper.* New York: Rand McNally & Company.

Zimbalist, Andrew. 1979. "Technology and the Labor Process in the Printing Industry." In *Case Studies in the Labor Process,* edited by Andrew Zimbalist, 103-126. New York: Monthly Review Press.

CHAPTER 5

"THINGS WILL NEVER BE THE SAME
AROUND HERE"

HOW *SEE IT NOW* SHAPED
TELEVISION NEWS REPORTING

Dinah Zeiger

LMOST EVERY HISTORY OF 1950S PUBLIC AFFAIRS
TELEVISION seems to begin and end with CBS's *See It
Now* and its legendary co-producers, Edward R. Murrow and Fred W. Friendly. *See It Now* debuted in November 1951, but it was "The Case of Milo Radulovich,"
predecessor to the more famous March 9, 1954 "Report" on Senator
McCarthy, that marked the beginning of its rise to iconic status. The
series became the benchmark of television public affairs programs,
brought to its full flowering in later broadcasts on McCarthy and several longer programs dealing with such issues as poverty and racial
inequality in America. By the time the network cancelled it in 1958,
See It Now had laid the foundation of norms and practices for television news reporting. What made *See It Now* so special? Many media
scholars agree that it set the standards of journalistic fairness and objectivity that initially defined the form, presenting reports based on
evidence and facts without resorting to staged or reconstructed events,
which had been common in newsreels and on radio programs. However, there is more to a form than its outward appearance and adherence to a set of practices. Form also implies an inner impulse, a guiding
ideology, produced by the social, economic, and political processes at
work in a given time and place.

The form *See It Now* pioneered transformed television newsgathering and reporting practices, simplifying and clarifying complex social

and political issues by focusing on what Murrow called "small stories" and ordinary people. That's not to say Murrow ignored experts and official comments, but as Alexander Kendrick, one of "Murrow's Boys," said, *See It Now* emphasized "human beings affected by events, rather than [focusing] on the events themselves" (Kendrick 1969, 121). That emphasis represents one of the major effects that Murrow's style of reporting had on journalism in toto—the shift from the event to the personal experience of the event. Much of *See It Now*'s appeal lay in its ability to tap into natural human interest in how other people live and work. The America into which this program emerged was one shaped by wars, insecurity and a shiny new technology called television, led by a man who was wary not only of its power to manipulate viewers, but also of any possible accusations that his efforts might be labeled "propaganda."

Mid-twentieth century Americans swung between the contradictions of hope and anxiety, intensified by competing mass media messages promising a bright economic future while warning of possible annihilation. Those messages, products of the Cold War, fueled the social and cultural changes of the 1950s, but they were rooted in attitudes formed after World War I and the historical role and changing nature of propaganda, which shaped American perceptions of and responses to the Cold War. Scathing assessments following the end of the Great War critiqued the means by which the United States had been drawn into that conflict and how the government conducted the war at home. That led many postwar Americans to see propaganda as a potent threat capable of almost "unlimited power to capture the minds and hearts of men" (Rawnsley 1999, 2). By the time the U.S. entered World War II, experts who had studied the techniques of persuasion had enlisted in the fight for hearts and minds and deployed a range of new weapons, including broadcasting, in their arsenals. The psychological warfare that emerged in the 1950s mobilized the persuasive powers of this medium, television in particular, to groom Americans for their role in waging Cold War.

FROM PROPAGANDA TO PERSUASION

More than a little marketing went into selling the American public on going to war in 1941. Mindful of the propaganda excesses of the Great War, the government trod lightly when setting up its Office of War Information in 1942. The propagandists working in various information bureaus, mainly recruited from the nation's newspapers and radio news operations, positioned the 1941-1945 war as a conflict between good and evil in which Americans were reluctant warriors forced to confront a treacherous, militaristic enemy. Almost every film, photograph, and article produced during World War II featured an iteration of this perspective. And, as photo historian George A. Roeder shows, those images played a particular role in forming American perceptions of other countries during World War II. Moreover, they established a pattern of visual framing that carried over into Cold War information campaigns, especially on the newly emerging medium of television.

American technological superiority was often a subtext of World War II images. For example, many photographs and films viewed the enemy through the bombsights of aircraft flying high above strategic targets. But, as Roeder points out, there are consequences to images that distance viewers from the "human meaning of the bombing" (Roeder 1993, 84). Overlaid on an already magnified sense of moral superiority that Americans "destroyed only bad things," many viewers came to believe that American bombs hit only military targets and were "the most humane of all weapons" (Roeder 1993, 84-85). Such images also led viewers to believe that the Allies, with their superior technology, did not hit civilian targets, as few photographs showed the humans on the ground affected by the bombs (Roeder 1993, 86). This bombsight view—with its particularizing and privatizing effect—foreshadows the shift *See It Now* introduced in television news and public affairs programs. It suggests a direct cause-and-effect, an easy solution, by minimizing the complex social, economic, and political relationships that create the conditions in the first place.

The propaganda disseminated at home and abroad during the 1941-1945 war conditioned Americans to see themselves as defenders of liberal democratic freedoms. By war's end, many Americans regarded propaganda as something the other side did, in contrast to the "information campaigns" mounted by the United States government to counter Soviet aggression. Americans generally accepted the proposition that media did not directly affect their opinions and ideas. Rather, scientific studies, largely devised and conducted by media industry researchers, proved that opinions derived from "personal influences" in daily interaction with other individuals and social institutions. Journalistic objectivity, couched in the language of scientific or professional expertise, worked in tandem with this theoretical perspective to help allay fears that media indoctrinated audiences (Sproule 1989, 238). Lance Bennett defines it as "documentary reporting," journalists reporting only events they have witnessed or facts gleaned from and confirmed by "credible sources" (Bennett 1988, 129). The problem, as he points out, is that those conditions also effectively narrowed the routines of objectivity, because the government controlled access to official information, especially during times of national emergencies.

Objectivity became a kind of shield for mid-century reporters, allowing them to present "just the facts" without requiring them to examine the nature or source of those facts. Thus, journalists could continue to rely on government sources and resources, which not only represented expertise but provided access to secret programs or initiatives. Beginning in the late 1950s, television documentaries increasingly based their authority on what Michael Curtain characterizes as "scientific anticommunism," linking objectivity and scientific and professional expertise as weapons in the Cold War arsenal (Curtain 1995, 22).

"HOLDING THE LINE AND HOPING FOR THE BEST"

The Cold War culture, carefully crafted by national security advocates, helped create the conditions for consensus about the nation's foreign policy objectives and practices among the media elite, including Murrow and *See It Now*. Two events occurring days apart framed the national-security argument. On June 22, 1950, an American anticommunist organization published *Red Channels: The Report of Communist Influence in Radio and Television*, a list of 151 names of writers, directors, and performers said to be members of subversive organizations. Three days later, on June 25, North Korean troops crossed the border dividing it from the south, launching the Korean War. These events represent the twin themes that dominated American culture in the 1950s: fears of internal subversion and external invasion. The simultaneous hot war in Korea and Cold War with the Soviet Union intensified feelings of vulnerability to harm from within as well as outside America's borders. The Korean War claimed 36,914 American lives over a three-year period, during which time television allowed viewers to see combat zones from their own living rooms. Korea was, as historian Thomas Doherty points out, the "bloody backdrop to superpower rivalry" that contained the seeds of Soviet domination in Asia (Doherty 2003, 7).

The threat of the spread of Soviet ideology in Asia and fighting in Korea coincided with the hunt for Russian spies at home, and television delivered a new kind of war into America's living rooms, a Cold War that provoked a sense of unease and foreboding. An orchestrated campaign led by Federal Bureau of Investigation Director J. Edgar Hoover and fanned by Wisconsin Senator Joseph McCarthy claimed that "communist influences" had infiltrated the American airwaves and were using these "channels ... for pro-Soviet, pro-Communist, anti-American, anti-democratic propaganda" (American Business Consultants 1950: 1). *Red Channels*, launched by three former FBI officials calling themselves American Business Consultants, claimed the nation's entertainment industries—film, radio, and television—were paving the way for the eventual communist domination of American broadcasting (Barnouw 1975:109-110). The front line of the "counterattack" included the loyal American companies sponsoring programs, as well as the holders of broadcast licenses, who were "duty-bound" to uncover those who held anti-American views and deny them access "to our microphones" (American Business Consultants 1950: 6). *Red Channels* named 151 individuals in media industries with ties to socialist and communist organizations. Journalists were not immune: several of Murrow's colleagues were among those targeted. The blacklist destroyed careers by creating a climate where corporate sponsors, with network support and collusion, routinely weeded out writers, filmmakers, and on-air talent whose names appeared in the pages of *Red Channels*.

This was a new kind of warfare. At the end of World War II, most Americans expected the fledgling United Nations to work out border disputes and reparations demands among the victorious allies. Instead, U.N. meetings turned into another contested arena, especially between the United States and the Soviet Union. What emerged was a state of "cold war" between these two ideological enemies. Journalist and speechwriter Herbert Bayard Swope introduced the term in a 1947 speech he wrote for Bernard Baruch. But it was Walter Lippmann, influential in exposing the propaganda tactics after the First World War, who defined the issues at stake as "[A] policy of holding the line and hoping for the best ... [that] the Soviet Union will break its leg while the U.S. grows a pair of wings" (Lippmann 1947,12-13). Cold war was indirect combat, a battle for hearts and minds that shifted the U.S. toward a national security state and its policy of containment.

The fundamental problem for cold warriors, as historian Michael J. A. Hogan points out, was how the United States could wage a long-term war with the Soviet Union without sacrificing the freedoms America sought to defend (Hogan 1998, 21). And convincing the public of the merits of a powerful executive and a military outside of civilian control presented formidable obstacles (Hogan 1998, 288-289). It required persuasion on a massive scale, but it had to be simultaneously subtle and terrifying.

The apparent lack of public interest initially could be attributed partly to the desire to return to some kind of normalcy. Americans wanted to get a job, settle down, and raise their families; that was what they'd fought for, historian Lizabeth Cohen argues. During the war, government agencies, business leaders, and mass media had worked together to construct mass consumption as a civic duty that would provide "full employment and improved living standards for the nation" (Cohen 2003, 113). Consumption had been framed as a patriotic duty, not a personal indulgence. Although prosperity rested on citizens' shoulders, government generosity stoked it through such programs as the Servicemen's Readjustment Act of 1944—better known as the GI Bill of Rights—and support for new housing loans and highway construction (Cohen 2003, 118). As Cohen observes, the postwar consumer "devoted to more, newer, and better was the good citizen" (Cohen 2003, 119). In the end, the mass consumption economy also provided one of the most persuasive propaganda weapons in the Cold War, linking the free choice of American consumers with political liberty.

Initially, however, that pleasure-seeking, consumer-oriented lifestyle worried many national security advocates: Did Americans have the resolve, would they make the sacrifices, necessary to win a prolonged Cold War (Oakes 1994, 21)? National security advisors argued that Americans needed information about the real state of Soviet aggression and its aim of world communist domination in order to arrive at an "intelligent" opinion and "consensus" support for U.S. policies (Hogan 1998, 301). How to accomplish that without resorting to government-supported propaganda was the question. A string of events supplied the material to convince Americans their way of life was threatened if they failed to act. One occurred in 1947 with the implementation of loyalty oaths, when President Harry S. Truman ordered the U.S. Justice Department to draw up a list of possible "subversives" in government and to administer loyalty oaths to all public employees. Under the terms of this program, the federal government could dismiss an employee "if reasonable grounds exist for belief that the person involved is disloyal" (Truman Papers "Loyalty Oath" 1947, n. pag.). Then, in 1949, the Soviets tested their first atomic bomb, igniting a nuclear arms race that consumed Americans until the last decade of the 20th century.

Congress had already responded to growing domestic fears by approving the National Security Act in 1947. Among other things, the act consolidated all branches of the military under a Department of Defense and established a civilian Secretary of Defense as a cabinet post. Its real importance, however, lay in language establishing the permanent structures of war planning, capable of responding to security problems even without a threat from hostile nations (Raskin and Le-Van 2005, 16). Thus, by 1950, a whole new institutional infrastructure had been built to service national security, and a massive information effort, largely through popular media, rallied public support (Cohen 2003, 125-126). Television became a major resource in the production and distribution of the ideology of the national security state, primarily through its ability to frame it as a contest between competing systems—the democratic values of the United States, which emphasized the inseparability of security and liberty, versus Soviet totalitarianism and expansionism, which sought world domination and the overthrow of capitalism. Embedded in the discourse of security was the threat of nuclear annihilation and the need for constant vigilance. Liberty was framed in traditional cultural narratives of private property, individualism, and the moral superiority of American democracy (Hogan 1998, 2).

DOMESTICATING COLD WAR—
HEARTH AND HOME

A subtler problem lay in how to prepare Americans to resist Soviet expansion. The deepest concern among officials was the emotional stability of the American people faced with a nuclear attack (Oakes 1994, 21). By the time Truman created the Federal Civil Defense Administration in December 1950, "a clear line connected national will and national security, but civil defense planners had to tread carefully between bucking up the national will and stampeding the people into a panic" (Oakes 1994, 39). Historian Laura McEnaney describes civil defense planning as "the militarization of everyday life," an all-out propaganda effort as well as a national security strategy in which the "gradual encroachment of military ideas, values, and structures infiltrated the civilian domain" (McEnaney 2000, 6). Civil defense involved the whole society, not just the military, in preparation for nuclear war. But the process of "domesticating" defense proceeded in unpredictable ways. Lawmakers faced a balancing act—on one side trying to reconcile massive security needs against fears of military rule; on the other, confronting the financial impossibility of defending the civilian population against nuclear attack. These conflicting values led, McEnaney argues, to the privatization of civil defense and the emergence of the self-help model, which shifted the financial burden of protection from the government to the individual (McEnaney 2000, 7). Civil defense became a personal matter, a housekeeping issue conveyed to homemakers through the language and institutions of domesticity, including popular women's magazines and television (McEnaney 2000, 8).

Mass media taught ordinary citizens about "preparedness," spreading what historian Guy Oakes characterizes as the "rules of nuclear household care" (Oakes 1994, 120). Films made for television by the Civil Defense Administration, such as _This is Your Civil Defense_ and _Facts About Fallout_, linked personal responsibility to national security, painting the Soviet Union as a ruthless opponent threatening to topple the United States by every means at its disposal from nuclear attack to infiltration of its institutions (Oakes 1994, 120). Because of the scope of the threat, the films warned Americans not to rely on military power alone but to be prepared to defend their own families and communities. Survival depended upon self-help and following a few simple rules. As Oakes observes, these films reduced fallout to a matter of hygiene, characterizing its as an "uncommonly troublesome form of household dirt" that could be removed by thorough cleaning (Oakes 1994, 122).

Into this heated atmosphere dropped Senator Joseph R. McCarthy, whose assertions of communist spies infiltrating every layer of the government further complicated the domestic information campaign so necessary to the advancement of the national security state. The Soviet nuclear test in 1949 offered McCarthy the perfect example of government malfeasance, as many in Congress believed the Russians could not have produced such a weapon so quickly unless they had attained top-secret information. McCarthy launched his attack in a speech in Wheeling, West Virginia, on February 9, 1950, claiming the U.S. State Department was "riddled" with 205 "known" communist sympathizers and traitors (Guth 2002, 20). The exact number of spies changed every time McCarthy spoke. And witnesses called before the Senate Committee on Government Operations and its Permanent Subcommittee on Investigations, led by McCarthy, seemed to testify to a creeping communist conspiracy at all levels of society, one that undermined the very values upon which the nation stood. McCarthy's histrionics served the ends of national-security-state building, as the public acquiesced in the need to prepare for total war to stave off the Soviet threat to the American way of life.

TELEVISION: "WE TRUST YOU ARE NOT OFFENDED"

Television became the preferred medium for delivering directly into the American living room the twin messages of Soviet expansionism and the winnability of a nuclear attack. By the time *See It Now* debuted in November 1951 the national security state was well entrenched in the national psyche, and the effects of *Red Channels* and the blacklist were well established in the TV industry. Why did the television networks cooperate in an arrangement perceived today as an unwarranted intrusion on the free expression rights and obligations of the media? The answer is tangled in the complex web of power relationships among those inside the executive and legislative ranks of government, the owners of the networks, and the structure of their arrangements with both station owners and advertisers.

Daniel Hallin characterizes the period between 1940 and 1960 as "the heyday of straight journalism," when the reporter's job was to tell "'who, what, when, where,' and leave it at that" (Hallin 1994, 25). When a reporter presents competing political views, it implies balance, but as Robert Hackett observes it also deflects viewers' attention from the question of why the issue is cast in those particular terms or why it is an issue at all. Moreover, it obscures the reasons why these individuals, usually government officials, have the right to define the issue (Hackett 1984, 248). What arises is a "ritualistic posture of antagonism between press and government" (Bennett 1988, 125). To the public, they appear to operate independently, says Bennett, but in reality no one questions the content or the possibility of a broader range of political perspective: "Such ritualistic posturing dramatizes the myths of a free press and an open government that have been important parts of American image" since before the American Revolution (Bennett 1988, 125). As historian Nancy Bernhard points out, broadcast news, in particular the fledgling television news and public affairs programs of the 1950s, gained public credibility by their access to official sources at a time when deference to military authority, corporate profitability, and community consensus were high: "Collaboratively produced programs did not seem to surrender television's public service responsibility. Indeed, the networks constructed the programs … as the exemplary *fulfillment* of their public service responsibility and as evidence of their highly detached professional objectivity" (Bernhard 1999, 67, emphasis added).

Television had captured the American imagination as early as the 1920s, but it only came to dominate mass communications after World War II. Its rise was spectacular: In 1948, less than 0.5 percent of Americans had a TV set. Within two years, 9 percent had one, and a year later almost 25 percent of all homes had a television (Castleman and Podrazik 2003, 20 and 101). By 1956, nearly two-thirds of every American home owned at least one TV set (Baughman 2006, 41-42).

From its beginning, *See It Now* innovated with the news form, partly in response to the new technology of television but also in response to Murrow's insistence on the primacy of the personal narrative. Murrow built a reputation for fearlessness during World War II, reporting from the rooftops of London amid German bombing runs during the Battle of Britain and following American troops into battle. By war's end, he had assumed almost legendary status within the journalistic community and with the American public. Murrow's background and education as a college debater and stage actor influenced everything from his choice of language to his selection of handmade suits. Experience as a debater propelled him on a path that ultimately intersected with William S. Paley, chairman and owner of the CBS radio network. When they met, Paley had just embarked on a new radio programming format—public affairs and news—that appealed strongly to Murrow. The rest is history. From daring live reports during the London Blitz to the stare-down with Senator Joseph McCarthy, Murrow seemed to define broadcasting practices in the 1940s and 1950s.

Murrow was a reluctant convert to television, but with co-producer Fred W. Friendly leading the way technically, CBS launched *See It Now* in November 1951 (Sperber 1986, 354). Although the television public affairs format shares attributes of cinema documentary and newsreels, it ultimately was shaped by its relationship to viewers watching at home. The medium's essential domesticity easily adapted to the intimacy of family life and daily routines, and *See It Now* offered viewers a new way to engage in important issues through the on-camera presence of a trusted guide and adviser. Murrow addressed viewers as intimates, almost face to face from a low camera angle, using an apparently extemporaneous conversational style that became a typical feature of television documentary. *See It Now's* impact rested on the aura of Murrow's professionalism—the public's acceptance of his expertise signaled by his position in front of the control panel, reinforced by his impeccable attire and on-camera mannerisms—and his storytelling. His focus on individuals offered alternative views of world events from the position of the ordinary person.

Telling small stories began with the very first episode of *See It Now*, which concluded with a segment featuring the 101st Army Infantry 24th Division's Fox Company in Korea. The segment ends with Murrow, looking into the camera, telling the audience the company had taken 50 casualties and asking if they could "spare a pint [of blood]." Two weeks later, *See It Now* sent its cameras to follow a pint of blood from a donation center in New York to a field hospital in Korea. The story of Bottle 14528HA aired the following week, "in order," Murrow says, "that [we] might know what use was made of it." The segment was a small tour-de-force in logistics and technical prowess as the pint of blood hopscotched across the United States to Hawaii, Tokyo and finally Kimpo Air Force Base Korea. The segment played on the sense of urgency arising from both the need for blood and its nature: whole blood expires rapidly and requires a constant cool temperature. Murrow narrates the journey, which he personalized by identifying precisely "our" pint of blood as Bottle 14528HA. Planes take off and land under the expert guidance of air traffic controllers, medical technicians diligently monitor the temperature and add ice to coolers containing multiple pints of blood. All along, the clock is running as Murrow ticks off the time: "14528HA arrives in Tokyo—37 hours after it left the States," he tells the audience. By the time Bottle 14528HA arrives in Kimpo, it "has come a long way from the comfort of the blood center in your hometown. The blood is almost a week old now, the wounds they must fight are only minutes old, and Kimpo is still not the front."

The precious pint is loaded onto a medical evacuation helicopter and lifted to the 121st Evac Hospital, where PFC Wayne Capson, "wounded less than three hours ago," will receive it and several more in an operation. Throughout the narration, Murrow addresses the audience intimately, bringing it into private spaces to listen in on, and sometimes initiate, conversations. In the operating room, Murrow carefully explains the procedures ("the patient has been shaved and scrubbed with benzene or ether to remove the oil from the skin. The scalpel cuts through the outer layer of skin"), and the camera follows the surgery from a distance, always keeping a close eye on a pint of blood dripping slowly into the patient's arm.

No one had ever seen war, or its effects, in their living rooms on a Sunday afternoon. The images were grainy and often overexposed, and the panning camera occasionally left viewers' heads spinning. Nevertheless, it was compelling viewing because it gave audiences access to real events—an actual operation from the frontlines of a war 3,000 miles away. Viewers heard the clink of metal-on-metal as the extracted bullet hit the waiting pan and listened in as air-traffic controllers cleared huge transport planes for take off. Murrow concluded the segment with an apology: "We trust that you are not offended by the clinical realism of these pictures. We debated for some time before deciding to bring them into your home. We determined that they were part of our flesh and blood—they weren't actors—and that we in this country are not required to live in cotton batting. And if those men can stand the experience, we concluded that *we* could stand to look at it."

"SPEAKING INFORMALLY TO EQUALS"

There is no record of whether the pint-of-blood segment resulted in an increase in donations the following week, but it became the basis of an episode of *M*A*S*H*, a popular television series about the Korean War that aired in the 1970s. It also exhibits many of the characteristic elements of the television public affairs form that came to dominate the medium for two decades, a form that simultaneously acknowledges its entrance into the intimate space of the home and its ability to affect people's actions and attitudes.

Murrow provided the guiding rationale, emphasizing the human impact rather than focusing on the event itself. That form of storytelling fit the new medium, which had become an ersatz member of the family. The focus on the individual caught up in events promotes the nuclear family, but it also, as Wendy Kozol argues, cultivates a trend toward privatization (Kozol 1994, 184). Such an orientation deflects attention from collective responsibility, situating the solution to systemic social, economic, and political problems within the family unit. The family also, importantly, provided the anchor for those "traditional American virtues of self-determination, personal responsibility, and voluntary cooperation" that Oakes points out were so necessary to waging the Cold War, where civil defense was linked to family values (Oakes 1994, 105-106).

The up-close-and-personal focus of *See It Now* may be attributed partly to the technical constraints of television, but it also acknowledges TV's social function within the intimate confines of home and family. Television reconfigured the intimacies of home and family in the 1950s. Its programs, available at set times on predictable days, were crafted to appeal to the tastes of probable viewers at given times—for example, children's programs in the late afternoons, soap operas for stay-at-home moms at midday, Westerns for early-evening family viewing. Initially, Cecelia Tichi points out, television disrupted household behaviors and norms, as the private home became more like such public places as the local theater, snack bar, or ballpark (Tichi 1991, 24). However, popular magazines like *Ladies Home Journal* and *Life* helped domesticate the medium, instructing homemakers where to place the cumbersome box, first in the living room, later in a family room dedicated to its use. At the same time, such publications helped normalize its screen as a window on the world, bringing into the family circle new faces and places (Spigel 1992, 41).

With *See It Now*, television news also began to develop specific forms of narration and story organization that differed from its newsreel and radio progenitors (Scannell 1991, 3). Talk on early television programs tended toward monologue—experts speaking at length to unseen listeners—rather than dialogue. However, television demanded a degree of naturalness in these exchanges, which meant broadcasters had to learn how to address the audience as intimates, how to behave in the domestic space of the home where people were "spoken to in the friendly, familiar, and informal manner of equals" (ibid.).

Murrow excelled at that. He regarded voice and speech as the vehicles of thought and persuasion, perhaps only natural in one trained in speaking and debate and an accomplished collegiate actor (Sperber 1986, 25-26). On *See It Now*, Murrow employed both direct speech to the audience and three-way "conversation"—the talk show-guest format that treats the audience as one of the participants (Goffman 1981, 227). The combination of on-the-spot interviews and voice over—alternating between Murrow and the reporter in the field providing context and background information—created a degree of intimacy previously unknown in film or radio documentary (ibid).

Each episode of *See It Now* was meticulously edited and scripted, and stories were selected based on reported events and the co-producers' interests. Early episodes ranged over an array of subjects, linked only by Murrow's presence in the studio. What set it apart were its stylistic contributions, for example the Korea segment from episode one ended with each soldier identifying himself and his hometown. These men represented the voices and faces of America, and viewers at home began to see and hear themselves on the small screen. At the same time, most of the stories had political agendas, prompted by government or industry interest in influencing public opinion. Insiders routinely fed ideas and events to news organizations like CBS and *See It Now*, which cast them into stories with standardized plots. As Bennett points out, the story format produces constraints on news content: "Criminal trials are dominated by 'mistaken identity' or 'victim of circumstances' ... Storytelling between friends often centers on recurring themes that define the relationship. ... In politics ... elites, leaders, define political situations [by] familiar themes [which] strike journalists and ordinary citizens as suitable framings of events ... [employing plot devices] characterized ... as ethnocentrism (American first, America the generous, America the embattled), altruistic democracy, responsible capitalism, individualism" (Bennett 1988, 130).

"A SMALL FOOTNOTE IN HISTORY"

Murrow and *See It Now* were relatively late in engaging McCarthy, who had already caught many prominent members of the publishing and entertainment industries in his net. His Senate subcommittee also had targeted the military and the U.S. State Department, accusing them of security breaches. These were powerful forces in American culture, with the ability to fight back to some degree, and some did.

Years before Murrow stepped into the fray, journalists had denounced McCarthy and exposed his factual lapses (Persico 1988, 373). Murrow himself had criticized McCarthy's tactics on his daily radio news program, and journalists from Walter Lippmann to Drew Pearson, and broadcasters Elmer Davis and H.V. Kaltenborn, had taken aim at the senator on television (ibid).

Some of the McCarthy hearings were televised, and the media presentation of them helped rally public opinion through the apparent exposure of lapses in government oversight. In many ways, McCarthy's histrionics served the ends of national-security-state building, as the public acquiesced in the need to prepare for total war to stave off the Soviet threat to the American way of life. Although mass media were not entirely silent about McCarthy's tactics, they generally reproduced the basic government line about the need for constant vigilance. Even *See It Now* aired a number of stories in the 1951-1953 period offering reassuring messages about preparedness and survivability in a nuclear attack. The program, however, did not address the threat of internal subversion directly until Murrow and Friendly began their assault on McCarthy with "The Case of Milo Radulovich." The episode, focused entirely on one man's struggle against the senator, resonated deeply with audiences. Media historian Rodger Streitmatter argues that television generally was "pivotal in exposing exactly how McCarthy operated," but the Radulovich episode marked the beginning of his take-down (Streitmatter 2007, 173).

CBS was not enthusiastic when Friendly and Murrow approached management about the episode they planned to air on the night of October 20, 1953. According to Friendly, there was a resounding silence from the executive offices and a refusal to pay for an ad in the *New York Times* publicizing the program. Murrow and Friendly paid for it themselves—$1,500 for a display ad that read: "The Case Against Milo Radulovich, A0589839," listing the time and station and signed by both. No CBS logo, no CBS eye. As it went on the air, Friendly recounts: "Murrow took a final sip from a glass of scotch at his feet, offered me my customary gulp and said, 'I don't know whether we'll get away with this one or not, and things will never be the same around here after tonight, but this show may turn out to be a small footnote to history in the fight against the senator'" (Friendly 1967, 3-4).

Most Americans would never become entangled in one of McCarthy's communist witch-hunts, but Murrow and Friendly needed a vehicle to convince the public of the danger of the senator's actions. They found it by linking the complex issues of national security and loyalty to one man's plight. Their story focused on Radulovich, a 26-year-old reserve officer in the Air Force studying physics at the University of Michigan. The issue revolved around the degree of security risk he represented because of his family.

McCarthy is never mentioned, but his specter hangs over the episode. *See It Now* picked up the original story from a Detroit newspaper, which reported that the Air Force, alarmed by the red scare histrionics unleashed by McCarthy, had labeled Radulovich a "security risk" for associating with communists or communist sympathizers, presumably his father, who read a Serbian-language newspaper, and sister, who may have belonged to a questionable political group. The Air Force asked him to resign his reserve commission. Radulovich refused. The Air Force then convened a board hearing at which sealed information was submitted but which neither Radulovich nor his attorney ever read. The board recommended that Radulovich be "severed" from the Air Force. When the *See It Now* episode aired, the case awaited a final decision from Secretary of the Air Force Harold E. Talbott.

The episode begins with Radulovich, seated on his living room sofa, speaking directly to the camera. He looks middle class, neatly dressed in casual clothes, surrounded by the comfortable furnishings of a 1950s-modern living room. His entire opening monologue speaks to patriotism and family values, beginning with the charge against him, which pits loyalty to his family against loyalty to his country, and ending with his question about who will employ him if the charge sticks.

The story that unfolds sidesteps ethnicity and overlooks any potential class differences with the father—who works in an auto assembly plant—by focusing on the son, whose accomplishments include pursuit of a physics degree while simultaneously providing for his wife and two children. Only the broken English of Radulovich senior pleading for "my boy" reveals a non-native speaker. Murrow ignores ethnic differences; yet ethnicity is intertwined with the allegations against Radulovich senior, whose crime appears to be reading a Serbian-language newspaper.

Murrow and Friendly visualize the cost of national security in terms of its threat to domesticity, relying on contemporary cultural values about family and home for a framework. Much of McCarthy's anticommunist hysteria focused on internal rather than external threats to the American way of life, and in the case of Milo Radulovich the home became the frontline, the contested space of both familial and national security. Yet, the episode's domestic narrative deflects attention from the underlying contradiction of a *national* security state that is the responsibility of the *individual* by focusing on the family that is to be protected and preserved. That approach, which becomes the broadcast norm by the 1960s, reduced the complexities of national security to a concrete example that ignores some important social and political issues. Murrow dilutes the larger institutional issue to a communication failure by the Air Force, which has not clearly expressed the rules of the game of national security. His summation does not question the idea of national security or the need for secrecy, which are taken for granted, nor does it directly address whether dissent is necessarily disloyal, which is the implication of the government's action. In this "whole area of the relationship between the individual and the state," which Murrow addresses in his closing monologue, no one questions the ideology of Cold War and all its implications. Such abstract ideas are difficult for television to capture; its inherent visuality begs for a dramatic narrative to clarify and simplify the issue. And by focusing on the Radulovich family, the episode certainly did that.

"The Case of Milo Radulovich" energized the public, at least the public that saw it. The audience for *See It Now* was not large, nor was it for any news program in the 1950s. *See It Now* averaged an 8.1 share and a 9.1 share, respectively, in 1952 and 1953, when it still ran on Sundays, although its move to a Tuesday-evening time slot shortly before the Radulovich episode aired probably boosted the audience somewhat (Stewart 1954, 396). *Who* was watching that night mattered: it was an audience still largely confined to the Northeast and North Central states. And its viewers were demographically prime territory—the affluent and influential who could affect change, a point often overlooked in critiques of the program. The Radulovich episode encouraged viewers to locate themselves with him at the center of this controversy. The class status implied in the episode suggests that the middle-class was not immune from threats to its freedom. Praise poured in for the episode, but that's a double-edged sword: for while it honors the integrity of the producers and the network for revealing the plight of one man, it also reflects the mass media echo chamber, which ignores other equally significant messages contained in the visual and verbal narrative.

CONCLUSION

See It Now played a key role in familiarizing television audiences, watching at home, with a way of seeing news framed in the small story of personal involvement rather than an extended narration of a complex issue or event. The program frequently located its viewers within the domestic spheres of home and work, which represented the opportunities and freedom of a capitalist society in contrast to the deprivations and limitations of communism. This strategy endowed *See It Now* with urgency and importance and helped sustain Cold War political tensions, even when episodes did not directly address those conflicts. In episodes like "The Case of Milo Radulovich," *See It Now* mobilized popular fears among a certain class of viewers about the frightening reach of McCarthyism, which undermined the very values epitomized in the American home and family.

See It Now's influence lives on in the many television news-magazine programs airing today, offering immediately accessible personal narratives of the American dream deferred by people caught up in circumstances beyond their control. Framing political, economic, and social issues within the domestic realm of the individual—coupled with the organizational and storytelling structure exemplified by Murrow in the control room directing reporters and cameramen in the field—defines the American television documentary form that prevails in such continuing popular public-affairs programs as *20/20* and *60 Minutes*.

Don Hewitt, who became one of CBS's top editors and producer of *60 Minutes*, appeared in the opening sequence of every episode of *See It Now*, seen only from the back (he's the figure wearing headphones and turning dials). He said he learned from working with Murrow and Friendly that "it is your ear as much as your eye that keeps you at a television set. It's what you hear as much as what you see" (Sperber 1986: 381). But Hewitt's emphasis on "personal" journalism as the format for *60 Minutes* was as much an economic-ratings decision as much as one driven by news values (Campbell 1991, 3). Richard Campbell, who analyzed extensively the first two decades of *60 Minutes*, argues that its emphasis on personalized narratives "redirected the structure of television news programs away from the appearance of facticity—describing and listing information in neutral reports—and toward the narrative intrigues of character, setting, plot and conflict. [Its] style of 'personal' reporting ... [applies] the techniques of realistic fiction to journalism" (Campbell 1991, 29).

News organizations of all stripes have adopted the story format in part because it seems to represent the authentic voice of the people involved in an issue or an event. And, as Bennett points out, authenticity plays to public expectations that the news is "true and believable" (Bennett 1988, 118). The small-story form is reproduced in journalism schools as the way journalists can engage big, complex issues. That's because drama and conflict attract audiences, and personal narratives often pit the "little guy" against an institution, playing into well-worn formulas that don't require expertise in specialized subject matter: "[G]eneralism is justified almost exclusively in normative terms. A key element of the journalism code is public service. The news is billed normatively as a democratic service to the mass public. ... [and] the standardized story format is justified as the best means of presenting comprehensible information to the average person. [Specialized] expertise run[s] the risk of complicating a story" (Bennett 1988, 132).

This personalized form of storytelling has become so naturalized most viewers never notice it. What better way to convey complicated ideas than by making a human connection? It is, after all, easier to visualize a person than a process (Jamison and Campbell 2001, 41). Taking the audience into the domestic space of an individual's family and home offers viewers both pleasure and a novel way of engaging important social and political issues through glimpses of others' lives. But the focus on the personal can distort underlying issues, and the overall effect may be profound. Privileging the individual experience over the collective impact of the issue or event ignores the possibility of widespread and widely different effects, depending on a person's class, gender, race, or ethnicity. Further, privatizing crises by focusing on a representative family or individual also can foreclose the possibility of community activism by deflecting attention to small problems that can be solved immediately (ibid.). In the end, some important social, political, and economic questions may remain unanswered or unnoticed.

REFERENCES

American Business Consultants. 1950. *Red Channels: The Report of Communist Influence in Radio and Television*. New York: Counterattack.

Barnouw, Erik. 1975. *Tube of Plenty: The Evolution of American Television*. London: Oxford UP.

Baughman, James. 2006. *The Republic of Mass Culture: Journalism, Filmmaking, and Broadcasting in America Since 1941*. 3rd Ed. Baltimore: Johns Hopkins UP.

Bennett, Lance W. 1988. *News: The Politics of Illusion*. Second Edition. New York: Longman.

Bernhard, Nancy E. 1999. *U.S. Television News and Cold War Propaganda, 1947-1960*. Cambridge Studies in the History of Mass Communication. Cambridge: Cambridge UP.

Campbell, Richard. 1991. *60 Minutes and the News: A Mythology for Middle America*. Urbana: Illinois UP.

Castleman, Harry and Walter J. Podrazik. 2003. *Watching TV: Six Decades of American Television*. The Television Ser., Robert J. Thompson, ed. Syracuse: Syracuse UP.

"Case of Lt. Milo Radulovich." *See It Now*. CBS. 3 Oct. 1953. Tape No. 112. Prod. Columbia Broadcasting System. New York.

Cohen, Lizabeth. 2003. *A Consumers' Republic: The Politics of Mass Consumption in Postwar America*. New York: Vintage.

Curtain, Michael. 1995. *Redeeming the Wasteland: Television Documentary and Cold War Politics*. New Brunswick, NJ: Rutgers UP.

Doherty, Thomas. 2003. *Cold War, Cool Medium: Television, McCarthyism, and American Culture*. Film and Culture Ser. New York: Columbia UP.

Friendly, Fred. 1967. *Due to Circumstances Beyond Our Control*. New York: Random House.

Gitlin, Todd. 1978. "Media Sociology: The Dominant Paradigm." *Theory and Society* 6. 209-245.

Goffman, Erving. 1981. *Forms of Talk*, Philadelphia: U of Pennsylvania Press.

Gould, Jack. 1953. "Video Journalism: Treatment of Radulovich Case History by 'See It Now' is Fine Reporting." *New York Times* 25 October.

Guth, David. 2002. "From OWI to USIA: The Jackson Committee's Search for the Real 'Voice of America.'" *American Journalism* 19, 20.

Hackett, Robert A. 1984. "Decline of a Paradigm? Bias and Objectivity in News Media Studies." *Critical Studies in Mass Communication* 1: 229-259.

Hallin, Daniel. 1994. *We Keep America on Top of the World: Television Journalism and The Public Sphere*. London: Routledge.

Hogan, Michael J. 1998. *A Cross of Iron: Harry S. Truman and the Origins of the National Security State, 1945-1954*. Cambridge: Cambridge UP.

Jamison, Kathleen Hall and Karlyn Kohrs Campbell. 2001. *The Interplay of Influence: News, Advertising, Politics, and the Mass Media*. Belmont, CA. Wadsworth/Thomson Learning.

Jowett, Garth S. and Victoria O'Donnell. 1992. *Propaganda and Persuasion*. 2nd ed. Newbury Park, CA: Sage.

Kendrick, Alexander. 1969. *Prime Time: The Life of Edward R. Murrow*. Boston: Little, Brown & Co.

Kozol, Wendy. 1994. *Life's American: Family and Nation in Postwar Photojournalism*. Philadelphia: Temple UP.

Lippmann, Walter. 1987. "The Cold War," Foreign Affairs 65 (Spring): 884-869

McEnaney, Laura. 2000. *Civil Defense Begins @ Home: Militarization Meets Everyday Life in the Fifties*. Princeton: Princeton UP.

Oakes, Guy. 1994. *The Imaginary War: Civil Defense and American Cold War Culture*. Oxford: Oxford UP.

Palmer, Allen W. and Edward L. Carter. 2006. "The Smith-Mundt Act's Ban on Domestic Propaganda: An Analysis of the Cold War Statute Limiting Access to Public Diplomacy." *Communication Law and Policy* 11: 1-34.

Persico, Joseph. 1988. *Edward R. Murrow: An American Original*. New York: Dell.

Rawnsley, G. 1999. *Cold War Propaganda in the 1950s*. New York: St. Martin's Press.

Raskin, Marcus G. and A. Carl LeVan. 2005. "The National Security State and the Tragedy of Empire." *In Democracy's Shadow: The Secret World of National Security*. Eds. Marcus G. Raskin & A. Carl LeVan. New York: Nation Books. 3-43.

Ross, Andrew. 1996. "Containing Culture in the Cold War." *Cultural Studies* 1: 328-48.

Roeder, George A. Jr. 1993. *The Censored War: American Visual Experience During World War Two*. New Haven: Yale UP.

Schiller, Dan. 1996. *Theorizing Communication: A History*. New York: Oxford UP.

Scannell, Paddy. 1991."Introduction: The Relevance of Talk." *Broadcast Talk*. Ed. Paddy Scannell. London: Sage.

Sperber, A. M. 1986. *Murrow: His Life and Times*. New York: Freundlich.

Spigel, Lynn. 1992. *Make Room for TV: Television and the Family Ideal in Postwar America*. Chicago, University of Chicago Press.

Sproule, Michael J. 1989. "Progressive Propaganda Critics and the Magic Bullet Myth." *Critical Studies in Mass Communication* 6: 225-246.

Stewart, Robert Hammel. 1954. The Development of Network Television Program Types to January 1953. Diss. Ohio State University.

Streitmatter, Rodger. 2008. *Mightier Than the Sword: How the News Media Have Shaped American History*. New York: Westview Press.

Tichi, Cecelia. 1991. *Electronic Hearth: Creating an American Television Culture*. New York: Oxford UP.

Truman, Harry S. Truman Public Papers."Truman Loyalty Oath, 1947." Dept. of History, Michigan State U. 10 Sept. 2006. http://coursesa.matrix.msu.edu/~hst203/documents/loyal.html.

U.S. Census. 1955. "Television Sets in Households in the United States June 1955," *Housing and Construction Reports: Housing Characteristics*. Washington, D.C. September.

CHAPTER 6

"WE CAN REMEMBER IT FOR YOU WHOLESALE"

LESSONS OF THE BROADCAST BLACKLIST

Carol A. Stabile

> What the world supplies to myth is an historical reality, defined, even if this goes back quite a while, by the way in which men have produced or used it; and what myth gives in return is a *natural* image of this reality. And just as bourgeois ideology is defined by the abandonment of the name 'bourgeois,' myth is constituted by the loss of the historical quality of things: in it, things lose the memory that they once were made. (Barthes 1989, 142)

I N PHILIP K. DICK'S STORY, "WE CAN REMEMBER IT FOR YOU WHOLESALE," Douglas Quail purchases implanted or "extra-factual" memories in order to inexpensively fulfill his dream of visiting Mars. But the implantation reveals that that Quail's memory has already been tampered with—he actually is a government assassin—and further attempts to implant memories reveal older suppressed memories. The metaphor of Quail's extra-factual, manipulated memories offers a starting-point for understanding why U.S. culture recalls the 1950s through a certain set of images and ideas. In particular, U.S. culture "remembers" the 1950s as the fountainhead of family and family values largely because our memories of family and the gender roles that underwrite this construction were in fact remembered for us "wholesale," through a process of industrial production that has repressed even the memory of any challenges to what would soon become the ideological status quo.

The following essay considers the ways in which the broadcast blacklist affected how media studies scholars think about and study the 1950s, as well how we understand the role of gender and family in 1950s popular culture. At the start of the 1950s—at the very moment in which television was emerging, in the words of blacklisted writer Shirley Graham DuBois, as "the newest, the most powerful, the most direct means of communication devised by Man .... [whose] potentialities for Good or for Evil are boundless"—a massive ideological crackdown occurred in broadcasting (Graham 1964, 1). By focusing on how the blacklist made struggles over gender, race, and class unspeakable in the new medium, this essay seeks to restore the memory of these struggles and their participants to accounts of the 1950s, to underscore the strategic manipulation of culture and memory by conservative forces, and to remind us just how crucial historical research is for media studies.

GENDER, HISTORY, AND PRODUCTION

Over the past thirty years, literature on Cold War television has focused on consumption and women-as-consumers of television produced for them by men. This focus has made sense in terms of our own intellectual history—for those interested in gender and women in particular, women were at least visible in front of the camera and, based on the assumption that women were excluded from production, the focus on consumption allowed media studies scholars to consider women as active agents in relation to media, rather than as passive spectators of content produced and structured by a male gaze. But as historian Michele Hilmes (1997) convincingly argues, women *were* working in the broadcast industry prior to the 1950s. The focus on women-as-consumers has had the unfortunate effect of reinforcing the gendering of producers as male and consumers as female and reproducing the belief that women were simply not present at the birth of either radio or television. While key scholarly works on 1950s television—Lynn Spigel's *Make Room for TV* (1992), George Lipsitz's *Time Passages* (2001), Nina Leibman's *Living Room Lectures* (1995), and Ella Taylor's *Prime Time Families* (1991)—all importantly offered ideological analyses of 1950s television and its content, none of these considered the material production of these images: namely, the producers and writers who created television content and the conditions in which they were working at such a formative moment in the history

of television. Of course, in order to document resistance to 1950s gender ideologies on the part of cultural producers we must also understand the impact of what Raymond Williams (2001) described as the
selective tradition in order to seek traces of content that never made
it onto the air. Focusing only on what was actually broadcast does not
allow us glimpses into alternatives to the gendered narratives that ultimately became hegemonic. Fundamentally, understanding the history
of what was made and broadcast on television also means researching
what it was not possible to make.

Although the blacklist played a determining role in what made it
onto the air, as well as what would make it onto the air in years to
come, the impact of the Red Scare on the content of 1950s television
has yet to be reckoned with. Scholarship on the broadcast blacklist
remains thin, although a large body of literature in film history and
studies addresses the blacklist in the motion picture industry. But no
research focuses specifically on the impact of the blacklist on women
working in film or television industries or the progressive feminist
ideas many of them were struggling to communicate to a larger audience. How do we account for these gaps in scholarship? After all,
media and cultural studies include many articles and full-length books
on 1950s television. Was the blacklist in broadcasting really such a
comparatively uninteresting or unimportant event in television history, with little impact on the industry itself? Following from these
questions, are there historical and political reasons for the ignorance
of the broadcast blacklist in popular culture that are homologous to
the silence in scholarly literature? Why do memories of the 1950s—
whether popular or scholarly—so seldom include mention of the
blacklist?

THE MAKING OF THE MAKING OF THE FAMILY

Fifties television programming contained a specifically androcentric
fantasy of family life. In it, women uncomplainingly did the work of
raising children, managing households, and volunteering in their communities, gratefully exchanging stressful work in the waged economy
for the promise of serenity in the domestic sphere. Those who popu-
lated this landscape were as white as the snow that often distorted
television signals. Judged solely on the basis of television images, it
seemed that the ideological shift that occurred in the years following
the war was a bloodless coup in which those working in the broadcast

industry and consumers alike—all of them apparently white people invested in whiteness—were swept off their feet by the seductive promises of postwar consumer culture.

The world that appeared in 1950s family sitcoms was a world in which father knew best; in which no one suspected that Margaret Anderson's obsessive cleaning might be a symptom of a problem that had no name, as Betty Friedan (1964) was to put it less than a decade later; or that June Cleaver's bland happiness may have come from a pill bottle. As Joanne Meyerowitz points out in her reassessment of postwar mass culture, "the conservative promotion of domesticity" (1994, 230) was neither blindly accepted nor unopposed. Women did not always joyously give up jobs that had afforded them a measure of autonomy. Rather than decreasing, women's workforce participation steadily increased throughout the 1950s, albeit in low paying and often part time positions. Black women and men did not quietly and passively return to lives limited by segregation and racial discrimination, as the civil rights movement was demonstrating.

The images that dominated television content in the 1950s ineluctably shaped beliefs and memories of family and gender in the U.S., their formulaic nature and cohesiveness erasing the struggles that were occurring off camera. Fearful of even referencing the blacklist, writers avoided hinting at its existence. Even fifteen years later, when the blacklist came up during publicity interviews with blacklisted actor Jean Muir, networks "bleeped" out references to the sponsors, networks, and ad agencies who had had a hand in her firing (Gould 1965, 29; 1966, 55). This silence is notable in an industry that has avidly mythologized its own history in a series of now iconic moments: the Army-McCarthy hearings, in which the new medium of television played the role of heroic defender of civil liberties (overlooking, of course, CBS' firing of Ed Murrow just a few years later, not to mention its assiduous enforcement of the loyalty oath among its rank and file); the quiz show scandal of 1956, enshrined as a triumph of self-regulation; coverage of the 1968 Democratic Convention; the inflated role that television was said to have played in ending the Vietnam War. That television has proved reluctant to narrate this one story about its own history is therefore significant, particularly insofar as this story hints at the powerful suppression of dissident views on family and gender.

Fig. 1: Jean Muir (Courtesy of Stephens College)

At the time, and for creative and often politically progressive people working in media industries, television held out new hopes and
dreams about the creative and cultural potential of broadcasting. Although there was no debate over whether the new medium was going to be commercial, a cohort of writers like Ruth Gordon, Garson
Kanin, Gore Vidal, and Arthur Miller all believed that television could
provide an important venue for political and creative expression. But
progressives underestimated just how far the U.S. government, media
executives, advertisers, and politicians were willing to go to ensure that
"controversial" content (particularly material that could be construed
as politically progressive on issues of race, gender, class, or immigration) would not appear. The family that came to appear in entertainment programming was thus very much the end result of a systematic
purge of dissenting voices and viewpoints from media industries; the
memory of that family very much the product of an active process of

Fig. 2: Hazel Scott at Piano (permission of Library of Congress)

memory implantation and manipulation. To remember the Red Scare and purges in the television industry thus is to understand the images produced in the 1950s as the effect not necessarily of consensus within the industry or in U.S. culture writ large, but as the result of abject cowardice, concessions to rightwing fears and paranoia, and the quashing of debate ironically attributed to communism itself. That the blacklist in the television industry occurred during a formative moment in television history, in which the routines and practices that would come to govern the industry for decades to come were beginning to coalesce, meant that television content from that moment on would bear the imprimatur of anti-communism and the racism and sexism that were a part of it.

THE BIBLE OF THE BLACKLIST

On June 22, 1950, *Red Channels: The Report of Communist Influence in Radio and Television* was published by the anti-communist journal

CounterAttack. The introduction's author was Vincent Hartnett, a former naval intelligence officer and later an employee for the Philips H. Lord Agency, where he supervised the writing of the radio series *Gangbusters.* Vincent Hartnett also served as an informant for the FBI (Jean Muir FBI Files 1953).[1] *Red Channels* began with testimony J. Edgar Hoover had presented to a U.S. Congressional Committee in 1947, that "The (Communist) Party has departed from depending upon the printed word as its medium of propaganda and has taken to the air. Its members and sympathizers have not only infiltrated the airways but they are now persistently seeking radio channels" (*Red Channels* 1950, 1). Although the publication of the slender volume was eclipsed by the start of the Korean War just three days later, over the course of the summer, anti-communist forces began to mobilize using *Red Channels* to pressure advertisers and sponsors to fire the "controversial" cultural workers listed in its pages. David Jacobson of Young & Rubicam told the FBI that General Foods "had stated they would put nobody on their sponsored program who had been listed in 'Red Channels'" (Nichols 1950). In August, CBS suddenly fired Jean Muir, who had been cast as the mother in the television sitcom *The Aldrich Family,* just hours before taping of the first episode was to begin. In September, NBC very quietly cancelled *The Hazel Scott Show.* Its star had appeared before the House Un-American Activities Committee just a week earlier. The firing of these two women—one white, one African American—ushered in the era of the broadcast blacklist.

Red Channels included the names of 144 women and men working in broadcasting, as well as the names of people the authors feared might move into broadcasting. Of the 144 names listed, a surprising 40 were women working in broadcasting, as producers, writers, actors, and dancers. The individuals identified in *Red Channels* were listed alongside various political affiliations that: a) showed "how the Communists have been able to carry out their plan of infiltration" of broadcasting; b) indicated "the extent to which" individuals had been "inveigled" or duped into lending their names "to organizations espousing Communist causes"; and c) that were intended "to discourage actors and artists from naïvely lending their names to Communist organizations or causes in the future" (*Red Channels,* 9).

---

1   Both Jean Muir and Hazel Scott's FBI files are available on my blog: cstabile.wordpress.com.

Red Channels had an effect disproportionate to its size or the veracity of its research. The firing of Muir, a longtime supporter of Civil Rights and the NAACP, close friend of NAACP president Walter White, and wife of the American Federation of Radio and Television Actors' head counsel, Henry Jaffe, sent a clear message to progressives in the broadcast industry, many of whom had watched in dismay as the Red Scare hit Hollywood a few years earlier. Shortly after the show's taping was cancelled, General Foods Corporation, the program's sponsor, announced that they had fired Jean Muir because she was "'a controversial personality' whose presence on the video show might adversely affect the sale of the advertiser's product" (Gould 1950a, 1). According to NBC and General Foods, the protests of outraged anticommunist consumers had forced them to make this difficult decision, even though they had received a scant twenty phone calls and two telegrams in protest—hardly a mandate, considering the thousands of letters some programs received from consumers (Everitt 2007, 150). When NBC moved to replace Muir, General Foods' position had become more absolute: they had cancelled Muir's contract because they were certain her presence "*would* provoke unfavorable criticism and even antagonism among sizable groups of consumers" (Everitt, 60).

The firing of Hazel Scott received considerably less attention in the mainstream press than did the firing of Jean Muir, although the African American press was swift to point out that both women had been politically active in the Civil Rights movement. A talented, Juilliard-educated musician and performer, like Jean Muir, Scott was married to a prominent New Yorker: Scott had married Adam Clayton Powell in 1945. Like Muir, Scott had used her stardom to advocate for Civil Rights. Throughout her career, Scott refused to play in segregated venues. In the late 1940s, while touring the Northwest, a diner in Pasco, Washington refused to serve Scott. When she complained to the local police, Scott was told that she could either leave town or be arrested for disturbing the peace. Instead, Scott filed a lawsuit against the diner owners, ultimately winning a settlement of $250,000, which she promptly donated to the NAACP (Chilton 2008, 139-140). Scott's role as host of her own variety show also challenged the color line in television: it was the first television show to star an African American (Nat King Cole's equally short-lived variety show would not premier until 1956) and a woman.

That the Muir and Scott cases involved politically active career women who had close ties to the NAACP, as well as husbands who were prominent liberal politicians (Jaffe was dealing with the impact of the blacklist in television and Powell was seeking re-election to the U.S. House of Representatives) was hardly coincidental. For as the ideology of the nuclear family took hold, women working in the broadcast industry found themselves vulnerable on two fronts. First, women were expected to be engaging in appropriate procreative activities in the domestic sphere rather than competing with men for employment. Professional women who had been combining careers and families in the 1940s became sitting ducks in the 1950s. Second, and as the right-twing vituperation aimed at Eleanor Roosevelt illustrated, not only should women not forsake their domestic duties to their families, to interfere in political matters (save only the most racist, rightwing, pronatalist politics) was as surely a sign of communism as disobedience to male authority was a sign of witchcraft in the seventeenth century.[2]

Once labeled a communist, moreover, these women had few resources for defending themselves. As scholar Marie Jahoda (1956) made clear in her landmark study of the blacklist in the entertainment industry, to even refer to the blacklist in public was to make one's self politically vulnerable, which made even sympathizers reluctant to express solidarity or support. The blacklist combined with legal action on the part of those dismissed to create a culture of silence and denial. John Frankenheimer, a director at NBC in the 1950s, later recounted: "Well, it was awful and what happened at CBS was that you would get a list of actors and you'd say Simon, Penn, Mulligan, Frankenheimer and you'd call into an extension and you didn't even know who was at the other end of it. And the next day somebody would call you back and say Mulligan fine, Penn fine, Frankenheimer no. And you never had, you never knew why or how and then you'd try to get to the bottom of it and you couldn't. It was a very, very serious horrible phase of our lives and our business. And people forget about that when they talk about the Golden Age of television" ("The Dynamics of Live Television" 1994). To defend one's self publicly—to name the namers—was to risk further smears and accusations, particularly for those who

---

2 Redhunters like Elizabeth Dilling and J. Edgar Hoover shared a dislike for Eleanor Roosevelt that bordered on the obsessive. See Gleason (1997) and Jeansonne (1996) on Elizabeth Dilling and Theoharis and Cox (1998) on Hoover.

Fig. 3: Gertrude Berg (George Karger/Time & Life Pictures/Getty Images)

did hold progressive beliefs, who had worked for social change, and who found themselves in the midst of a culture war intent on demonizing a wide range of progressive opinions.

Jean Muir is a case in point. Accusations that Muir was a communist were based on a transcription error made by an FBI agent who worked for the infamous New York Anti-Red Squad. At the advice of her counsel (husband Henry Jaffe), Muir sought to explain her connections with the progressive organizations with which she had been associated for two decades, first to the FBI's New York Field Office and then several years later to the FBI in Washington, D.C. Mistakenly believing that the Communist Party was the problem, Muir criticized her naïvete in relation to a variety of ostensibly Communist-related causes. Not realizing that in the eyes of the FBI, Civil Rights activism was largely identical with membership in the Communist Party, Muir staunchly defended her role in Civil Rights activism and her unconditional support for the Roosevelt administration and the late president. According to an FBI report of her interview with the D.C. headquarters, "The subject proudly admitted membership in this organization stating she belonged to the New York Section of the Southern Conference for Human Welfare" (Jean Muir FBI Files 1953, 4). Shortly after this meeting, the FBI discovered that their informant had NOT identified Muir as being a member of the Communist Party and they closed their file on her. Although they corrected internal documents concerning Muir, the damage to her career was irreparable.

The first two blacklist cases involved performers, but many of the women whose names appeared in *Red Channels* or whose professional lives were affected by the broadcast blacklist were writers whose perspectives diverged significantly from the status quo on family values emerging during the early 1950s. Jean Muir was an outspoken critic of the racist and sexist roles available to people of color and women, but as an actor she had little control over them. Women producers and writers, in contrast, like Gertrude Berg, Shirley Graham, and Joan LaCour Scott could exert some influence over the content of television programming. Gertrude Berg, for example, wrote, produced, directed, and starred in the long-running hit *The Goldbergs*. Throughout its two-decade run, *The Goldbergs* wore its New Deal, pro-immigrant sentiments on its sleeve, offering warm representations of Jewish life and culture during a viciously anti-Semitic era.

Thousands of Jewish listeners, Jewish organizations, and non-Jews wrote fan letters in appreciation and support of Berg's efforts during the 1930s and 1940s. A rabbi Berg had consulted about a wedding ceremony concluded his fan letter by saying, "I am glad to help any little way that I can, because I think that you are doing more for 'better understanding' and 'good will' of an international and interracial character than all the organized movements" (De Sola Pool 1932). A listener from Arkansas shared this sentiment, posing the following rhetorical question in a letter to Berg: "I wonder Mrs. Berg if you realize what you are doing to carry on the Jewishness we are used to—there is so much of our traditions, so many of our folk expressions—so much of the real things that makes us Jews—of which so many of our race is ashamed? From the bottom of my heart I thank you and sincerely I feel your fifteen minutes each night is a Kadish and memorial to my darling mother—may you and your little group continue!" (Dreyfus 1934, 2-3). Jewish organizations, like the National Council of Jewish Women and the Anti-Defamation League, added their own testimonials in fan letters. In the opinion of one representative of the Cleveland Board of Education, "this series from your facile pen has done more to *set us Jews right* with the 'Goyim' than all the sermons ever preached by the Rabbis" (Benesch 1931).[3]

Berg's audience support gave her some protection from the blacklist, as did her cultivation of a star persona based on traditional maternal ideology. Nevertheless, blacklisters dropped hints and innuendoes about Berg's ostensible red affinities in interviews with the press. Vincent Hartnett, who wrote the introduction to *Red Channels*, singled out *The Goldbergs* as evidence that the broadcasting industry was "indirectly but effectively" helping to "subsidize Stalinism in this country" (1950, 161). "It is believed," Hartnett slyly added, "Miss Gertrude Berg, the 'Mollie Goldberg' who also writes and produces the series, had disavowed her past Communist-front affiliations" (1950, 167). [4]

Gertrude Berg thus became a secondary target of the blacklist. Jewish actor Philip Loeb, who played the role of Molly's husband Jake, became the vehicle for a frontal assault on *The Goldbergs*. According to Hartnett, Loeb's "affiliations over the years hardly denote sympathy for our American capitalist system, let alone complete loyalty to our form of government" (1950, 168). The assault that followed his listing in *Red Channels* was vicious and protracted: "So low were the blows that an elderly actor, a brass-collar Republican who had voted for Coolidge, Hoover, Landon and Wilkie, defended the accused in *Equity Magazine*: 'The charges against you, Mr. Loeb,' he wrote, 'seem to be four in number. 1. That you are a Jew. 2. That you are a Communist. 3. That you are a troublemaker, a rabble-rouser. 4. That you are personally ambitious. I will have no truck with these charges'" (Kanfer 1973, 4).

When Berg refused to fire him, additional pressures were brought to bear. In 1951, sponsor General Foods dropped *The Goldbergs*, publicly asserting that "It was the *least lucrative* of all General Foods' evening TV properties," but neglecting to mention that the drop in

---

3   Berg also managed to do this during the 1930s, when there was a virtual blackout on information about the worsening situation of European Jews. See Weinstein 2007 for a provocative discussion of this.

4   In response to this author's Freedom of Information Act request, the FBI denied maintaining a file on Berg.

revenue resulted from a sponsor boycott, rather than lower ratings ("General Foods to Drop the Goldbergs" 1951). Elsewhere, General Foods stated that their reason for cancelling the show involved a "trend on the part of food sponsors to drop expensive TV shows because of the new price cutback," although *The Goldbergs* could hardly have been more expensive than programs like *Arthur Godfrey & His Friends* and the *Frank Sinatra Show*, both of which featured established male stars (*Herald American* 1951). In a moment of uncharacteristic honesty, one advertising executive wrote to Berg in 1952, confirming that "the only disappointment which either we or the client [at that point Ekco Products Company, a manufacturer of bakeware] have had in connection with the show has been in regard to clearances" ("Earle Ludgin and Company Advertising" 1952).

Shortly after General Foods terminated its sponsorship of *The Goldbergs*, CBS dropped the series in 1951. NBC agreed to pick up *The Goldbergs* in 1952, but sponsors made it clear that they would not touch the program as long as Loeb was involved. Loeb subsequently "left" the program in 1952. In response to continued network pressures, and in a last ditch effort to save the show and the livelihoods of those who depended on it, Berg made concessions about the content of the program. Having resisted the move to the suburbs for years, at long last, the family made the move from 1030 East Tremont Avenue to a suburb named "Haverville." But removed from its original milieu—the tenement in the Bronx—the series lost heart and meaning. Her moral and cultural authority diminished, Molly Goldberg seemed lost in the suburban environment. Episodes like one in which she went to a "fat farm" rang hollow and ended badly (the final shot in this episode showed Molly alone in the kitchen, furtively shoveling spaghetti into her mouth directly from a pot). Episodes recycled from radio scripts also appeared strained, with Molly's frugality and immigrant ethos at odds with incitements to the new consumerism.

Even these changes were insufficient to remove the taint of the blacklist, for *The Goldbergs* continued to experience "sponsor troubles" (a euphemism for problems related to the blacklist). NBC moved *The Goldbergs* around the prime time schedule before it was picked up by the financially troubled DuMont network, where it died a quiet death in October 1954. Gertrude Berg continued to work in theater, winning a Tony Award for best actress for her role in *A Majority of One* in 1959. She attempted yet another comeback on television in the series

Fig. 4: Shirley Graham (Permission of Schlesinger Library)

Mrs. G. Goes to College, which ran for a single season on CBS in 1961-1962. Berg died suddenly of heart failure in 1966, at the age of 67. The ending to Philip Loeb's career was swifter and more tragic. In 1955, out of work, homeless (he had been living with blacklisted actor Zero Mostel's family), and depressed about his inability to provide medical care for his schizophrenic son, Philip Loeb took an overdose of sleeping pills and died in a hotel room in New York City.

The example of *The Goldbergs* contradicts network, sponsor, and advertiser attempts to blame the blacklist on consumer protests, instead underscoring the fact that the series had never been popular among those who owned and controlled production. Over its lifetime, the series was cancelled three times in total, constant reminders that as a woman and a Jew, Berg's position in the broadcast industry was tenuous at best. Networks resented Berg's successful financial negotiations on her own part as well as that of her cast and crew. The networks disapproved of the show's politics—its antiquated pro-immigrant beliefs, its commitment to social welfare, and its large, powerful female star. Just a few weeks before the publication of *Red Channels*, the entire cast of *The Goldbergs* honored a walkout on the part of the technician's union—their refusal to perform left CBS having to deal with the problem of dead air time. Berg routinely hired performers and writers who were either blacklisted or would go on to be blacklisted: actor

Burl Ives, who played himself; African American actor Fredi Washington; and she had announced her desire to once again break the color line by writing in a part for actor Eartha Kitt. The blacklist thus gave the network and sponsors an alibi for abandoning a cast and program they had never particularly liked. By blaming the audience for their decision, they disavowed their part in cancelling a popular and much-loved show—the decision had not been theirs but the result of their sensitivity to the audience's demands.

In addition to eliminating influential women like Berg from the television industry, the blacklist also served to prevent other progressive cultural workers from making the move from other media industries into television. From the standpoint of her professional activity, for example, Shirley Graham was an unlikely target of the broadcast blacklist. Graham had made some limited forays into radio, researching audiences with NBC, for example, while she attended graduate school at Yale in the 1930s. In addition, her opera *Tom-Tom: An Epic of Music and the Negro* and play *Track Thirteen* had been broadcast on NBC. CBS had broadcast two of her teleplays (on George Washington Carver and Phillis Wheatley). But Graham's commercial successes had largely been in the area of adolescent fiction and her blacklisting in the pages of *Red Channels* caught her completely by surprise. Of her blacklisting, she wrote in disingenuous and cynical mimicry of the language demanded by HUAC: "I am not now and never have been employed in the radio and television fields."

Graham's FBI records make it clear that Graham's novels were a source of concern for the FBI and its anti-communist allies. Frequent references to Graham's novels about Paul Robeson and Frederick Douglass appear in FBI reports throughout the 1950s, as in the following excerpt from a 70 page FBI "synopsis," that reported that Graham, "is best known for her biographies of famous Negroes, written for young people. She is co-author of the book, 'Dr George Washington Carver: Scientist' (1944), written for teen-age readers. Her second biography for young people, 'Paul Robeson, Citizen of the World,' was published in 1946. Scheduled for early 1947 publication, was her next book, 'There Was Once a Slave.'" (Shirley Graham FBI Files FBI Memorandum 1956). One FBI summary of Graham's activities cited a letter received by J. Edgar Hoover from a confidential informant, who complained that "*Paul Robeson, Citizen of the World*, by Shirley

Graham" was a book not "fit for formative young minds" (Shirley Graham DuBois FBI Files Report 1961).

Graham's successes in popularizing progressive ideas and her access to what one FBI special agent in charge referred to as "the subversive press" also gravely concerned the FBI. A report from the FBI's New York City Red Squad urged caution in approaching Graham herself, because "the subject is an Editor of a Communist Publication and she is a lecturer and writer of Communist propaganda having access to publication in both Domestic and Foreign Communist publications" (Shirley Graham DuBois FBI Files 1961). Not only were Graham's ideas dangerous, that is, she also had access to national and international distribution networks that could not be easily controlled by the FBI.

Although Graham had been the subject of various diatribes in the pages of *CounterAttack*, dating back to a 1949 article that objected to CBS's broadcast of *The Story of Phillis Wheatley*, the publication of *Red Channels* renewed anti-communist attention to her work. Fearless and outspoken, Graham was one of the few blacklistees to openly discuss the effects of *Red Channels* on her life and livelihood. Fresh from husband W.E.B. Du Bois' indictment under the Foreign Agent's Registration Act and trial (which was finally dismissed by a federal judge for lack of evidence), Graham's responses to inquiries about the blacklist from Joseph Goldstein, editor of the *Yale Law Journal*, and Elmer Rice, Chairman of the Committee on Blacklisting established by the Authors League of America, paint a picture of widespread, organized political repression. Graham described the multiple venues through which the blacklist operated: "As an author it is extremely difficult to put one's finger on such things as 'denial of employment' and the like. Books can be attacked through distribution channels, publicity, handling in stores. My income has steadily decreased" (Graham 1952, 2). She told Goldstein that inclusion of her name in *Red Channels* resulted in demands "that my books be withdrawn from the schools and libraries" of Scarsdale, New York (Graham 1952, 1). Calls to ban Graham's books from public libraries also followed from upstate New York, home of American Business Consultants, as well as Wheeling, West Virginia, where Joseph McCarthy had made his infamous speech about Communist infiltration of the U.S. government just six months before. In addition, publicity appearances for *Your Most*

Humble Servant (Graham's award-winning book about Benjamin Banneker) were inexplicably cancelled, never to be rescheduled.

Although *Red Channels* purported to focus on the communist takeover of the airwaves, as the blacklisting of Graham illustrates, its effects rippled across media industries. Although Graham's novel about white journalist and abolitionist Anne Newport Royall received enthusiastic reviews from readers, five major publishing houses rejected it. As Graham put it in her letter to Goldstein, *"No publisher has criticized the manuscript as a piece of writing. This we could understand and accept. Novels are always worked on after being accepted by some publisher. But these refusals have each time been vague and in certain cases obviously reluctant"* (Goldstein, 2). The novel was never published.

Harassed by the FBI and the INS, Graham and DuBois left the U.S. for Ghana in 1961. Other blacklisted writers and producers saw the writing on the wall earlier, leaving the U.S. for work in Europe and Mexico in the early 1950s. In the UK, the ATV's *The Adventures of Robin Hood*, which first appeared on British televisions in 1955, was produced by a small production company named Sapphire Films. Sapphire Films was founded by writer Hannah Weinstein, an American who had worked professionally for a Hearst newspaper and politically for communist pressure groups in the U.S., like the Progressive Citizens of America, which criticized the House Un-American Activities Committee, and called for its abolition. Weinstein founded Sapphire Films in London in 1951. Over the next decade, she hired a cohort of American writers who could no longer find work in the U.S. because of the blacklists in the film and television industries. Hollywood Ten members Ring Lardner and Adrian Scott, as well as Scott's wife Joan LaCour Scott, wrote scripts for *The Adventures of Robin Hood*, as well as a later production of *The Adventures of Sir Lancelot*, finding much-needed employment during the leanest years of the blacklist. Scripts for both these programs reflected the concerns and political beliefs of these progressive writers, who believed in Civil Rights, gender equality, and economic justice.

The Adventures of Robin Hood could not have been made in 1950s America—its themes of solidarity and economic justice too obviously at odds with the individualism and consumerism promoted by television; its references to the Cold War suppression of dissent too open. In an episode written by Scott and LaCour Scott entitled "The Cathedral," Robin criticizes the Sheriff of Nottingham's monopoly ownership of property only to be accused of "being a tool of an inter-national conspiracy, anti-church and anti-Christ" (Scott and La Cour Scott 1957, 4). Indeed, progressive beliefs and themes as a whole were eradicated from American television entertainment program in the early 1950s by the anti-communist crusaders who promoted the blacklist.

One can, of course, find traces of progressive ideas in the program-ming to which blacklisted writers contributed, often under pseud-onyms. As writer and producer Adrian Scott put it, "when things were bad for me I did not, as most did, look for the best programs on the air—which everybody hoped to write for. I looked for the worst. My theory was that the worst program, or programs, were the ones who needed scripts the most" (Adrian Scott, 1966: 2). In practice, this squeezing in "the back door," as Scott put it, meant writing scripts for programs like *Lassie*, which became Scott and his wife Joan's most reli-able source of income.

Relegated to the margins of television production, writers like the Scotts smuggled progressive content into the scripts of the children's programs they wrote for in the U.S. *Lassie* (1954-1973) resonates with the cadences of this generation's political vocabulary and con-cerns. *Lassie* often featured animals that, like those cultural workers who had been blacklisted, had been falsely accused of vile acts and had to be redeemed by the resourceful collie. Originally, *Lassie* fea-tured a widowed, single mother, who later adopted a second child, and lived with her elderly father on a farm rather than in the consumer-oriented suburbs that were the backdrop for virtually all family sit-coms and dramas of the 1950s. Over the years, *Lassie*'s familial re-lations included a series of young boys, forestry workers, and finally the inmates of a home for "troubled" children—hardly the ingredients for the making of a nuclear family. One hears echoes of a forgotten generation's language when Timmy accuses Lassie of being "a reaction-ary" because of her dogmatic attachment to tradition; when a forest ranger comments on eagles' egalitarian "division of labor" in caring for their young (Court, 1972); or when a priest adopts an orphaned boy whose parents had worked with him in South America "to improve crop yield among peasants" (Court, n.d.). But confined as they were to children's programming or exiled from cultural memory altogether, these viewpoints did not appear in the mainstream of 1950s enter-tainment programming.

Images and ideas like those created by blacklisted talent would not be part of the culture from which later writers would grow new programming. Perhaps most importantly, that progressive ideas had ever been debated, held legitimate, and fought for by women and men of intellect and principle was erased from television's memory of the past. The blacklist chilled the speech of all television writers, issuing a clear warning about the kinds of content and representations the new medium would tolerate. As Berg put it in a 1956 interview: "You see, darling, don't bring up anything that will bother people. That's very important. Unions, politics, fund-raising, Zionism, socialism, intergroup relations. I don't stress them. And after all, aren't all such things secondary to daily family living?" (qtd in Zurawik 2003, 45).

In the end, understanding the images produced in the 1950s solely on the basis of those that made it to prime time has contributed to reifying a particular memory of this era, based on the suppression of intense class, gender, and racial discrimination. The images upon which we base our memories of the 1950s were made by forces that had every intention of erasing these struggles from sight and memory. The family that is remembered, that is, has erased the fact that *it once was made*. It took a culture war of unprecedented proportions—a war that brought together forces of industry, white supremacy, and government—to still the voices of protest and opposition to Cold War politics of gender, race, and class. By this war's end, images of interracial solidarity, working women, and even the presence of people of color in television programming became evidence of heresy.

What writer David Zurawik observed of Berg can be usefully applied to the historical suppression of the blacklist as a whole: "the founders of the networks were uncomfortable with that history and their role in it and so she sort of became a story they didn't want to tell because it brought up the narrative of the blacklist. And so she sort of fell by the wayside" ("From the Goldbergs to 2005" 2005). Rightly uncomfortable about what the narrative of the blacklist revealed about the ideological beliefs and practices of the broadcast industry in the 1950s, invested in the promotion of conservative beliefs about the family and gender as cultural universals, memories of the blacklist were consigned to the margins of cultural production, to comedic representations in film like *The Front*, and to the embittered and painful memories of a silenced generation of progressives who had fought and lost the culture war over television.

WELCOME TO THE PHANTASMAGORIA

> Don't ask him questions about his actions or question his judgment or integrity. Remember, he is the master of the house and as such will always exercise his will with fairness and truthfulness. You have no right to question him. ("The Good Wife's Guide" 1955)

Although Raymond Williams' (1978) phrase "structure of feeling" has been appropriated most frequently by theorists interested in affect, I have always found the term more useful in terms of thinking about the importance of historical research in media and cultural studies. Williams was clear in saying that those studying historical periods could never "know" a given generation's structure of feeling in any immediate sense. The partiality of our ability to capture and understand the past, however, does not mean that we cannot and should not approach it through the material culture that remains. Shirley Graham's anguished letters to friends and colleagues about the banning of her books give us some sense of the impact of the blacklist on her creative life. Similarly, a yellowed and creased piece of paper in Vera Caspary's papers, one that listed her response to the questions asked her by California's anti-Red Tenney Committee; one that had been nervously folded and re-folded, speaks volumes about the anxiety and fear blacklisted writers experienced. And the scripts and abstracts and unpublished novels carefully and tenderly placed in archives by these women and men tell us much about the aspirations they had for the new medium and their hope that it would be expansive enough to include stories about women who did not conform to the 1950s domestic ideal, about women and men of color who made history, about environmental activism and anti-consumerist values.

Watching the products of the 1950s television industry gives us no sense of these struggles over television content or the alternatives that were in the air at the dawn of the era of television. A focus on consumption alone serves the interests of a bourgeois mythology that would rather have us believe that these alternatives were never a part of broadcast history than acknowledge the strenuous efforts that were undertaken to force them out of the industry. Analyses of 1950s television that focus on the ideological, or what some might describe as rhetorical, dimensions of media texts cannot account for the repressive, punitive measures taken to purge broadcasting of progressive ideas. The case of the blacklist also challenges the focus on women and consumption in media studies, suggesting that much research remains to be done on women's roles in broadcast production. Perhaps the most important lesson of the broadcast blacklist lies in its challenge not only to how we remember the 1950s, but how we remember the history of the industry and its complex myth-making abilities as well. Historical research serves as an absolutely crucial corrective to media's efforts to erase and elide how control of the means of production affects the content of what we consume. Grounding analyses not by reference to vague and often abstract generalizations, attention to concrete examples of how control is exercised, maintained, and institutionalized in media industries can help us understand, to take just one example, the shallowness of the television industry's efforts to blame audiences for its shortcomings, errors, and censorship of content.

In a series of interviews she gave in the early 1950s, Shirley Graham noted that she began writing adolescent fiction because of her awareness that African Americans "were misunderstood, and were not known, and were outside of history." As her research progressed, she told her interviewer, she "became aware that this was not as narrow a problem as I had thought. It is not only the Negro, it is not only the Indian, who is dropped out of history—it is also the dissenter, the person who didn't go along with the majority!" (Graham 1954, 4-5). Presenting narratives about African Americans, Native Americans, and dissenters, Graham wanted to restore the role they had played "in the making of American history" (Graham 1950).

For Graham and a generation of progressive cultural workers, presenting histories that U.S. culture refused to represent across a range of media was an act of political faith intended to educate and inspire. Although new media are once again transforming our ability to do historical research (digitizing, for example, historically black newspapers like the *Chicago Defender*), control over the means of production and access to materials like these is reproducing selective traditions. Working against those strong and easy currents—restoring political struggles to our own accounts of media history, understanding the powerful structuring structures of media industries, researching content that could not be made within these strictures or that remains difficult to access and marginalized—remain acts of political faith.

ACKNOWLEDGMENTS

I am grateful, first of all, to Jon Sterne, who heard something in a conference paper I gave ages ago and encouraged me to chase it. Although she may not have known it at the time, Rachel Ida Buff's enthusiasm for this project and kind words about it kept me going during a lean period. My enduring gratitude to David Price, who for years has patiently and graciously answered ALL my questions about Freedom of Information Act Requests. This project would not have been possible without the labor of some fantastic research assistants. I was endlessly fortunate in having the skills of Mary Erickson at the University of Oregon and Zach Sell at the University of Wisconsin-Milwaukee at my service. Eric Lohman and Sarah Mick at the University of Wisconsin-Milwaukee provided tremendous support as well, helping me to locate often-arcane materials and track down hard-to-find resources. Stephanie Schuessler and Janine Zajac from the University of Pittsburgh offered research assistance in the very early stages of this project. The librarians and staff at the Schlesinger Library were wonderfully patient and helpful, especially Sarah M. Hutcheon, Lynda Leahy, and Caitlin Stevens. I am grateful, too, for the support of the Morris Fromkin Memorial Lectureship from the University of Wisconsin-Milwaukee which allowed me to travel to three different archives during the course of a single summer, as well as funding from the University of Wisconsin-Milwaukee and the University of Oregon.

ARCHIVAL RESOURCES

Adrian Scott and Joan LaCour Scott Papers. Laramie, WY: American Heritage Center, University of Wyoming.

Gertrude Berg Papers. Syracuse, NY: University of Syracuse Library.

Larry Adler Papers. Laramie, WY: American Heritage Center, University of Wyoming.

Shirley Graham DuBois Papers. Cambridge, MA: Schlesinger Library, Harvard University.

Vera Caspary Papers, Madison, WI: Wisconsin Historical Society.

REFERENCES

Barthes, R. 1989. *Mythologies.* New York: Noonday Press.

Benesch, A.A. 1931. Letter to Gertrude Berg, d. 31 December. *Gertrude Berg Papers*. Correspondence (scrapbooks), Volume 5.

Berg, G. 1948. *Me and Molly: A Play in Three Acts.* New York: Dramatists Play Service.

———. 1961. *Molly and Me.* New York: McGraw-Hill.

———. 1931. *The Rise of the Goldbergs.* New York: Barse Company.

Buhle, P. 1995. "The Hollywood Blacklist and the Jew: An Exploration of Popular Culture." *Tikkun* 10(5): 35-40.

Buhle, P. and D. Wagner. 2004. *Hide in Plain Sight: The Hollywood Blacklistees in Film and Television, 1950-2002.* New York, Palgrave Books.

Caspary, V. 1945. *Bedelia.* London: Eyre and Spottiswoode.

———. 1960. *Evvie.* New York: Harper & Brothers.

———. 1944. *Laura.* London: Eyre & Spottiswoode.

———. 1946. *Stranger than Truth.* New York: Random House.

———. 1932. *Thicker Than Water.* New York: Liveright, Inc.

———. 1929. *The White Girl.* Kingsport, TN: Kingsport Press.

Chilton, K. 2008. *Hazel Scott: The Pioneering Journey of a Jazz Pianist from Café Society to Hollywood to HUAC.* Ann Arbor: University of Michigan Press.

Court, J. n.d. "A Boy and His Dog, Part I." *Lassie. Adrian Scott and Joan LaCour Scott Papers.* Box 19, Folder 2.

———. 1972. "The Golden Eagle." *Lassie. Adrian Scott and Joan LaCour Scott Papers.* Box 29, Folder 15, 21 June.

De Sola Pool, D. 1932. Letter to Gertrude Berg, d. 8 June. *Gertrude Berg Papers.* General Correspondence, Volume 3.

Dick, P.K, 1987. "We Can Remember It For You Wholesale." *The Collected Stories of Philip K. Dick.* Volume V. New York: Underwood-Miller.

Doherty, T. 2003. *Cold War, Cool Medium: Television, McCarthyism, and American Culture.* New York: Columbia University Press, 2003.

Dreyfus, D.S. 1934. Letter to Gertrude Berg, *Gertrude Berg Papers*, General Correspondence, Volume 3, Pine Bluff, Arkansas, 12 January.

"The Dynamics of Live Television: A Conversation with Three Prominent Directors (John Frankenheimer, Robert Mulligan, Arthur Penn)." 1994. *Museum of Television and Radio Seminar Series.* Los Angeles, CA: 24 February.

Earle Ludgin and Company Advertising. 1952. Letter to Gertrude Berg, d. 14 July. *Gertrude Berg Papers*. General Correspondence (Scrapbooks), Volume 9.

Everitt, D. 2007. *A Shadow of Red: Communism and the Blacklist*. Chicago: Ivan R.

Friedan, B. 1964. *The Feminine Mystique*. New York: Dell.

"From the Goldbergs to 2005: The Evolution of the Sitcom." 2005. *Museum of Television and Radio Satellite Seminar Series*, New York: Museum of TV and Radio.

"General Foods to Drop the Goldbergs." 1951. "Newsletter, Tide: The Newsmagazine for Advertising Executives," 25 May. *Gertrude Berg Papers*. General Scrapbooks, Volumes 28-32.

Gleason, M.D. 1997. *In Defense of God and Country: Elizabeth Dilling, a Link Between the Red Scares*. Unpublished PhD Dissertation, University of Arkansas, August.

"The Good Wife's Guide." 1955. *Housekeeping Monthly*. 13 May.

Gould, J. 1965. "A.B.C. Puts Off Jean Muir Blacklist Interview." *New York Times*. 25 December 1965: 29.

————. 1966. "TV: Blacklisting's Effect." *New York Times*. 15 January 1966: 55.

————. 1950a. "'Aldrich' Show Drops Jean Muir; TV Actress Denies Communist Ties." *New York Times*. 29 August: 1.

————. 1950b. "Case of Jean Muir: Principles of Fair Play Yield to Pressures." *New York Times*. 3 September: 49.

————. 1950c. "Critic Backs Miss Muir's Rights; Mrs. McCullough Shuns Clean-Up." *New York Times*. 7 September: 1.

————. 1950d. "Publicity Pledged on Anti-Red Actors." *New York Times*. 8 September: 33.

————. 1950e. "'Red Purge' for Radio, Television Seen in Wake of Jean Muir Ouster." *New York Times*. 30 August: 33.

————. 1950f. "TV Play Cancelled in Fight on Actress." *New York Times*. 28 August: 1.

————. 1950g. "TV 'Red Ban' Lifted by General Foods." *New York Times*. 27 September: 32.

Graham, S. 1964. "Address to Kwame Nkrumah Ideological Institute." *Shirley Graham DuBois Papers*. Box 44, Folder 9, 26 May.

———. 1954. "As a Man Thinketh in His Heart, So Is He." *The Parish News: Church of the Holy Trinity.* Brooklyn: NY, Vol. LVII, No. 4, February 1954, 1-5, *Shirley Graham DuBois Papers,* Box 27, Folder 3.

———. 1952. Letter to Elmer Rice, d. 30 January. *Shirley Graham DuBois Papers.* Box 17, Folder 9.

———. 1951. Letter to Mr. Joseph Goldstein, d. 22 December. *Shirley Graham DuBois Papers.* Box 17, Folder 5.

———. 2001. *It's Morning: A One-Act Play.* In *Plays by American Women: 1930-1960.* Ed. Judith E. Barlow, 235-262. New York: Applause Books.

———. 1962. *Jean Baptiste Pointe DeSable: Founder of Chicago.* New York: Julian Messner.

———. 1946. *Paul Robeson: Citizen of the World.* New York: Julian Messner, Inc.

———. 1949. *The Story of Phillis Wheatley.* New York: J. Messner.

———. 1953. *The Story of Pocahontas.* New York: Grosset and Dunlap.

———. *There Once was a Slave ... the Heroic Story of Frederick Douglass.* New York: J. Messner, 1947.

———. 1991. "Tom-Tom: An Epic of Music and the Negro." In *The Roots of African American Drama: An Anthology of Early Plays, 1858-1938.* Ed. by L. Hamalian and J.V. Hatch, 238-286. Detroit: Wayne State University Press.

———. 1950. WMEX Boston: Interview. 18 February. *Shirley Graham DuBois Papers.* Box 27, Folder 3.

———. 1949. *Your Most Humble Servant,* New York: J. Messner.

———. 1974. *Zulu Heart.* New York: The Third Press.

Hartnett, V. 1950. *Catholic World,* July: 161-7.

"Hastie, Jean Muir to Talk at NAACP Student Meet." 1943. *The Chicago Defender* (National Edition). 11 September.

"Hazel Asks Boycott in Red Whirl." 1950. *Chicago Defender* (National Edition). 7 October: 21.

"Hazel Scott Denies Any Red Sympathies." 1950. *New York Times.* 16 September: 5.

"Hazel Scott Makes Denials at Inquiry." 1950. *New York Times.* 23 September: 11.

Herald American. 1951. Chicago, IL, 23 May. *Gertrude Berg Papers.* General Scrapbooks, Volumes 28-32.

Hilmes, M. 1997. *Radio Voices*. Minneapolis: University of Minnesota Press.

"Hit Ban on Jean Muir." 1950. *The Chicago Defender* (National Edition). 23 September: 21.

Jahoda, M. 1956. "Anti-Communism and Employment Policies in Radio and Television." In *Report on Blacklisting*. J. Cogley. New York: The Fund for the Republic, 221-281.

Jean Muir FBI Files. 1953. Teletype d. 22 May.

———. Report d. 1953.

Jeansonne, G. 1996. *Women of the Far Right: The Mother's Movement and World War II*. Chicago: University of Chicago Press.

Kanfer, S. 1973. *A Journal of the Plague Years*. New York: Atheneum.

Leibman, N. 1995. *Living Room Lectures: The Fifties Family in Film and Television*. Austin: University of Texas Press.

Lipsitz, G. 2001. *Time Passages: Collective Memory and American Popular Culture*. Minneapolis: University of Minnesota.

Meyerowitz, J. 1994. "Beyond the Feminist Mystique: A Reassessment of Postwar Mass Culture, 1946-1958," in J. Meyerowitz, *Not June Cleaver: Women and Gender in Postwar America, 1945-1960*: 229-262. Philadelphia: Temple University Press.

"Miss Muir is Ready to Deny Communism." 1950. *New York Times*. 2 September: 22.

"Newark Schools' Head Buys 'Red Channels,' Anti-Communist Pamphlet, for Reference." 1950. *New York Times*. 13 September: 9.

Nichols, F.L. 1950. "Memorandum to C. Tolson." Washington, DC: FBI, 29 August.

Red Channels: The Report of Communist Influence in Radio and Television. New York: American Business Consultants, 1950.

Scott, A. 1966. Letter to Allan Scott, d. 11 September. *Adrian Scott and Joan LaCour Scott Papers*. Box 6, Folder 13.

Scott, A. and J.L. Scott. 1957. "The Cathedral." *Adrian Scott and Joan LaCour Scott Papers*. Folder 2, "1957-1958 *Robin Hood* Episodes."

Shirley Graham DuBois FBI Files. 1956. Memorandum from SAC New York to J. Edgar Hoover. 14 June.

———. 1956. Report d. 16 May.

———. 1961. Report d. June 19.d

Smith, G.D. 2007. *"Something on My Own': Gertrude Berg and American Broadcasting, 1929-1956.* New York: Syracuse University Press.

Spigel, L. 1992. *Make Room for TV: Television and the Family Ideal in Postwar America.* Chicago: University of Chicago Press.

Taylor, E. 1991. *Prime-Time Families: Television Culture in Post-War America.* Berkeley: University of California Press.

Theoharis, A. and J.S. Cox. 1998. *The Boss: J. Edgar Hoover and the Great American Inquisition.* Philadelphia: Temple University Press.

Weinstein, D. 2007. "Why Sarnoff Slept: NBC and the Holocaust." In *NBC: America's Network.* Edited by M. Hilmes, 98-116, Berkeley: University of Chicago Press.

Williams, R. 2001. *The Long Revolution.* New York: Broadview Press.

———. 1978. *Marxism and Literature.* New York: Oxford University Press.

Zurawik, David. 2003. *The Jews of Prime Time.* Hanover, NH: Brandeis University Press.

CHAPTER 7

FOREIGN CORRESPONDENTS, PASSPORTS, AND MCCARTHYISM

Edward Alwood

J OURNALISTS HAVE A LONG HISTORY OF RESISTING GOVERN-
MENT INTERFERENCE WITH THE PRESS. American journalists
successfully fought newspaper licensing and punitive libel laws
during the colonial era. The Constitution specifically protects
the press from government interference in the First Amendment. Passport restrictions that prevent journalists from reporting
from abroad have amounted to a hidden restriction that runs counter
to a free press. There has been little recognition that travel restrictions
placed on Americans are adopted at the discretion of the secretary
of state. In effect, government passport policies represent an unrecog-
nized form of licensing of the press since travel by journalists has been
restricted at the whim of the State Department. The clearest examples
of how this process can be politicized come from the 1950s during the
McCarthy era when government policies violated civil liberties and
from the 1960s. The Cold War between the United States and the Soviet Union was the basis of restrictions during the 1960s but, as this
article argues, little prevents such restrictions from being used against
journalist today.

THE AMERICAN PASSPORT

Americans see the right to travel as a fundamental liberty of citizenship akin to freedom of religion, freedom of speech, and freedom of
assembly. Though it is not protected by the Constitution per se, citizens have long considered travel restrictions anathema to democratic
principles. For journalists, travel is essential if they are to provide the
public with an understanding of world events. Interwoven with travel

is the First Amendment protection of the press and its antecedent freedom to gather news and information. Travel restrictions on journalists have the potential of undermining democratic self-government by placing the secretary of state in the position of determining the terms and conditions under which the public is informed. This authority essentially empowers the government to decide which journalists will be permitted to report on important events overseas.

Congress enacted the nation's first passport law in 1856 in an effort to centralize issuance; it had been the responsibility of local police departments. The new law provided the secretary of state with absolute discretion in evaluating passport applications as delegated by the president. Before the early 1900s, passports amounted to little more than a ceremonial voucher that attested to an individual's citizenship, but it was not needed for travel abroad (Fagen 1973, 387; Ehrlich 1966, 129). Congress imposed the first restrictions during the War of 1812 when the government briefly banned travel into enemy territory unless the traveler held a valid passport (Mott 1962, 196). The restrictions held little consequence for journalists since most of the war coverage originated from reporters in Washington, individuals living near battlefields, or from journalists who fought in the army (Rogers 1985, 497; Whelan 1952, 72).

World War I marked the first time the government required a passport for entry into the United States and departure. The State Department automatically issued one to anyone who could prove citizenship with a valid birth certificate or some other official voucher. Statutes adopted in 1918 authorized issuance but it did not empower the secretary of state to deny one (Parker 1954, 863; Ehrlich 1966, 130). The policy enabled more than five hundred American journalists to travel to Europe during the war to satisfy their readers' insatiable demand for news (Emery, Emery, and Roberts 2000, 258).

The political atmosphere changed in 1939 as fascism threatened Europe. President Franklin D. Roosevelt declared a national emergency, and the secretary of state initiated a policy that "no passport heretofore issued shall be valid for use in traveling from the United States to any country in Europe unless it is submitted to the State Department for validation" (*Federal Register* 1939, 3892). Roosevelt declared another emergency on May 27, 1941, when the United States entered World War II, prompting the State Department to prohibit a citizen from entering or leaving the country "unless he bears a valid passport"

(*State Department Bulletin* 1941, 384). Wartime restrictions remained in place as the Cold War developed between the United States and the Soviet Union, marking the first travel limitations on American citizens in peacetime (*Washington Law Review* 1967, 875).

During the Red scare of the late 1940s and 1950s, anti-Communist sentiment burrowed deep into the American psyche and became federal policy. In its extreme, anti-Communism became known as McCarthyism, a pejorative term that reflected the influence of Wisconsin Senator Joseph McCarthy. It was characterized by the public leveling accusations of disloyalty, subversion, or treason with little regard for evidence, or for protection of civil liberties (Fried 1990, 131–32). Initially, the House Committee on Un-American Activities was the most public face of McCarthyism, but by the early 1950s anti-Communism had become policy throughout the federal government and most states (Schrecker 1998, 86).

As international tensions rose with the onset of the Korean War, passport policies became politically charged; Congress passed the Internal Security Act of 1950, which made it a crime for "members of the Communist Party or a Communist-front organization to obtain or use an American passport" (Boltax 1982, 402; Whelan 1952, 80). The historian David Caute estimates that the law prevented about three hundred Americans from traveling abroad between May 1951 and May 1952 alone (1978, 246). Though not specifically aimed at journalists, the policy presented noteworthy concerns for journalists given the First Amendment guarantee that precludes the government from abridging freedom of the press. The first example of how it affected journalists involved writers at two Communist newspapers published in the United States, the *Daily People's World* and the *Daily Worker*. When the writers attempted to travel to Europe and Asia in 1951, the State Department blocked their passport applications, ruling in each case that "'the purpose of the trip was deemed to be contrary to the interest of the United States,'" the *New York Times* reported on February 11. The next day the paper applauded the decision but with reservations. "If … the refusal was wholly or partially based on the belief that the two men would send dispatches displeasing to the Administration or to the population in general … we would have to ask if this were not a denial of the guarantees of the First Amendment."

Congress expanded the 1950 restrictions two years later with the Immigration and Nationality Act, which made it a crime to enter or leave the United States without a valid passport. This marked the first travel limitation placed on American citizens in peacetime and became the justification for a string of passport application denials involving prominent figures (*Washington Law Review* 1967, 875–80; Association of the Bar 1958, 22). Two of the most celebrated denials involved the actor Paul Robeson and the playwright Arthur Miller. The State Department revoked Robeson's passport from 1950 to 1958 based on his outspoken criticism of racism in the United States. Similarly, the government revoked Miller's passport when he tried to attend the opening of one of his plays in Brussels in 1954 because he was thought to be closely tied to the Communist party (Caute 1978, 166, 247).

Though Robeson and Miller were the best-known examples, the restrictions also fell on hundreds of lesser-known individuals (Saltzman 1952, 177; Klehr 1984, 378–85). In the case of journalists, it is difficult to determine how many have been affected because the State Department's 192 million passport files are protected by federal privacy laws (Kessler 2008). Denials of passport applications became public only when applicants challenged federal policies in court. Two examples illustrate how the policies worked against journalists. The first involved Anne Bauer, a freelance American writer whose passport was revoked in 1951 while she was in Paris. Bauer had written for the *American Scholar* and *Jet*, the "Weekly Negro News Magazine," on racial issues in South Africa (Bauer 1951, 33; *Jet* 1952, 32–33). Like the cases against the journalists at Communist newspapers, passport examiners based their decision about Bauer on the view that her activities were "contrary to the best interests of the United States," the *New York Times* reported on July 10, 1952. The American Civil Liberties Union filed suit, claiming the decision violated her due process rights and that the passport law was unconstitutional. The State Department argued that "the Secretary of State has discretionary authority … both as a power inherent in the exercise of the Presidential authority to conduct foreign relations and as a matter of statutory law" (*State Department Bulletin* 1952a, 919–23).

Newspaper editorial pages remained silent as Bauer battled the State Department, although the policy raised issues that potentially affected every American journalist. One explanation for their reticence may have been that Bauer worked as a freelance writer, not as a full-time employee of any news organization. The historian John Lofton has argued that newspapers' defense of the First Amendment has been based "more on self-interest than on principle" (1980, 283–84). In 1952 publishers were more concerned about government censorship of nonmilitary news than any intrusion on the rights of journalists to travel (Porter 1952, 22). Nevertheless, the ACLU took up the issue, arguing that the government interfered with Bauer's work as a journalist. The ACLU called on Congress to enact a law that would mandate issuance of passports to American citizens and prohibit revocation "except for specifically stated reasons," the *New York Times* reported on April 23.

In July 1952 a three-judge federal District Court upheld the State Department restrictions but ruled that the government had overstepped its power. "Denial of an American passport has a very direct bearing on the applicant's personal liberty to travel outside the United States," it said. The court ordered the State Department to return Bauer's passport or provide a full hearing on the reasons for its revocation (*Bauer v. Acheson* 1952, 452). The State Department instituted a formal appeals process; however, the rate of revocations and denials continued unchanged (*State Department Bulletin* 1952b, 417–18; Boudin 1956, 73–74). The appellate ruling did not address the free press implications, sending a clear message to journalists that if their politics did not conform to the mainstream, they could be denied travel abroad.

THE CASE OF WINSTON BURDETT

Another example of how journalists were affected came in 1952 when the State Department held up the passport of the CBS correspondent Winston Burdett. Unlike Bauer's case, where there was no evidence that she was targeted solely because she was a journalist, there is ample evidence that Burdett ran into trouble because he was a journalist who had once belonged to the Communist Party. As the historian Frank Donner has noted, the government did not target every party member during the McCarthy era but selectively chose individuals like Burdett who would generate the greatest exposure for its campaign, often on the flimsiest of evidence (Donner 1961, 147–49).

A prominent figure in the heyday of broadcast news, Burdett began his broadcast career when he covered battle zones in Europe for Transradio Press during the early years of World War II. He later gained national prominence as a member of the elite CBS broadcast team assembled by Edward R. Murrow (Cloud and Olson 1996, 174). In

1951, as anti-Communist sentiment escalated, CBS adopted a corporate loyalty oath to counter its conservative critics. When asked to sign, Burdett acknowledged that he had been a Communist Party member during the late 1930s when he worked as a writer at the *Brooklyn Eagle* (Alwood 2006a, 153–54). Colleagues, including Charles Collingwood, Eric Sevareid, and Murrow, rallied to Burdett's defense and persuaded CBS to retain him, provided he made a full disclosure to the FBI (Persico 1988, 340–41; Cloud and Olson 1996, 320).

Between September 1951 and July 1953, the FBI interviewed Burdett on seven occasions, and he laid out details of his experiences as a party member. In one session he disclosed that he had spied for the Soviets, then an ally of the United States, during World War II. He assured the FBI that he had severed his party ties and had ended his contacts with the Soviet espionage apparatus in the early 1940s.[1] In the spring of 1954, after CBS assigned him to a story in Paris, Burdett submitted an application to the State Department to renew his passport. It soon became clear that the renewal had hit a snag after passport examiners became aware of his disclosures to the FBI.[2]

Like FBI Director J. Edgar Hoover, the head of the State Department's Passport Office, Ruth Shipley, was a devout anti-Communist who exploited anti-Communist sentiment to impose her own agenda on public policy. Her office was concerned that Burdett had not sufficiently purged himself and questioned why he had kept his party activities secret until 1951. Passport examiners told Burdett that his story sounded incomplete and instructed him to produce a sworn statement in which he would state his innocence before they would rule on his renewal application (Caute 1978, 246). "I think that a careful investigation should be made of the banking activities of Mr. Burdett," observed an examiner in the Passport Office. "I also think that his connection with [name deleted] and the Transradio Press and the Columbia Broadcasting in 1940, 1941, and 1942 should be investigated." Another examiner questioned whether CBS and the *Eagle* had

---

1 Scheidt to [name deleted], August 30, 1951, FBI 100-376050-9; Report by [name deleted], October 27, 1951, FBI 100-376050-19. [Hereafter cited as FBI Files.]

2 "Case of Winston Burdett," Department of State, RPS/ISP, June 9, 1954, FBI 100-376050-73, FBI Files.

kept Burdett on their payrolls "to cover for his espionage activities."[3] The FBI monitored his mail, canvassed informants for additional information, checked his bank records, reviewed his travel records, examined his voting records, and watched his newscasts on CBS, then forwarded information to the State Department (Alwood 2006b, 104).

Burdett filed a signed affidavit with the Passport Office to explain his delay in stepping forward. "The fact is that working and residing abroad, far from the American scene, I did not fully appreciate how the question presented itself in my own country," he said. "I came to this appreciation much more rapidly once I had returned home. I came to see my personal situation in the light of the larger political situation, and consequently to see my personal duty to face the facts and to report them to the proper authorities."[4] Rather than allay concerns, the affidavit fueled suspicion. "There seems to be a discrepancy in the date of Burdett's final break with the Communists," the FBI told passport officials. "A review of the Bureau files and Burdett's signed statement reflects that the Bureau has not been advised heretofore of Burdett's contact with a female Soviet official in Turkey in February or March 1942."[5]

Burdett sought help from the New York attorney Morris Ernst, a long-time anti-Communist activist who was CBS's general counsel. Ernst referred Burdett to New York Municipal Judge Robert Morris, an ardent anti-Communist who had served as counsel to the Senate Internal Security Subcommittee (Alwood 2006a, 164–65). Morris was part of an anti-Communist network that had worked behind the scenes for many years to cripple the Communist Party, helping transform domestic communism into a dominant political issue. He suggested that Burdett could clear his name by purging himself before a congressional investigative committee and arranged for a subpoena to a closed session in October 1954 (Alwood 2006b, 109). Justice Department lawyers determined that it was not clear whether Burdett

---

3 [Louis] Nichols to File, June 9, 1954, attached to memo, Flinn to J. Edgar Hoover, March 30, 1955, FBI 100-376050-73; SAC Washington Field Office, to Director, July 8, 1954, FBI 100-376050-65, all in FBI Files.

4 Affidavit of Winston Burdett, June 29, 1954, FBI 100-376050-65, FBI Files.

5 [Alan] Belmont to Boardman, March 22, 1955, FBI 100-376050-71, FBI Files.

had violated any federal law since his activities were conducted on foreign soil, and there was no evidence that he had spied against the United States, but his passport remained in limbo.[6]

By late June 1955 Burdett agreed to testify before the Senate Internal Security Subcommittee to clear his name. State Department documents show that the FBI used the denial of Burdett's passport as leverage to induce him to name twenty-three individuals he had known as members of the Communist party. It is not clear, however, that CBS understood the intimidation tactic used by the government to gain Burdett's testimony, but the network exploited his public announcement that he had dropped out of the Communist Party a decade earlier. On June 30 the *Washington Post* quoted the network as saying, "It is our judgment that Mr. Burdett's break with communism was complete and final thirteen years ago and that he has been a loyal and honest citizen ever since." Following his testimony, the Passport Office approved his application and issued him a passport to travel to Rome, where he would head the CBS bureau for the remainder of his career. The role of his passport did not become public until well after his death (Alwood 2006a, 167).

Anticommunism began to abate in the mid-1950s after McCarthy fell from political grace and the U.S. Supreme Court began to rein in the abuses associated with it. Between 1955 and 1964, the Court issued a string of rulings that limited the powers of congressional investigative committees to coerce witnesses to testify and began to curtail State Department powers to deny passports. Though only a few cases involved journalists directly, the challenges resulted in protections for journalists that had not been previously available.

One of the first battles was waged by Otto Nathan, a professor at New York University who was the executor of the estate of Albert Einstein. Nathan applied for a passport and tried for two-and-a-half years to obtain a hearing, only to be told that his travel "would be contrary to the best interest of the United States" (Abel 1955). In June 1955 the U.S. Court of Appeals for the District of Columbia Circuit ruled in *Nathan v. Dulles* that the government must give reasonable grounds for denying a passport to an U.S. citizen, saying it could not simply issue a vaguely worded reference to safeguarding the "best interest of the United States." The same court reached a similar conclusion

---

6   [name deleted] to [name deleted], March 4, 1954, FBI 100-376050-64, FBI Files.

three weeks later in *Shachtman v. Dulles*, in which it overturned a U.S. District Court ruling that the secretary of state had exercised proper discretion in denying a passport to Max Shachtman, chair of the Independent Socialist League. The appeals court ruled that the government could not arbitrarily deny a citizen a passport without providing a compelling reason; its decision marked the first time the courts had recognized the passport as an inherent right.

PASSPORTS TO CHINA

Although the postwar era produced economic prosperity for Americans, international events brought a sense of foreboding as the "grand alliance" of the United States, Great Britain, and the Soviet Union crumbled. Russia's development of an atomic bomb and the fall of China in 1949 only exacerbated public fears of communism. In 1950, following the outbreak of the Korean War, the State Department declared passports invalid for travel to Communist nations, including Albania, China, Cuba, North Korea, and North Vietnam (Graham 1966, 140).

Government officials argued that the United States would be unable to protect citizens traveling in these areas. Tensions between the State Department and journalists reached a high point in September 1955. "Reliable information from Peiping [*sic*] indicated that Communist China would be willing to allow at least two American reporters to go to Peiping and travel throughout Communist China," the *New York Times* reported (Reston 1955). The announcement triggered a spate of applications from American journalists. One of the first test cases involved the freelance writer Homer A. Jack. When his application arrived at the State Department, documents show that passport officials privately questioned his journalistic fitness. "Mr. Jack may not be the best choice," said one official. "Were he among the American correspondents allowed to enter China, his stories might not reflect the reportorial skill and insight which is usually associated with American international press representatives."[7] The memo implied that only journalists who favorably reflected administration foreign policy would be permitted to travel abroad. Rather than make its justification public, the State Department denied Jack's request, telling him

---

7   American Embassy, Djkarta, to Department of State, telex, May 17, 1955, 911.6293/5-1755, box 338, State Department Central Decimal File, 1955-59, RG 59. [Hereafter cited as State Department Files.]

that travel to China would place him in danger. "The presence of over thirty Americans unjustly held in Communist jails is indicative of the disregard of the Chinese for the rights of nationals of other countries," it said.[8]

In the summer of 1956 China invited eighteen reporters to visit for one month, but the State Department remained adamantly opposed, citing China's refusal to release ten Americans imprisoned during the Korean War, the *New York Times* reported on August 8. The decision prompted protests from major news organizations, the paper reported the next day. "Correspondents going in there and asking the government embarrassing questions about those prisoners and everything else might help rather than hinder," an officer in the American Society of Newspaper Editors suggested to the State Department.[9] The State Department learned that NBC News, the Associated Press, United Press, and the *Chicago Daily News* were threatening to defy its ban (MacGregor 1956, 4). "The Associated Press has informed the Department that it is considering instructing its correspondent in Hong Kong to deposit his passport with the American Consulate General and proceed to Communist China," the U.S. embassy told State Department officials in Washington. "If AP is successful in getting their man in, other organizations may rapidly follow suit and we would be faced with the collapse of our policy."[10]

On Christmas Eve 1956 three American journalists crossed from Hong Kong into China. William Worthy was a respected African American reporter for the *Baltimore Afro-American*, one of the most influential African American newspapers in the United States, and a freelance reporter for CBS News. He felt strongly that the First Amendment guaranteed journalists the right to travel abroad in order to listen to voices that were not heard (Coleman Broussand and Chance Cooley 2009, 386–88). He was joined on his trip by Edmund

---

8   Hover, State Department, to American Embassy, Djkarta, July 22, 1955, 911.6293/5-1756, box 338, State Department Files.

9   [Herbert] Brucker to Lightner, August 17, 1956, 911.6293/8-1756, box 338, State Department Files. Brucker was a writer at the *Hartford Courant*, and E. Allen Lightner was acting assistant secretary for public policy at the State Department.

10 Sebald to Acting Secretary, August 17, 1956, 911.6293/8-1756, box 338, State Department Files. William J. Sebald was a State Department political adviser in Japan.

Stevens and the photographer Philip Harrington from *Look* magazine, but Worthy attracted the greatest attention. "[Worthy] is willing [to] become [a] test case if [the] State Department objects to his visit," a State Department official told Washington in the abbreviated style used in telex transmissions.[11] Faced with an embarrassing public relations blunder, passport officials avoided spelling out whether any penalties would be imposed against the journalists. "If asked what action the United States Government proposes to take he should state that the matter is under study," Raymond E. Murphy of State Department's Office of European Affairs wrote in a private memo.[12] Publicly, the department downplayed the situation. "As a result of this misuse of the passports issued to them, their passports will be made valid only for return to the United States," a State Department official announced. "Their cases are being called to the attention of the Treasury Department in view of the relevant provisions of the Trading With Enemy Act."[13] At the same time the CIA could hardly wait to debrief Stevens. "Ambassador Bohlen feels that the correspondent's long residence in the Soviet Union makes him particularly well qualified to compare current Chinese and Soviet conditions," said an intelligence memo. "Stevens was favorably impressed by the relative availability of consumer goods and by the absence of the atmosphere of fear and restraint so pervading in the USSR" (*Current Intelligence Bulletin* 1957).

The uproar over China triggered protests from professional organizations. The Overseas Press Club condemned the State Department's decision, saying it produced a climate in which "the American public is receiving information from Red China solely from non-American journalists or from official Communist Chinese sources," the *New York Times* reported on January 8, 1957. Two months later representatives of newspapers, magazines, and other journalistic organizations testified before Congress in support of the journalists' right to travel (Trussell 1957, 6). "The State Department has in times past ... permitted exceptions to general practices that will allow the American people to continue to have information and knowledge about areas

11   Hong Kong to Acheson, telex, December 24, 1956, 911.6293/12-2456, box 299, State Department Files.

12   Raymond E. Murphy to Sebald, December 24, 1956, 911.6293/12-2456, box 338, State Department Files.

13   John Foster Dulles to American Embassy, Moscow, telex, December 28, 1956, 911.3293/12-2856, box 338, State Department Files.

in which general travel is not permitted," said Russell Wiggins of the *Washington Post*, who represented the American Society of Newspaper Editors (U.S. Senate 1957, 16).

William Worthy received a less sympathetic reception when a three-judge panel of the U.S. Court of Appeals upheld the State Department's ban on travel to China, and the Supreme Court subsequently declined to review the decision. "Merely because a newsman has a right to travel does not mean he can go anywhere he wishes," wrote Chief Judge E. Barrett Prettyman in *Worthy v. Herter* (1959, 909).

Two months later several other news organizations threatened to send even more correspondents. Arthur Hays Sulzberger, publisher of the *New York Times*, warned that any restriction would be "abridging the freedom of the press." Secretary of State John Foster Dulles, an eminent Washington lawyer, brushed the argument aside. "The constitutional 'freedom of the press' relates to publication, and not to the gathering of news," he told Sulzberger. (*Time* 1957, 45).

Meanwhile, the Supreme Court chipped away at the State Department's restrictions. When Rockwell Kent, a New York artist, wanted to travel to Europe in the late 1950s, the State Department denied his passport application. Officials cited his "consistent and prolonged adherence to the Communist Party line" (*Kent v. Dulles* 1957, 600). Kent claimed that a government affidavit that was required of all applicants concerning Communist Party membership was unlawful. By the time his appeal reached the Supreme Court, the Court's views on civil liberties had begun to shift as a result of the appointment of Chief Justice Earl Warren. Though Dwight D. Eisenhower had been elected president on a conservative Republican platform, his appointee to the Supreme Court to succeed the late Justice Fred Vinson turned out to be a social liberal (Sabin 1999, 106–14). This was especially evident in the 1954 decision in *Brown v. Board of Education* that struck down school segregation.

Four years later the Court ruled 5–4 against the State Department in the *Kent* case, establishing for the first time that foreign travel is a constitutionally protected liberty and can be restricted only by due process of law, as spelled out in the Fifth Amendment. The decision meant that passports could be withheld only under authority specifically granted by Congress, striking at the "discretionary" underpinning of the secretary of state's actions. The Court specifically noted that "foreign correspondents and lecturers on public affairs need first-hand information," but the justices again skirted the constitutional arguments. They wrote: "We deal with beliefs, with associations, with ideological matters. We must remember that we are dealing here with citizens who have neither been accused of crimes nor found guilty. … We would be faced with important constitutional questions were we to hold that Congress had given the Secretary authority to withhold passports to citizens because of their beliefs or associations. Congress has made no such provision in explicit terms; and absent one, the Secretary may not employ that standard to restrict the citizens' right of free movement" (*Kent v. Dulles* 1958, 130).

Rather than risk a constitutional crisis, the Court focused on the scope of delegated authority rather than the First Amendment issues (Emerson 1970, 197–98; Bickel 1962, 111–198). The decision prompted the State Department to revise its passport procedures. On June 29 the *New York Times* reported this announcement from the agency: "Pursuant to the recent Supreme Court decision, the Passport office of the State Department no longer requires applicants for passports or renewals to fill in the Communist oath part of the form."

Frustrated by the State Department's ill-defined policies, William Worthy again challenged the restrictions in 1961 after the United States banned travel to Cuba without citizens' first obtaining approval from the State Department.[14] Cuba had been a concern for Americans since the 1956 revolution that installed Fidel Castro as its Communist leader. Castro soon allied the island nation with the Soviet Union. Worthy traveled to Cuba following the 1961 Bay of Pigs invasion, a failed attempt by U.S.-trained forces to overthrow Castro (Ambrose and Brinkley 1997, 168–69). Upon his return in October 1961, Worthy was arrested by federal agents in Miami and charged with illegally entering the United States. A federal court brushed aside his claim to First Amendment protection, convicted him of unlawfully reentering the country without a valid passport, and sentenced him to three months in jail (Lewis 1964). The *New York Times* rallied to Worthy's defense on March 4, 1964, but, like the courts, did not distinguish the First Amendment right of a journalist from the right of any other citizen. "We do not think Americans should have to have a Government

---

14 "Termination of Relations," White House Press Release, January 3, 1961, in "U.S. Breaks Ties With Government of Cuba, Maintains Its Treaty Rights In Guantanamo Base," *State Department Bulletin*, January 23, 1961, 103.

official's approval to travel anywhere," the paper said. "The Government must be able to stop a trip designed to carry out some illegal act, such as smuggling or espionage. But it is not the American system to make travel itself a crime merely on the say-so of an official."

When the case came before a U.S. appeals court, a three-judge panel reversed the conviction but left Worthy's First Amendment defense unaddressed. "Travel abroad, like travel within the country, may be necessary for a livelihood," wrote Judge Warren L. Jones of the Fifth Circuit. "We do not think that a citizen, absent from his country, can have his fundamental right to have free ingress thereto subject to a criminal penalty if he does not have a passport" (*Worthy v. U.S.* 1964, 393, 394). Some observers credit Worthy for "helping to transform the role of modern foreign correspondence" (Coleman Broussard and Chance Cooley 2009, 387).

Battles continued in the Supreme Court. In 1963 the Court heard the case of Herbert Aptheker, editor of the Communist publication *Political Affairs*, combining it with another by party chairman Elizabeth Gurley Flynn. Although a U.S. District Court had upheld the passport denial as a "valid exercise of power," the Supreme Court reversed the decision 6–3. "We hold that ... section 6 of the Control Act too broadly and indiscriminately restricts the right to travel and thereby abridges the liberty guaranteed by the Fifth Amendment," wrote Justice Arthur Goldberg for the majority. "Under the statute it is a crime for a notified member of a registered organization to apply for a passport to travel abroad to visit a sick relative, to receive medical treatment, or any other wholly innocent purpose. ... Congress has within its power less drastic means of achieving the congressional objective of safeguarding our national security" (*Aptheker v. Secretary of State* 1964, 512–13). As the *New York Times* noted in its report on June 23, the decision was a landmark in that it recognized constitutional restraints on the power of Congress to restrict foreign travel by U.S. citizens. However, it left the State Department free to curtail travel to certain specific locations.

Another case that held implications for journalists involved Louis Zemel, a Connecticut ski lodge owner, who sued to overturn the travel ban as the United States entered the politically charged atmosphere of the Cuban Missile Crisis. A U.S. District Court upheld the State Department's denial of Zemel's passport application and in 1965 a divided Supreme Court rejected his appeal in *Zemel v. Rusk*, leaving the government's ban on travel to Cuba intact. Though not a journalist, Zemel had presented arguments that were the closest of any to confronting the free press issue, saying that the purpose of his trip was "to satisfy my curiosity about the state of affairs in Cuba" (*Zemel* 1965, 4). The Court's decision specifically noted, "The right to speak and publish does not carry with it the unrestrained right to gather information" (17). Justice Hugo Black dissented, saying that the discretion delegated to the secretary of state amounted to "delegation running riot" (22). Justice William O. Douglas, with whom Justice Arthur Goldberg concurred, wrote, "Restrictions on the right to travel in times of peace should be so particularized that a First Amendment right is not precluded unless some clear countervailing national interest stands in the way of its assertion" (26). A January 1966 *New York Times* headline noted, "Right to Travel Is Still Undefined." The article explained, "The Government's position has been compromised by an inconsistency between the reasons it gives for the travel bans, and the use to which they have been put" (Graham 1966). Yet nearly fifty years later *Zemel* stands as the Supreme Court's last word on the subject.

Passports are supposed to be a right of citizenship without regard to an individual's thoughts or beliefs. However, as the experiences of the 1950s and 1960s demonstrate, the process is easily politicized in a manner that excludes individuals who are seen as outside the mainstream. Unlike the passport denials suffered by actors, artists, lawyers, and other left-leaning Americans, restrictions against journalists held broad implications that went beyond an imposition. At a time when international tensions ran high, it was essential for Americans to have access to news and information beyond that provided by news agencies operated by foreign governments.

Between 1952 and 1966 courts recognized travel as a form of free speech, but they were unwilling to recognize free press arguments, leaving journalists with no more protection than any other citizen. And by leaving passport policies to the discretion of the secretary of state, the courts left an unelected official in the position of determining the terms and conditions under which the public is informed on international affairs. Deciding when journalists are allowed to travel abroad and which ones are to be granted the privilege means the secretary of state decides how the press is to be permitted to report to the public on important events overseas. In the 1950s passports became a political tool despite the First Amendment protections against government interference with the press.

Though examples involving journalists are anecdotal, there is evidence that passport restrictions have abrogated the constitutional protection of journalists who may hold political beliefs outside the mainstream but have committed no crime. The cases of Anne Bauer and Winston Burdett reveal the manner in which McCarthyism was aimed at journalists during the 1950s. Evidence also indicates that passports have been denied based on the government's assessment of the quality of a journalist's work, as in the case for Homer A. Jack. It is not possible to determine how many journalists have been denied passports. Nor is it possible to determine how many chose to forgo a foreign assignment rather than risk humiliation and unemployment, as did Winston Burdett. Media owners silently tolerated government encroachment for fear they would become targets of McCarthyism themselves. It wasn't until journalists wanted to travel to China that the owners began to object to government interference. Competitive pressure prompted them to support journalists' demands for unrestricted travel.

One legacy of the McCarthy era is that American foreign correspondents have no greater right to hold a valid passport than any other citizen, despite First Amendment protection of the press. At the whim of the secretary of state, a passport becomes an ideological leash, the length of which rests with an unelected federal official and the courts.

REFERENCES

Abel, Elie. 1955. "U.S. Appeals Court Rules a Passport Is Inherent Right." *New York Times*, June 24, 1.

Alwood, Edward. 2006a. "CBS Correspondent Winston Burdett and His Decision to Become a Government Witness in the Age of McCarthyism." *American Communist History* 5, no. 2 (December): 153–67.

———. 2006b. *Dark Days in the Newsroom: McCarthyism Aimed at the Press.* Philadelphia: Temple University Press.

Ambrose, Stephen, and Douglas G. Brinkley. 1997. *Rise to Globalism: American Foreign Policy Since 1938.* 8th ed. New York: Penguin.

Aptheker v. Secretary of State, 378 U.S. 500 (1964).

Association of the Bar of the City of New York. 1958. *Freedom to Travel: Report of the Special Committee to Study Passport Procedures.* New York: Dodd, Mead.

Bauer, Anne. 1951–52. "South Africa's New Racial Order." *American Scholar* (winter): 33.

Bauer v. Acheson, 106 F. Supp. 445 (D.C.D.C. 1952).

Bickel, Alexander M. 1962. *The Least Dangerous Branch: The Supreme Court at the Bar of Politics.* 2d ed. New Haven, Conn.: Yale University Press.

Boltax, Phyllis E. 1982. "The Right to Travel and Passport Revocation." *Brooklyn Journal of International Law* 8: 391–428.

Boudin, Leonard B. 1956. "The Constitutional Right to Travel." *Columbia Law Review* 56: 45–75.

Brown v. Board of Education, 347 U. S. 483 (1954).

Caute, David. 1978. *The Great Fear.* New York: Simon and Schuster.

Cloud, Stanley, and Lynne Olson. 1996. *The Murrow Boys: Pioneers on the Front Lines of Broadcast Journalis.* Boston: Houghton Mifflin.

Coleman Broussard, Jinx, and Skye Chance Cooley. 2009. "William Worthy (Jr.): The Man and the Mission." *Journalism Studies* 10: 386–88.

Current Intelligence Bulletin. 1957, February 3. "American Correspondent Reports on Communist China." CIA-RDP79T00975A002900420001-3, Central Intelligence Agency.

Donner, Frank J. 1961. *The Un-Americans.* New York: Ballantine.

Ehrlich, Thomas. 1966. "Passports." *Stanford Law Review* 19: 129–49.

Emerson, Thomas I. 1970. *The System of Free Expression.* New York: Vintage, 1970.

Emery, Michael, Edwin Emery, and Nancy L. Roberts. 2000. *The Press and America.* 9th ed. Boston: Allyn and Bacon.

Fagen, Leslie G. 1973. "The Right to Travel and the Loyalty Oath." *Columbia Journal of Transnational Law* 12: 387–400.

Federal Register. 1939, September. U.S. Department of State, Departmental Order no. 811, 3892.

Fried, Richard M. 1990. *Nightmare in Red: The McCarthy Era in Perspective.* New York: Oxford University Press.

Graham, Fred P. 1966. "Right to Travel Is Still Undefined." *New York Times,* January 2, 140.

Jet. 1952, January 31. "Press Digest," 32–33.

150 *A Moment of Danger*

Kent v. Dulles, 248 F. 2d 600 (D.C. Cir. 1957); 357 U.S. 116 (1958).

Kessler, Glenn. 2008. "Celebrity Passport Records Popular." *Washington Post*, July 4, A-1.

Klehr, Harvey. 1984. *The Heyday of American Communism: The Depression Decade.* New York: Basic.

Lewis, Anthony. 1964. "'Right to Travel' Pressed in Courts." *New York Times*, March 8, E-5.

Lofton, John. 1980. *The Press as Guardians of the First Amendment.*

MacGregor, Greg. 1956. "4 U.S. Newsmen Awaited in China." *New York Times*, August 20, 4.

Mott, Frank Luther. 1962. *American Journalism.* 3d ed. New York: Macmillan.

Nathan v. Dulles, 225 F.2d 29 (D.C. Cir. 1955).

New York Times. 1951, February 11. "Passports Denied to Two Reporters," 1.

———. 1951, February 12. "Those Communist Reporters," 21.

———. 1952, July 11. "Acheson Aides Study Ruling on Passport," 4.

———. 1952, April 23. "Passport Revoking Tested in U.S. Court," 20.

———. 1952, July 10. "State Department Upset," 14.

———. 1956, August 8. "U.S. Firm in Ban on Red China Trip," 7.

———. 1956, August 9. "U.S. Press Protests on China Ban Here," 6.

———. 1957, January 8. "Protest Aids Newsmen," 3.

———. 1958, June 29. "Regulations on Passports," XX9.

———. 1964, March 4. "Freedom to Travel," 36.

———. 1964, June 23. "Ruling Ends Passport Ban Restricting Travel by Reds," 1.

Parker, Reginald. 1954. "The Right to Go Abroad: To Have and to Hold a Passport." *Virginia Law Journal* 40: 863–65.

Persico, Joseph E. 1988. *Edward R. Murrow: An American Original.* New York: McGraw-Hill.

Porter, Russell. 1952. "Publishers Assail Censorship Trend." *New York Times*, April 23, 22.

Reston, James. 1955. "U.S. May Ease Ban on Red Area Trips." *New York Times*, September 12, 1.

Rogers, Alan. 1985. "Passports and Politics: The Courts and the Cold War." *Historian* 47: 497–511.

Sabin, Arthur J. 1999. *In Calmer Times: The Supreme Court and Red Monday.* Philadelphia: University of Pennsylvania Press.

Saltzman, Warren Hall. 1952. "Passport Refusals for Political Reasons." *Yale Law Journal* 61: 171–203.

Schrecker, Ellen. 1998. *Many Are the Crimes: McCarthyism in America.* Boston: Little, Brown.

Shachtman v. Dulles, 225 F.2d 938 (D.C. Cir. 1955).

State Department Bulletin. 1941. "Requirements for the Departure and Entry of American Citizens," November 15, 384.

———. 1952a. "Department Policy on Issuance of Passports." June 9, 919–23.

———. 1952b. "New Passport Regulations Issued." September 15, 417–18.

Time. 1957, May 13. "The Press: Blank-Page Policy," 45.

Trussell, C. P. 1957. "Newsman Cites Pressure by U.S." *New York Times,* March 30, 6.

U.S. Senate. Committee on the Judiciary. Subcommittee on Constitutional Rights. 1958. *The Right to Travel,* 85th Cong., 1st sess., March 29, 1957, pt. 1. Washington, D.C.: GPO.

Washington Law Review. 1967. "Judicial Review of the Right to Travel: A Proposal" 42: 875–80.

Washington Post. 1955, June 30. "4 Statements on Inquiry," 8.

Whelan, Charles M. 1952. "Passports and Freedom to Travel." *Georgetown Law Journal* 41: 63–90.

Worthy v. Herter, 270 F.2d 905 (D.C. Cir. 1959); *cert. denied,* 361 U.S. 918 (1959).

Worthy v. U.S., 328 F.2d 386 (5th Cir. 1964).

Zemel v. Rusk, 381 U.S. 1 (196

CHAPTER 8

"LOVE THAT AFL-CIO"

ORGANIZED LABOR'S USE OF TELEVISION,
1950-1970

Nathan Godfried

"It's not like selling soap. You can't just sing a jingle that says, 'Love
that AFL-CIO.'" (Labor publicist quoted in Pomper 1959-60, 490)

IN 1952 THE CONGRESS OF INDUSTRIAL ORGANIZATIONS (CIO)
warned that labor's failure to utilize television would leave "the
wealthy conservative and big business propaganda agencies...to
present, uncontested, their reactionary viewpoints" (quoted in
Douglas 1986, 32). A few years later in San Francisco, Local 9
of the Shipfitters Union moved its regular meetings from Wednesday to Tuesday evenings so that the rank-and-file could watch televised boxing matches. But Milton Berle and other entertainers proved
equally attractive to working-class viewers on Tuesday nights. Taken
aback, Local 9's secretary suggested that the union have "a TV set at
our meeting and conduct business during commercials" (*Federation
News* February 26, 1955, 5).

By the mid-1950s, organized labor recognized that television attracted Americans, including union members, and that it had the
potential to mold public opinion, either for or against trade unions.
Knowing that they had to use the medium in some fashion, labor officials confronted two sets of problems. The first set dealt with how
to gain access to television. A small group of union staff encouraged
the labor movement to secure its own television broadcasting stations,
arguing that the existing system, dominated by large corporations
such as the National Broadcasting Company (NBC), the Columbia

Broadcasting System (CBS), and a host of industrial and advertising firms, would seldom allow trade unions unfettered or uncensored access to the airwaves. The majority of labor groups disagreed, preferring to gain admission to television either by purchasing time on stations and networks or by securing the free time that stations were obligated to devote to public service programming.

A second set of problems dealt with what to say once organized labor got on television. Some groups envisioned using television as a means of communicating specific information concerning union activities, collective bargaining disputes, or public policy discussions directly with their membership or with the larger public. Others wanted television to improve their overall image in the community via institutional advertising, especially to demonstrate that organized labor was a "loyal" participant in America's Cold War domestic and foreign policies. Few if any labor activists wished to use television to offer a working-class challenge to the postwar order.

Labor had not always been reticent to use broadcasting to struggle against the status quo: during radio's heyday, labor radicals in city federated bodies and in various CIO unions envisioned labor radio as a progressive force supporting a collective social unionism. By the time that television supplanted radio as the major broadcasting venue, however, the U.S. trade union movement had lost much of its political and cultural radicalism. Succumbing to the imperatives of the Cold War, labor purged radicals from its ranks and embraced the individualistic business unionism characteristic of the American Federation of Labor (AFL).

This article explores why and how organized labor used television during the 1950s-1960s, analyzing the assumptions that national union officials made regarding the role of television in the labor movement and evaluating the messages conveyed to the audience. It recognizes that labor's approach to television reflected ongoing tensions within the labor movement and between organized labor and the corporate and state sectors. Before turning to a discussion of labor's efforts at television programming, it is necessary to outline the structure and perspectives of the U.S. labor movement during the early Cold War.

LABOR AND COLD WAR AMERICA

In 1945, after a decade of organizing and political maneuvering, the trade union movement, including the AFL and the CIO, appeared on the cusp of significant economic and political power. More than one-third of the labor force belonged to unions in 1946 and at least 80 percent of the workers in most basic industries held union cards. Membership grew from approximately 14 million workers in 1948 to more than 20 million by the end of the 1960s. Some labor leaders believed that massive membership could lead to increased political power. Although the press and business sector exaggerated their influence, political action committees created by both national unions educated and mobilized working-class voters and opposed a nascent coalition of anti-labor Republicans and southern Democrats. The merger of the two unions in 1955 seemed to mark a united front of labor and to portend greater political influence (Moody 1988, 41-69; Green 1980, 174-209).

U.S. labor's growth coincided with a booming postwar economy. Prosperity was based on increases in worker productivity, government fiscal policies, and the nation's hegemonic role in the global economy. Organized labor, according to Nelson Lichtenstein, "helped determine the extent to which the working class could win its share of that growth dividend" (2002, 57). Union workers enjoyed relatively high wages and substantial fringe benefits in part because they remained combative. "From the late 1940s through the early 1970s, strike levels in the United States stood higher than at any time, before or since" and such union activism helped to keep businesses in line, "making certain that the standards won in the union sector would flow to millions of non-union workers" (136-137).

The trade union movement circa 1945 contained competing worldviews. The AFL emphasized organizing craft unions of skilled workers and achieving "bread and butter" issues (Lichtenstein 2002, 68). For presidents Samuel Gompers (1886-1924), William Green (1924-1952), and George Meany (1952-1979), the union's top goal was to secure more money, fewer hours, and better working conditions for workers. The AFL was not a class movement; it neither embraced an overt political role for itself nor sought broad social goals; rather it desired a partnership with business and the state in the capitalist system. By favoring the organization of craft workers, officials often ignored the plight of unskilled labor, especially racial and ethnic minorities and women (Lichtenstein 2002, 63-71; Fletcher and Gapasin 2008, 14-17). The CIO, formed in the mid and late 1930s, promoted the organization of all workers, regardless of skill level, in a particular industry. CIO unions generally recognized the need to include women and racial minorities within their ranks and they often unequivocally demanded "nondiscrimination, fair employment, [and] political enfranchisement" for workers (Lichtenstein 2002, 79). To the extent that explicit job rules—such as seniority rights and grievance procedures—limited the unilateral power and abuses of management, CIO organizers struggled for greater industrial democracy. Industrial unionism thus initially had a broad social agenda.

Leftists, including Communists, played crucial roles in building and developing CIO unions. Adhering to the concept of class struggle, leftists saw unions as vehicles for organizing workers in their self-interest, educating them to the necessity of transcending capitalism, and helping them achieve societal change (Fletcher and Gapasin 2008, 23). Throughout the 1930s and 1940s, leftists helped to construct powerful and democratic unions in the CIO. "Indeed, the effectiveness of the Left in championing U.S. democracy and social reform, with a strong base in the CIO and other unions, is precisely why it became a target of the Cold War witch hunts" (25).

As Elizabeth Fones-Wolf (1994) has explained, the postwar era witnessed a business assault on New Deal activism and on the growing power and legitimacy of the labor movement. This involved an ideological campaign—waged against organized labor in the mass media, in educational and religious institutions, and in local communities—that proclaimed the sanctity and benefits of the free enterprise system. Many large corporations renewed welfare capitalist policies to undermine worker loyalty to unions. Executives turned to Boulwarism—named after the General Electric Company's postwar personnel manager—"to establish a new hard-line labor relations strategy that would reassert the ideological authority of management" in the workplace (Davis 1999, 120). In addition to this vast arsenal of weapons, the business community utilized the developing Cold War itself to weaken worker organizations.

Labor became a target of Red hunters because CIO unions and others were home to a significant number of leftists and Communists. Business and government leaders, aided by conservative union officials who had long sought the elimination of leftists in the ranks, consciously manipulated fears of Soviet actions abroad and an international Communist conspiracy at home. Out of both genuine concern and political expediency, leaders in the AFL and the CIO increasingly embraced Cold War liberal ideology—i.e., they supported New Deal-type social welfare programs, labor-management cooperation, economic growth rather than class struggle, and the destruction of domestic and foreign Communists and political radicals. The anti-labor Taft-Hartley Act (1947) mandated "a set of constraints that encouraged trade-union parochialism and penalized any serious attempt to project a classwide political-economic strategy" (Lichtenstein 2002, 122). In 1949-1950 the CIO purged eleven unions whose leaders refused to sign anti-Communist affidavits. By eviscerating leftist influences in their ranks, the CIO and the AFL deprived the union movement "of those activists who could have most effectively mounted a strong defense of collective action and challenged the business community's promotion of privatization and individual gain" (Schrecker 2004, 16).

The loss of labor radicals profoundly affected how the organized labor movement approached the mass media, including the new medium of television. Within radical unions and among independent leftists were those who believed that radio, film, and television could and should be used to organize and mobilize the working class and to create alternative and oppositional culture to that of consumer and corporate capitalism. In 1946, for example, the United Electrical, Radio, and Machine Workers' Union—soon to be purged from the CIO—began producing films that exposed the faults of corporate capitalism and agitated workers to take action. Corporate executives were horrified that UE films "preach class hatred toward business" (*The Dispatcher* January 24, 1947, 9; Godfried 2008, 326-327). Corporate, state, and conservative union officials legitimately feared what leftists might do with television.

By the mid-1950s the "moment of danger" had passed. The combination of Cold War politics, the business attack, and economic growth helped assure business unionist domination of organized labor's operations and policies. "Content to negotiate, sign, and administer labor contracts," AFL and CIO leaders embraced the capitalist system to such a degree that they ran their own unions like businesses and sought partnership with the private sector (Moody 1988, 56; Fletcher and Gapasin 2008, 251n18). The 1955 merger of the AFL and

CIO—made possible by the systematic purging of leftists from the CIO—exemplified this triumph of business unionism. When labor turned to the question of television broadcasting in the 1950s, it did so from a business unionist perspective.

Given their belief in the harmony of interest with capital and the state, AFL-CIO President George Meany and other business unionists saw no need to formulate, let alone communicate to a wider audience, an alternative to Cold War liberalism. But, because a business unionist perspective per se did not obviate labor-capital clashes, the AFL-CIO had a vested interest in a narrowly oriented public relations and mass media campaign. Throughout the 1950s and 1960s organized labor and corporations continued to battle over wages, hours, and benefits, and they vied for influence in and access to local and national political institutions (Fones-Wolf 1994). Labor leaders recognized the need to shape public opinion in general and workers' opinion in particular and this made television important to them.

LABOR-OWNED TELEVISION STATIONS

While acknowledging television's value for organized labor under certain conditions, most unions argued against the establishment of labor-owned stations. The financial requirements of securing a broadcasting license and building studios, hiring staff, etc., led media consultants to favor securing time on existing stations and networks. Not a single expert invited to speak at a labor television workshop in New York City in September 1954 even mentioned the option of labor-owned television stations.[1] Certainly the failure of the FM radio stations owned and operated by the International Ladies' Garment Workers' Union (ILGWU) and the United Automobile Workers (UAW) during the late 1940s and early 1950s did not bode well for labor television (Fones-Wolf 2006, 184-201). The few advocates of labor stations argued that the dominant mass media were "almost entirely owned and operated by business groups" whose economic and political interests overwhelmingly opposed those of labor (Pomper 1959-1960, 493). But no prominent AFL or CIO official accepted the suggestion that the unions create "a network of TV stations, operated

---

1 "Television: Labor's New Challenge," proceedings of First Annual Television Workshop, National Labor Service, September 7-8, 1954, File 17, Box 4, Novik Papers.

in the interest of the public and organized labor" (*American Federationist* May 1952, 30).

The labor organization coming closest to establishing its own television station in the Cold War era was the Chicago Federation of Labor. In 1950, officials of Chicago's central labor body—an amalgam of dozens of individual unions in the city—talked about establishing a television station to complement radio station WCFL. The opening of ultra-high frequency channels in the 1960s allowed the CFL to secure a license for Channel 38. CFL President William Lee promised that labor television would "add new dimensions to the Chicago television scene" by telling "the union story to all the people in an interesting and colorful style" (*Federation News* September 1969, 1). But only two programs in the CFL's proposed schedule dealt directly with labor issues: a daily 15-minute news show promised to report on labor matters, interview guest experts, and offer film clips and short documentaries on relevant topics. A 30-minute panel discussion show, slated for Saturday nights, would invite representatives from management, labor, civic organizations, or legislative bodies (Godfried 2002, 121-125, 130).

Lee's rhetoric notwithstanding, two labor programs hardly distinguished WCFL-TV as labor television. In the 1920s-1930s, progressive, social democratic leaders of the CFL created WCFL radio to broadcast oppositional perspectives on contemporary issues and to contest corporate values (Godfried 1997, 19-136). Decades later, quintessential business unionists proposed a television station. Lee and his colleagues favored "negotiations to strikes and conciliation to confrontation" and rarely challenged the economic or political status quo in Chicago or the nation (*Chicago Tribune* June 17, 1984, sec. 3, 8). Working with local business and government elites, they supported the prevailing distribution of economic and political rewards while maintaining labor peace and the image of a cross-class harmony of interests. In 1957 Lee declared that Chicago labor "*knows* that we are *not* a 'working class' that's abusive of our economic system, management and the public interest" (*Federation News* July 13, 1957, 4). CFL leaders, like their counterparts at the national level, had no interest in developing programming with a sharp class-conscious edge. Rather they desired providing quality entertainment for a wide audience; demonstrating to corporate officials and the public at large that the labor perspective paralleled that of Cold War liberal government and big business; and generating revenue for the CFL. They soon realized, however, that few television stations made profits during their first years of operation. Technical and conceptual problems further hampered labor television's development. The CFL sold Channel 38 in 1975, leaving the television world without broadcasting a single program (Godfried 2002, 129-131).

PUBLIC SERVICE PROGRAMMING AND INSTITUTIONAL ADVERTISING

With the exception of CFL officials, by the early 1950s supporters of labor broadcasting advocated that unions develop programming rather than establish stations. Morris S. Novik and Harry W. Flannery, in particular, recommended that organized labor engage in a fusion of public service broadcasting and institutional advertising. Novik, a socialist in his youth, worked for the ILGWU during the 1920s, served as program director for the Socialist Party's radio station WEVD during the 1930s, and advised the ILGWU and UAW on the development of their radio stations in the late 1940s (Godfried 2001, 350-352; Fones-Wolf 2006, 42-43, 157-158). Flannery, a print and broadcast journalist, worked as a news analyst for CBS during the 1940s and for the AFL during the 1950s.

In 1951 Flannery and Novik formulated a strategy that the AFL adopted when it entered television production. The two argued that a labor program had to appeal to the AFL membership because not all members accepted union policies or candidates for elective office. In addition, the program had to "sell the AFL and its ideas" to non-union members. "The program must attract non-AFL listeners, and it must sell them." Catchy commercials asking viewers to "love that AFL" would not suffice. Instead the two contended that selling the union movement required a good news program that avoided "emotional crusading" and appeared "fair." Given the misconception that labor was leftist—a "particularly silly [idea] in the case of the AFL"—Flannery warned that, "a program that rants, one that seldom deviates from attacks on Congress and Congressmen, one that finds little but fault helps to perpetuate the wrong idea in the minds of anti-Labor people. On the other hand, a program that is none the less fearless, that is none the less determined, but which also tries to be fair, which is less of a patent medicine barker, and more of a conscientious servant of the people, such a program will win friends and get results."[2]

Thus Flannery and Novik favored public service news shows that used the commercial breaks to tout the virtues of the trade union movement. Almost all of the shows examined below were paid for by the trade union movement and aired at no cost by networks and stations seeking to meet their public service requirements.

Both Sides, a 30-minute panel discussion moderated by the liberal commentator Quincy Howe, appeared over the American Broadcasting Company (ABC) for thirteen weeks in the spring of 1953. With this "first venture into television," the AFL hoped to inform the public about current affairs and to call "attention to its own contributions to the general welfare in the 'commercial periods' available to the sponsor" (*Federation News* March 7, 1953). Howe opened the inaugural program, which aired on a Sunday afternoon over New York station WABC-TV, by asking whether the new Soviet leader wanted peace or war and where President Dwight Eisenhower's foreign policy might lead. "I'm in the middle but in a moment we will bring you *Both Sides.*" Forum guests, Democratic Senator Hubert H. Humphrey and Republican Senator Homer Ferguson, did not represent "both sides" of the U.S.-Soviet confrontation, but rather contending sides in a domestic political battle (*New York Times* March 16, 1953).[3]

At the outset AFL spokesperson Flannery announced that the program was the first in a series of weekly forums "brought to you in the public interest by the eight million men and women who make up the American Federation of Labor, the world's largest labor organization." Midway through the program he returned, explaining that, "right in line with today's discussion, our foreign policy, is the campaign against communism which the American Federation of Labor has been carrying on, not only in our country, but" throughout the world. Leading American political figures briefly attested to how effectively the AFL defended freedom and opposed communism. Flannery concluded: "This is only one of the ways in which the American Federation of Labor is trying to serve the public interest and defend the free way of life." When the show ended, Flannery informed viewers that the AFL

2   Letter, Harry W. Flannery to Morris Novik, Sept. 16, 1951, File 32, Box 2, Novik Papers.

3   Memorandum, M. S. Novik to Ellen Bogner, March 13, 1953, Box 1, File 7, Novik Papers.

pamphlet, "American Labor in World Crisis," detailing the labor movement's international efforts, was available free of charge.[4] In the weeks
that followed, Howe and his guests discussed a variety of issues while
the mid-program commercials publicized the patriotic role of the AFL
in American society.[5]

AFL affiliates and members had conflicting assessments of *Both
Sides*. The Cincinnati Central Labor Council ranked the program
among the best current affairs programs on television. "It shows a
clear desire by the A.F. of L. to select the best informed participants
available to present both sides of important issues without Labor itself
actually participating."[6] A California labor council praised the show's
"unbiased motif" and "stimulating logic."[7] The program's detractors
questioned the efficacy of presenting "balanced" viewpoints. They argued that most public affairs programs on radio and television rarely
gave trade unions or liberal organizations equal time with the National Association of Manufacturers, the U.S. Chamber of Commerce,
or the American Legion. Conservative broadcast commentators and
newspaper columnists, contended these critics, inundated American
society with pro-corporate propaganda. Given this situation, wrote
one labor activist from Pittsburgh, the AFL should be spending its
members' money "in presenting the workingman's side of the story
exclusively." There was something to be said for "monopoliz[ing] our
own program in favor of our side."[8] Despite this criticism, the AFL
and then the AFL-CIO continued to produce "balanced" current affairs programs for television well into the 1960s.[9] At the same time,
the labor movement began to diversify its television fare.

---

4   Memorandum, Novik to Bogner, March 13, 1953, Box 1, File 7, Novik
    Papers.

5   Scripts, Both Sides, March 29, 1953, April 19, 1953, File 7, Box 1, Novik
    Papers.

6   Letter, Jack Hurst to George Meany, May 5, 1953, Folder 24, box 39,
    Meany Papers.

7   Arthur K. Hutchings, San Gabriel Valley Central Labor Council to G.
    Meany, June 19, 1953, Folder 24, Box 39, Meany Papers.

8   Letter, Edward J. Blotzer, Jr., to Meany, March 23, 1953, File 24, Box 39,
    Meany Papers.

9   See, for example, the 20-week run of *Briefing Session* in 1961. Transcripts,
    Briefing Session, Box 4, File 2, Novik Papers.

On September 20, 1954 at 8:00 p.m., the AFL sponsored *Operation Entertainment* over the NBC network. This special program honored the entertainers who performed for U.S. armed forces during World War II and the Korean War. As AFL convention delegates sat in the Los Angeles audience, Bob Hope, Danny Kaye, Debby Reynolds, and Edward G. Robinson, among many others, appeared, as did General Matthew Ridgeway, the Army Chief of Staff and former Korean War commander (*New York Times* September 20, 1954, 30). Halfway through the program, actor William Holden told the television audience that although it had not seen a commercial, "we do, in a non-commercial sense, have a sponsor...a great organization which symbolizes the American system of Free Enterprise and represents the welfare of more than ten million free Americans." While Holden spoke of the AFL members who helped "turn the wheels of our colossal industrial machines," the camera showed film of workers at their jobs. The audience heard about union workers' role in creating the nation's high standard of living and "the weapons to protect it." George Meany then talked about how the unknown majority of union workers—the television audience's neighbors and fellow citizens—built the nation's homes, cities, and infrastructure, manufactured the country's consumer goods, and toiled "to keep America strong and secure" by constructing atomic submarines and "fleets of jet bombers." The AFL, explained Meany, vehemently opposed "Communism and all forms of dictatorship," while dedicated "to the free American way of life."[10] Similar to many other union efforts at institutional advertising, *Operation Entertainment* sought to impress upon its audience the indivisibility of "labor and America;" of the symbiotic linkage between unions, on the one hand, and anti-communism, a high standard of living, community services, and freedom, on the other (Pomper 1959-1960, 488). Events at the end of the 1950s made such efforts at institutional advocacy more imperative.

Fears that television would generate negative publicity for unions were realized in 1957-1959 as a U.S. Senate committee, chaired by John L. McClellan, held televised hearings on union corruption, especially in the Teamsters' Union. The McClellan Committee's message that the union movement had become too powerful, corrupt, and

---

10   Letter, Morris Novik to Lt. Colonel Allison A. Conrad, Aug. 13, 1954; and Script, *Operation Entertainment*, Sept. 20, 1954, Box 1, File 12, Novik Papers.

undemocratic led to the passage of the anti-labor Landrum-Griffin Act (1959). This law fashioned new legal barriers to union-organizing campaigns and established regulations on union governance (Fones-Wolf 1994, 275-278). In response to the hearings, the AFL-CIO instituted a $1.2 million public relations program. As the *Wall Street Journal* reported, the AFL-CIO planned "a new television campaign aimed at convincing the public that union workers are nice people—and thus counteracting the effects of the labor scandals of the past year" (July 29, 1958, 15).

The first installment of the AFL-CIO's series, *Americans At Work*, appeared in 1959. By 1967, the union had aired 104 fifteen-minute episodes. The series paralleled the structure of *Industry on Parade* produced by the National Association of Manufacturers (1950-1960). NAM and the AFL-CIO each offered its series for free to commercial and educational television stations throughout the country as public service programming. Whereas each episode of *Industry on Parade* touted a specific wonder of U.S. industrial technology and its centrality to the nation's economic welfare, general health, and national security, *Americans at Work* depicted how laborers—from bookbinders to potters—did their jobs. The labor program aimed to enhance workers' pride in their occupations and skills and, indirectly, to convince the public of the value of union members. NAM's "public service announcement," aired during each of its episodes, "generally promoted capitalism, the American way, and the rewards of a free economy and society" (*Industry on Parade Collection 1950-1960*; *AFL-CIO News* August 16, 1958, 1-2, December 27, 1958, 7; *Federation News* July 4, 1959, 1, January 5, 1963, 2). Albert J. Zack, director of the AFL-CIO's Department of Public Relations, admitted in early 1959 that the labor shows were not "designed to show the scope or jurisdiction of any union." "There is," he told his superiors, "a delicate problem in the amount of direct union propaganda that can be included in the films and still get them on the air on free public service time." Nevertheless, Zack and his associates constantly scrutinized ways "to get as much of the union message in as possible."[11]

While the national labor movement used television to sanitize its image, unions at the local and state levels engaged the medium in a different way. From 1951 until 1967, Local 100 of the Transport

---

11   Memorandum, Albert J. Zack to William Schnitzler, Feb. 12, 1959, Box 2, File 3, William F. Schnitzler Papers.

Workers' Union in New York City produced more than a hundred television shows that "typically took the form of scripted, studio-based reports to the union's membership and/or the riding public, or televised mass membership meetings of the union in large public auditoriums" (Gottfried 2008, 508-512). The United Steelworkers of America (USWA) created *The USWA TV Meeting of the Month* in 1957-1958 for stations located in areas with heavy union membership. According to USWA President David J. MacDonald, the series, which highlighted major union activities, aimed at "those members who can't—or don't—get to their regular local union meetings." But it also "let the general public look over our shoulders and see how a big, influential union operates" (*AFL-CIO News* January 11, 1958, 5). The UAW and other unions also utilized television as a direct link to their rank and file (Fones-Wolf 1994, 119, 149).

During the 1950s several major corporations sponsored drama anthologies. Rather than selling specific products, the *Ford Theater* (1949-1957), *United States Steel Hour* (1953-1963), *General Electric Theater* (1953-1962), and *DuPont Cavalcade of America* (1954-1957) merchandised "brand awareness, corporate identity," and the free enterprise system (Raphael 2009, 127). Organized labor never seriously considered mounting such productions because of the enormous expense involved. Buying airtime, concluded the CIO Executive Council in 1954, was "perhaps the least expensive problem." Even if the union built a popular program and got its "message across," it still faced economic and political opponents "who have millions and millions of dollars in television" and who could "figure out a way to put the highest powered program on at the same hour ours is and just take away our audience."[12] This reasoning reinforced the AFL-CIO preference for short-term series or one-time special programs.

A logical date for organized labor's television productions was Labor Day, which always had been "a day on which unionists defined themselves in confident tones to the nation at large" (Kazin and Ross 1992, 1311). In the 1930s and 1940s, radio station WCFL broadcast elaborate Labor Day programs that included speeches, music, dramatizations of labor history, and parades (Godfried 1997, 186-187, 232-233). On September 6, 1954, the San Francisco Labor Council paid for and produced a 30-minute scripted program, *Labor Day: San Francisco*, for the ABC affiliate KGO-TV, which provided free air time.

12 CIO Executive Meeting, June 29, 1954, 115 (quotes), Reel 16.

Viewers watched as a union business agent—the emcee—walked about his office, explaining the principles, objectives, and practices of unions; reviewing Northern California's labor history; and discussing labor's contributions to Bay Area development. "Occasionally, he walked over to the 'window' of his office where a rear-screen projector was used to show newsreel clips of past parades and other materials to illustrate the account" (Howard 1955, 33-34). The program emphasized labor's legitimate role in American society and how union gains benefitted all workers.

For Labor Day 1960, the AFL-CIO borrowed from these earlier efforts. In cooperation with the ABC network and educational stations, the union produced *Land of Promise*, written by Sheldon Stark and narrated by actor Melvyn Douglas (*Federation News* August 27, 1960, 1). Opening with Woody Guthrie's "This Land is Your Land," the 30-minute program explored the role of labor in American history, from the Revolution through the mid-20th century. Along the way the production utilized historical paintings, sketches, photographs, and film clips and era music performed by a folk singing group. During the segment on the Great Depression, for example, the audience heard the "Soup Song" as newsreels showed unemployed workers crowding around factory gates and bread lines. Pictures of hopeful faces replaced the images of despair as President Franklin D. Roosevelt intoned that "the only thing we have to fear is fear itself." Douglas explained that, "for the first time in American history," the government sanctioned democratic working-class organization. Clips of union meetings and crowds of happy workers dissolved into a montage of working hands and the narration that organized labor generated benefits for all workers. World War II came next with a sequence of images of the war at home and abroad and the message that, "Free men out-produced slave labor. Free soldiers buried Hitler and Tojo and won a war!"[13]

The remainder of the program highlighted postwar middle-class suburban development. Douglas reiterated that trade unions brought security, dignity, and pride to U.S. workers and generated benefits for entire communities and the nation. When the standard of living of union members went up, so did that of their neighbors. Union struggles produced better schools, child labor laws, and paid holidays and vacations. As an image of a rocket replaced that of playing children,

---

13   "The Land of Promise," draft script, no date, 12-13 (quotes) Box 2, File 33 "George Meany Foundation 1960-1967," Novik Papers.

the narrator declared: "We must give those who follow us *more* life, *more* liberty and the never-ending, everlasting pursuit of happiness!"[14] Like earlier television productions, *Land of Promise* emphasized the legitimacy of organized labor and its key role in the nation's social and economic advancement. It downplayed the militant actions and radical demands of labor that had advanced the union movement and achieved societal reform. Indeed, reviewers praised the program for ignoring these aspects of American labor history (*AFL-CIO News* September 17, 1960, 10).

LABOR DRAMA AND *THE ETERNAL LIGHT*

During the 1960s the AFL-CIO experimented with a different form of television program, one that added to the standard Cold War message, but hinted at the social unionism of an earlier era and, consequently, opened the possibility of more oppositional viewpoints in the present. This development came about as the AFL-CIO created the George Meany Foundation, which became linked to the Herbert H. Lehman Institute of Ethics and the NBC religious anthology, *The Eternal Light*. Both the Lehman Institute and *The Eternal Light* were creations of the Jewish Theological Seminary of America (JTSA) and its president Louis Finkelstein. Established in 1957, the Lehman Institute reflected Finkelstein's interest in applying the study of Talmudic ethics to "the area of human rights" (Ellenson and Bycel 1997, 564; Greenbaum 1997, 199). *The Eternal Light*, another Finkelstein innovation, debuted on the NBC radio network in 1944 and offered "a popular presentation of Jewish tradition and its ideals." The show developed a reputation as "one of the best religious programs on the air" and "one of the leading dramatic shows in all radio." The radio program continued well into the 1950s and 1960s even as a television version emerged (Greenbaum 1997, 188-189; Parker, Inman, and Snyder 1948, 7). It is not surprising that as they confronted public perceptions of union corruption in 1959-1960, AFL-CIO officials welcomed an association with organizations dedicated to the study and dramatization of ethical behavior.

In 1960 Novik and several union leaders discussed creating a foundation honoring George Meany. Self-consciously characterizing

---

14 "The Land of Promise," 16-18 (quotes), Box 2, File 33 "George Meany Foundation 1960-1967," Novik Papers.

Meany as an ethical and principled leader devoted "to the welfare of the working class," Novik and his colleagues sought to make the argument for an affiliation with the Lehman Institute.[15] Although people inside and outside the labor movement disagreed with this assessment—critics, for example, characterized Meany as "judgmental, dogmatic, and disdainful of the masses of unorganized workers" (Zieger 1987, 324)—Novik and his colleagues nevertheless recommended, in June 1961, the establishment of a George Meany Foundation within the Lehman Institute. Among other activities, the Meany Foundation would produce an annual television program—featured on *The Eternal Light*—dealing with the lives of labor leaders or union-related topics.[16]

The first of the Meany Foundation-sponsored programs aired over *The Eternal Light* in November 1962. Entitled, "Never Ask What Country," the 30-minute drama, written by Morton Wishengrad, depicted the life of William Green. The author of television, theater, and film productions, Wishengrad was an award-winning radio writer and head writer of the Jewish series. He had worked as an education director for the ILGWU during the 1930s when social unionism still defined the union's worldview (Godfried 2008, 316). A reviewer for the trade journal *Variety* praised the scriptwriter's approach to his subject: Wishengrad "used the adult Green to relate events from his childhood on screen while those events were enacted behind him." The end result effectively portrayed Green's career from coal miner to state senator to national labor leader (November 28, 1962, 29). Wishengrad elegantly depicted the hard life of coal miners and their families while precisely conveying Green's "vision of a society perfected through trade unionism" and religious values (Phelan 1987, 142). In the play's final scene, set in June 1940, Green and ILGWU President David Dubinsky

15 "Proposal for the Establishment of a George Meany Foundation by the American Labor Movement in the Herbert H. Lehman Institute of Ethics," no date, 1 (quotes), Box 2, File 34, Memo, M. Novik to David Dubinsky, June 8, 1961, and Letter, Howard D. Samuel to Morris Novik, June 20, 1961, Box 2, File 34, Novik Papers; Letter, M. Novik to Joseph Keenan, June 2, 1962 and Draft Letter from J. Keenan, June 2, 1962, Box 12, Folder 6, Keenan Papers.

16 Letter, M. Novik to Joseph Keenan, June 2, 1962, Box 12, Folder 6, Keenan Papers; "Proposal for Meany Foundation," 1, 5 (quotes), Box 2, File 34, Novik Papers.

request that Franklin Roosevelt have the United States issue visas for Jews endangered by the Nazi conquest of France. Paraphrasing Louis Pasteur, Green says: "We do not ask of an unfortunate, what country do you come from, what is your religion? We say to him: you suffer, that's enough; we shall make you well."[17] Wishengrad thus captured some of the social unionism of an earlier era.

The play also reflected the AFL-CIO's fidelity to Cold War liberalism. Warning of the futility of violent strikes, Green characterized "collective bargaining and peaceful negotiation" as "the only civilized procedures" for workers to follow. The AFL-CIO's aversion to fundamental challenges to American capitalism came across in a scene in which Green and Gompers first meet and the latter complains: "These days everybody seems to have a system. I hate systems. Too neat. Too tidy. A system is a box. Put your neighbor in it, and if a part of his leg or arm sticks out, saw it off for the sake of the neatness. The true believers are a dangerous crowd. They pretend they love people, but what they truly love is their system. They want to take a chaotic, disorderly world and arrange it into flower-bordered rows, as neat and as orderly as Arlington Cemetery."[18] Labor unions therefore must not embrace "grandiose schemes" of societal change leading to the violent and deadly "systems" of socialism or communism. Rather, labor unions should serve as mechanisms to secure "a little more in the workingmen's paychecks every year." Gompers urges Green to promise workers "More, more, more, now" and "the better world of twenty minutes from now, not Utopian pie in the sky tomorrow."[19] The script thus echoed the thoughts of Meany who frequently contended that "essentially conservative" union members desired only "bread and butter, not crusades" (quoted in Goulden 1972, 465).

The Meany Foundation returned to these themes when it portrayed the careers of CIO President Philip Murray ("A New Earth" November 1963), New York Governor and Senator Lehman ("The Moral Dimension" December 1965), and Franklin Roosevelt's Secretary of Labor Frances Perkins ("The Vine and the Fig Tree" December 1968).

---

17 "Never Ask What Country," Morton Wishengrad, Box 2, File 33, Novik Papers.

18 "Never Ask What Country," 8 (first quote), 11 (second quote), Box 2, File 33, Novik Papers.

19 "Never Ask What Country," 11 (quotes), Box 2, File 33, Novik Papers.

"The Liquid Fire" (December 1966) written by John Vlahos, again featured Gompers, emphasizing his dedication to workers ("in religion I am a workingman"), his mental discipline (the product of "my study of the Talmud"), and his commitment to international labor cooperation. The program highlighted Gompers's efforts to forestall a possible war between the United States and Mexico in 1914. In reenacting a meeting between President Woodrow Wilson and Gompers, Vlahos incorporated a familiar Cold War premise. Wilson notes that Gompers's reference to American oil, land, and mineral interests in Mexico raised the specter of an "international capitalist conspiracy." Gompers responds: "Have I ever suggested that, sir? Have I once quarreled with the American system? I'm no socialist, and you know it, Mr. President. I believe in the free enterprise system, I have no desire to destroy it or even to change it. All I have ever asked is a fair share for the worker and decent conditions in the shops. And that is all I seek for our Latin brothers."[20]

Emphasizing U.S. labor support for Latin American workers had contemporary relevancy. In 1961-1962, the AFL-CIO created the American Institute for Free Labor Development (AIFLD) with the ostensible goal of educating and training Latin American union officials and members in basic union skills. But the AIFLD—administered and financed jointly by the AFL-CIO, the U.S. Government, and corporations—also aided the interests of U.S. multinationals in the hemisphere and, via secret funding from the Central Intelligence Agency, assisted right-wing Latin unions in destabilizing indigenous progressive labor organs (Buhle 1999, 151-154; Scipes 2010). Having a play underscore long-standing labor concerns for the plight of "our Latin brothers" sought to place contemporary AFL-CIO hemispheric operations in a more favorable context.

An interesting respite from AFL-CIO television's adherence to Cold War liberalism came with the 1964 production of Millard Lampell's "The Ballad of Isaac and Jacob." Lampell, like Wishengrad, was "a socially conscious writer who communicated in every medium he could," including radio, television, film, and theater (*New York Times* October 11, 1997, B7). Before World War II, Lampell was a journalist and folk musician—an original member of the Almanac Singers (McGilligan and Buhle 1999, 390-392). He briefly joined the Communist Party before entering the military in World War II. During

---

20   John Vlahos, "The Liquid Fire," no date, Box 2, File 33, Novik Papers.

and after the war, Lampell wrote radio scripts, developing a reputation "as a consummate craftsman" (*Hollywood Quarterly* 1947-1948, 207). But his participation in leftist politics and unions led to his blacklisting in 1950. Lampell overcame the blacklist by 1960, when his adaptation of a John Hersey novel about the Warsaw Ghetto uprising made its Broadway debut (McGilligan and Buhle 1999, 390-391, 399-400). Within a few years he was writing episodes for a provocative television series dealing with racial issues and scripting a film documentary on immigration, class struggle, and unions (Watson 2008, 40; *New York Times* November 9, 1964, 42).

"The Ballad of Isaac and Jacob" captured the dilemma of David Miller, a mathematician and computer programmer trying to complete an automation program that would allow one textile machine to do the work of 300 people. The task troubles David because he is haunted by his grandfather's religious belief that human dignity derives from a person's labor. He eventually asks: "Who am I? David Miller, grandson of Isaac…Talmudic scholar, sweatshop tailor, silk weaver…Who am I? David, son of Jacob…loom fixer and master mechanic." After wondering why workers remain "unsung" and "anonymous," David narrates a brief history of immigrant labor in America, aided with commentary from Isaac and Jacob, and augmented with the screening of contemporary engravings, paintings, and photographs and the playing of appropriate musical numbers performed by three folk singers.[21] When the chronology reaches the early 20th century, the play directly incorporates the stories of David's grandfather and father. Isaac Miller tells of leaving the slums of Manhattan's Lower East Side and making his way to the silk mills in New Jersey. His son, Jacob, grows as World War I and the roaring twenties swirl around him. The onset of the Great Depression forces Jacob to abandon his plans for college and to hit the road looking for a job, comforted by his father's admonition—drawn from Jewish teachings—that "if one falls, he shall be supported by the other. Woe to him that is alone, for when he falls, he has none to lift him up." Here Lampell indirectly refers to the importance of both family and working class community. The chronology quickly moves to World War II, allusions to the Holocaust, and Jacob's military service in Europe.[22]

21 Millard Lampell, "The Ballad of Isaac and Jacob," December 13, 1964, 1, 5-6, Box 2, File 33, Novik Papers.

22 "The Ballad of Isaac and Jacob," 9, 13, Box 2, File 33, Novik Papers.

In its last segment, Lampell's play focuses on the shifting character of work in modern society. David explains to his father that his automation program is "just a tool, like any other tool. To take over the kind of work that for a person is meaningless." Jacob immediately understands the dilemma: "And grandpa's work—my work—that's also meaningless?" "What becomes of the workers your machine replaces? What becomes of a man like your grandpa? What becomes of me?" David's reply—that people could enjoy shorter work days and weeks and, perhaps, at some point, get paid not to work—remains inadequate. Jacob persists: "God worked. Creation is work. A person who doesn't work…I do not understand such a person." David insists that the computer/automation is a tool; "It can destroy us or it can free us. It all depends on how we use it." But David himself remains dissatisfied with this answer and uncertain about the future. Any solution to the problem of automation, David realizes, must contain his grandfather's faith that work "honors the workman."[23]

The subtext for the "Ballad of Isaac and Jacob" would have been clear to contemporary audiences, especially workers. In the spring of 1964, a group of social activists, economists, and scientists had sent President Lyndon Johnson a memorandum warning of a "triple revolution," one part of which had been generated by the amalgamation of "the computer and the automated self-regulating machine" (Ad Hoc Committee 1964, 85-89). The increasing use of automation in steel mills, automobile plants, and in the shipping industry had affected tens of thousands of workers by the early 1960s. While AFL-CIO leaders feared that automation would become a societal curse, they remained unwilling to "directly challenge management's prerogative to determine the means and ends of production, or to question the form or direction of technological change itself" (Noble 1984, 250-251).

When Lampell's characters invoke the Jewish tradition that human labor afforded dignity to an individual, they also echo a militant trade union and socialist tradition that "labor itself is a kind of redemption by which spiritual and social needs are fulfilled" and that workers must control the production process (Aronowitz 1985, 21). Lampell raised profound questions about workers' control and dignity, as well as America's transformation from a production to consumption ethos. But he offered no solutions. Indeed David remained oblivious to the way in which computerization of the workplace not only transferred

23 "The Ballad of Isaac and Jacob," 14-16, Box 2, File 33, Novik Papers.

routine tasks to machines and eliminated the need for workers, but how it simultaneously restricted the "sphere of autonomy" for those remaining workers, and concentrated workplace control in the hands of a "narrow layer of computer scientists and engineers responsible for devising the systems" (22). "The Ballad of Isaac and Jacob" embraced the collective memory of immigrant workers; it utilized these memories to remind viewers of how workers once helped each other in times of need and how the work itself gave people a sense of value and dignity. The play offered few options for dealing with automation and the loss of workers' control.

While the Meany Foundation productions for *The Eternal Light* were thought provoking, they were short-lived, ending by the early 1970s. The overall AFL-CIO commitment to television production remained tenuous at best. Expenditures for television amounted to only a fraction of organized labor's total spending on general public relations efforts, including radio operations—and even this spending fell rapidly during the 1960s as organized labor's negative publicity dissipated for a time. Between the fiscal years of 1961-1962 and 1968-1969, total annual AFL-CIO spending on television fell from $70,327 to $8,170 (AFL-CIO 1963, 20; AFL-CIO 1969, 21). Meany Foundation expenditures were separate from the general union funds, but these too diminished over the course of the decade, dependent, as they were, on donations from the AFL-CIO's constituent unions.

CONCLUSION

Throughout the 1950s and 1960s organized labor conceived of television broadcasting as a way to shape public opinion and inform union members of its stand on political and economic issues. Most officials did not perceive of television programs as opportunities to shape class-consciousness, to create working-class culture, or to agitate for societal reform. While embracing the history of the American labor movement and its militant and often aggressive efforts to challenge the prevailing economic, social, and political status quo in the nation at any one time, the AFL-CIO in the Cold War era engaged in a delicate balancing act. It still saw the need for change—certainly with regard to the regressive Taft-Hartley and Landrum-Griffin acts—but it also wished to portray itself as an integral part of the nation's economic growth and international mission.

Labor's business unionist outlook meant that, like corporate America, unions used television to spread propaganda about their political and economic ideology and agenda. Little innovative thought went to larger cultural or social issues. Few union officials or their media advisers saw a need to build a progressive community or to construct an alternative or oppositional culture or even to raise questions about automation, inequality, nuclear weapons, corporate power, or race relations. Organized labor took existing corporate capitalist culture and American societal myths and reformulated them to incorporate labor. But using television in this way fundamentally limited the union movement's goals and results.

On rare occasions union programs did open spaces for alternative and oppositional readings. The plays of Lampell and Wishengrad had a harder edge and more intellectual content than most AFL-CIO offerings on television—in large part because the two writers were products of an earlier more radical age of social unionism. Even when their plays served to reinforce the business unionist and Cold War liberal ideology of the AFL-CIO hierarchy, they often raised troubling questions in the minds of their audience. Unfortunately the plays on *The Eternal Light* had limited audiences because they aired during the ratings wasteland of Sunday mornings or early afternoons and were restricted to one production per year. Despite the small hopeful experiments found on *The Eternal Light*, the AFL-CIO's excursions into television programming during the 1950s and 1960s achieved little more than a reaffirmation of business unionist and Cold War liberal dogma.

ACKNOWLEDGEMENTS

The author thanks Beth McKillen, Janice Peck and Inger Stole for their constructive critiques of earlier versions of this article.

ARCHIVAL SOURCES

George Meany Papers. Silver Spring, MD: George Meany Memorial Archives.

Joseph D. Keenan Papers. Washington, DC: Archives and Manuscript Division, Catholic University of America.

Minutes of American Federation of Labor Executive Council. Silver Spring, MD: George Meany Memorial Archives.

Minutes of the Executive Board of the Congress of Industrial Organizations, 1935-1955. Microfilm edition.

Morris S. Novik Papers. Silver Spring, MD: George Meany Memorial Archives.

William F. Schnitzler Papers. Silver Spring, MD: George Meany Memorial Archives.

REFERENCES

Ad Hoc Committee. 1964. "The Triple Revolution," *International Socialist Review* 24: 85-89.

AFL-CIO. 1969. *Proceedings of the Eighth Constitutional Convention of the AFL-CIO, vol. II, Report of the Executive Council, October 2-7, 1969.* Washington, DC: AFL-CIO.

———. 1963. *Proceedings of the Fifth Constitutional Convention, vol. II, Report of the Executive Council, November 14-20, 1963.* Washington, DC: AFL-CIO.

AFL-CIO News.

The American Federationist.

Aronowitz, Stanley. 1985. "Why Work?" *Social Text* 12: 19-42.

Buhle, Paul. 1999. *Taking Care of Business: Samuel Gompers, George Meany, Lane Kirkland and the Tragedy of American Labor.* New York: Monthly Review Press.

Chicago Tribune.

Davis, Mike. 1999. *Prisoners of the American Dream: Politics and Economy in the History of the U.S. Working Class.* London: Verso.

The Dispatcher.

Douglas, Sara U. 1986. *Labor's New Voice: Unions and the Mass Media.* Norwood, NJ: Ablex Publishing.

Ellenson, David and Lee Bycel. 1997. "A Seminary of Sacred Learning: The JTS Rabbinical Curriculum in Historical Perspective." In *Tradition Renewed: A History of the Jewish Theological Seminary,* vol. II, ed. Jack Wertheimer, 527-591. New York: Jewish Theological Seminary of America.

Federation News.

Fletcher, Bill, Jr. and Fernando Gapasin. 2008. *Solidarity Divided: The Crisis in Organized Labor and A New Path Toward Social Justice.* Berkeley: University of California Press.

Fones-Wolf, Elizabeth. 1994. *Selling Free Enterprise: The Business Assault on Labor and Liberalism, 1945-60.* Urbana: University of Illinois Press.

————. 2006. *Waves of Opposition: Labor and the Struggle for Democratic Radio.* Urbana: University of Illinois Press.

Godfried, Nathan. 2008. "Revising Labor History for the Cold War: The IL-GWU and the Film, *With These Hands.*" *Historical Journal of Film, Radio and Television* 28: 311-333.

————. 2002. "Identity, Power, and Local Television: African Americans, Organized Labor, and UHF-TV in Chicago, 1962-1968." *Historical Journal of Film, Radio and Television* 22: 117-134.

————. 2001. "Struggling Over Politics and Culture: Organized Labor and Radio Station WEVD during the 1930s." *Labor History* 42: 347-369.

————. 1997. *WCFL, Chicago's Voice of Labor, 1926-78.* Urbana: University of Illinois Press.

Gottfried, Erika. 2008. "'TWU on TV!' - The Transport Workers' Union and Television in the Early 1950s and 1960s." *Film History* 20: 508-512.

Goulden, Joseph C. 1972. *Meany.* New York: Atheneum.

Green, James R. 1980. *The World of the Worker: Labor in Twentieth-Century America.* New York: Hill and Wang.

Greenbaum, Michael B. 1997. "The Finkelstein Era." In *Tradition Renewed: A History of the Jewish Theological Seminary,* vol. I, ed. Jack Wertheimer, 163-232. New York: Jewish Theological Seminary of America.

Hollywood Quarterly. 1947-48. 3: 207.

Howard, Jack. 1955. "Labor Day: San Francisco." *The Quarterly of Film, Radio, and Television* 10: 32-43.

Industry on Parade Film Collection. 1950-1960. www.americanhistory.si.edu/archives/d4507.htm, accessed January12, 2011.

Kazin, Michael and Steven J. Ross. 1992. "America's Labor Day: The Dilemma of a Workers' Celebration." *The Journal of American History* 78: 1294-1323.

Lichtenstein, Nelson. 2002. *State of the Union: A Century of American Labor.* Princeton: Princeton UP.

McGilligan, Patrick and Paul Buhle, eds. 1999. *Tender Comrades: A Backstory of the Hollywood Blacklist.* New York: St. Martin's Press.

Moody, Kim. 1988. *An Injury to All: The Decline of American Unionism.* London: Verso.

New York Times.

Noble, David F. 1984. *Forces of Production: A Social History of Industrial Automation.* New York: Alfred A. Knopf.

Parker, Everitt C., Elinor Inman, and Ross Snyder. 1948. *Religious Radio: What To Do and How.* New York: Harper & Brothers Publishers.

Phelan, Craig. 1987. "William Green and the Ideal of Christian Cooperation." In *Labor Leaders in America,* ed. Melvyn Dubofsky and Warren Van Tine, 134-159. Urbana: University of Illinois Press.

Pomper, Gerald. 1959-1960. "The Public Relations of Organized Labor." *The Public Opinion Quarterly* 23: 483-494.

Raphael, Tim. 2009. "The Body Electric: GE, TV, and the Reagan Brand." *TDR: The Drama Review* 53: 113-138.

Schrecker, Ellen. 2004. "Labor and the Cold War: The Legacy of McCarthyism." In *American Labor and the Cold War: Grassroots Politics and Postwar Political Culture,* ed. Robert W. Cherny, William Issel, and Kieran Walsh Taylor, 7-24. New Brunswick: Rutgers UP.

Scipes, Kim. 2010. *AFL-CIO's Secret War Against Developing Country Workers: Solidarity or Sabotage?* Lanham, MD: Lexington Books.

Variety. November 28, 1962: 29.

Watson, Mary Ann. 2008, 2nd edition. *Defining Visions: Television and the American Experience in the 20th Century.* Malden, MA: Blackwell Publishing.

Zieger, Robert H. 1987. "George Meany: Labor's Organization Man." In *Labor Leaders in America,* ed. Melvyn Dubofsky and Warren Van Tine, 324-349. Urbana: University of Illinois Press.

CHAPTER 9

THE POSTWAR "TV PROBLEM" AND THE
FORMATION OF U.S. PUBLIC TELEVISION

Laurie Ouellette

N 1967, FOLLOWING THE PASSAGE OF THE U.S. PUBLIC BROAD-
CASTING ACT, *Life* magazine celebrated the "oasis" of the wasteland, sight unseen ("Public TV," 14). The article imagined the
newly authorized Public Broadcasting Service, which became
operational in 1969, as a beacon of excellence in a sea of me-
diocrity. Public television would bring quality to the airwaves, elevate
habits and tastes, and serve discriminating viewers fed up with standardized and unintelligent programming. In making these assumptions, *Life* drew from a high level discussion of the nation's "TV
Problem" that gained momentum during the postwar period. Social
scientists, philanthropists, public policymakers, journalists, and critics expressed anxieties about television's output and potential danger
to liberal ideals of culture and democracy. This chapter revisits this
prominent "discursive formation"[1] and its role in the conceptualization
of noncommercial public broadcasting in the United States. Drawing

---

1 My study follows Michel Foucault's genealogical approach to historiog-
raphy (1972), adopting his understanding of sense-making discourses as
"productive" forces that shape the institutions (what Foucault called technologies) of modern societies. I also draw from Tony Bennett's approach to
culture as a "reformer's science," a phrase he uses in reference to the English
reformer Matthew Arnold (1992, 1995, 1998). Bennett develops the cultural dimensions of Foucault's analysis of governmental power, showing
how the emergence of late-19th century public museums combined progressive gains with efforts to shape and guide the populace and differen-
tiate the educated classes. Bennett connects the "political rationalities" or
reform logics that gave birth to new "cultural technologies" to ongoing policy debates, providing a helpful conceptual framework for understanding
public television's formation in the 1960s and early 1970s.

from archival research and social and cultural theory, I show how anxieties steeped in the widening contradictions of consumer capitalism informed critical diagnoses of the TV Problem, setting the stage for public television's belated emergence—and narrowly corrective role. In the process, I also unravel the origins of public television's ambivalent relationship with the "people" it claims to represent. Because a negative construction of the unsophisticated, hedonistic mass audience was commonly blamed for the contested condition of commercial television, public television was to avoid the "perils" of popularity. It was *for* the people, not *by* the people, because its *raison d'être* hinged on their presumed failures as cultural subjects.[2]

DIAGNOSING THE TV PROBLEM

The postwar TV Problem can arguably be traced to "irresolvable" tensions at the heart of U.S. broadcasting (Hilmes 1999). On one hand, the private corporations that controlled radio were held accountable to an ethic of public service interpreted as the transmission of legitimated knowledge and culture. On the other hand, broadcasting was a business that profited from the sale of advertising, and therefore the ritualized listening of as many potential consumers as possible. When amusement became the principal conveyor for the mass movement of merchandise, radio became the target of critical contempt as well as a reform movement orchestrated mainly (but not only) by foundations, university educators and prominent citizen groups. The bid to recast radio as a noncommercial venture (as it had been during its experimental years) was blunted by corporate lobbying campaigns that pledged public service compliance while demonizing "haughty" reformers and the highbrow alternatives they championed (McChesney 1994). Public broadcasting was authorized three decades after the

---

2   This chapter draws from the Introduction and Chapter 1 of my book *Viewers Like You: How Public TV Failed the People*. Parallel reform logics of the late-1960s, including demands for Black inclusion, active citizenship, and educational leveling among children, are more fully addressed in the larger study. I would like to thank Justin Lewis, Toby Miller, Anna McCarthy, and Tony Bennett for encouraging and supporting this work. For an analysis of contemporary U.S. public television in the wake of privatization, fragmentation, new technologies, and neoliberal reforms, see my essay "Reinventing PBS: Public Television in the Post-Network, Post-Welfare Era."

1934 Communications Act—contrary to the national public broad-casting systems being created in Europe—established private own-ership and commercial sponsorship as the American system of "free" broadcasting. Why? When the new medium of television emerged at the center of postwar culture and society, the residual tension between high expectations and the commercial drive to manufacture popular-ity resurfaced with a vengeance.

Some doomsayers deemed television an inherent threat to civiliza-tion. Other critics lamented the rapid demise of its "golden age," when they could find operas and symphony performances (NBC had its own orchestra), live theatre, educational and arts programming, and expert discussions of public affairs. The networks had briefly sched-uled "prestige" programs alongside variety shows and situation com-edies adapted from radio; the shows were often underwritten by spon-sors hoping to reach influential opinion leaders or sustained by the networks as a public service gesture. Such fare was phased out as TV set ownership mushroomed and executives realized that they could maximize profit by selling multiple advertising spots within standard-ized entertainment filmed in Hollywood. By the late-1950s, the in-dustry's operational goal was to attract the largest audience possible and facilitate its smooth flow from one program to the next.

At a time when instruments for differentiating viewers on the basis of demographics and lifestyle had not been invented and hundreds of cable channels were the stuff of science fiction, competition for gross numbers among ABC, CBS, and NBC shaped the television beamed into everyone's homes. Concerns about the cultural consequences trig-gered an intensified discussion of the TV Problem that had much in common with the postwar debate over mass culture. According to Jackson Lears, the economic boom of the 1950s led intellectuals (crit-ics, academics, policy advisors, professional thinkers) across partisan lines to pressing "new problems" that often coalesced around the con-tested quality and homogenizing effects of mass culture (Lears 1998, 44). The growth of public universities and expansion of a white-collar professional middle class comprised of college-educated people who "worked with knowledge instead of making things," made it possible to conceive the power dynamics of the postwar era as "treatable" cultural symptoms, Lears contends. Intellectuals took the level of mass cul-ture as "proof" that upwardly mobile Americans needed (and perhaps wanted) the "guidance of a cultural elite" (ibid. 46-48).

Diagnoses of the TV Problem shared an aversion to mass culture rooted in the unacknowledged contradictions of postwar capitalism. Broadcasters' quest to maximize profits was sanctioned by free enterprise—yet spawned cultural products that mocked the nation's claim to pluralism and ignored the taste and authority of the white, educated, male bourgeoisie. Commercial television was perfectly in sync with the "fun morality" noted by sociologists of the day, and thus helped circulate the values (enjoy! indulge! spend!) of the consumer economy.[3] Yet, its perceived association with hedonism, passivity, and mental escape also clashed with ideals of enlightened citizenship, the competitive image of a world superpower, and the ethic of hard work and self-improvement long associated with the American Dream.

Instead of unpacking these contradictions, researchers, commentators and policymakers routinely displaced the cause of the TV Problem onto an unsophisticated, presumably working class and feminized mass audience. In the eyes of some supercilious observers, the medium addressed an uncultivated crowd at the expense of an intelligent and tasteful minority. The *Report of the President's Commission on National Goals*, prepared for the outgoing Eisenhower administration, contained a scathing assessment of "The Quality of American Culture" by August Heckscher, the president of the 20th Century Fund, a New York philanthropy. Zeroing in on the TV Problem, Heckscher accused broadcasters of undermining the public interest by pandering to an "audience eager for fourth-rate material." He also worried that increasingly affluent Americans had become a "great mass prepared to listen long hours to the worst of TV or radio" (Heckscher 1960, 128). Paradoxically, if the hoi polloi were setting the sights for broadcasting, the mass market was simultaneously "virtually abolishing" class distinctions (ibid. 131), rendering the United States too close to Communism for Hecksher. The TV Problem gained urgency around the

3   Barbara Ehrenreich (1983) argues that the "new consumer ethic" promoted by advertisers and the "fun morality" scrutinized by sociologists were one and the same. Likewise, the hedonism ascribed to the childlike masses by the discourse of the vast wasteland was not a character flaw, but a complex economic and cultural phenomenon. The postwar consumer boom was fueled in part by business campaigns designed to direct the "average American" accustomed to traditional values like thrift and hard work toward a new "life of pleasurable consumption." Seeking to "demonstrate that the hedonistic approach" to life was moral, corporations and advertisers contributed to the anxieties routinely blamed on television (44-45).

time social scientists and cultural critics embraced pluralism as the "distinguishing difference between free societies and totalitarian ones" (Curtin 1995, 22). Mass culture, especially television, wasn't easy to reconcile with this assumption. Heckscher's assessment exemplified the conflation of anti-Communism and elite anxieties about diminished class distinctions, his dismay to see everyone offered the same culture on their ubiquitous TV sets rivaled by his perception that "women at different levels of income dress indistinguishably" while the "most luxurious housing units boast the same dish washing machine available in almost any worker's home" (Heckscher 1960, 131).

For other commentators, the issue was that a potentially edifying medium had become another crude amusement in the service of hawking soda pop and shaving cream. As one commentator put it, "We have triumphantly invented, perfected, and distributed to the humblest cottage throughout the land one of the greatest technical marvels in history, television, and have used it for what? To bring Coney Island into every home" (Steiner 1963, 235). The year after *National Goals* appeared in paperback, John F. Kennedy was in the White House, and his appointee to head the Federal Communication Commission brought a combination of Camelot cultural tastes and a reformist sensibility to the regulator's chair. In a 1961 speech to the Association of Broadcasters, Newton Minow called television a "vast wasteland," coining an influential and enduring metaphor in the ongoing discussion of the TV Problem. Whereas conservatives like Heckscher perceived mass culture as a threat to class hierarchies, Minow's critique was articulated to the Kennedy Administration's promotion of the arts, education and "public interest" goals for *all Americans*. "It is not enough to cater to the nation's whims—you must also serve the nation's needs," he told executives, attempting to revive voluntary compliance. And yet, concepts such as cultural value and the public interest are not obvious—they are socially constituted within historical conditions and power dynamics. Despite his progressive intentions, Minow's approach to the TV Problem managed the cultural contradictions of postwar capitalism without addressing their messy origins. As with other postwar critics, his common sense definition of "good" television was a product of his own social privilege, reflecting his white, upper middle class family origins and background as a Northwestern graduate and lawyer.

Minow did not question the issue of private ownership, treating television's "screaming, cajoling and offending" ads less as structural determinants than as cultural offenses. His critique of "assembly line" entertainment geared to mass audiences stemmed from postwar television's growing redundancy and lack of innovation—but it also evoked sociologist Pierre Bourdieu's (1984) assertion that the ranking of culture is related to the ranking of people in capitalist democracies. Bourdieu suggests that cultural value is not obvious or innate, but the result of class hierarchies. In 1961, "good" culture was defined by and associated with an educated, upper middle class population bound by family networks, elite universities, and social ties. While this elite grouping did not necessarily own factories or possess huge trust funds, it was socialized from infancy into the knowledges and dispositions that comprise legitimate tastes. As Bourdieu points out, "cultural capital" facilitates class privilege, in part by naturalizing the cultural preferences of those who possess it as "inherently" superior. When Minow told broadcasters they must present a "wider range of choices, more diversity, more alternatives," he evoked pluralist ideals, but took for granted that diversity meant *upgraded* programs imbued with legitimacy, such as live plays and panel discussions. Similarly, television formats closely associated with women and the working classes during the 1960s—situation comedies, soap operas, Westerns, quiz shows— were singled out as evidence of cultural malaise.

In the context of university growth and white-collar class mobility, Minow's speech implied that *all* TV viewers could be conditioned to accept better television, as he defined it. What they needed—and what commercial broadcasters should provide—were more opportunities for maturation and uplift. While humanitarian, this logic also cast the "people" as infantile and flawed in their constitution as a mass audience. Implicitly held responsible for commercial television's flaws, the public was thought to require "discipline, regulation and rule," not a participatory role in the medium's governance (Hartley 1992, 111). It's a textbook example of what John Hartley calls protective "paedocracy," the regulatory flip side of the pleasure regime orienting commercial broadcasting.

Just as for Raymond Williams (1983) there were no masses, only ways of "seeing people as masses," Hartley approaches audiences as institutional "fictions" created and circulated by the television industry and its regulatory bodies for their own purposes. To maximize profits, commercial broadcasters often imagine hypothetical viewers as child-like, says Hartley; they are especially apt to paedocrize in the name of pleasure when courting the broadest audience possible. Broadcasters use appeals that cut across social and educational differences, so that popularity is organized around inclusiveness and pleasure, not pedagogy or exclusion. Instead of judging these cultural products on aesthetic grounds, Hartley stresses the controlling, corporatized dimensions of the paedocratic regime. He rejects "innate" cultural hierarchies without alternately celebrating the commercial marketplace—providing a useful conceptual model from which to recognize the programs condemned by the logic of the vast wasteland as popular in a paedocrized and corporatized form.

Regulatory institutions like the FCC often infantilize television viewers too, by speaking about and for them, says Hartley. So too did Minow's famous speech, casting the mass audience as immature, uncultivated, and unable to distinguish between wants and needs. TV was corrosive of the public interest, for "given a choice between a Western or a symphony, most people will watch the Western." This argument *presumed* the corrosive status of the Western, ascribing the correct taste to those who prefer the symphony. It also ascribed the ability to recognize quality, and solve the TV Problem, to well-placed experts. Why consult the public when, as one critic lamented, it "chooses—again and again and again—the frivolous as against the serious, 'escape' as against reality, the lurid as against the tragic, the trivial as against the serious, fiction as against fact, the diverting as against the significant" (Roe 1962, 84).

The tendency of the mass audience to choose "wants" over "needs" was often presented as a discipline problem that needed to be managed by regulators and broadcasters. Concerns about television's debased cultural quality intersected with anxieties about its promotion of trivial and escapist amusement over respectable activities like work and learning. In a telling analogy, Minow argued that if parents and teachers followed "ratings," children would be "spoiled by ice cream and holidays." Class and gender were implicit to this troubling portrait of the common id. As Curtin notes, the valorization of the "productive labor" involved in watching edifying programs over the "passive consumption" ascribed to mass entertainment correlates to stereotypical assumptions about the lazy, feminized masses (Curtin 1995, 237). Broadcasters were not being asked to discipline professors or CEOs;

nor did *New York Times* critic Jack Gould refer to white male newspaper readers when he opined that the "mass audience can be childlike; it will generally choose candy over spinach" (Steiner 1963, 239). *TV Guide*, on the other hand, dutifully informed its much broader readership that it stood accused of gorging on "popcorn and candy" instead of selecting a "nutritious meal." Extending protective paedocracy to micro processes of self-discipline, the headline read "Not Until You Finish Your Vegetables" (Armbruster 1962, 2).

Minow's critique of the vast wasteland ignored commercial television's failure to serve every minority except one: college-educated people with "respectable" tastes. Those who shared Minow's criticisms tended to be "well-heeled upper-middle class"; although "expert at mobilizing a PTA, they made for a minor constituency, an elite," and conspicuous by their absence were "members of the working class or racial and ethnic minorities who, while arguably victimized by television, evinced little displeasure with the medium" (Baughman 1985, 170). Social scientific studies and public opinion polls frequently reported that the "most literate and alert Americans" were least happy with television, as did newspapers and magazines (Shayon 1967, 60) casting an aura of innate sophistication around television's mostly white, upper-middle class disaffected. While this group's right to function as a cultural elite was sometimes called into question, the structural issue of private ownership and commercial control was consistently displaced onto the stakes of television's alleged acquiescence to "majority rule."

In the CBS documentary "The Ratings Game" (1965), Minow protested the problem of "slide rule," or television's tendency to favor "crowd pleasers" over better programs. Other critics argued that ratings had killed good plays, symphony performances and serious public affairs. Against this discourse, TV executives championed ratings as a measure of cultural democracy in television. Comparing the ratings to the election of political candidates, the vice president of CBS argued that in a cultural democracy as in a political democracy, there's "nothing wrong with finding out what the people want." Television's critics betrayed a "serious distrust of a people in a democracy," echoed another executive. "Why," he demanded to know, should a "committee at the top" dictate what is shown on TV? Equating ratings with people's democratic participation, the industry's spokesmen obscured their own role as shapers of a profitable television culture.

Since the 1950s commercial broadcasters had been casting their critics as haughty elites who snobbishly looked down on "plain folks"—
a discursive strategy drawn from the corporate lobbying campaigns
against the broadcast reform movement of the 1930s (Boddy 1990).
As the TV Problem intensified, so did the myth of cultural democracy and the demonization of "anti-democratic" elites. The television
industry reconstructed the fictionalized mass audience as empowered
decision-makers, defying and replacing the patronizing and childlike
portrait constructed by reformers with the image of an active body
politic. While it sounded respectful, this corporate rationalization
provided no "real voice for audiences to speak within the institution,"
to use Hartley's argument (Hartley 1992, 118). By aligning itself with
a "voting" majority of its own construction, the industry justified its
cultural power in populist-democratic terms.

Arguments put forward by the industry spilled over into cultural
forums as well. The magazine *American Mercury* agreed "in this one
respect the leaders of the nation do exactly what the people want them
to do." *TV Guide* concluded if television was a "belt-line assemblage
of repetitive inanity," it was because viewers liked it that way (Rob-
binson 1960, 14).[4] Having accepted industry fiction, others pondered
the consequences. Other commentators agreed with Edward Murrow,
host of the acclaimed but cancelled news program *See it Now*, when
he claimed that catering to a majority desire for trivial amusements
jeopardized "the virtue of the republic if not the security of Western
democracy" (Baughman 1985, 30).

As James Baughman (1985) has shown, anxieties about the decline
of television journalism were harder to dismiss as cultural elitism, as
they signaled a "crack" in the liberal corporate faith that broadcasters
could be free marketeers *and* serve the public interest. The industry's
myth of cultural democracy had further implicated the masses in what
Toby Miller (1990) calls the conflicting demands of the consumer
economy (selfishness, pleasure, indulgence) and the political order
(ethics, discipline, civic duty). This logic, in turn, further alienated the
"people" from public interest goals inevitably crafted from above. As
one reformer put it, "we are in trouble as we unconsciously confuse the
interests (tastes) of the public with the public interest, which is what
broadcasting, under law, is charged to serve. For the public interest

---

4   For parallel arguments in trade publications see Ratner (1969, 54-55)
    and "Public Taste Molds TV," 1961, p. 26).

has little to do with our appetites and desires, however widely shared. It has everything to do with our needs, as human beings and citizens of this democracy. In both realms our whims and appetites must be subordinate to our needs and duties" (Seipmann 1964, 4).

THE BIRTH OF PUBLIC TELEVISION

The TV Problem spawned dual reform logics, both of which informed public television. The first plan for change advocated the development of national public service television, presuming it would bypass the indiscriminate mass audience altogether and operate at a higher level. At an intellectual summit on the problem of American mass culture attended by philosopher Hannah Arendt, social scientist Paul Lazarsfeld, and CBS president Frank Stanton, among other prominent people, author and Kennedy advisor Arthur Schlesinger urged the government to "rescue" a portion of television (Schlesinger 1961, 149). Conceding that since "horse opera sells more autos than Ed Murrow, then the advertiser has to go for horse opera," John Fischer, the editor of *Harper's* magazine, promoted the creation of a nonprofit National Broadcasting Authority to be run by a board of distinguished directors that might include the "president of Harvard, the heads of the Carnegie and Rockefeller foundations, and the director of the Metropolitan Museum." The proposed Authority would plan "public service" programs, defined as in-depth news, serious music, and good theater. Under the arrangement, which drew praise from public officials, civic leaders, and cultural critics, people "not interested" in the superior offerings could simply "turn to a western on CBS or a song-and-dance number on ABC" (Fischer 1959, 12-18).

Walter Lippmann's declaration that there was something fundamentally wrong with U.S. television policy is another example of this exclusive reform logic. Writing in his *New York Herald Tribune* column in the wake of the quiz show scandal, the influential scholar and policy advisor called television a "prostitute of merchandising." His main complaint, however, was that a "superb scientific achievement" was being misused at the expense of "effective news reporting, good art and civilized entertainment." While he strongly believed in American free enterprise, Lippmann concluded that culture was an exception and proposed that "the people at Harvard and Yale and Princeton and Columbia and Dartmouth" find a way to run a public service network that would show "not what was popular but what was good."

Presuming that good television would never attract a substantial viewership, he unapologetically reasoned that it would make "up in influence what it lacked in numbers" (Lippmann 1959, 26).

Lippmann's solution was so arrogant it had little chance of attracting public funding and broad support. However, it coexisted with a pedagogic logic that promised to extend the benefits of public broadcasting, effectively serving the people by guiding and improving them. Like the proverbial chicken and egg, the question was what comes first—an audience predisposed to appreciate culture, or culture that viewers would, through exposure, learn how to appreciate? Opinions among decision makers split down the line. Minow believed that the people could be steadily uplifted by the upgrades he championed, while the president of the American Council for Better Broadcasts thought that "the surest way to get programming of higher quality and taste is to have audiences with better taste" (Hausman 1961). According to Lazarsfeld, researchers at Columbia University's Bureau of Applied Social Research felt that the level of popular taste might be raised with increased exposure to the best, despite the failure of NBC's "Operation Frontal Lobe," a short-lived plan to insert bits of "enlightenment" into popular entertainment so as to raise capacities for excellence. While often humanitarian, this logic presumed that cultural authorities should (and indeed could) manage public taste by merging behaviorist strategy and cultural expertise (Lazarsfeld 1963, 414).

The pedagogic reform logic adopted a more egalitarian tone when Great Society rhetoric emerged in the 1960s. The idea of diffusing the best culture was bound to the promise of equal opportunity and improved quality of life for *all* Americans. "Many people are not rejecting the best—they simply had never had the opportunity to chose it," said one supporter (Dale 1967, 3). The possibility tempered industry accusations of cultural elitism and attracted people like Senator (and later President) Lyndon Johnson to the cause. In 1964, FCC Chairman William Henry, along with Commissioner of Education Francis Keppel, declared in a joint speech that it was time to overcome "our electronic Appalachia." We "must find ways to make the medium serve one of its highest and most natural uses—as a means of eliminating cultural poverty" by making culture and enlightenment "available to everyone" not just an elite, they argued ("ETV's Job" 1964, 2). While these solutions to the TV Problem differed on the issue of exclusivity, both called for public television to operate against the destructive grain of mass appeal. For practical reasons, both visions also initially hinged on the expansion of educational television, a spattering of low-budget noncommercial stations licensed to communities, universities, and school systems across the states.

As the TV Problem accelerated, educational television's overtly instructional image was phased out. For one thing, social scientific discourse reported that its viewership, while "well-placed," was tiny and sporadic. For another, Minow's ultimate failure to upgrade the vast wasteland put hopes for better television on the existing educational stations. In the mid-1960s, National Educational Television (NET), a hub for educational broadcasters funded by private foundations, repositioned itself as a fourth network known for cultural and informational programs, not pedantic lessons delivered by tweed clad professors scrawling on chalkboards. The order came from the Ford Foundation, whose new president, an Ivy League-educated Boston Brahmin named McGeorge Bundy, envisioned educational television as a superior program service, not an electronic schoolroom. A Cold War liberal intellectual, Bundy was a former Harvard professor of government and dean; he had also planned Vietnam War strategy as Special Assistant of National Security Affairs to Kennedy and Johnson. After graduating Harvard, he assisted his mentor Walter Lippmann with an unfinished attempt to update Lippmann's *The Good Society*, a 1937 blueprint for the state to play an active role in culture, framed within an overall "defense of laissez-faire capitalism" (Bird 1998, 102). For Bundy, noncommercial television, like the "strong government" he also championed (Bundy 1968) would strengthen American capitalism by improving culture and society.

NET attempted to revive the golden age of commercial television by sponsoring live drama, performing arts, concerts, sophisticated treatments of current events, documentaries, and prestigious BBC imports like "The Age of Kings," a series of Shakespeare plays. While pursuing the good over the popular, as Lippmann had stated, it also stressed the benefits for the less fortunate, insisting that "few by few, through accidental or unintentional exposure, they will come to realize that the 'finest' is indeed the best" (Elman 1965, 217). But Ford's checkbook wasn't bottomless, NET programming was limited to ten hours per week, and the distribution of programming by mail was slow and cumbersome. Educational television was still a very a long way from a national public service network.

In the late 1960s, the discourse of the vast wasteland, coupled with the uplifting spirit of the Great Society and the precedent set by the National Endowments for the Arts and Humanities created a moment hospitable to more substantial policy interventions. Once dismissed as unnecessary and even unAmerican, the idea of public broadcasting gained credence and legitimacy, within important boundaries. In 1966, the blueprint for such a service was conceived by a "blue-ribbon" panel of business, educational, and cultural leaders who had been assembled by Carnegie Corporation, the philanthropy established by steel magnate Andrew Carnegie. In 1967, the U.S. Congress adopted most of the Carnegie Commission's recommendations, legislating a national solution to the TV Problem in the form of a nonprofit Corporation for Public Broadcasting (CPB) and, shortly thereafter, a national Public Broadcasting Service (PBS).

The Carnegie Commission and the public-private institution it spawned was not too far removed from the liberal corporate approach to broadcast policy that has always prevailed in the United States. As Tom Streeter argues, the "social vision" that gave shape to radio and later television, was corporate liberalism, defined by its tendency to conceptualize the "public interest" as an expert-planned component of capitalist principles (Streeter 1996, xii, 43). Likewise, the Carnegie Commission envisioned public television as a rationally planned, complimentary supplement to the commercial broadcasting system, not a fundamentally new way to organize television culture. Whereas the establishment of a major public broadcaster (along the lines of the BBC) or the opening of the medium to grassroots interests would have undermined corporate liberalism, a modest public-private intervention to correct cultural gaps in the free enterprise system made perfect sense to the commissioners.

The solution to the TV Problem was also in sync with the liberal corporate approach to social welfare policy critiqued by late 1960s activists. Students for a Democratic Society member Richard Flacks, for example, protested the extent to which Great Society reforms were designed at the national level by elites and experts, not publicly elected officials or grassroots constituencies (Flacks 1966). The Carnegie Commission, which operated outside public jurisdiction in consultation with business leaders, academics and intellectuals, public officials, and token representatives from labor unions and racial minority groups, exemplifies the liberal corporate governmentality Flacks describes.

The panel was a culmination of the "old boys" network that moved among private foundations, the Ivy League, the corporate sector, and the federal government during the 1960s. Several people—including Scott Fletcher, who had retired from the Ford Foundation and Ralph Lowell, a wealthy banker and chairman of Boston's educational station WGBH—suggested the presidential commission to Lyndon Johnson. Johnson agreed that public broadcasting complemented his national Great Society programs, but had no qualms outsourcing its conception to the private sector. John Gardner, Johnson's appointee to head the Department of Health, Education, and Welfare and former president of the Carnegie Corporation, arranged for the Corporation to undertake the study (Robertson 1993, 231-234; Weischadle 1989). The Commission's members, who had been hand picked by Carnegie executives, were all business and academic "big wigs," reported the trade magazine *Broadcasting* ("Architects" 1967, 24). Novelist Ralph Ellison and Leonard Woodcock of the United Automobile Workers of America were appointed, providing the only representation of blacks and laborers. Retired MIT president James Killian served as chairman, embodying the Carnegie Corporation's emphasis on educational credentials and technocratic expertise as the solution to social problems. Described as having vast "scientific knowledge in the communication field," Killian had been Eisenhower's science advisor before landing at MIT. Characterized as a renaissance man by the press, he owned a "prized" art collection, served on the corporate boards of AT&T and General Motors, and published scholarly articles advocating "science as a cultural force" (Killian 1964). In a speech prior to his Commission appointment, Killian announced a strong commitment to the arts and humanities, promoting them as essential to the "strength and welfare" of the United States ("Educational Ecumenist" 1967, n.p.).

The Carnegie Commission solicited written and oral testimony from four sources: cultural experts (professors, respected cultural figures, staffers at prestigious magazines like *Atlantic Monthly* and the *New Yorker*); government appointees; educational television personnel; and commercial broadcasters. The discursive formation surrounding the TV Problem figures heavily in the statements of these almost exclusively university credentialed male advisors (race is never mentioned, suggesting the normalization of whiteness). In a letter reminiscent of his call for a noncommercial National Broadcast Authority, the editor of *Harper's* complained about insufficient "programming for the minority," by which he meant well-educated cultural connoisseurs (Fischer 1966). Similarly, a professor of broadcasting testified that "quality" had disappeared the day commercial television decided it must draw a "crowd" ("Programming Panel" 1966). Many advisors cautioned against "entertainment for a mass audience," believing it frivolous and, in the words of Douglass Cater, special assistant to the President, antithetical to the purpose of a "major social institution of defined character" ("Proceedings" 1966). Network executives, happy to monopolize popular culture while surrendering unprofitable high cultural expectations, couldn't have agreed more. Philanthropist-turned-policymaker Gardner and CBS board president William Harley were in sync, anticipating a serious but modest complement to commercial television analogous to a university press. There were objections: union leader Leonard Woodcock suggested that many people might welcome noncommercial entertainment as did Franklin Patterson, president of Hampshire College, who called for programs that were joyous and fun ("Proceedings and Statement" 1966). But these suggestions were difficult to reconcile with public television's cultural positioning as the wasteland "oasis."

Public television was also called upon to restore pluralism, a goal that was presumed incompatible with "mass appeal." With expert planning, it could provide more cultural choices to differentiated "subgroups," claimed supporters—some of whom envisioned public television as a stepping stone to the smorgasbord of options awaiting "pay TV" subscribers. The social movements of late 1960s and the struggles over cultural representation they spawned had very little impact on these discussions. Prior to 1968, social class was the principal, yet unacknowledged "difference" which public television was poised to affirm. The Carnegie Commission's report made no direct mention of the word class, yet the fragmented taste cultures it conjured up under the banner of excellence did not extend beyond the well-placed university crowd. This limitation was made explicit by an unpublished "draft" profiling the potential audiences for public television that was not included in the Commission's published findings (White 1966).

Demonstrating Hartley's point that audiences are institutional creations, the document characterizes viewing groups defined according to their likely tastes and needs. Despite their specialized interests, the core beneficiaries are said to collectively comprise the "elite ten percent" of the population, on the basis of education, taste, and influence as much as wealth and income. The first of these segments was called the "intellectual elite," a "small and compact" subgroup comprised of highly educated people who were more affluent than the average and, more importantly, "engaged in occupations that occupy the mind." Passionate about reading and discussing, this specialized audience would be served by news analysis, documentaries, discussion shows, and serious treatments of intellectual topics. Next was the "cultural elite," or people interested in good "drama, fine and applied arts, music, ballet, dance." While not quite as "narrow as the intellectuals," this group was similarly educated and concentrated among the "higher economic brackets." Programs that "mirrored the theater or the concert hall" were its priority. The "political audience," an "extremely influential" subgroup concerned with the "soundness and welfare" of the community, was also comparatively educated and affluent and would be served with serious treatment of news and discussion of civic issues. Together, these specialized (but overlapping) audiences comprised what the report's author, Carnegie Commission staffer Stephen White, called the "elite ten percent."

The groups described by the unpublished Carnegie Commission document added up to an "elite" quite a bit larger than the tiny ruling class envisioned by Karl Marx. They were a representation of the white collar middle class—the "educated and affluent persons who like to think of themselves as intellectual and cultivated"—obsessively reported by the news media during the 1960s. Educational credentials were said to be integral to what Vance Packard called the diploma elite. According to _U.S. News and World Report_, between 1956 and 1967, the number of bachelor's degrees awarded more than doubled, master's degrees rose by more than 250 percent and Ph.D.s more than tripled ("Heyday" 1969). That public television would serve the cultural and informational needs of this population was taken as a given; the question under debate was: would it cater to the cream of the crop, or to the still upwardly-mobile? The report was ambivalent about potential viewers who felt a "need for self-improvement," envisioned as the newly-minted, state university-educated middle class and its aspirants (Cunningham, 1966). Sandwiched between the "elite ten percent" and the masses served by commercial TV, this grouping of self-improvers was presumed to be looking for "expert guidance," whether in culture, bridge instruction, French cooking lessons, or "College of the Air." While receptive to cultural uplift, self-improvers were also seen as a threat: if public television catered too much to people "bent on self-improvement," said the report, it would probably repel the intellectual, cultural, and political elite.

This assumption did not go unquestioned by advisors and consultants. One critic summed up the prevailing concern when he warned that the "average Congressman" would not support public television unless it promised all Americans the chance "to improve and upgrade their minds." The suggestion that a supposedly non-existent ruling class, however diffuse and expanded, was poised to benefit the most from public television would have doomed tax funding. The Carnegie Commission's published report, *Public Television: A Program for Action* (1967) treated the "elite ten percent" less as beneficiaries than as resources, positioning public television as a "continuing learning experience" in sync with the long-standing American quest for "self-improvement." Public television would harness broadcasting for "great purposes," bringing expert "analysis of art and philosophy, music and literature, science and technology" to the people. Catering to those who yearn for "something they do not find in their everyday lives" and which they "cannot afford unless it comes to them free," it would be an agent of classlessness, not privilege (Carnegie Commission 1967, 7).

Reflecting a broader vision, *A Program for Action* noted the nation's geographical, cultural, and ethnic variety when it described public television's orchestration of "excellence in the service of diversity." The report promised "choice" to all television viewers, defined as the chance to select "from an ensemble of transmitted alternatives" one that is "most appropriate" to individual "needs and interests." (Carnegie Commission 1967, 13-15, 204). The ability to choose was restricted, however, to the consumption of preselected options; little was said about public involvement in the cultural "selection" process. While it struggled to present an encompassing vision of specialized audiences, the report was unable to transcend a narrow definition of respectable leisure and culture steeped in class and racial privilege. The suggested programs (live plays, science specials, serious public affairs) echoed the earlier prestige formats, situating the orchestration of pluralism within education and class privilege.

Diversity and popularity were incompatible within this discourse, for public television's taken-for-granted purpose was to rise *above* commercial television's cultural level. This too was made clear by the document on potential audiences. While no one had ever offered a mass audience "courteous treatment," it was possible to "conceive of a noncommercial station which would offer exactly the same schedule as its commercial competitor but which would do it better in some manner." Such a service, speculated the draft document, might present popular variety shows, sitcoms, and light entertainment without advertisements. However, this idea was an oxymoron, incompatible with prevailing expectations for the "oasis" and was dropped. *A Program for Action* called on public television to provide "all that is of human interest and importance," except the "desire to relax and be entertained," a role that commercial television was thought to be already filling. CBS president Frank Stanton so approved of this division of responsibilities, he pledged one million dollars to the proposed Corporation for Public Broadcasting (Stanton 1967).

In January 1967, *Public Television: A Program For Action* was published in paperback and hardcover, catapulting the push for public broadcasting into the media spotlight. Many reporters and commentators cheered the report as the long-awaited answer to the TV Problem, drawing from assumptions about the vast wasteland to reiterate the lowness of the mass audience. Typifying this response, the *San Francisco Examiner* approved the Carnegie Commission's proposal on the grounds that "all private television networks have expended huge sums and energies in trying to elevate programming but usually, when they read the ratings, their ambitious efforts have been shunned and Joe Public is still back there gawking at *Bonanza* or *Gomer Pyle* and *Red Skelton*." (Newton 1967, n.p.).

While the report drew heady praise, it also triggered vociferous opposition to tax-supported "caviar TV." The two percent excise tax on TV sets proposed by the Carnegie Commission was especially controversial. The Johnson White House had warned against the idea, predicting the "cost of supporting public broadcasting through an excise tax would be inequitably borne, primarily by the poor, who were probably the least interested in the passage of such a bill." (Burke 1979, 150). Consultants concurred that the people would likely "revolt" at the prospect of paying such a tax. The Commission wanted a permanent revenue stream, but its vision was vulnerable to complaints that "self-selected guardians" were trying to create the television *they* wanted at the people's expense. It was "an ingenious system of taxing the poor to furnish culture to the rich" declared an editorial *Washington Post* ("Educational Television" 1967, E6). Why, the *Seattle Daily Times* wanted to know, should Joe Q. Public be a "captive subsidizer of the noncommercial system?" ("Subsidized TV" 1967, n.p.)

Republican FCC commissioner Lee Loevinger's opposition to the proposed "culture tax" reverberated throughout media coverage of the Carnegie Commission's report. Loevinger, who was also an opponent of broadcast regulation, turned the logic of the oasis on its head, defending television as "the literature of the illiterate; the culture of the low-brow; the wealth of the poor; the privilege of the underprivileged; the exclusive club of the excluded masses" (Lagemann 1989, 222). "The common man has every right to be common … we shouldn't criticize the golden goose for not laying caviar," he told the *Milwaukee Sentinel*. "Let those who want it, or want to force it on others, pay for it themselves," he opined ("Distasteful Caviar" 1967, n.p.). Also equating commercial television with cultural democracy, Carnegie Commissioner Joseph McDonnell, president of Reynolds Metals, went on the record with a dissenting opinion, telling a Dallas newspaper it was unfair to tax the "mass of the public, whose program preferences determine what television we have," to provide another service we believe they should have as well (Shain 1967, n.p.) Even Jack Gould of the *New York Times*, a crusader for public television, wondered whether the excise tax implied a "reward" to the mass public antithetical to the service's mission (Burke 1979, 129). The excise was nixed for a temporary fiscal appropriation, and to this day Congress decides how much to give public television every few years.

Despite some opposition to the "New Deal" in television, most commentators cheered the Carnegie Commission's push for "excellence, not just acceptability" (Laruent 1967, n.p.). Johnson pitched public broadcasting in his State of the Union address, staffers at the White House and the Department of Health, Education, and Welfare prepared the legislation, Congress deliberated and within ten months the Public Broadcasting Act was signed into law (Lagemann 1989, 225). The debate in the House, overseen by Torbert MacDonald, a Democrat from Massachusetts, was conducted within the discursive parameters established by *A Program for Action* (House Committee on Interstate and Foreign Commerce 1967a). The presidents of the commercial networks testified that the "economic realities of commercial broadcasting made it impossible to produce and distribute educational and cultural programs which do not have mass audience appeal" ("Hearings" 1967, 151). Public television would prioritize quality not viewer quantity, solving the TV Problem with good plays, studio documentaries, opera, symphony performances, and an "experimental program now and then," testified one supporter. It would provide a choice, not "between two or possibly three stations programming similar kinds of entertainment," but between "programs of entertainment and programs of cultural worth" (Hyde 1967, 180, 199). Public television would be "first class," but it wouldn't compete for mass audiences or advertising dollars, promised Ford Foundation President McGeorge Bundy. Stitching its mission into the logic framing the postwar TV Problem, he told legislators: "Commercial television is commerce first, and with the marginal exception it exploits only that part of the promise of television which gives the most assurance of the most profit. To the commercial networks, time is money, and they cannot give much of it away. It follows that noncommercial television must do the job that commercial television cannot do" (McBundy 1967, 371-372).

Since quality was thought to be incompatible with "large numbers," public and commercial television were considered the equivalent of apples and oranges. One would entertain the millions; the other would serve a small and selective "fragment" of the audience. "We have to serve the greatest number of people in order to do our job," explained CBS President Frank Stanton. "They will be able to do types of special interest programming that we cannot do" (Stanton 1967, 244-245). While it was promoted as noncompetitive and geared to what Stanton called "occasional" viewers of commercial fare, public television was also paradoxically pitched as an instrument that would educate and uplift the broader populace. Just as early radio broadcasts of the New York Philharmonic and Toscanini-conducted concerts made "great music" familiar to more people, public television would expose all Americans to "the best in our cultural tradition," promised Gardner (Gardner 1967, 20-24).

Since entertainment was already "plentiful" on television, public television would enlighten, said Carnegie Commission President James Killian, who conceded that cultural uplift "made to appear" more fun, while quasi-entertainment for "specialized" groups such as tennis buffs (an upper-middle class sport in the 1960s) might be appropriate (Killian 1967, 378). Fred Friendly, former president of CBS News and television advisor to the Ford Foundation, further defined "appropriate" entertainment against amusement geared to the mass audience, arguing "Public television must not be permitted to become a honky-tonk midway of action games, violent fantasies, and contrived farces with fake laughter and applause, designed to appeal to the lowest common denominator all of the time" (Friendly 1967, 378). The House version of the legislation forbade the Corporation for Public Broadcasting from funding programs designed to "amuse and for no other purpose," a clause that was modified to account for those "which coat the philosophic pill with innocent merriment" (House Committee on Interstate and Foreign Commerce 1967b; Witherspoon and Kovitz 1986). While the prohibition did not appear in the final legislation, its contemplation speaks to the discursive formation in which public television was formed. It was for the people, not by them, because its imagined purpose was to offset the consequences of their alleged cultural sovereignty.

THE OASIS OF THE WASTELAND

During the postwar years, high anxieties about the TV Problem gained currency, setting the stage for the belated creation of public television. Following the national debut of the Public Broadcasting Service (PBS) in 1969, its purpose was restated by a wave of publicity. PBS press kits promising a "Chance for Better Television" (1970) and countless newspapers and magazines drew from prior assumptions about television's cultural decline at the hands of the indiscriminate mass audience, and posited the new public channel as a solution. Across institutional statements and popular media, the basic message was the same: public television's role, in the words of Corporation for Public Broadcasting President John Macy, was to serve the "purposeful" (light and selective) viewer while attempting to uplift and "convert" those who watched commercial television habitually and presumably, indiscriminately (Macy 1974).

Cast as a redemptive and marginalized "oasis," public television soothed anxieties but posed no real threat to commercial broadcasters, from which it inherited a narrow interpretation of public interest responsibilities. Envisioned apart from mass culture but not inimical to "discreet" commercial sponsorship, it was susceptible to upscale niche marketing that cemented its upper middle class associations. Because of its small but disproportionately upscale viewership (particularly for adult programming), public television was (and is) also vulnerable to recurring conservative-populist accusations of "elitism" and attempts to privatize public television that began with the Nixon Administration. Today, public television struggles to survive in an expanded television marketplace that caters to precise consumer demographics and upscale lifestyle clusters. The TV Problem that preoccupied postwar influentials and opinion leaders commands less urgency in the wake of proliferating commercial channels and new media technologies. As we have seen, U.S. public television's role as an expert-planned solution to the class-coded ills of mass culture was not inevitable, but socially-constituted within the sense-making discourses of the 1950s and 1960s. For that reason, its mission could still be reinterpreted *by the people*, including the ethnically, sexually, and gender diverse working classes ignored by the abundance of commercial options now available.

REFERENCES

"Architects of CPTV." 1967. *Broadcasting*, 30 Jan: 24.

Armbruster, Walter. 1962. "Not Until You Finish Your Vegetables." *TV Guide*, 1 Sept: 2-5.

Baughman, James. 1985. *Television's Guardians: The FCC and the Politics of Programming, 1958-1967.* Knoxville: University of Tennessee Press.

Beirne, Joseph. 1967. "Testimony to the House Committee on Interstate and Foreign Commerce, Public Television Act of 1967." *Hearings on H.R. 6736*: 668.

Bennett, Tony. 1992. "Putting Policy Into Cultural Studies." In *Cultural Studies*, ed. Lawrence Grossberg, Cary Nelson and Paula A. Triechler. New York: Routledge, 23-50.

———. 1992. "Useful Culture." *Cultural Studies* 6.3: 395-408.

———. 1998. *Culture: A Reformer's Science Culture.* London: Sage.

———. 1995. *The Birth of the Museum.* London, Routledge.

Bird, Kai. 1998. *Color of Truth: McGeorge Bundy and William Bundy.* New York: Simon & Schuster.

Boddy, Williams. 1990. *Fifties Television: The Industry and its Critics.* Urbana: University of Illinois Press.

Bourdieu, Pierre. 1984. *Distinction: A Social Critique of the Judgment of Taste.* Cambridge: Harvard University Press.

Bundy, McGeorge. 1967. "Testimony to the House Committee on Interstate and Foreign Commerce, Public Television Act of 1967." *Hearings on H.R. 6736*: 371-372.

———. 1968. *The Strength of Government*. Cambridge, MA: Harvard University Press.

Burke, Edward. 1979. *Historical-Analytical Study of the Legislative and Political Origins of the Public Broadcasting Act of 1967*. New York: Arno Press.

Carnegie Commission. 1967. *Public Television: A Program for Action*. New York: Bantam.

CBS Television. 1965. *The Ratings Game* (video recording). Paley Center for Media, New York.

Cunningham, John P. 1966. "Letter to Hymin Goldin, 7 July." Wisconsin State Historical Society. Carnegie Commission papers, box 1, file 2.

Curtin, Michael. 1995. *Redeeming the Wasteland: Television Documentary and Cold War Politics*. New Brunswick, NJ: Rutgers University Press.

Dale, Edgar. 1967. *Can You Give the People What They Want?* New York: Cowles Education Corporation.

"Distasteful Caviar." 1967. *Milwaukee Sentinel*, 27 Jan: n.p. Wisconsin State Historical Society. Carnegie Commission papers, press clippings, box 6 file 2.

"Educational Ecumenist: James Rhyne Killian Jr." 1967. *New York Times*, Jan. 26: n.p. Wisconsin State Historical Society. Carnegie Commission papers, press clippings, box 6, file 2,.

"Educational Television." 1967. *Washington Post*, 5 Feb: E6.

Ehrenreich, Barbara. 1983. *The Hearts of Men: American Dreams and the Flight from Commitment*. Doubleday: Anchor Press.

Elman, Richard. 1965. "Educational TV." *The Nation*, March 1: 217.

"ETV's Job: Close the Culture Gap." 1964. *Broadcasting*, 14 Dec: 42.

Fischer, John. 1959. "TV and its Critics." *Harper's*, July: 12-18.

Fore, William F. 1967. "Testimony to the House Committee on Interstate and Foreign Commerce, Public Television Act of 1967." *Hearings on H.R. 6736*: 362.

Friendly, Fred. 1967. "Testimony to the House Committee on Interstate and Foreign Commerce, Public Television Act of 1967." *Hearings on H.R. 6736*:

Foucault, Michel. 1972. *The Archaeology of Knowledge*. New York: Pantheon.

Gardner, John W. 1967. "Testimony to the House Committee on Interstate and Foreign Commerce, Public Television Act of 1967." *Hearings on H.R. 6736*: 20-24.

Hartley, John. 1992. *Tele-ology*. London: Routledge.

Harley, William G. 1966. "Statement to Carnegie Commission by William G. Harley, 14-16 April." Wisconsin State Historical Society, Carnegie Commission papers, box 1, file 10.

————. 1967. "Testimony to the House Committee on Interstate and Foreign Commerce, Public Television Act of 1967." *Hearings on H.R. 6736*: 446.

Hausman, Louis. 1961. "Television and the Pursuit of Excellence." Speech Delivered Before the American Council for Better Broadcasts. Ohio State University, 26 April.

Heckscher, August. 1960. "The Quality of American Culture." In *President's Commission on National Goals, Goals for Americans*. New York: Prentice Hall, 127-148.

"Heyday for Intellectuals." 1969. *U.S. News & World Report*, 21 July: 74-75.

Hilmes, Michele. 1999. "Desired and Feared: Women's Voices in Radio History." In *Television, History, and American Culture: Feminist Critical Essays*, ed. Mary Beth Haralovich and Lauren Rabinovitz. Durham, NC: Duke University Press, 17-35.

"House Committee on Interstate and Foreign Commerce, 1967." Public Television Act of 1967: Hearings on H.R. 6736.

"House Committee on Interstate and Foreign Commerce, 90th Congress, 1st Session, 1967." *Report No. 572, to accompany H.R. 6736*. 11-21 July.

Hyde, Rosel. 1967. "Testimony to the House Committee on Interstate and Foreign Commerce, Public Television Act of 1967." *Hearings on H.R. 6736*: 180, 197, 199.

Killian, James R. 1964. "Toward a Research-Reliant Society: Some Observations on Government and Science." In *Science as a Cultural Force*, ed. Harry Wolfe. Baltimore: Johns Hopkins University Press, 9-34.

————. 1966. "Letter to John Fischer to James Killian. 22 Nov." Carnegie Commission papers, box 1, file 1.

————. 1967. "Testimony to the House Committee on Interstate and Foreign Commerce, Public Television Act of 1967." *Hearings on H.R. 6736*: 130.

Lagemann, Ellen Condliffe. 1989. *The Politics of Knowledge: The Carnegie Corporation, Philanthropy, and Public Policy.* Middletown, CT: Wesleyan University Press.

Laurent, Lawrence. 1967. "Carnegie Study Proposes New TV Deal." *Washington Post,* 27 Jan: n.p. Wisconsin State Historical Society, Carnegie Commission papers, press clippings, box 6, file 2.

Lazarsfeld, Paul F. 1963. "Some Reflections on Past and Future Research on Broadcasting." Afterword to Steiner, Gary, *The People Look at Television.* New York: Alfred A. Knopf. 409-414.

Lears, Jackson. 1989. "A Matter of Taste: Corporate Hegemony in a Mass-Consumption Society." In *Recasting America: Culture and Politics in the Age of Cold War,* ed. Larry May. Chicago: University of Chicago Press. 38-60.

Lippmann, Walter. 1959. "The TV Problem." *New York Herald Tribune,* 27 Oct: 26.

Macy, John. 1974. *To Irrigate a Wasteland.* Berkeley: University of California Press.

McChesney, Robert. 1994. *Telecommunications, Mass Media & Democracy: The Battle for Control of U.S. Broadcasting, 1928-1935.* New York: Oxford University Press.

Miller, Toby. 1993. *The Well-Tempered Self: Citizenship, Culture and the Postmodern Subject.* Baltimore: Johns Hopkins University Press.

Minow, Newton. 1961. "The Vast Wasteland." Address to the 39th Annual Convention of the National Association of Broadcasters. Washington, DC, 8 May.

Newton, Dwight. 1967. "Seeking Excellence, Not Just Acceptability," *San Francisco Examiner,* 29 Jan: n.p. Wisconsin State Historical Society, Carnegie Commission papers, press clippings, box 6, file 2.

Ouellette, Laurie. 2009. "Reinventing PBS: Public Television in the Post-Network, Post-Welfare Era." In *Beyond Primetime: Television Programming in the Post-Network Era,* ed. Amanda Lotz. New York: Routledge. 180–202.

————. 2002. *Viewers Like You: How Public Television Failed the People.* New York: Columbia University Press.

"Public TV: A Wasteland Oasis." 1967. *Life,* 17 Feb: 4.

Packard, Vance. 1959. *The Status Seekers: An Exploration of Class Behavior in America.* New York: David McKay.

————. 1963. "New Kinds of Television," *The Atlantic:* Oct: 51-53; 69.

"Proceedings, Carnegie Commission on Educational Television." 1966. 17-19 March. Wisconsin State Historical Society, Carnegie Commission papers, box 1, file 9.

"Programming Panel Minutes." 1966. 20-21 June. Wisconsin State Historical Society, Carnegie Commission papers, box 2, file 1.

"Public Taste Molds TV." 1961. *Broadcasting*, 18 Sept: 26.

Public Broadcasting Service. 1970. "A Chance for Better Television," press release. University of Maryland, National Public Broadcasting Archive, reference.

Ratner, Victor. 1969. "The Freedom of Taste." *Television Magazine*, Nov: 54-55.

Robertson, Jim. 1993. *Televisionaries*. Charlotte Harbor, FL: Tabby House Books.

Robinson, Hubbell. 1960. "You, The Public, Are to Blame." *TV Guide*, 26 Nov: 14.

Roe, Yale. 1962. *The Television Dilemma: Search for a Solution*. New York: Hasting House Publishers.

Schlesinger, Aurthur Jr. 1961. "Notes on a Cultural Policy." In *Culture for the Millions?* ed. Norman Jacobs. Princeton, NJ: D. Van Nostrand Company, Inc. 148-154.

Shayon, Robert Lewis. 1967. "When Everybody Loses." *Saturday Review*, 25 Feb: 60.

Siepmann, Charles. 1964. "What Is Wrong with TV—and with Us." *NAEB Journal*, Sept. Oct: 4.

Shain, Percy. 1967. "New Public TV System Proposed." *Dallas Morning News*, 26 Jan: n.p. Wisconsin State Historical Society, Carnegie Commission papers, press clippings, box 6 file 2.

Steiner, Gary. 1963. *The People Look at Television*. New York: Alfred A. Knopf.

Stanton, Frank. 1967a. "Letter to James Killian, 27 January." Wisconsin State Historical Society, Carnegie Commission papers, Box 1 file 4.

———. 1976b. "House Committee on Interstate and Foreign Commerce, Public Television Act of 1967." *Hearings on H.R. 6736*: 244-245.

"Subsidized TV Easy Prey for Politicians." 1967. *Seattle Daily Times*, 27 Jan: n.p. Wisconsin State Historical Society, Carnegie Commission papers, press clippings, box 6 file 2.

Weischadle, David E. 1982. "The Carnegie Corporation and the Shaping of American Educational Policy." In *Philanthropy and Cultural Imperialism*, ed. Robert F. Arnove. Bloomington: Indiana Univ. Press. 363-384.

White, Stephen. 1966. Unpublished draft. n.p. Wisconsin State Historical Society, Carnegie Commission papers, box 2 file 8,.

Williams, Raymond. 1983. *Culture and Society*. New York: Columbia University Press.

Witherspoon, John P. and Roselle Kovitz. 1986. "A Tribal Memory of Public Broadcasting Missions, Mandates, Assumptions, Structures." Unpublished report for the Corporation for Public Broadcasting. National Public Broadcasting Archive, University of Maryland, College Park, MD.

CHAPTER 10

LOCKOUTS, PROTESTS, AND SCABS

A CRITICAL ASSESSMENT OF THE
LOS ANGELES HERALD EXAMINER STRIKE

Bonnie Brennen

T HE *LOS ANGELES HERALD EXAMINER* STRIKE, 1967–
1977, offers important insights into the impact of institutional power on the development of labor and news
work in American journalism. The decade-long strike
had devastating economic consequences for both the
newspaper and the unions. According to Robert J. Danzig, Hearst
Corporation Vice President in the 1980s, although the unions and the
newspaper finally reconciled, the strike "crippled labor relations and
caused an exodus of advertisers and subscribers" (quoted in Mathews
& Farhi 1989, E-3). As a result of the strike, the *Los Angeles Herald
Examiner* eventually ceased publication and the viability of the Los
Angeles Newspaper Guild was severely undermined. Although the
"facts" of the labor conflict are well known, this essay addresses issues
of identity, work, and economics in the power struggle between Los
Angeles Newspaper Guild members and Hearst management. Specifically, this critical cultural study assesses the Guild-based publicity
efforts as well as the local and national press coverage of the strike
in an effort to understand the political and social implications of this
labor struggle. It also attempts to explain publisher George R. Hearst's
potential motives for refusing to negotiate with the unions and pro-
longing a strike that eventually destroyed his newspaper.

Critical communication studies offer historically grounded and politically informed examinations of culturally situated media practices
that may expose power relations in the communication process and
provide alternative readings of the relationship between media and

society (Hardt 2001). Historically based critical cultural analyses go beyond considerations of catastrophe, crisis, domination, and oppression to also consider regenerative processes, oppositional strategies, and challenges to dominant ideological positions. As Raymond Williams (1989, 322) explains, "It's the infinite resilience, even deviousness, with which people have managed to persist in profoundly unfavorable conditions, and the striking diversity of the beliefs in which they've expressed their autonomy." Understanding the political ramifications of history, critical cultural assessments of labor relations consider the "often troubled" (Garnham 2000, 33) relationships between the cultural and economic realms within organizations and professions.

During the past decade critical scholars have urged a more interdisciplinary approach to media studies, linking cultural considerations directly to the political economic realm. The political economy of communication examines relationships between media ownership, advertising, and government policies, particularly as they influence media practices and content (McChesney 2000). Showcasing theoretical connections between cultural studies and political economy, Nicholas Garnham (1995, 71) maintains that because in capitalist societies, "waged labor and commodity exchange constitute people's necessary and unavoidable conditions of existence," these elements must be included in any analysis of cultural practices. While cultural studies theorists remain concerned with the reductionist potential of political economy, Lawrence Grossberg (1995, 79) notes that economic practices may even help to shape the cultural agenda, albeit "always and only in part." Eileen Meehan (1999, 162) suggests that a dialogue between cultural studies and political economy is "essential" to critique the complex "relationships among corporations, audiences, makers, and regulators."

Pointing to Hanno Hardt's 1990 study of newsworkers, technology, and journalism history as an example, Mosco (1996) finds that recent studies of newsroom labor are one contemporary area of research that attempts to reconcile political economic concerns with critical cultural studies. This essay responds to Meehan's interdisciplinary call by integrating central concerns of political economy into a critical cultural analysis.

This historical study of the *Los Angeles Herald Examiner* strike draws on government documents on antitrust and monopoly, as well as hearings regarding the Failing Newspaper Act, which considered joint operating agreements including "price fixing, profit pooling and market allocation" (Barwis 1989, 27) for at risk newspapers. It uses strike-related materials from the Los Angeles Newspaper Guild collection at the Los Angeles Urban Archives Center; *Los Angeles Herald Examiner* labor conflict files from the Freedom of Information Center at the Missouri School of Journalism; and two telephone interviews with Charles Dale, an International Representative of the Newspaper Guild who served as co-director of the strike.

CONSTRUCTING A COLLECTIVE IDENTITY

The strike began on December 15, 1967 when approximately 1,100 members of the Los Angeles Newspaper Guild, Local 69 walked out of the *Los Angeles Herald Examiner*. At the time of the labor conflict, the Guild negotiated for all *Herald Examiner* newsroom, circulation, and business employees ("Guild strike idles 1900" 1967). Guild members had asked for a $25.20 a week salary increase for reporters, photographers, and copy editors, achieved over a two-year period, to bring them in line with their colleagues on the *Los Angeles Times* and the *Long Beach Independent Press-Telegram*. At the time of the strike, full time professional Guild reporters, known as journeymen, with four to five years experience earned a minimum of $174.50 a week at the *Herald Examiner*. Comparable wages on the city's non-union morning newspaper, the *Los Angeles Times*, were $208 a week ("Where do we stand" 1967). Negotiations had broken down after *Herald Examiner* management had offered Guild members a $13 weekly increase over a two-year period (Stone 1968).

In support of the Guild, members of the International Association of Machinists, Local 94 also walked out of the *Herald Examiner* that morning. That afternoon members of the International Typographical Unions, Printers Local 174 and Mailers Local 9 were locked out by management after they refused to do editorial work such as gathering wire copy and running stories from the news office to the back-shop print facilities. Later that day Web Pressmen, Local 18, Stereotypers, Local 58, and Paper Handlers, Local 3 were forced out of the newspaper "under threat of arrest" ("Strike fact sheet" 1968, 1). In sympathy, Building Services Employees, Local 399, Teamsters General Warehousemen, Local 598, Photoengravers, Local 262, and News Vendors, Local 75-A stopped working. In total approximately 2,000 union members were affected by the labor conflict.

A few months before the strike began, the Los Angeles Newspaper Guild *Bulletin* evaluated minimum weekly pay rates for newspaper reporters and photographers in urban newsgathering centers guaranteed in Guild contracts. It found that Guild reporters in Los Angeles received the lowest contract pay. For example, experienced Guild reporters in St. Louis and San Francisco earned at least $200 a week while *Herald Examiner* and *Independent Press-Telegram* reporters earned $174.50 each week ("Where do we stand" 1967). That fall, *the Long Beach Independent Press-Telegram* Guild unit successfully negotiated a new contract that would bring reporters' salaries up to $200 a week within two years.

In negotiating sessions held before the strike, *Herald Examiner* management maintained that it was "economically impossible" to match the salaries and benefits of those recently negotiated at the other Guild newspaper, the *Long Beach Independent Press-Telegram*. In response, Robert J. Rupert (1967), Chief Negotiator of the Los Angeles Newspaper Guild, urged Hearst to provide the Guild with evidence that the *Herald Examiner* was losing money. Hearst management did not respond. In the early weeks of the strike, Hearst negotiators changed their position regarding the salary dispute and said that while the newspaper could afford the new wage proposals, they "did not see fit to do so" ("No heart in Hearst position" 1968, 1).

Throughout the decade-long labor conflict, the Los Angeles Newspaper Guild organized a variety of public relations activities and utilized several publication venues to keep strikers informed and to publicize and promote their views on the progress of the strike. More than 1,400 daily editions of the newsletter *On the Line* reported on labor activities during the first four years of the *Herald Examiner* strike. The Los Angeles Newspaper Guild *Bulletin* regularly covered strike-related issues and events as did the official publication of the Los Angeles County AFL-CIO unions, *the Los Angeles Citizen*. In addition, significant labor related news and opinion were announced in press releases sent to local, regional, and national media outlets throughout the ten years.

Strike-related promotional activities and news coverage focused on three major intertwined issues: the economic aspects of the strike, the use of professional strikebreakers to crush the unions, and Hearst's refusal to negotiate with labor. Consistent with Douglas Kellner's (1995) suggestion that in modernity group or individual identity is self-reflexive and changeable, Guild strike strategies may be seen to have also aided in the development of a collective identity as workers.

One economics-based strategy of the Guild was to try to persuade local companies to stop advertising in the *Herald Examiner* during the labor conflict. Letters were sent to major advertisers and members talked with businesses about canceling their advertising. Rupert (1968) maintained that advertisers held the key to the strike: "They are the life line of the newspaper. Without them, Hearst could not further pursue his union-busting campaign." Urging major advertisers to support the labor boycott, Rupert rejected the use of violence or other illegal actions by union members, yet he warned that the Guild would take every legal action possible to disrupt businesses that failed to support the strike.

More than three years into the strike the Guild continued to encourage businesses not to buy advertising during the strike and consumers not to purchase products from companies that continued to advertise in the *Herald Examiner*. For example, the January 27, 1970 issue of the Los Angeles Newspaper Guild *Bulletin* urged workers not to buy Coors, Seagrams, or California grapes because the companies still advertised in the *Herald Examiner*. In an effort to sway major advertisers' continued support of the newspaper, Guild members picketed *Herald Examiner* advertisers and held large demonstrations at major local retailers. While many businesses continued to advertise in the *Herald Examiner*, demonstrations and related activities continued to increase public awareness of the strike and helped to bring Guild members together and re-energize them for the extended strike.

In addition to daily picket lines at the *Herald Examiner*, Guild crews went door to door, discussing the strike with residents and asking them to cancel their subscriptions to the *Herald Examiner* during the dispute. This strategy not only hurt the newspaper's circulation but it also further increased community awareness of the issues involved in the strike. Decreases in circulation and advertising lineage reductions were regularly reported in pro-Guild publications as evidence of labor's progress in the strike. Hearst's discontinuation of the newspaper bowling tournament and the closing of the *Herald Examiner* library were showcased as further evidence of the strike's economic damage to the newspaper (Dale and Pattison, n.d.).

Such strategies had devastating consequences for the *Herald Examiner*'s circulation and revenue figures. Audit Bureau figures for

September 30, 1967 ranked the *Los Angeles Herald Examiner* as the largest circulation daily afternoon newspaper in the United States, with a Monday through Friday average of 731,473 ("Guild strike idles 1900" 1967). Six weeks into the strike, *Herald Examiner* daily circulation dropped 28 percent to about 450,000. Circulation continued to decrease throughout the strike ("No apparent end seen" 1968). Advertising revenue declined sharply and *Time* magazine estimated that after one year the strike had cost the *Herald Examiner* $15 million in advertising sales revenues alone ("Defeat of the strikers" 1968).

Charles Dale, an International Representative of the Newspaper Guild, was sent by labor leaders to Los Angeles to work with the other unions on the strike. As co-director of the *Herald Examiner* strike, Dale focused on making strike related activities as effective as possible. He oversaw the economic aspects of the conflict, made sure that strike benefits were paid and all money was spent wisely, and worked to bring the strike to a positive conclusion. According to Dale, to keep strikers motivated during the lengthy conflict, the Guild held many meetings and organized numerous events for the striking workers, including an annual Thanksgiving food drive. As the strike dragged on Guild members became discouraged. Nonetheless, Dale said, the low pay and old, outdated equipment at the newspaper motivated union members. Most remained determined to negotiate a fair contract (Dale 2002, pers. comm., February 21 and 26).

Appeals for donations to help fund the strike frequently appeared in pro-labor publications. In March 1969, fifteen labor organizations in Southern California pledged $250,000 for a radio, newspaper, and television advertising campaign to encourage the public to boycott companies who continued to advertise in the *Herald Examiner* (Joint Council of Teamsters 1969). Although unions throughout the country and in Canada helped out financially, by August 1971 the Los Angeles Newspaper Guild had borrowed $100,000 from the AFL-CIO because costs associated with the *Herald Examiner* strike had reached five million dollars.

SHOWCASING SCAB LABOR

The most strident rhetoric found in Guild strike materials focused on the *Herald Examiner*'s use of professional strikebreakers, also known as scabs. Author Jack London coined the term "scab" in 1903 to describe a professional strikebreaker who readily works in the place of a striking employee and refuses to join or support the actions of labor. London (1953, 1) insisted that "the modern strikebreaker sells his birthright, his country, his wife, children and his fellowmen, for an unfilled promise from his employer, trust or corporation." From a labor perspective, the use of professional strikebreakers undermines the collective bargaining process, since when scab labor is used, employers are trying to "bust" the unions, reject contract negotiations, and operate an open shop without union influence. During the *Los Angeles Herald Examiner* strike, Hearst used at least 200 professional strikebreakers "imported" from other cities and states. The Guild judged this a betrayal of all working people and condemned it as unethical and amoral. *The Guild Bulletin* and *On the Line* frequently referred to professional strikebreakers as "parasites," "criminals," and "mercenaries" with no redeeming value. Specific information on professional strikebreakers working for the *Herald Examiner* was repeatedly included in pro-Guild publications. For example, the January 1968 edition of *Strike Lockout Extra* prominently displayed photographs of strikebreakers and identified them not only by skill areas but also by name, background, criminal record, and past strikebreaking activities.

Twelve days into the strike, AFL-CIO Leader Thomas L. Pitts charged that Hearst's use of professional strikebreakers was part of a concerted effort to destroy collective bargaining at the *Herald Examiner* and ultimately "crush the unions" (Peevey 1967). An undated editorial cartoon in *The Guild Bulletin* by "Strobel" titled "A Killer on the Loose!" illustrated labor's concern about "George R. Hearst's Anti-Union Drive," with huge feet smashing free collective bargaining in America, and destroying employees' rights, union shops, decent wages, working conditions, and the gains of labor during the last 30 years.

Strike leaders also maintained that professional strikebreakers were used to destabilize the working class community of Los Angeles ("Dynamics of aggression" 1968). With nearly 2,000 employees out of work, the economic and social well being of the community was challenged by "transient mercenaries" who collected excessive wages and then moved on without contributing anything to the community. Labor leaders maintained that professional strikebreakers' lack of respect for union work generally escalated into a total lack of respect for the community as a whole ("Community is loser" 1968, 4).

Executive Secretary of the Los Angeles County Federation of Labor Sigmund Arywitz (1968a) maintained that Hearst management had been preparing for a strike for at least one month before it began. Newsprint, cots, and food were stockpiled at the plant, a chain link wire fence was installed around part of the building, and arrangements were made with the Western Newspaper Industrial Relations Bureau, a company that specialized in providing newspapers with non-union labor, to hire professional strikebreakers. Three weeks into the strike, Hearst negotiators announced that professional strikebreakers hired at the beginning of the strike would become permanent employees and would have "super-seniority" over striking workers regardless of any final agreement reached. Finding Hearst's actions "wholly unacceptable, immoral and a deterrent to peace" ("Labor calls Hearst boycott" 1968, A-3), Arywitz (1968b) insisted that such decisions made negotiations impossible. He said that until the *Herald Examiner* dismissed all professional strikebreakers and began negotiating with the unions, they must be considered the enemy of labor. In response to Hearst's actions, 2,000 union members participated in an anti-strikebreaker march from the *Herald Examiner* to Los Angeles City Hall ("Labor socks Hearst," 1968). The Los Angeles County Federation of Labor called for a nationwide boycott of all Hearst enterprises. People were urged not to purchase any Hearst newspapers, magazines, or Avon Pocket Books and to cancel subscriptions to Hearst publications.

Hearst's unwillingness to negotiate continued throughout the strike. Los Angeles Mayor Sam Yorty, members of the Los Angeles City Council, and ten prominent Jewish and Protestant clergy urged Hearst to negotiate with the unions; however, he refused ("Strike fact sheet," 1968). Eight months into the strike-lockout, Guild negotiators said they were willing to work with any arbitrator chosen by the *Herald Examiner*. Hearst management replied:

> We will not turn the management of this paper over to an outsider. We are not going to give any outsider the authority to make decisions regarding the operation of this paper. We will not agree to arbitrate any of the outstanding issues we have in dispute with the Guild. (Rupert & Dale 1968, 1)

Nearly four years into the strike, the Los Angeles Newspaper Guild and the other unions involved in the *Herald Examiner* strike-lockout volunteered to comply with President Richard Nixon's call for a three-month end to all labor conflicts. In exchange for ending the strike, union members asked Hearst to end his lockout and immediately rehire all union members who were still available to work. Hearst refused to agree with their terms (Abraham 1971). Although Hearst's unwillingness to deal with the unions frustrated negotiators, it reinforced the union's zeal for gaining an equitable contract and helped to keep strikers motivated as to the righteousness of their cause, again reinforcing a collective identity among Guild members as part of the labor movement.

PRESS COVERAGE OF THE STRIKE

Over the ten years, an extensive amount of pro-Guild strike information and publicity was produced. However, Dale explained that the anti-labor sentiment in Los Angeles made getting other newspapers interested in covering the *Herald Examiner* strike difficult (Dale 2002, pers. comm.). Dale's comments regarding an anti-labor environment are supported by research into the American labor movement during the twentieth century. Robert McChesney (1999, 298) finds that in mainstream media labor coverage is limited to stories about the negative or violent aspects of strikes. "If one read only the commercial media, it would be difficult to determine what on earth good was served by having labor unions at all." As early as the 1940s and 1950s "unionists charged that it was impossible to find unbiased coverage of labor issues in the daily press" (Fones-Wolf & Fones-Wolf 1995, 48). An assessment of more than 50 articles on the *Los Angeles Herald Examiner* strike published in local and national newspapers, collected in the Los Angeles Urban Archives and the Freedom of Information Center, also supports Dale's charges. From the 1950s through the 1990s the Missouri Freedom of Information Center clipped all newspaper articles available on freedom of expression, including the *Los Angeles Herald Examiner* strike. A pro-labor perspective is virtually absent from the reportage of the *Herald Examiner* strike. Consistent with McChesney, the strike coverage in local and national newspapers, *Time* newsmagazine, and the trade publication *Editor and Publisher*, focused on the violence of the strike and the damage the unions were inflicting on the newspaper.

In most cases a pro-management perspective was framed through word choice and an emphasis on negative consequences of the strike for Hearst management. Headlines such as "Mob invades Walnut Creek, attacks Times" (1968), "Strike violence at L.A. paper" (1968), and "Herald strike throng pays city hall visit" (Bernstein 1968a) illustrate how the strikers' actions were cast in a negative light. The coverage frequently compared the strikers to an unruly mob. For example, supporters of the strike were referred to as a "massive throng" of demonstrators who "demanded" an audience with the Mayor (Bernstein 1968a, 1). When labor picketed other Hearst properties the *Los Angeles Times* reported that picketers were participating in an "illegal secondary boycott" (Bernstein 1968b, 1). In contrast, Hearst was portrayed as a courageous individual battling with the evil unions. *Time* magazine maintained that the grandson of William Randolph displayed "determination rarely displayed these days by a publisher confronted with a strike" ("Frustrating the unions" 1968, 72). The *Wall Street Journal* showcased Hearst's ability to keep publishing the newspaper during the strike and several newspaper articles lauded Hearst for working in the newsroom and pressroom, answering the phone and even composing type. "Powerful" support from the non-union *Los Angeles Times* and Mayor Yorty was showcased to illustrate the righteousness of Hearst's stance. Yorty was quoted as saying, "I think the unions should get wise to themselves. They're putting the newspapers out of business" ("Defeat of the strikers" 1968, 48). Financial costs associated with the strike were used to reinforce the need to fight the unions; no articles mentioned the circulation and advertising losses to illustrate public support of strikers.

The consequences of professional strikebreakers were downplayed in most of the coverage. The term "professional strikebreaker" was rarely used; instead scabs were referred to as "non-union personnel." To deemphasize the use of professional strikebreakers, reporters explained how Hearst managers worked in the newsroom to augment the use of wire-service copy and syndicated columns from other Hearst writers. *Time* magazine reported that during the strike jurisdictional disputes ceased, because non-union labor and management worked together wherever they were needed. The article noted approvingly that "even reporters are called on to run copy and dirty their hands in the backshop" ("Frustrating the unions" 1968, 72).

Violence was a significant aspect of the strike coverage in the press. During the strike Hearst management was quick to define any issues or problems as violent pro-labor actions. The *Herald Examiner* distributed flyers and ran display advertisements offering a reward for evidence resulting in the arrest and conviction "of any person, or persons, damaging the property of any Herald-Examiner advertiser through strike- related criminal activity" ("Hearst reward" 1970).

Newspapers showcased Hearst's accusations in strike-related coverage, even when the charges were unfounded. Ten days after the strike began the *Los Angeles Times* reported that the *Herald Examiner* was offering a $5,000 reward for information on shots fired at a newspaper delivery truck. The *Times* quoted *Herald* management as saying that since the strike began there had been repeated incidents and threats of violence against newspaper dealers and carrier boys and sabotage at the newspaper's offices. While the front-page article focused on strike-related violence, it mentioned that the Los Angeles County Sheriff's office had found no bullet holes or other evidence to indicate a shooting (Reich 1967). Also within days of the strike's onset, *Editor and Publisher* reported that union members had sabotaged the *Herald Examiner*. Hearst management had charged that glue was poured onto the newsprint conveyor belts, ink tanks were emptied onto the pressroom floor, and composing room type and materials were destroyed ("Guild strike idles 1900," 1967). Similarly, *Time* magazine described the "cold blooded murder" of a non-union printer as the worst of some 150 strike-related violent actions. While the newsmagazine admitted that police had not tied the crime to the unions, the article showcased *Herald Examiner* opinion that blamed the shooting on the strikers ("Frustrating the unions," 1968, p. 72). Ultimately, no charges were ever filed against any union members connected with the *Herald Examiner* strike.

Lack of evidence was also apparent in the *Des Moines Register* report that a January 1968 pro-labor demonstration "erupted into violence" when windows were broken with rocks and sticks. The newspaper article added that a television cameraman was "attacked" but sustained no injury. Missing from the news story was any estimation of the numbers of protestors, the extent of the violence, or the cost of the damage. Nor did the article include any sources to support the accusations ("Strike violence at L.A. paper" 1968, 1). No follow-up coverage of the demonstration was found in the archived articles.

Reporters connected other arguably unconnected newspaper industry violence to the *Los Angeles Herald Examiner* strike. For example, when a large group of men damaged machinery at the Walnut Creek printing plant used to publish the *Contra Costa Times* and the *Concord Transcript*, news reports blamed union sympathizers for the damage.

Although no evidence was included to support such an accusation, articles quoted owner/publisher Dean Lesher as saying that he did not know why union sympathizers harmed his plant because his newspapers had "no connection" with strike. Lesher noted that the *Herald Examiner* had hired some of his employees, but he maintained that the workers left "without consent" ("Printing shop wrecked" 1968, 8).

While much of the coverage included some mention of the union perspective, if only to counter Hearst's charges, some *Editor and Publisher* articles were openly and blatantly anti-labor. For example, an *E & P* article published one month after the strike began emphasized the efforts of labor to try to close down Hearst's newspapers. Calling picket lines at the *Los Angeles Herald Examiner* and at Hearst-owned newspaper the *San Francisco Examiner* "strong-arm" techniques that "turn collective bargaining into a farce" (Brown 1968, 64), *E & P* urged Guild members to be reasonable and equitable. No mention whatsoever of the Guild's position appeared in the *E & P* article. Hearst's use of professional strikebreakers and his unwillingness to participate in collective bargaining were omitted from the coverage as were wage inequities.

Overall, the U.S. press showcased a pro-management perspective on the strike, dismissing union charges and accusations as insignificant. None of the news articles presented both sides of the labor conflict fairly, much less showcased a pro-labor position. Even labor's charge that Hearst would not negotiate was downplayed and challenged as merely a "claim" by union members ("Frustrating the unions" 1968, 72). None of the articles archived at Missouri questioned Hearst's determination that union members were responsible for all strike-related violence. No articles considered the possibility that police and/or professional strikebreakers might be involved in some of the violence. In fact, Dale said that he met often with the Los Angeles Police Department to complain about brutality on the picket lines, but he found police were clearly pro-management (Dale 2002, pers. comm.). In at least one case, a police officer framed a strike leader for destroying newspaper delivery boxes and threw him in jail for ten days. Dale noted that the professional strikebreakers often assaulted the strikers. The strikebreakers walked through the picket lines with long neck soda bottles and hit the picketers with them. They also injured strikers with filed down printing tools.

HEARST'S UNWILLINGNESS TO NEGOTIATE

Why did George Hearst refuse to negotiate with the unions and allow the strike eventually to destroy his newspaper? A definitive answer is impossible, given that Hearst himself has remained mute on this topic. He never commented publicly on the strike and repeated requests for an interview have been denied. [1] No *Herald Examiner* archive exists. As *California Business* reporter Dan Goodgame (1987, 46) suggested, as a private corporation, "the Hearsts don't have to tell anybody anything about their business, and generally they don't." The Hearst corporate web site offers a brief history of the corporation and a timeline that begins on March 4, 1887 when William Randolph Hearst became proprietor of the *San Francisco Examiner*. Although the vast majority of acquisitions are included here, the site never mentions the *Los Angeles Herald Examiner* (or any other Hearst-owned Los Angeles papers), although at one time it was the largest circulation afternoon newspaper in the United States.

While the Hearst corporation may have erased the *Herald Examiner* from its history, some strong evidence remains that provides clues as to Hearst's motivation for his actions during the strike. Early in his career William Randolph Hearst was not actively opposed to the labor movement. Ironically, the *Los Angeles Examiner* began publication in 1903 after labor activists encouraged Hearst to start a union newspaper in Los Angeles to compete with the non-union *Los Angeles Times* (North 2003). Hearst agreed and in November 1903 the *Los Angeles Herald Examiner* began publication.

Initially, Hearst seemed to respect the role of labor and he negotiated equitable contracts with craft and trade unions. However, Hearst was actively opposed to the American Newspaper Guild from its inception in 1933. Envisioning reporters as romantic figures, Hearst felt that the Guild would undermine editorial policies and could ultimately compromise the integrity of journalism (Lee 1937). He ordered his editors and publishers actively to oppose the Guild. Newsroom employees were warned not to join the Guild; those who disobeyed were reprimanded and even fired (Carlisle 1969). In 1934, the firing

---

1   This author made numerous attempts by letter, email and telephone to contact George Hearst or any Hearst managers willing to comment on the *Herald Examiner* strike. To date, no one connected with the Hearst organization has been willing to comment.

of the respected *San Francisco Examiner* editorial writer Louis Burgess for union activities exemplified Hearst's anti-Guild policy. During the development of the American Newspaper Guild, Hearst refused to negotiate with any of the local Guilds; when the *Milwaukee News* went on strike, Hearst vowed to spend as much money as necessary to defeat the Guild. After a tentative agreement had been reached between editorial workers and the newspaper, H. L. Bitner, General Manager of Hearst newspapers, informed Milwaukee Guild members, "The Hearst management will not enter into any agreement written or verbal that recognizes the Guild" (quoted in Leab 1970, 250). For Heywood Broun (1936), the American Newspaper Guild's first president, Hearst's strident non- recognition of the Guild became a unifying force among editorial workers. Initially the Guild was organized as a semi-professional organization that worked with publishers to represent the economic and professional needs of editorial workers. As publisher resistance and non-recognition escalated, the Guild became a union committed to collective bargaining.[2]

George Hearst's actions during the *Herald Examiner* strike solidified an anti-Guild bias first established by his grandfather William Randolph Hearst. During the twentieth century the Los Angeles Newspaper Guild and Hearst management had maintained a contentious relationship. Strikes occurred in the late 1930s and again in 1946. The Guild held a one-day strike in November 1965 after a contract deadline passed without resolution. Apparently shocked by the strike, George Hearst settled with the Guild within hours but "vowed that he would oust the unions" ("History of the *Herald Examiner* strike" n.d.). The November 1965 strike is generally considered the precursor of the 1967–1977 *Herald Examiner* strike. Dale suspects that Hearst wanted to destroy the unions as a way to keep the *Herald Examiner* economically competitive with the non-union *Los Angeles Times* (Dale 2002, pers. comm.). While this is an interesting explanation, it does not fully explain Hearst's actions because at that time employees at the *Times* were paid considerably higher wages than workers on the *Herald Examiner*. Although the problems between the Hearst organization and the Guild were at least in part historically situated, Hearst's actions probably were also a conscious effort to weaken the

---

2   For further discussion on the development of a union perspective in the American Newspaper Guild, see Brennen (2004).

Guild specifically because it represented the most vocal opposition
to the development of monopolistic practices in the newspaper business. Over the years, the American Newspaper Guild repeatedly questioned the growth of newspaper chain ownership, single newspaper
communities, and local media monopolies. Concerned with the influence of newspaper concentration on the overall economic well-being
of communities, the Guild asserted that newspaper trends toward
monopolization eliminated the diversity of information, opinion, and
news sources that were essential to a democratic society (The Failing
Newspaper Act 1968a).

MEDIA CONGLOMERATION & MONOPOLIZATION

By the 1960s, single ownership or combination newspaper monopolies existed in most U.S. cities (Arywitz 1968a). In 1955 chains controlled about 28 percent of the daily newspapers in the U.S.; ten years
later they controlled 43 percent of daily newspapers (Failing Newspaper Act 1968a). In 1962 only 55 U.S. cities still had competing daily
newspapers, whereas 552 cities had competing daily newspapers in
1920. According to William Randolph Hearst, Jr., "when monopoly is
substituted for two formerly competitive papers, the profit is two and
a half times the total profit under independent operation of the two
papers" ("Growth of monopoly and concentrated ownership" 1963,
1291).

Interestingly, the creation of the *Herald Examiner* was the result of
a combination newspaper monopoly in Los Angeles. Until January
1962, four newspapers operated in Los Angeles. The Hearst-owned
Herald and the Chandler-owned *Times* were morning papers. Hearst's
Herald-Express and Chandler's *Mirror* were afternoon newspapers.
Cross-ownership agreements arranged in 1962 between Hearst and
Chandler consolidated the *Examiner* and the *Herald-Express* and dis-
continued the *Mirror*. These actions resulted in one morning newspa-
per, the *Los Angeles Times*, and one afternoon paper, the *Los Angeles
Herald Examiner*.

During House of Representatives hearings on news media concentration of ownership, Hearst General Manager G.O. Markuson said
that the Hearst and Chandler actions in Los Angeles were undertaken
because the Los Angeles area "could not profitably support four metropolitan papers" (Failing Newspaper Act 1968a, 212). Markuson
maintained that some of the newspapers were consolidated because

they were losing money. Yet in hearings before the judiciary subcommittee of antitrust and monopoly, Executive Secretary of the New York Newspaper Guild Thomas Murphy attributed the Los Angeles situation to corporations creating a monopoly rather than encouraging the "free flow of news as a competitive press" (Failing Newspaper Act 1968b, 2677). Murphy noted that the Los Angeles newspapers had been profitable before the consolidations. Doubting the claim that newspapers were losing money, he said that for many years the Los Angeles papers had been profitable but that profits had been drained off to subsidize other corporate ventures. Further doubt about Hearst's consolidations came from Samuel Shulman of the General Accounting Office. In 1963, Shulman testified to a House antitrust subcommittee on newspaper business practices and ownership trends that "more realistic bookkeeping" would have changed Hearst's claimed $2,037,000 five-year loss on the *Los Angeles Examiner* into a $6,124,000 profit (Failing Newspaper Act 1968a, 209).

In a concerted effort to halt the newspaper industry's trend toward monopolization, in 1959 the Guild asked the Justice Department to investigate possible antitrust violations in a rumored newspaper merger between Scripps-Howard and Hearst in New York City. In the previous eighteen months Hearst and Scripps-Howard newspapers in San Francisco had merged and Scripps-Howard's United Press had acquired Hearst's International News Service. The Guild noted that before each of these business transactions, the newspapers had publicly denied plans for any merger. This time the Guild wanted the Justice Department to consider potential antitrust violations before a merger was completed. In response, Hearst sued the American Newspaper Guild for spreading unfounded rumors regarding a new Hearst and Scripps-Howard merger. William J. Farson, Executive Vice President of the Guild, said that the purpose of Hearst's lawsuit was to divert public attention from the Justice Department's recent scrutiny of business transactions between Hearst and Scripps- Howard ("Comment on Hearst suit"1959). The suit was eventually dropped but not before the Guild spent thousands of dollars in legal costs. However, the Guild's call for an antitrust inquiry was successful in the short run in that it forestalled new mergers between Hearst and Scripps-Howard.

The American Newspaper Guild was also a vocal opponent of the Failing Newspaper Act because it would accelerate the trend toward monopolization and chain ownership of newspapers. The Failing

Newspaper Act was originally designed to maintain the diversity of editorial voices in a community when at least one newspaper was in serious financial straits and no prospective buyer could be found. Under the Act, newspapers established joint operating arrangements that allowed them to "reduce costs by combining the economic and business aspects of their papers' production, while at the same time maintaining separate editorial and reportorial staff" (Barwis 1989, 28). Under the Act, jointly operating newspapers may fix joint advertising rates and pool their profits—actions that the Sherman and Clayton Antitrust Acts otherwise expressly prohibited.

At its board meetings and national conventions the Guild repeatedly raised opposition to the Failing Newspaper Act. State and national officers also testified during Senate and House of Representatives hearings. During Congressional hearings Thomas Murphy, Executive Secretary of the New York Newspaper Guild, maintained that the proposed bill violated current antitrust laws and infringed on freedom of the press. Murphy said that, if passed, the Failing Newspaper Act:

> would encourage greater monopoly, not only by giving existing publishers greater freedom to make agreements for producing newspapers more cheaply through common production and distribution facilities, but most importantly by giving the blessings of law to unregulated price and rate fixing and profit-pooling arrangements that make it financially impossible for a potential new competitor to even consider attempting to enter a market. (Failing Newspaper Act 1968b, 2674)

While other individuals and organizations also testified against the Failing Newspaper Act, most of the commentary against the bill came from Guild members. In contrast, newspaper owners and publishers lobbied Congressional members for the Act and testified that the Act would maintain a diversity of voices and actually prevent newspaper monopolies. After extended hearings, and a series of legislative compromises, including a more optimistic sounding name, the Newspaper Preservation Act became law on July 24, 1970. Just as the Guild had warned, a retrospective assessment of the Newspaper Preservation Act (Barwis 1989) found that joint operating agreements had saved no newspapers from failure; instead it had increased the profits of successful newspapers and encouraged monopolistic business practices that inhibited freedom of the press.

A Moment of Danger

The Guild's vocal opposition to chain ownership and monopolization and the Justice Department's repeated investigations into antitrust violations directly targeted Hearst. Each time Guild members testified before Congress, they offered examples from the Hearst Corporation to support their concerns regarding monopolization and chain ownership. With the lure of huge financial gains tempting Hearst, he may have decided that his economic plans for the corporation depended on destroying union viability. Certainly the issue of monopolization at least partially influenced Hearst's decisions in the *Herald Examiner* strike.

A STORY OF FAILURE

A critical assessment of the *Los Angeles Herald Examiner* strike showcases strategies of opposition, challenge, and resistance to the dominant ideological power structure. It illustrates the formation of a collective identity as well as the power struggles between the unions and Hearst. However, the *Herald Examiner* strike is also a story of failure. Throughout the decade-long strike, *Herald Examiner* advertising revenue and circulation dwindled. In the decade after the strike, the newspaper was unable to rebuild its circulation and advertising base. In 1989 when the Hearst Corporation attempted to find a buyer for the newspaper, its circulation had fallen to 242,000. Unable to sell the newspaper, the *Herald Examiner* ceased publication on November 2, 1989. Meanwhile, the viability of the Newspaper Guild and the other unions involved in the labor conflict was severely undermined, because they were unable to negotiate a settlement. In 1976 a series of elections decertified all of the original unions involved in the strike and created a new union, the International Printing and Graphic Communications Union, which immediately began negotiations with Hearst. Interestingly, the new union included striking workers who had not found other jobs and non-union employees who currently worked for the newspaper. Eight months later, in March 1977, the International Printing and Graphic Communications Union successfully negotiated a new three-year contract for *Los Angeles Herald Examiner* employees ("Union pack" 1977).

Although the Guild ultimately failed to bring the strike to a positive outcome it does not diminish the years of effort and the resilience of its campaign to raise wages for reporters on the *Herald Examiner* in line with other Southern California newspapers. During the decade-long strike Guild members used a variety of promotional strategies to showcase their struggle. Their sustained efforts informed the public about the labor conflict and helped to influence adversely the *Herald Examiner*'s circulation numbers and advertising revenue. Although the vast majority of the local and national newspaper coverage was pro-management this stance had more to do with the newspapers' anti-labor ideological position rather than any failing of the Guild to make its views heard. Certainly *Editor & Publisher*'s coverage of the strike reinforced an anti-Guild position among editors and publishers that began in the 1930s when the American Newspaper Guild first turned to collective bargaining (Brennen 2004).

Hearst refused to negotiate with labor despite sustained pressure from community leaders and the public to settle the strike. The continued losses of revenue and circulation were offset by his intention to destroy union involvement at the *Los Angeles Herald Examiner*. The same strategy used by Hearst and other corporations to hide profits from individual newspapers, by funneling income from one company within the corporation to another, was used to sustain the *Herald Examiner* during the decade-long strike. The assets of Hearst's multi-million dollar media empire allowed the newspaper's continued losses to be diffused throughout the corporation, Hearst was thereby able to hold out for ten years until the existing unions had been decertified and rendered powerless. Hearst's refusal to negotiate with labor was repeated by other media conglomerates. Today union influence is at an all time low in the newspaper industry.

As Hardt (1993, 90) suggests, the "anti-labor attitudes of media owners may offer explanations for the contemporary status and working habits of newsworkers, the production of content matter, and the understanding of audiences as consumers." At the time of the *Herald Examiner* strike, while many newspapers were anti- labor, they also covered labor issues as a regular beat. Some newspapers, such as the *Los Angeles Times*, employed a labor editor. Today, even on daily urban newspapers, labor is no longer a regular area of coverage. McChesney describes labor reporting as "nearly extinct" (2004, 88). Linking the lack of labor coverage directly to the decline of the labor movement, McChesney notes, "People still work, poverty among workers is growing, workplace conflicts are as important as ever, but labor issues are no longer considered newsworthy because organized labor is no longer powerful" (2004, 76). Current labor coverage is routinely a historical, fragmented, and superficial because it lacks background or understanding of the role of labor.

The relationship between the strike and the Guild's active and sustained opposition to monopolization also provides insights for future research into conglomeration and consolidation, central concerns of political economy. In the twenty-first century, the structure and control of media conglomerates are central concerns of a global market economy. Ben Bagdikian notes that as of 2003, five media corporations—Time Warner, Walt Disney Company, Murdoch's News Corporation, Viacom, and Bertelsmann—dominate mass communication in the United States. Linking media conglomeration to an increasingly limited flow of diverse information as well as to changes in public policy and political power, Bagdikian (2004, 29) suggests that political leaders now "treat the country's most powerful media corporations with something approaching reverence." Yet, for many policy makers, media monopolization is a new issue, because they do not understand that media consolidation has been a concern throughout the twentieth century (Sterling 2000). At a time when the FCC is working to relax media ownership rules even further, understanding the efforts of the Newspaper Guild to alert Congress about the problems of monopolization might aid critics and researchers trying to counter questionable FCC processes.

ACKNOWLEDGEMENT

An earlier version of this chapter appeared in *Critical Studies in Media Communication*, Vol. 22, No. 1 (2005) pp. 64-81. Reprinted by permission of Taylor & Francis.

REFERENCES

Abraham, N. 1971. "Los Angeles Newspaper Guild memo." August, 23. In Los Angeles Urban Archives Center, Oviatt Library, California State University.

Arywitz, Sigmund. 1968a. "Are we to become a one-paper town?" *Strike Lockout Extra*, January, 3.

Arywitz, Sigmund. 1968b. "In this corner. Strikebreaker seniority tightens Hearst screws," *Los Angeles Citizen*, January 12, 8.

Bagdikian, Ben H. 2004. *The New Media Monopoly*, Boston: Beacon Press.

Barwis, Gail. L. 1989. "The newspaper preservation act: A retrospective analysis." *Journalism Quarterly* 66: 27–38.

Bernstein, Harold. 1968a. "Herald strike throng pays city hall visit," *Los Angeles Times*, January 13.

Bernstein, Harold. 1968b. "Hopes for newspaper settlements still dim," *Los Angeles Times*, January 11.

Brennen, Bonnie. 2004. "The emergence of class consciousness in the American Newspaper Guild." In *Class and News*, edited by Don Heider, 233–247. Boulder: Rowman and Littlefield.

Broun, Heywood. 1936. "Broun's page," *The Nation*, Vol. 142, May 6.

Brown, R. U. 1968. "Shop talk at thirty. Labor's rights and illegal acts." *Editor & Publisher*, Vol. 101, January 14, 64.

Carlisle, Rodney. 1969. "William Randolph Hearst's reaction to the American Newspaper Guild: A challenge to New Deal labor legislation." *Labor History* 10: 74–99.

"Comment on Hearst suit: Guild denies rumor action violates law." 1959. *Editor & Publisher*, November 14, 14.

"Community is loser." 1968. *Strike Lockout Extra*, January, 4.

Dale, Charles, & Pattison, D. n.d. "Memo to all Herald-Examiner Guild Members." In Los Angeles Urban Archives Center, Oviatt Library, California State University.

"Defeat of the strikers." 1968. *Time*, December 26, 92.

"Dynamics of aggression. Hearst's target: Hit unions." 1968. *Los Angeles Citizen*, January 19, 1.

Fones-Wolf, Ken, & Fones-Wolf, Elizabeth. 1995. "A mighty voice for labor: The struggle to create a national daily labor newspaper, 1952–1958." *Labor Studies Journal* 20: 42–65.

"Frustrating the unions." 1968. *Time*, March 8, 91.

Garnham, Nicholas. 1995. "Political economy and cultural studies: Reconciliation or divorce?" *Critical Studies in Mass Communication* 12: 62–71.

Garnham, Nicholas. 2000. *Emancipation, the Media, and Modernity. Arguments about the Media and Social Theory.* Oxford: Oxford University Press.

Goodgame, Dan. 1987. "Citizen McCabe." *California Business* 46: 22.

Grossberg, Lawrence. 1995. "Cultural studies vs. political economy: Is anybody else bored with this debate?" *Critical Studies in Mass Communication* 12: 72–81.

"Guild strike idles 1900: 250 publish Hearst paper. Los Angeles Herald-Examiner has 32 and 40-page editions." 1967. *Editor & Publisher*, December 23, Vol. 9, 100.

Hardt, Hanno. 1990. "Newsworkers, technology, and journalism history." *Critical Studies in Mass Communication* 7: 346–365.

Hardt, Hanno. 1993. "Alternative visions of democracy: Theories of culture and communication in the United States." In *Communication and Democracy*, edited by S. Splichal, & J. Wasko, 87–102. Norwood, NJ: Ablex.

Hardt, Hanno. 2001. *Social Theories of the Press. Constituents of Communication Research 1840s to 1920s*. Boulder: Roman and Littlefield.

"Hearst reward for capture of criminal strikers." 1970. Flyer, April. In Los Angeles Urban Archives Center, Oviatt Library, California State University.

"History of the Los Angeles Herald Examiner strike." n.d. In Los Angeles Urban Archives Center, Oviatt Library, California State University.

The International Typographical Union. 1963. *Growth of monopoly and concentrated ownership*. Presented to the Antitrust Subcommittee of the House Committee on the Judiciary Investigation of Monopoly Practices in the Newspaper Industry, Washington, D.C.

"Joint Council of Teamsters." 1969. Press release, March 28. In Los Angeles Urban Archives Center, Oviatt Library, California State University.

Kellner, Douglas. 1995. *Media Culture. Cultural Studies, Identity, and Politics between the Modern and the Postmodern*. London: Routledge.

"Labor calls Hearst boycott." 1968. *Citizen News*, January 6, A-3.

"Labor socks Hearst. 9th column. L.A. strike-lockout drive gains speed." 1968. *Los Angeles Citizen*, January 19, 1.

Leab, Daniel. 1970. *A Union of Individuals. The Formation of the American Newspaper Guild, 1933–1936*. New York: Columbia University Press.

Lee, Alfred McLung. 1937. *The Daily Newspaper in America. The Evolution of a Social Instrument*. New York: Macmillan.

London, Jack. 1953. "What is a scab?" *Columbus Dispatch*, November 20, B-1.

Mathews, Jay & Farhi, Paul. 1989. "L.A. Herald Examiner to fold after 118 years." *The Washington Post*, November 2, E-3.

McChesney, Robert. 1999. *Rich Media Poor Democracy. Communication Politics in Dubious Times*. Urbana: University of Illinois Press.

McChesney, Robert. 2000. "The political economy of communication and the future of the field." *Media Culture and Society* 22: 109–116.

McChesney, Robert. 2004. *The Problem of the Media. U.S. Communication Politics in the 21st Century.* New York: Monthly Review.

Meehan, Eileen. 1999. "Commodity, culture, common sense: Media research and paradigm dialogue." *The Journal of Media Economics* 12: 149–163.

"Mob invades Walnut Creek, attacks Times. Composing room hit, damage near $50,000." 1968. *Contra Costa Times,* January 31, 1.

Mosco, Vincent. 1996. *The Political Economy of Communication. Rethinking and Renewal.* London: Sage.

"No apparent end seen." 1968. *Wall Street Journal,* January 26, 7.

"No heart in Hearst position." 1968. *Strike Lockout Extra,* January, 1.

North, G. 2003. "Social media Guild history." Southern California Media Guild. Accessed February 11, 2003. http://216.71.122.154/history.htm.

Peevey, M. 1967. "Press release," December 27. In Los Angeles Urban Archives Center, Oviatt Library, California State University.

"Printing shop wrecked; link to Herald denied. Walnut Creek publisher says theory that plant was helping L.A. paper is untrue." 1968. *Los Angeles Times,* January 31, 8.

Reich, K. 1967. "Herald offers reward in reported shooting." *Los Angeles Times,* December 25, 1.

Rupert, Robert. J. 1967. "Wire to William Randolph Hearst." In Los Angeles Urban Archives Center, Oviatt Library, California State University.

Rupert, Robert. J. 1968. "Correspondence to James B. Woods," October 24, 1. In Los Angeles Urban Archives Center, Oviatt Library, California State University.

Rupert, Robert. J., & Dale, Charles. 1968. "Special negotiating report— Guild company meeting." *Los Angeles Newspaper Guild Bulletin,* August 28.

Sterling, Christopher. H. 2000. "US communications industry ownership and the 1996 Telecommunications Act. Watershed or unintended consequences." In *Media Power, Professionals and Policies,* edited by H. Tumber, 56–69. London: Routledge.

Stone, R. 1968. "No apparent end seen in walkout involving paper in Los Angeles. Herald-Examiner is publishing with nonunion workers, but circulation and pages decline." *Wall Street Journal,* January 26, 8.

"Strike fact sheet." 1968. Herald-Examiner Joint Strike-Lockout Council, April. In Los Angeles Urban Archives Center, Oviatt Library, California State University.

"Strike violence at L.A. paper." 1968. *Des Moines Register,* January 27, 1.

"Union pact ends 10 years of strike." 1977. *Editor & Publisher,* March 12, 13.

U.S. Congress, House. Committee on the Judiciary. Subcommittee on Antitrust and Monopoly. 1963. *Hearings on concentration of ownership in news media.* 19th Cong., 1st &2nd sess., part 5. March 13-14, April 9.

U.S. Senate. Committee on the Judiciary. Subcommittee on Antitrust and Monopoly. 1968a. *The Failing Newspaper Act.* 19th Cong., 1st sess., part 1. S.1213. Washington: DC: Government Printing Office.

U.S. Senate. Committee on the Judiciary. Subcommittee on Antitrust and Monopoly. 1968b. *The Failing Newspaper Act.* 19th Cong., 2nd Sess., part 6. S.1213. Washington, DC: Government Printing Office.

"Where do we stand?" 1967. *Los Angeles Newspaper Guild. Bulletin,* August 23, 1.

Williams, Raymond. 1989. *Resources of Hope.* London: Verso.

CHAPTER 11

THE REPORTERS' REBELLION

THE *CHICAGO JOURNALISM REVIEW* 1968-1975

Steve Macek

I N THE WAKE OF THE UNPROVOKED POLICE VIOLENCE that greeted demonstrators during the tumultuous 1968 Democratic National Convention in Chicago, a group of young reporters—many of whom had been beaten or arrested while covering the action and all of whom were upset by the anti-protestor slant of their own papers—created a magazine called the *Chicago Journalism Review*. Its aim was to "report on the news media and open up their internal processes to public scrutiny" (Dorfman 1978, 189) and, in particular, to call attention to the distortions and errors in the Chicago media's convention coverage. It was, in many ways, the first publication of its kind in the U.S.: a journalism review with a local focus, published not by academics (like the *Columbia Journalism Review*) but by members of the working press, and devoted to honestly examining the constraints imposed on journalists by the corporate structure and conservative management of the media organizations that employed them. And while CJR—as its supporters called it—started out as a reaction against the Chicago news media's knee-jerk support of the crackdown on dissent during the '68 convention, it quickly developed a broader purpose: critiquing biased media representations of the New Left, the Black Panthers, and the women's movement; printing stories intended for publication in mainstream papers that had been spiked by timid or ideologically reactionary editors; and at the same time championing the idea of "reporter power" and "newsroom democracy."

At a time when commercial magazines in the Chicago market found it difficult to stay afloat for even a year, the noncommercial, nonprofit CJR enjoyed a 7-year run. Moreover, the magazine exercised an influence far beyond that indicated by its modest peak circulation of 10,000. Media critic and onetime CJR editor, Michael Miner, now of the *Chicago Reader*, credits the review with nudging the once staunchly right-wing *Chicago Tribune* in the direction of more balanced, honest, less ideologically-driven reporting (Miner 2004). Indeed, it's a testament to the review's importance that by the early 70s it had spawned some two dozen imitators around the country, from the high profile *MORE* out of New York to less well known publications like the *Hawaii Journalism Review* and Denver's *The Unsatisfied Man* (see Granitsas, 1970). But the case of the *Chicago Journalism Review* is worth studying for at least two other reasons: first, because it highlights an all but forgotten antecedent and progenitor of the current media reform movement; and second, because CJR, and the journalism review movement it helped inspire, represent one possible response to the dilemmas journalists committed to social justice face as workers in hierarchical, profit-driven, corporate media institutions.

In this chapter, I first sketch out the circumstances surrounding the founding of the *Chicago Journalism Review*, focusing specifically on the impact of the police riots at the 1968 Democratic National Convention on the young, progressive-minded reporters assigned to cover it. Then, I explore CJR's wide-ranging and often groundbreaking criticism of the local press, analyze its relationship to the New Left and the other social movements of the 1960s, and examine its role in promoting the notion of "reporter power." I conclude by briefly discussing why the experience of the review is still relevant today.

CHICAGO 1968

Chicago in the late 1960s was a city marked by civic strife, racial tension, and sharp political divisions. In 1967, Dr. Martin Luther King had arrived in town to coordinate a drive to integrate the city's all white neighborhoods and was greeted with such vitriolic hostility that he quipped that "the people of Mississippi ought to come to Chicago to learn how to hate" (Biles 1995, 128). When King was assassinated on April 4, 1968, destructive rioting broke out on the city's predominantly black West Side and Chicago's law and order mayor Richard J. Daley famously demanded that the police "shoot to kill any arsonist...and shoot to maim or cripple anyone looting" (Farber 1988, 94). Meanwhile, President Lyndon B. Johnson's unpopular and costly war in Vietnam had swelled the ranks of a vibrant local anti-war movement led by Students for a Democratic Society and the Chicago Peace Council. Throughout 1967 and '68, activists associated with these groups were repeatedly hassled by the Chicago Police Department and one peace march through the Loop in the spring of 1968 had degenerated into a brawl with truncheon-wielding cops (ibid. 151-152). Thus, when anti-war and New Left leaders around the country announced plans to stage massive demonstrations to protest U.S. involvement in Vietnam outside the Democratic National Convention—scheduled to take place in the city in late August 1968—observers on all sides expected trouble.

The leaders of the main national umbrella organization behind the proposed demonstrations, the National Mobilization to End the War in Vietnam (aka "the Mobe"), expected to attract as many as 100,000 protestors to Chicago for the demonstrations (Walker 1968, 21). Throughout the summer, Mobe officials negotiated unsuccessfully with the mayor's office to obtain permits for a rally in Grant Park and a parade to the International Amphitheater where the convention was to be held. In the end, a last minute Mobe lawsuit failed, ensuring that most of the marches and events they were organizing would be illegal in the city's eyes (Farber 1988, 113). Exacerbating an already tense situation, the Yippies—a small, theatrically-minded group of radicals led by veteran New Left organizers Abbie Hoffman and Jerry Rubin—announced that they were organizing a "Festival of Life" in Lincoln Park to counteract the Democrats' "Convention of Death." It would feature nonstop rock music, free food, poetry, dancing in the streets, illicit drugs and public nudity. "We demand the politics of ecstasy," proclaimed the Yippie manifesto. "We will create our own reality, we are Free America. And we will not accept the false theater of the Death Convention" (Farber 1988, 17).

Mayor Daley—who had worked hard to bring the Democratic National Convention to Chicago for the first time since 1956—was not about to allow a pack of "miscreants" and "Reds" ruin his party. To meet the threat posed by the Yippies and by the Mobe's promised legions of demonstrators, he arranged to supplement his 12,000 member police force with 5,000 Illinois National Guardsmen, 6,000 riot-trained federal troops, a sizable contingent of secret service agents and hundreds of state and county police (Biles 1995, 152). The Chicago Police Department's in-house anti-subversive unit, the Red Squad, planted undercover operatives in several local anti-war groups to keep tabs on their convention plans (Farber 1988, 149). The convention site itself, the International Amphitheater, was turned into a fortress: "Encircled by a seven-foot-tall barbed-wire fence, the aged structure contained virtually every piece of sophisticated security equipment available. Bulletproof panels enclosed the building's main entrance; fifteen hundred patrolmen occupied the *cordon sanitaire* surrounding the edifice; policemen with rifles positioned themselves on the roofs of adjacent buildings; helicopters swooped and dived overhead" (Biles 1995, 155). Such draconian security measures scared away many potential demonstrators. By the start of convention week, only 5,000 protestors had made their way to the city and their numbers never grew higher than 15,000 for even the largest marches (Schultz 1998, 285).

In the end, of course, the events that unfolded on the streets of Chicago during the 1968 DNC turned out to be more savage and bloody than even the most pessimistic commentators had feared. The entire week of the convention was marked by escalating clashes between police and protestors during which several police officers committed what an official inquiry into the confrontations labeled "violent acts far in excess of the requisite force for crowd dispersal or arrest" (Walker 1968, 5). On Sunday, August 25, some 400 officers dispersed hundreds of demonstrators gathered in Lincoln Park using tear gas and batons, injuring several (Schultz 1998, 68-92). The following two nights, gangs of police in riot gear repeatedly attacked demonstrators and bystanders in Lincoln Park, often removing their badges beforehand so as to avoid identification (Farber 1988, 186-187). The spiraling violence culminated in a pitched battle in front of the Conrad Hilton hotel on the night of Wednesday, August 28, during which club-wielding cops pushed 20 or so demonstrators through the plate glass windows of the Haymarket bar and sent dozens of people to the hospital (Walker 1968, 215-282). Much to the chagrin of Democratic Party officials, the TV networks intercut scenes of the carnage at the Conrad Hilton with their coverage of final convention balloting for the party's presidential nominee. The following day several marches organized by mainstream peace groups futilely attempted to reach the Amphitheater; by the time they gave up, hundreds of marchers had been gassed and dozens more arrested (ibid. 204). All told, 668 people were arrested (Walker 357) and more than a thousand protestors and 192 police were injured in the convention week mayhem.

Observers found the brutality of the police assault on members of the press covering the protests particularly outrageous. According to the official inquiry into the convention violence, at least forty-nine reporters were beaten or arrested in the course of the convention, although the real figure was likely much higher (Walker 1968, 330). Moreover, this was not merely a case of a few unfortunate journalists accidentally being swept up in the general melee. The evidence reviewed by the official investigation indicated that members of the press had been "singled out for assault and their equipment deliberately damaged" (ibid. 1). Thus, on Monday the 26th, a *Newsweek* photographer was taking pictures of demonstrators being chased near Lincoln park by a line of police when he heard the cops yell "Get the cameras" and "Beat the press" immediately before they began striking him on the arms and shoulders with their batons (ibid. 311). CBS cameraman Delos Hall was clubbed over the head by an officer and sustained a deep cut to his scalp while attempting to tape the action (ibid. 312). Predictably, the heads of TV networks, newspapers and news magazines vigorously protested the rough treatment of their personnel, lodging complaints with both the mayor's office and the Convention organizers (ibid.). On Tuesday the 27th, the *Chicago Sun-Times* and the *Chicago Daily News* both carried stories about the cops' vicious attack on the city's "newsmen." On Wednesday morning, Chet Huntley told the audience for his national NBC radio broadcast that the Chicago police were "going out of their way to injure newsmen and prevent them from filming or gathering information" and declared that "[t]he news profession in this city is now under assault by the Chicago police" (ibid. 322).

Mayor Daley and his supporters responded to such condemnations by assailing the media for its "distorted and twisted" accounts of the convention violence (ibid. 329). They charged that television in particular had allowed itself to become a willing "tool" of "groups of terrorists" (ibid. 329). "The television industry," Daley told NBC news on August 29, "is part of the violence and creating it all over the country" (Farber 1988, 252). The official spokesperson for the Chicago police department, Frank Sullivan, claimed that the protestors were "bent on the destruction of the United States. They are a pitiful handful. They have almost no support. But, by golly, they get the cooperation of the news media. They are built into something really big" (Walker 1968, 327). Convention coordinator John Meek denounced criticism of the

convention as "unfair and unwarranted" and blamed "incomplete reporting by television newsmen as the major source and cause of the
criticism" (Smith 1968, 12).

THE FOUNDING OF THE
CHICAGO JOURNALISM REVIEW

During the convention, the city's newspapers dutifully reported the
atrocities being perpetrated by Daley's police. But shortly after the riots subsided and the national TV networks and newsmagazines had
left town, they rapidly changed their tune. As soon as the delegates
departed, the editors of the city's four major dailies began selectively rewriting the history of what had happened and retrospectively
blamed the protestors for the bulk of the violence. For instance, the
Daily News, at the time the highest circulation afternoon paper in the
city, gave prominent coverage to the mayor's interpretation of the convention disturbances. On September 6, the paper ran the full transcript of a long, self-serving interview Daley did with Walter Cronkite
on CBS on the front page under the headline "Mayor Daley's Side
of Riots Story" ("Mayor Daley's Side" 1968, 1). The following day it
carried a front page story on the city's hastily produced "white paper"
on the DNC violence, "The Strategy of Confrontation," which pinned
exclusive responsibility for the disorders on out of town "revolutionaries" and lauded police for their moderation (O'Conner 1968, 1); it
also published extensive excerpts from the report itself, including a
series of unflattering "biographical sketches" of demonstration leaders Tom Hayden, David Dellinger and Abbie Hoffman that framed
them as Communist trouble makers with "disregard for orderly processes of dissent" ("Who are the radicals?" 1968, 16). A week later, the
city's one-sided hour-long "documentary" about the convention week
riots, "What Trees Do They Plant?," was broadcast on WGN-TV and
over a hundred other TV stations nationwide. The *Daily News* gave
it lavish front page coverage and breathlessly repeated its charge that
the radicals responsible for the upheaval in Chicago had threatened
to "create further disorders around the nation" ("U.S. sees city's side"
1968, 1).

Meanwhile, the market's top morning paper, the *Chicago Tribune*,
ran one article or editorial after another singing the praises of the Chicago Police Department and demonizing the convention protestors.

"Citizens who are wasting sympathy on youthful revolutionaries had better start understanding them," it lectured readers. "These agitators aren't fooling. Their blueprint calls for provocation, violence and the collapse of established order" ("Chicago was just a warmup", Sept. 3, 1968, 16). It also used its news columns to publicize the city's self-serving explanation of the convention debacle. Thus, on September 7, it printed the full text of "The Strategy of Confrontation" beginning on page 3 and "turned over two-thirds of page one to the beginning of its news story" (Diamond 1968, 15). And it hailed Daley's propaganda film, "What Trees Do They Plant?" as "a great achievement" (Schreiber 1968, 4).

Rank and file reporters reacted to this backtracking and revisionism with understandable indignation. Shortly after the convention, some thirty-five reporters from every news outlet in the city gathered in a room above Riccardo's bar on Rush Street to discuss how best to respond (Dorfman 2004). After two additional meetings—and after ruling out a protest, a sit-in and a press conference—they settled on the idea of putting out a local journalism review. The group also decided to create a new professional organization, dubbed the Association of the Working Press, to cut across the lines of existing media unions and professional organizations. Due to lack of interest, the Association dissolved within a few months but the *Chicago Journalism Review* lived on. An editorial board was appointed that included representatives from each of the four major daily papers as well as WCFL, Chicago's labor owned radio station. As the editors explained in the first issue, CJR aimed to provide a "continuing critique of media coverage in the city" and to "explore problems created by official news management and by the newsgathering system that now exists."[1] Furthermore, they resolved to raise "professional consciousness" among other working journalists and "to provide pressure from below for change." As longtime editor Ron Dorfman explained in the magazine's 5th anniversary issue, the founders intended the magazine to be a forum "where we could tell stories that couldn't be told in the establishment press and where we could tell non-journalists something about how media institutions operate."

Most of the reporters who became the organizers and writers of the *Chicago Journalism Review* were young and relatively unknown at

---

1   Unless otherwise noted, all direct quotations are taken from the pages of *The Chicago Journalism Review*.

the time (though among their ranks were a few who would eventually become famous like movie critic Roger Ebert and Pulitzer Prize-winning urban affairs reporter Lois Wille). Indeed, for this reason, CJR's detractors tended to dismiss it as little more than "a safety value for one college generation afflicted with extraordinary irritability and impatience, and an ideological vogue" (Hill 1971, 60). Yet a handful of respected older figures like radio host and raconteur Studs Terkel, *Daily News* columnist Mike Royko, and editorial cartoonist Bill Mauldin also lent the enterprise moral and financial support. Virtually all of the contributors were broadly sympathetic to what was at the time called "The Movement" and many had been active in civil rights activism or campus political struggles in college; "most of the people involved with CJR were very sympathetic to the counterculture movement" notes founding contributor Dan Rottenberg, "and many of them were involved in it" (Rottenberg 2008). For instance, Dorfman, who was either editor or managing editor for much of CJR's existence, had gone from participating in various civil rights demonstrations as a student to covering King's Chicago marches for the *Chicago American* (Dorfman 2004). Henry De Zutter, the review's editor for the first two years, was an education reporter for the *Daily News* with a background in the New Left (De Zutter 2008). Some CJR writers, like Michael Miner, lacked activist pasts but "felt like history was being made" all around them and wanted to "find a way to participate in the '60s while still being a journalist" (Miner 2004). A significant number of the publication's backers saw it as vehicle for exploring issues that had been raised by the social movements of the 1960s—issues of participatory democracy, racism, sexism, class conflict etc.—within the journalistic field.

The group behind the review decided early on against carrying advertising[2]. As Dorfman explained, the compromises that came with advertising were "the shit we put up with everyday" and the group wanted the magazine to be fearless and uncompromising in its critique of the press (Dorfman 2004). Instead, a couple of wealthy patrons put up the money to print the debut issue and a collection was taken up among friends to cover other expenses (ibid.). The first issue

2 Eventually, financial exigencies forced CJR to take a limited number of classified ads. From April 1972 on, the magazine carried a handful of classifieds per issue, usually advertising for other progressive publications like *The Nation* and *Harper's Magazine*.

was published in October and mailed out free to 1500 people. Its appearance immediately sent ripples though the nation's journalistic establishment. The *New York Times* and *Newsweek* both mentioned its release; a little later, the review was covered in *The Columbia Journalism Review*, *Time* and *The Nation*; CBS even did a story about it on Walter Cronkite's show (see Diamond 1968; Janson, 1968). Many in the press regarded the review as a shocking—but perhaps justified—deviation from the conspiracy of silence that traditionally kept newsroom politics out of the public eye; "[t]here is something distinctly disturbing about newspaper employees in effect snitching on their own bosses in public," observed *Time* magazine, "[y]et the Review can clearly serve a useful purpose in Chicago" ("Reporters" 1968, 71). The free publicity that greeted CJR's launching resulted in subscription requests and inquiries from bookstores and newsstands. And newsstand sales, subscriptions, donations from wealthy benefactors and a grant from the Playboy Foundation allowed the review to grow. Within two years, circulation had reached almost 10,000 and in 1970 the review was able to open its own office with Dorfman as editor and two other paid staffers (Dorfman 2004).

CRITIQUING THE CONVENTION COVERAGE

Understandably, the review's first three issues (October 1968, December 1968, and January 1969) focused almost exclusively on what Don Rose called "the two-faced press coverage of convention brutality" (Rose 1972, 43).

The debut issue skewered the anti-demonstrator slant of the convention coverage in the city's four main dailies, *Chicago's American*, *The Chicago Tribune*, *The Daily News*, and *The Chicago Sun-Times*. It noted, for instance, that the *Sun Times* relegated stories about the repeated police use of tear gas and billy clubs against people camped out in Lincoln Park to its inner pages. It attacked the *Tribune* for labeling all the protestors "hippies" and for claiming that the crowd in front of the Conrad Hilton on Michigan Avenue had intentionally broken the window of the hotel bar when in fact they'd been pushed into it by rampaging police. The magazine also condemned the nominally liberal *Daily News* for dwelling on the demonstrators' alleged "provocation" of the cops without ever mentioning "the steady stream of obscenities from the police."

But considerably worse than the flawed initial coverage, the editors of the review argued, was the way the papers' follow-up stories rewrote and distorted what had actually happened on the streets of Chicago in the last week of August. In the week after the convention, *The Chicago American* ran a front page interview with Police Superintendent James Conlisk that—according to CJR sources—had actually been edited by Conlisk and Police Department PR man Frank Sullivan. And the review naturally took *The Daily News* and other papers to task for publishing the mayor's self-serving "white paper" on the convention violence "without comment or correction," despite its numerous serious factual inaccuracies.

Subsequent issues of CJR closely followed the National Commission on Violence's special investigation into the convention disorders, especially its inquiry into police attacks on journalists. Daniel Walker, general council for Montgomery Ward and head of the Commission's Chicago staff, asked the city's newspaper publishers for copies of articles and photographs about the convention and solicited written statements from reporters who had witnessed the street clashes. Yet, not all of the city's news outlets cooperated. As Frank Joseph documented in his front page article in the December 1968 CJR, Larry Mulay, the general manager of the City News Bureau—a local news service reporting on the police and city hall that served all four major dailies—censored his reporters' statements to the commission. Mulay demanded that all City News writers submit their statements for the commission directly to him and then redacted the statements in a way that minimized police violence and cast the demonstrators in the worst possible light. As a sidebar, CJR ran the full text of a memo from Mulay to his night city editor ordering him not to cover press conferences called by anti-war activists who were referred to as "yippes, hippies and all other rabble."

After the Walker Report was finally released, the January 1969 CJR featured a long article by Christopher Chandler of the *Sun Times* that lauded the facts collected during the investigation, but took issue with the report's conclusions, which linked the convention violence to a few rogue cops instead of to the upper echelons of the Daley administration. As he put it, "the Walker Report at times seems inspired by the curious brand of upper middle class morality that always contrives to blame society's ills on the character failings of the lower classes—in this case, the overworked, underpaid, propaganda-inflamed, badly directed Chicago cop." Chandler also pointed out that the Walker report credulously accepted the notion perpetrated by Daley that the city was "under the threat of a fearsome attack" by demonstrators. The same issue carried a critical analysis of *Chicago Tribune* coverage of the Report that, CJR claimed, "was a joke to most working newsmen and most people with heads. It seemed to proclaim so loudly that 'the world is really flat' that even some Tribsmen are laughing off the sad spectacle." In particular, the article highlighted the *Tribune's* misuse of Walker Report statistics to portray the convention riots as "the work of outside agitators" and to make it seem as if more police than peace marchers had been injured in the fighting.

MEDIA CRITICISM IN SERVICE OF "THE MOVEMENT"

While the first few issues of CJR were devoted to combating the hegemony of Daley's convention narrative in the local press, the magazine soon embraced more ambitious aims. Central among them was challenging the media's unthinking support for the political status quo being contested by the radical social movements of the late '60s (Dorfman 2004). Throughout its seven-year existence, the magazine dissected and debunked mainstream reporting on anti-war activism, the New Left, the Black Panthers and the women's movement. It also regularly published stories of concern to radicals that had been ignored or glossed over by the commercial daily newspapers and broadcast news outlets.

For instance, long before Todd Gitlin published *The Whole World is Watching* (1980)—his now famous study of the New Left's complex relationship with the media—CJR had already articulated the basic argument advanced in Gitlin's book: namely, that media representations of SDS, and the anti-war movement more generally, fixated on the bravado, unconventional attire and nonconformist behavior of some of the movement's participants while ignoring their substantive claims and reasoned criticisms of U.S. military involvement in Southeast Asia. For example, in an analysis of the sensationalistic coverage of the Weathermen's window smashing rampage through Chicago's Gold Coast during their October 1969 "Days of Rage," Henry De Zutter pointed out that the city's papers avoided "the basic neglected topic: ...why are the Weathermen running in the streets?" The press, he argued, had failed to ask "why are some of the children from the suburbs and the universities tearing up the cities at this moment in history? Why would grown men and women do such things?" Though De Zutter was hardly sympathetic to the Weathermen's militant posturing, he objected that the "lurid treatment" given their exploits left readers with a decontextualized image of the Weathermen as savage "New Left demons" and no real understanding of why they resorted to such extreme tactics. A September 1970 essay surveying the national media's reporting on three large rallies in support of imprisoned Black Panther leader Bobby Seale found a similar pattern: "As soon as trouble broke out, no matter how minor, the rhetoric or political significance of the gathering was displaced, and the story of the rally became a story of confrontation."

Perhaps more significant for local New Left activists than CJR's critique of the media's sensationalized coverage of demonstrations was the magazine's willingness to scrutinize the activities of the Chicago Police Department's Anti-Subversive Unit, the so-called Red Squad, at a time when most major news outlets in town either ignored the unit's existence or actively colluded with them. The February 1969 edition of the magazine was given over almost entirely to a 5000-word exposé about the Red Squad co-authored by Lois Wille and the review editors. Among other things, the story revealed that the police were covertly spying on black alderman Sammy Rayner and other black politicians critical of the Daley regime. And it documented that Students for a Democratic Society, Citizens for a Democratic Society, and the Medical Committee on Human Rights had been infiltrated by Red Squad spies and agent provocateurs. According to the exposé, one Red Squad operative posing as a "tough talking merchant seaman" told "a living-room full of gray-haired members of the Citizens for a Democratic Society that they had to 'meet violence with violence.'" At another CDS meeting, "two of the eight participants were Red Squadders." The article also detailed Red Squad break-ins at the offices of Chicago area peace groups and at the temporary offices of the National Conference for New Politics when the organization met in the Palmer House in 1967.

One reason CJR was so concerned about the Red Squad is that its operatives routinely posed as reporters in order to gather information on political dissidents. "One Red Squadder, Joe Hall, carries U.P.I. Credentials," Wille's 1969 article explained, "Police have easy access to credentials in Chicago, since local media rely on press cards issued by the police." An update on the Red Squad story printed in the January

1971 issue of CJR reported on two agents of the Illinois Bureau of Investigation who monitored a peace rally at Northern Illinois University (in Dekalb) disguised as TV news cameramen for the nonexistent cable station WJJO-TV.

Beyond exposing the disturbing frequency with which police spies in Chicago tried to pass as journalists, CJR highlighted the fact that friendly relationships between "anti-subversive" agents and the local media had kept domestic surveillance of peaceful activists out of the news. In early 1971, the mainstream press broke the story that Army intelligence agents—often in cooperation with members of the Red Squad—had spied on hundreds of civilians in Illinois. Following up on the explosive revelations, David Anderson's April 1971 story in CJR, "The press and the spies", demonstrated that "the *Chicago Tribune*, for one, has had detailed information on the operations of the Evanston-based 113th Military Intelligence Group for a number of years—but instead of publishing its information...the *Tribune* used the 113th as a source of information." *Tribune* reporter Ron Koziol admitted to CJR that he'd known about the Army's spying activities but never wrote about them because "no one ever asked me to." As a result of CJR's ongoing investigation of the Red Squad and its relationship with the press, high ranking officers in the Chicago Police Department were ordered not to speak with anyone associated with the magazine (Dorfman 2004).

In late 1960s Chicago, the only group the media disdained more than the hippies and the student radicals were the Black Panthers, who had been alarming authorities and recruiting substantial numbers of the city's African American youth since first bursting on the scene in 1968. As with its critique of coverage of the New Left and the anti-war movement, CJR frequently took the local press to task for ignoring the substance of the Panthers' politics and laudable community organizing efforts and focusing instead on their macho, gun-toting image. But the *Chicago Journalism Review* played an even more crucial role in documenting the factual omissions and errors that marred the mainstream media's reporting on one notorious event involving the Panthers: the police raid that resulted in the death of charismatic Panther leader Fred Hampton.

Early on the morning of December 4, 1969, a group of fourteen police officers descended on a West Monroe apartment inhabited by several members of the Chicago Black Panthers party. Gunfire ensued.

When the gunfire died down, Fred Hampton and another occupant of the apartment were dead. The police claimed they were attempting to serve a warrant so they could search for illegal weapons when the Panthers fired on them and their story was backed by Cook Country State's Attorney Edward Hanrahan (for a complete chronology of the raid and its aftermath, see Haas 2010). Yet, as African American politicians, the Panthers and reporters associated with CJR probed the official story about the raid, it began to unravel: eyewitnesses said police fired on the Panthers first, the bullet holes in the apartment indicated that the shots had come from outside, and an independent autopsy showed Hampton was shot from above, in his bed, while lying down—consistent with the theory that he was still asleep when he was killed (see Haas 2010, 89-108).

Within days of the shooting, core members of CJR set to work on a special report about the incident and about the media's role in the cover up. Chris Chandler wrote a story summing up all the evidence contradicting the Hanrahan version of events. Dan Rottenberg did a piece on the misleading photographs from the Black Panther apartment run by the *Chicago Tribune*. Another article reported that a *Sun-Times* reporter quit "when editors buried his story—the first report that the location of the bullet holes did not square with the police version of the raid." The special issue also included a profile of Hampton and a chronicle of Hanrahan's previous efforts to target the Panthers. Rounding out the issue was Bill Mauldin's powerful cover illustration of bullets carving a swastika through an apartment door. According to Dorfman, the Hampton issue sold more copies than any other issue in the magazine's history (Dorfman 2004).

Even after its special report, CJR continued to monitor the Chicago press' handling of the official inquiry into the Panther raid and the ensuing court cases. The March 1970 issue probed State's Attorney Hanrahan's suspect prosecution of other political cases and described the extensive public relations operations run out of his office. The July 1970 CJR featured a meticulous analysis of the initial grand jury report on the Panther raid, including extended comments from two law professors and a rundown of several important questions that "were not asked" written by Francis Ward. When the grand jury voted to indict Hanrahan for obstruction of justice and to name Police Superintendent James Conslick as an unindicted co-conspirator, CJR again provided a comprehensive account, including a lengthy examination

by Dorfman of the "crucial role" played by the media "in both illumi-
nating and obscuring the circumstances surrounding the death of
Fred Hampton and its aftermath."

CJR AND WOMEN'S LIBERATION

Like other "Movement" affiliated periodicals, the *Chicago Journalism
Review* was deeply affected by the "gender revolution" of the late 1960s
and early '70s. Chicago in this period had become a center of radical
feminist organizing; groups like the Chicago chapter of the National
Organization of Women, the socialist-feminist Chicago Women Liberation Union and the National Black Feminist Organization conducted consciousness raising sessions, advocated for abortion rights
and decent childcare, sued the city for sex discrimination in employment and engaged in direct action to combat gender oppression (see
Strobel 1995). Inspired by this explosion of activism, the women involved in CJR used its columns to attack the persistent sexism of the
local media establishment.

Gender discrimination in hiring and promotion at the city's various news outlets was one of CJR's recurring concerns. A piece in the
March 1969 issue by *Daily News* reporter Diane Monk demonstrated
that women were dramatically underrepresented as newsroom employees at the city's main dailies—for instance, holding less than eight
percent of the jobs at the *Sun-Times*—even though they constituted
nearly half of all graduates of Illinois' journalism schools. She also observed that "there isn't one woman managing editor, city editor, assistant city editor or staff photographer at any of the four major Chicago
newspapers." Two years later, CJR produced an entire special issue
on "Women and the Media" that exhaustively explored employment
discrimination and working conditions for women in the Chicago
media. The lead article updated Monk's 1969 report and concluded
that, despite modest improvements, women in Chicago's newsrooms
were "still begging crumbs." A photo spread at the center of the issue
entitled "The many uses of women journalists" documented the city
papers' tendency to run demeaning or highly sexualized pictures of
their female staffers. Also included in the special issue was a surprising piece of self-criticism: a pointed essay by Pat Badertscher, CJR's
office administrator, lamenting the sexism she'd had to cope with from
the review's own male editors who expected her to make their cof-
fee and mend their clothes. And the August 1972 CJR carried a two

page-long story about *Chicago Tribune* reporter and sometimes-CJR contributor Terri Schultz's decision to quit the paper and sue for sex discrimination after being repeatedly passed over for assignments and promotions.

The review also regularly dissected the local news media's hostile treatment of the women's liberation movement in the city and around the country. One article in the 1971 special issue underscored the Chicago press' preoccupation with the mythic figure of the "bra burning feminist," which turned up in news articles and columns about everything from young women at college to the YWCA. As author Joanna Martin explained, the trivialization of feminist concerns evident in what she called "the bra business" was typical of the way local media "report minor actions of the movement—such as integrating men's grills—as though they were the major thrust" while ignoring weightier issues like employment discrimination, affordable child care and reproductive rights.

Perhaps even more significantly, a March 1972 article by Joanne Galka criticized the Chicago papers' practice of segregating want ads by gender, an arrangement which she charged typically gives men "first choice at positions of leadership while women have a multitude of choices among flunky jobs." Galka argued that full-time want ads for high paying professional and sales jobs were typical listed in the male section and that for a number of lower paying jobs the same ad was run in both the male and female sections, a redundancy that financially benefited the newspaper "which [got] two or three ads instead of one." The review's attention to the inefficiency and injustice of gender-specific want ads—together with pressure from the local chapter of NOW—eventually persuaded the four major dailies to drop the practice.

THE FIGHT AGAINST COMMERCIAL CENSORSHIP
AND MEDIA CONSOLIDATION

Though the bulk of CJR's criticism centered on the media's blinkered coverage of the New Left, the Panthers and the women's movement, the review also tried to draw attention to what some of its writers called "commercial censorship," the suppression of news stories motivated not by political ideology but to protect the financial interests of media owners or advertisers. The magazine recognized that, as David

Deitch put it in a 1973 piece entitled "The political economy of American newspapers", "newspapers are a mass production industry, no different, say, than the automobile industry," and that "the newspaper business, like the auto business, requires workers who do as they are told." Deitch went on to suggest that, like the auto worker, the news worker in the corporate news organization has "nothing to say about the final product that comes off the assembly line" and emphasized that the average reporter "in fact regularly suffers from management censorship in a variety of forms when it suits their purposes." Over the years, CJR carefully assembled evidence of such censorship and ran a number of articles that had been spiked by editors because they threatened the interests of newspaper owners, executives, or advertisers.

Perhaps the most explosive such story was a November 1969 piece by Christopher Chandler of the *Sun Times* that examined the questionable city land dealings of Charles Swibel, head of the Chicago Housing Authority. Swibel was a close friend of Mayor Daley and of Emmet Dedmon, the vice president of Field Enterprises, publisher of both the *Sun Times* and the *Daily News*. After Chandler endured a series of conferences with Baily K. Howard, president of the news paper division of Field Enterprises, Dedman, the *Sun Times* editor, and a team of libel lawyers, the story was killed, briefly resurrected and then killed again for good. Chandler quit the paper and published his story in the *Chicago Journalism Review* along with a blow by blow account of how it was suppressed. "There is a structural problem at the *Sun-Times* and probably at many other papers," wrote Chandler. "Increasingly, important decisions are made above the level of editor. The Field papers have a publisher, a president, and four vice presidents who are to varying degrees involved in editorial policy."

When Chandler a few months later wrote a story for CJR about Field's Bailey Howard allegedly stifling "an investigation into the Illinois insurance rackets because it displeased his friends," the piece nearly cost a fellow review contributor his job. Henry De Zutter, who worked for the Field afternoon paper the *Daily News*, appeared on the magazine's masthead as senior editor and after Chandler's piece on Howard he was given an ultimatum by Field management: "Either De Zutter's name would disappear from the masthead of the CJR or he would be reassigned to a position less sensitive than the education/radicals beat, like maybe writing obituaries or reading race track copy." In response, the executive board of the Chicago Newspaper Guild held a special meeting to plan De Zutter's defense while petitions supporting him circulated through the city's newsrooms; in the end, De Zutter kept his job at the *Daily News* and his name remained on the CJR masthead as a member of a newly created "editorial board."

While CJR delighted in blowing the whistle on owner and publisher tampering with editorial content, it also worked to raise awareness about the nefarious influence of big advertisers on the news. For example, the June 1970 issue carried an article by Ken Pierce that questioned the Chicago dailies' avoidance of bad news about the supermarkets who purchased millions of line of advertising in their pages each year. Similarly, the December 1973 CJR featured a Dorfman piece about how *The Daily News* omitted names of specific supermarkets from a story about contaminated hamburger because "they were afraid of losing advertisers."

Already by the late 1960s, ownership of the city's dominant media, as in the rest of the country, was becoming increasingly concentrated in the hands of a few very large multimedia conglomerates, with predictably dire consequences for the quality of their journalism and the diversity of viewpoints they presented to the public. CJR examined this trend on more than one occasion. For instance, the centerpiece of the December 1971 issue was a breakdown of the ownership of the city's media written by Duane Lindstrom, former executive director of Illinois Citizen's Broadcast Committee. Lindstrom's article demonstrated that a single corporation—the Tribune Co.—at the time controlled two of the city's main newspapers, one TV station, and one radio station that combined commanded 46 percent of the total ad revenues pulled in by all Chicago media. Even more sobering, it revealed that the Tribune together with Field Enterprises and the big three broadcast networks controlled some 92 percent of the "Chicago's marketplace of ideas." As Lindstrom remarked, "the way the major media of Chicago have wrapped up the city makes Mayor Daley's patronage army look like a Sunday school class." What made this especially alarming, he argued, is that the facts rehearsed in the article constituted "material the mass media for the most part have taken great pains to say nothing about."

VOICE IN THE PRODUCT

It would be a mistake, however, to see the CJR as merely finding fault with the Chicago increasingly oligarchic media institutions and the shoddy journalism they produced. What distinguished the magazine from less radical sources of media criticism such as the *Columbia Journalism Review* or *Editor and Publisher* was that it had a positive, profoundly democratic vision of how news organizations should operate that it offered as an alternative to what it saw as a bankrupt status quo. Throughout its existence, the *Chicago Journalism Review* promoted the cause of "reporter power" or, as the magazine sometimes called it, "voice in the product," the notion that most important decisions governing the gathering, selection, editing, and dissemination of news should be made by working reporters. The argument for such an arrangement, as Ron Dorfman put it, was that "the press could not be truly free until journalists had some protection from corporate power as well as from state power" (Dorfman 1978, 190). In a January 1972 editorial, Dorfman declared that insurgent reporters want "not simply the right to chant a different cotton-chopping rhythm, but a piece of the plantation." From time to time, CJR even dared to envision a "noncapitalist journalism" in which workers collectively owned and operated the news organizations in which they worked.

The immediate inspiration for the "reporter power" movement was the expanded editorial control won by reporters at some of Europe's most powerful newspapers and news magazines, although no doubt the New Left ideal of "participatory democracy" played some role as well (Dorfman 2004). At *Le Figaro* in France editors and reporters had closed down the paper in 1969 in order to preserve their control over important editorial decisions; workers at the West German magazine *Stern* had won veto power over the naming of editors and department heads. The review kept its readers informed about these initiatives and encouraged American reporters to replicate them.

Not only that, but longtime editor Ron Dorfman also proselytized in favor of "reporter power" at Guild meetings, conferences, panel discussions, and journalists' gatherings around the country (Dorfman 2004). In 1972, Dorfman and other review contributors helped to organize a gathering of dissident journalists hosted by the journalism review *More* in New York—The A.J. Liebling Counter-Convention—at which a "Journalist's Declaration of Independence" was drafted in hopes of sparking a larger national movement. Attended by some 2,000 to 3,000 people, the event included a panel on "Democracy in the Newsroom" and was marked by what CJR characterized as a "surprising consensus" about the idea that "journalists—not the owners, not the editors, not the broadcast producers—should have control over what they cover and how they present it." CJR staffers held a special session at the convention to dispense advice about starting a local journalism review (Dorfman 2004).

In Chicago, at least, the CJR's campaign for newsroom democracy enjoyed some support among working journalists and on a couple of occasions groups of rank and file reporters at the city's papers attempted to put the rhetoric of "reporter power" into reality. In March 1971, the Field papers—the *Sun-Times* and *The Daily News*—endorsed Mayor Daley for reelection. Reporters at both papers collected signatures demanding that the papers either endorse Daley's challenger, Richard Friedman, carry no endorsements in the mayor's race or "set aside space on the editorial page for dissenting staff opinion." When the newspapers' owner, Marshal Field V, refused this ultimatum, 174 staffers at both papers—including 85 percent of the daytime staff at the *Daily News*—collected money to buy ads that lambasted Daley's "bossism"; though at first the editors of the Field papers resisted, eventually they gave in and carried the ads. *Daily News* staffer and CJR contributor Lois Wille wrote the ad copy and as usual the review carried a candid account of the entire episode. As Dorfman reported in the January 1972 CJR, emboldened by their partial victory in the endorsement battle, the following year the Chicago Newspaper Guild and staffers at the Field papers pressed for "a significant voice in determining the quality and the editorial direction of their publications" in labor contract negotiations with the *Sun-Times* and the *Daily News*. Among their demands were a third representation on the editorial board, veto power over department heads and the right to exercise a first option to buy if the papers were ever put up for sale. These proposals were quickly set aside once the negotiations began but the very fact that they were raised at all was a symbolic victory for "reporter power" and its backers.

Yet, despite CJR's strenuous advocacy for "voice in the product," the cause of newsroom democracy ultimately failed to gain much of a following nationally (Dorfman 2004; Miner 2004). At the *New York Times*, for instance reporters were "unreceptive"; as Dorfman explained, J. Anthony Lukas, the leader of the "insurgent group at the *Times*" viewed the very idea that journalists should take control of the papers they wrote for as "preposterous" (Dorfman 1978, 190). By 1973, the review itself was debating whether it made more sense for dissident journalists to try to reform existing newspapers or to break away from capitalist media institutions altogether to form "alternative media."

Only a few short years after the A.J. Liebling Counter-Convention, CJR and the journalism review movement was dead. By the mid-70s CJR—never financially stable—was facing dwindling circulation numbers and declining revenues. "The steam went out of the movement," explained Michael Miner, "people became less and less impassioned about it" (Miner 2004). In 1974, Dorfman departed to pursue his own projects and left Leonard Aronson and Miner running the magazine. When Miner got an opportunity to go to Vietnam to cover the end of the war in April of 1975, he also moved on (ibid.). The remaining staffers managed to put out one last issue before the magazine closed down for good.

CONCLUSION: WHY CJR MATTERS

The *Chicago Journalism Review* is not just another colorful episode in Chicago's rich media history, although it certainly is that. Nor is it simply a precursor to the current surge of popular media criticism and commentary, though a case can be made that it is a vital link in an unbroken tradition of radical media criticism that extends back to George Seldes and I.F. Stone. In my view, CJR is significant because it represents a novel response on the part of working journalists to the flaws and contradictions of the capitalist press so thoroughly anatomized in its pages during its seven-year run, one that might well be worth imitating today.

Reporters working for the commercial news media learn very early on the various ways corporate ownership of the media and reliance on advertising shape and limit news coverage. They also learn, as Ben Bagdikian points out, that every newspaper has its collection of politically powerful "friends" whose interests are to be protected and whose failings must be studiously ignored (Bagdikian 2004, 154). And they discover rather quickly that the individual reporter is relatively powerless to change any of this, a cog within the profit-driven media machine, and that disrupting the assembly line—disregarding the suggestions of editors or offending the advertisers, for instance—can get one fired or at the very least bumped to a less desirable beat. Historically, one strategy rank and file reporters have used to overcome their relative powerlessness to shape the news agenda has been to organize labor unions as a countervailing force against the owners and their editors. Columnists like Mike Royko have from time to time developed such large and loyal followings that they could write what they wanted with at least partial impunity. CJR, I think, offers us a glimpse at a third option which to some degree complements the other two: rank and file reporters collectively training a critical light on the institutions in which they work, describing what stories got killed and why, pointing out biases in their papers and newscasts, demanding a "voice in the product" and in the process helping to change the culture (while at the same time striving to change the institutional structure) of the news. At a time when more and more journalists are complaining about the way corporate ownership and bottom line pressures have corrupted the news, perhaps what is needed is a forum in which angry journalists can sound off about their employers and honestly "explore problems created by official news management and by the newsgathering system that now exists." Perhaps what is needed, in other words, is something like the *Chicago Journalism Review.*

REFERENCES

MANUSCRIPT COLLECTIONS

Chicago Journalism Review Records (1968-1975), Chicago History Museum, Research Center, Chicago, IL.

TRADE JOURNALS

Chicago Journalism Review, October 1968–July1975

BOOKS, ARTICLES AND INTERVIEWS

Bagdikian, Ben. 2004. *The New Media Monopoly.* Boston, MA: Beacon Press.

Biles, Roger. 1995. *Richard J. Daley: Politics, Race, and the Governing of Chicago.* Dekalb, IL: Northern Illinois University Press.

"Chicago was just a warmup." 1968. *Chicago Tribune.* September 3.

De Zutter, Henry. 2008. Telephone interview by author. August 14.

Diamond, Edwin. 1968. "Chicago Press: Rebellion and Entrenchment." *Columbia Journalism Review,* Fall, 10-17.

Dorfman, Ron. 1978. "Truth, Justice and the American Way." *Revue Francaise D'Études Américaines* Vol. 3, No. 6: 183-193

Dorfman, Ron. 2004. Interview by author. Chicago, IL. September 6.

Farber, David. 1988. *Chicago '68.* Chicago: University of Chicago Press.

Gitlin, Todd. 1980. *The Whole World Is Watching: Mass Media in the Making and Unmaking of the New Left.* Berkeley and Los Angeles, CA: University of California Press.

Granitsas, Spyridon. 1970. "Counter-media Press picks up Agnew line." *Editor and Publisher,* August 1.

Haas, Jeffrey. 2010. *The Assassination of Fred Hampton: How the FBI and the Chicago Police Murdered a Black Panther.* Chicago: Lawrence Hill Books.

Hill, Norman. 1971. "The Growing Phenomenon of the Journalism Review." *Saturday Review,* September 11, 59-60.

"In Darkest Daleyland." 1968. *Newsweek,* October 28.

Janson, Donald. 1968. "Newsmen Assail Chicago Papers." *The New York Times,* October 13.

"Mayor Daley's side of the riots story." 1968. *Chicago Daily News,* September 6.

Miner, Michael. 2004. Telephone interview by author. September 8.

O'Connor, Philip. 1968. Daley's report: City blames revolutionaries. *Chicago Daily News.* September 7.

Rottenberg, Dan. 1969a. "Chicago Reporters Criticize their Papers, in Writing." *The Wall Street Journal,* February 11

Rottenberg, Dan. 1986. "CJR, RIP." *The Quill,* April, 24-27.

Rottenberg, Dan. 2008. Telephone interview by author. August 13.

Rose, Don. 1972. "New Voices of Newsmen." *The Nation,* January 10, 43-46.

Schreiber, Edward. 1968. "Daley's reply called a great achievement." *Chicago Tribune.* September 13.

Schultz, John. 1998. *No One Was Killed.* Chicago, IL: Big Table Publishing Company.

"Self-Criticism in Chicago." 1969. *Time,* March 21, 71.

Smith, Michael. 1968. "Criticism of Convention Week is Unfair: Meek." *Chicago Tribune.* August 31.

Strobel, Margaret. 1995. "Consciousness and Action: Historical Agency in the Chicago Women's Liberation Union." In *Provoking Agents: Theorizing Gender and Agency.* Ed. Judith Kegan Gardiner, 52–68. Urbana, IL: University of Illinois Press.

"U.S. Sees city's side of disorder." 1968. *Chicago Daily News,* September 16.

Walker, Daniel. 1968. *Rights in Conflict: Convention Week in Chicago, August 25-29, 1968*. New York, NY: Dutton.

Wille, Lois. 1971. "'Our girl at the Daily News.'" *Chicago Journalism Review*, July, 5-6.

"Who are the radicals?" 1968. *Chicago Daily News*, September 7.

CHAPTER 12

OPRAH WINFREY AND THE POLITICS OF RACE IN LATE TWENTIETH CENTURY AMERICA

Janice Peck

SINCE HER DEBUT ON THE NATIONAL SCENE IN 1986, OPRAH WINFREY has been hailed as a public figure unusually adept at bridging the black/white racial divide in American society. Her majority white following (81 percent) has stood as proof of that cross-racial popularity (Mediamark 2003). Early in Winfrey's career a *Newsday* article observed, "Though she makes race an undercurrent of her message, and it is part of her bearing, it does not define her following. She has what the business calls broad appeal" (Firstman 1989). More than a dozen years later, sociologist Eva Illouz declared it "unprecedented in American history" that a black talk show host had become "a model and a guide for mainstream white women" (2003, 228). Winfrey has explained her cross-racial appeal in similarly dramatic terms: "I transcend race, really. I believe I have a higher calling. What I do goes beyond the realm of everyday parameters. I am profoundly effective. I know people really, really, really *love* me, *love* me, *love* me. A bonding of the human spirit takes place" (Adler 1997, 261).

In a nation where the racial "wealth gap" between white and black households increased fourfold between 1984 and 2007 (Shapiro 2010; also Dillahunt et al. 2010, Ford 2010), where racial segregation of housing and schools is an entrenched and worsening problem (Massey 1996 & 2004; Kozol 2005; Adelman & Gocker 2007), and where presidential candidates since the 1960s have capitalized on white hostility to blacks to consolidate electoral support, what does it mean to say that a TV personality has "transcended" race? What is the extent of the social influence of such media figures, and what historical aspirations and anxieties endow the idea of "transcending race" with rhetorical and political power? This chapter seeks to answer those questions by situating Oprah Winfrey's rise to "cultural icon of mainstream [i.e., white] America" (Brown 2002, 242) in the context of a bi-partisan rightward turn in U.S. politics over the last three decades. That political sea change marked the shift from the Keynesian economic model that fueled the post-World War II "long boom," to the "long downturn" that has accompanied the rise of neoliberalism since the late 1970s (Brenner 2006).

A key challenge in studying the media is how to think about the relationship of media, culture, and society. Theorist Raymond Williams advises media historians to search for "the indissoluble connections between material production, political and cultural institutions and activity, and consciousness" (1977, 80). Sociologist C. Wright Mills advocates an approach he terms the "sociological imagination," which allows us "to grasp history and biography and the relations between the two within society" (2000, 6). Applying this holistic perspective, this chapter proposes that placing Oprah Winfrey's journey to fame and fortune—including her "transcendence of race"—in the context of the rise and triumph of the neoliberal political-economic project will provide a deeper understanding of both processes. In addition to tracing the political history of late twentieth-century America, the chapter draws on literary critic Fredric Jameson's (1992) argument that popular cultural texts—such as *The Oprah Winfrey Show*—have complex "relations of repression" with "fundamental social anxieties and concerns" (25). From this perspective, a vital task of cultural texts is managing those concerns by providing symbolic or "imaginary" resolutions to pressing societal problems that resist easy solution in reality (26). In the case examined here, the notion of "transcending race" signals deep-seated concerns about the persistence of racial inequality, the continued black/white divide, and the residual injuries of a national history grounded in slavery. At the same time, it points to powerful desires to be relieved of that troubling historical legacy. In looking at the political-economic context in which Oprah Winfrey became a widely-acclaimed symbol of racial transcendence, the chapter seeks to reveal something about the subterranean anxieties—or the "moments of danger—to which "transcending race" is posed as a solution, and about the utopian longings that endow this notion with its symbolic power.

BUILDING AN UNTHREATENING RACIAL BRIDGE

In February 1987, six months into the first season of her newly syndicated national talk show, Oprah Winfrey traveled to Forsyth County, Georgia—where blacks had been officially banned since 1912—to shoot a live episode at a restaurant in the county seat. Forsyth County had made the headlines in January on the Martin Luther King Jr. holiday when a "brotherhood march" of blacks and whites had been met with "Ku Klux Klan-inspired rock and bottle throwing." A week later, 25,000 predominantly black demonstrators had marched through the county backed up by Georgia state police and National Guardsmen (Brotherhood March 1987; Oprah's Show on Ga. March 1987). In a controversial move, Winfrey decided to ban African Americans from her broadcast, claiming it was to be a forum exclusively for the "beleaguered people" of Forsyth Country so they would feel comfortable speaking openly (Brown 2002, 242). According to biographer George Mair, Winfrey worried that "allowing militant blacks" on the show "would have been disruptive" (1994/1998, 126).

A group of African Americans, including Reverend Hosea Williams, an Atlanta civil rights leader who had organized the previous two marches, picketed outside the restaurant during the live broadcast (Brotherhood March 1987). He and seven other black protestors were arrested for disturbing the peace; meanwhile, inside, Winfrey "quickly cut off several more liberal members of the audience because she feared they might bring retribution down on themselves with their pro-black comments" (ibid.). Afterward, Winfrey said she was "disappointed" Reverend Williams was arrested, but made no apologies for excluding blacks (Black Picket 1987). African-American critics subsequently interpreted her exclusion of blacks and her conciliatory attitude toward Forsyth's white residents as proof Winfrey "was not the liberal civil rights crusader she would like some people to believe" (Mair 1994/1998, 127).

Anyone who has closely examined Winfrey's career, however, would not describe her as a civil rights crusader. From the beginning she distanced herself from the category of "black people who are angry and bitter" (174)—a stance that has been amply documented in interviews, biographies, compilations of Winfrey's thought, and in her talk show, website, magazine, and public appearances. In a 1987 interview with *People Weekly*, for example, Winfrey revealed she "hated" her time at all-black Tennessee State University, where she "did not relate well to the racially militant mood" of fellow students. They "hated and resented me," she said, "because I refused to conform to the militant thinking of the time" (Richman 1987, 56). Winfrey contrasted herself to fellow TSU students who were "into black power and anger," whereas she was "just struggling to be a human being." She also described being ostracized as a child by other black youngsters because she did not speak in dialect and wanted to "excel," and as a high school student, where she was labeled an "oreo" for refusing to work with African-American students organizing votes for a student council. "I thought their candidate wasn't the best qualified," she explained in the interview. Throughout her teenage and college years, Winfrey recounted, "whenever there was an conversation on race, I was on the other side, maybe because I never felt the kind of repression other black people were exposed to." Consequently, she explained, "Race is not an issue. It has never been an issue with me. …Truth is, I've never felt prevented from doing anything because I was either black or a woman" (ibid.).

By asserting that she harbored no racial resentment and had never personally been harmed by racism, while also castigating African Americans who might entertain such sentiments, Winfrey showed herself early on to be a model of racial reassurance for the white audience she hoped to attract (Mair 1994/1998, 174). Adopting a public persona that *People* described as "a comfortable and unthreatening bridge between the white and black cultures" (Richman 1987, 56), the "queen of talk" solidified her relationship with her white following. The value of that relationship is undeniable. By 2010, Winfrey enjoyed a net worth of $2.7 billion (Forbes 400, 2010) and oversaw a media empire that included her talk show, which in 2010 reached 40 million U.S. viewers a week and aired in 145 countries (Oprah Winfrey's Biography 2010); Oprah's Book Club, which made every selection a bestseller (Max 1999); *O: The Oprah Magazine*, widely considered one of the most successful magazine launches in publishing history (Wilson 2001); Oprah.com, with an average 86 million page views and more than 7 million unique visitors per month (Oprah Winfrey's Biography 2011); the multimedia production company, Harpo Entertainment Group; a radio satellite channel; and OWN, cable television channel, jointly owned with Discovery Communications, that launched in January 2011.

The loyalty of Winfrey's largely white following helped reinforce the view from early on that not only had she managed to "transcend race," but that racism itself was being transcended. This idea—that racism was on the verge of being relegated to America's past—found fertile ground in the 1980s as Ronald Reagan and the New Right backlash politics that brought him to office sought to "realign the electorate along racial, rather than class, lines" (Reeves and Campbell 1994, 157; also Macek 2006). That political shift also marked the beginning of what by century's end would be a fundamental redefinition of the "problem of race" in the U.S. based on the idea that "the American race problem no longer consists of White racism, which is steadily declining, but rather of racialism, defined as the misguided tendency of minorities (especially Blacks) to cry racism and/or emphasize their racial identity as a strategy for getting ahead" (Kim 2002, 62). In the emerging new consensus, Claire Kim argues, the perpetrators of America's "race problem" were not the white majority, who was being penalized for long past transgressions, but racial minorities, who were promoting a "'cult of victimization'" to "leverage white guilt" (ibid.). The notion of "transcending race" must be situated within the political-economic context of this redefinition.

REAGANOMICS AND THE POLITICS OF VICTIM-BLAMING

Fueled by bitterness over Supreme Court rulings on school prayer (1962, '63) and abortion (Roe v. Wade 1973), opposition to Lyndon Johnson's Great Society federal programs (e.g., Civil Rights, War on Poverty, etc.), and discomfort with social changes wrought by the 1960s political movements, the New Right emerged as a political force amid a crisis in U.S. capitalism that would bring the end of the post-World War II economic boom. The extended economic growth and stability from 1945 to the early '70s that economist Robert Reich has termed "the Great Prosperity" (2010) was driven by Keynesian policies, including the development of the welfare state as a safeguard against economic crises, a commitment to full employment through government spending, and state regulation of sectors of the economy. The postwar boom began to falter by the late 1960s and early '70s as unemployment and inflation increased together. Confronted with mounting debt from the Vietnam War, competition from the recovered economies of Europe and Japan, and political challenges from Third World national liberation movements, the U.S. began losing its grip on the competitive advantage it had enjoyed for more than two decades. The post-Vietnam shift to a peacetime economy, the 1973 oil crisis, and the global recession in 1973-74 marked the end of the 25-year boom and launched the beginning of the "long downturn" (Brenner 2006).

The end of the boom created divisions and polarization "not only between classes, but *within* classes" (Davis 1986, 178). The New Right's political strategy was to fashion an explanation for the economic downturn that would appeal to middle-class professionals and entrepreneurs, while also exploiting divisions within the working class to siphon off a bloc of Democratic support. That explanation identified three sources of national decline: "big government" excesses (e.g., high taxes, unrestrained spending, overregulation); privileging of "special interests" at the expense of "average" Americans; loss of "traditional values" of hard work, individual initiative and self-sufficiency. Weaving together these elements, New Right leaders and their candidate, Ronald Reagan, crafted a narrative in which hard-working Americans were being victimized by a voracious government that took their money, handed it over to undeserving social groups, and undermined the work ethic by punishing the diligent and rewarding the lazy. The proposed solution lay in reversing this unfairness, restoring economic growth, and reviving appropriate values. The racialization of this narrative—in which people of color were designated "special interests" and "traditional" values were associated with whites—would be central to its ideological and political power.

Joining the emerging Religious Right and coordinating an array of conservative single-issue campaigns—anti-busing, anti-affirmative action, anti-gun control, anti-communism, anti-property taxes—New Right leaders "mobilized widespread support from classical New Deal, blue-collar constituencies, thus demonstrating that social conservatism, racism, and patriotism provided powerful entrees for New Right politics" (Davis 1986, 170; also Wuthnow & Liebman 1983; Peck 1993; Perlstein 2001; George 2008). These forces swept Ronald Reagan into office in 1980 and provided support for a dramatic restructuring of U.S. economic policy, including cutbacks to social programs, increased military expenditures, aggressive deregulation (e.g., airlines, utilities, telecommunications, finance), major tax cuts for corporations and the wealthy, and high interest rates benefiting banks and speculators. Organized under the banner of "Reaganomics," these policies accelerated trends that had started in the late 1970s: the export of jobs in search of cheap labor from the unionized "Frostbelt" to the union-weak "Sunbelt" and to developing nations with low-cost, non-unionized labor and minimal regulation; a shift from relatively high-wage factory work in heavy industry to low-wage service occupations; growing dependence on part-time and temporary employment; and a large-scale movement of women into the workforce to offset declining household incomes. The tensions generated by this climate of scarcity provided a rich medium for backlash politics, in which people of color and the poor could be blamed for the financial hardship and individual and social problems resulting from those same economic policies. As Davis argues, "faced with a genuinely collapsing standard of living in many sectors of the traditional working class," skilled workers and the lower stratum of the white-collar middle class "increasingly visualized themselves … as locked into a desperate zero-sum rivalry with equality-seeking minorities and women" (Davis 1986, 228).

A chief target of the Reagan administration and Republican congressional allies was the nation's cities, which were seen as strongholds of Democratic support and home to a significant proportion of African Americans. A strategy of "permanently shrinking the federal budget" aimed to "deepen the schism between inner-city and suburban Democrats by increasing the competition for scarce revenue sharing" (ibid., 268–269). By the end of Reagan's second term, federal assistance to local governments had been cut by 60 percent, revenue sharing with cities had been eliminated, public service jobs and job training—which, thanks to Civil Rights legislation had provided many blacks entrée into middle-class employment—were drastically reduced, federally-funded legal services for the poor had nearly disappeared, and Community Development block grants and public transit funding had been slashed (Drier 2004; also Macek 2006, 17-35; Paget 1998). Coupled with de-industrialization, the decimation of the urban manufacturing base, middle-class and/or white flight, dwindling property taxes, and the growth of a drug economy in income-starved neighborhoods, black rates of unemployment, poverty, homelessness, school dropouts, incarceration, and addiction rose. This fallout of the political-economic policies of Reaganomics could then be configured rhetorically as evidence of cultural pathology among black Americans, who purportedly had been made dependent and irresponsible by over-indulgent government policies and/or misguided beliefs about their own victimization. This is where the ideological work of Oprah Winfrey's "transcendence of race" becomes important.

THE DESERVING AND THE UNDESERVING

In the inaugural fall of her new national program, Winfrey opened the first episode devoted to the subject of welfare by warning viewers to "hold onto your hats today, because this show is probably going to be pretty hot." Indeed it was, thanks in part to Winfrey's provocative introduction: "You know, welfare has become a way of life for millions of people in this country. We want to know how you feel about able-bodied welfare recipients sitting at home with their feet up, as you trudge off to work to support them with the tax dollars that are taken from your paycheck each week. Does it make you angry? A lot of people are" ("Pros and Cons of Welfare," *Oprah Winfrey Show* Nov. 17, 1986). This framing of the issue echoed Reagan's apocryphal and oft-repeated "welfare queen" anecdote from his 1976 presidential campaign ("Welfare Queen Becomes Issue" 1976), which relied on gender, race and class stereotypes to tap into "the white majority's growing unease with the perceived expansion of the social welfare apparatus" (Gilliam 1999). It was also filtered through the lens of "underclass ideology" promulgated by books such as Ken Auletta's *The Underclass* (1982), Charles Murray's *Losing Ground, American Social Policy 1950 –1980* (1984), and Michael Novak's *The New Consensus of Family and Welfare: A Community of Self-Reliance* (1987). Based on the argument that poverty and dependence are effects of defective cultural attitudes and weak familial values, the "theory of the underclass emerged in the early 1980s with a surprisingly wide spectrum of liberal support—the first sign of changing times," according to Ann Withorn (1996, 501).

Embraced by both conservative and liberal journalists and social scientists, underclass ideology focused on a specific sector of the poor: people living in core urban neighborhoods marked by high rates of poverty, crime, drugs, joblessness, and school dropouts, as well as high rates of female-headed households, teenage pregnancy, out-of-wedlock births, and use of welfare. This supposedly distinctive "underclass" was distinguished from the "ordinary" poor in that it was "depicted as a rootless population that functioned outside mainstream values and institutions, whose dependence and antisocial behavior was transmitted generationally (in homes headed by women) and which was stubbornly resistant to change" (ibid.). Thus, the underclass was seen as "not merely poor, disorganized and marginal, but also deficient and deviant" (502). The portrayal of the underclass was further linked to a second element of the emerging discourse on poverty in the 1980s: that the federal welfare program violated core American values and therefore neither had nor deserved public support.

Both liberal and conservative strains of underclass theory contained implicit racial and gender premises by identifying the underclass with central city neighborhoods and female-headed households. The supposedly self-reproducing nature of the underclass has been laid at the feet of women for failing to instill responsibility and morality in their offspring. Thanks to this "feminization" of the underclass that began under Reagan, Withorn argues, "welfare mothers were discussed in the same breath as drug users, criminals and other antisocial groups" (1996, 502). For example, the image of the "crack mother" pervaded 1980s media portrayals of drug problems in poor urban neighborhoods, becoming a potent symbol in Reaganism's "war on drugs" and contributing to the demonization of poor—especially minority—women (Reeves & Campbell 1994, 207-216; also Macek 2006, 161-164).

Winfrey's "Pros and Cons of Welfare" episode must be viewed within this political context. Panelists on the show included Lawrence Mead, whose underclass ideology tome *Beyond Entitlement* (1986) argued that welfare recipients—even mothers with young children—should be forced to work for their benefits; California State Senator Diane Watson, who compared this "workfare" approach to slavery and was trying to overturn the requirement that welfare recipients work in public service jobs without pay; and welfare recipient and single mother of three, Valencia Dodson. Two things stood out in the episode: the extent of audience and caller involvement (twenty-seven audience members, four callers) and the depth of hostility directed at "welfare mothers" by Mead, Winfrey, the callers and studio audience members. Mead set the tone with his assertion that "welfare mothers are out of step with other mothers who are working today. It is normal for single mothers to work, and if welfare mothers do not work, then they're not part of the United States. They actually are outside of the mainstream." Although Senator Watson argued that forcing welfare recipients to work in public service jobs without pay was not just "punitive," but "loses sight of the reason why welfare, AFDC—aid to families with dependent children—was designed, and that was to provide the necessary support for children," and Valencia Dodson and other AFDC recipients in the audience defended their need for public assistance, which they described as inadequate to begin with, Winfrey's and Mead's introductory remarks paved the way for the ensuing assault. All four callers and sixteen of the twenty-seven audience participants accused welfare recipients of being "lazy."

Winfrey would return to the issue of a parasitic "underclass" as a burden on responsible citizens in subsequent episodes, including "Three Generations of Underclass" (*Oprah Winfrey Show* March 22, 1989) and "Angry Taxpayers/Angry Tenants: Public Housing Controversy" (*Oprah Winfrey Show* June 18, 1991). She opened the first episode as follows: "… we have all heard stories of how being on welfare takes a hold of some families, about two and three generations of mothers and daughters and sons that get stuck in a cycle of poverty that provides little inspiration to the next generation to do better. People who work and pay taxes have a lot of big gripes about those who spend decades and generations on welfare. … today we asked families—mothers who have raised their children on welfare and their daughters who are also raising their children on welfare—why the cycle gets repeated" ("Three Generations"). During the program, Winfrey repeatedly described public aid recipients being stuck in a "cycle of poverty" caused by their "welfare mentality." In the "Public Housing" episode, she cited the "psychological programming" that afflicts residents of government-funded housing: "How do you even pull yourself up when your mother had lived there and her mother had lived there? It's what we now refer to as, you know, the underclass system." Later in the show, when panelist raised the question of the legacy of slavery, Winfrey asserted: "I think a lot of people still use the slavery experience as an excuse."

A key function of underclass ideology is that it shifts "attention away from [the] political-economic production of poverty to the 'pathological' behavior of the poor" (di Leonardo 1999, 59). The idea that the poor could change their circumstances if they simply acknowledged and took responsibility for their own deficiencies has been a recurring theme in *The Oprah Winfrey Show*'s treatment of public assistance, welfare, and poverty because that analysis corresponds with the core message of its host's entire enterprise. *Fortune* writer Patricia Sellers observes that "essence" of the "Oprah brand" can be distilled into a "simple message"—"You are responsible for your own life" (2002, 54). Winfrey's consistent representation of own biography through a Horatio Alger narrative of hard work and self-determination reinforces that message. The power and appeal of that message—as evidenced in Winfrey's ascent to the status of cultural icon—derives in part from its resonance with the political-economic agenda of the Reagan Revolution, with its mantra of "personal responsibility" and strategies of racialization.

As minorities, and especially black Americans, were defined as "special interests," beneficiaries of government largesse at the expense of whites, privy to unfair advantages in a shrinking job market and preferential access to education and training, and a threat to "law and order," the Reagan-era assault on social spending and campaign of privatization and deregulation could be justified by painting welfare recipients and the poor as "the creators of the problem of social order rather than its casualties, as dependents on society rather than claimants from society" (J. Smith 1997, 178). At the same time, the 1980s witnessed the rise of hugely popular black TV stars—Winfrey, Bill Cosby, Arsenio Hall—whose appeal was hailed as proof they "transcend race" ("Television" 1991, 52), and whose success could be framed as an argument against the existence of structural racial discrimination. Jimmie Reeves and Richard Campbell argue that the "right-wing appropriation of the celebrated mainstream media achievements of a handful of prominent African-American 'individuals'" served as evidence to support its claim that any lingering problems of black Americans were the result of cultural or individual pathology (1994, 100; see also Cloud 1996). Indeed, Winfrey regularly framed her life story in these terms.

By denying the existence of institutionalized racism, attributing black failure to lack of initiative or faulty values, and adulating black stars as proof that racial barriers to success had evaporated, the Reagan Revolution tapped historical undercurrents of racism in American culture while absolving whites of implication in that history (see also Jhally & Lewis 1992).). In the process, it "facilitated the upward redistribution of wealth in the 1980s by releasing people in the suburbs from any responsibility for—or identification with—the economic distress in the inner city" (Reeves & Campbell 1994, 157). Recasting poverty as the distinct sphere of "black Americans living in ghettoized neighborhoods" (J. Smith 1997, 179), underclass ideology deflected attention from the general effects of deregulated markets and the redistribution of wealth and turned it into the pathology of a specific segment of the population. Using economic scarcity to drive a wedge between the upper and lower sectors of the working class, between the working class and the poor, between suburbanites and inner-city residents, and between whites and racial minorities, the Reagan Revolution reconfigured class alliances through a "divide-and-conquer/unite-and-mobilize" strategy (Reeves & Campbell 1994, 157).

CLINTON, THE DEMOCRATIC LEADERSHIP COUNCIL AND RACIAL BREACH MANAGEMENT

Reagan wasn't the first president to recognize the political value of the racial divide. Lyndon Johnson famously predicted in the mid-1960s that the passage of the Civil Rights and Voting Acts would ultimately "cost Democrats the south" (Toner 2004). In 1968, Richard Nixon's political strategist, Kevin Phillips, seized the opportunity to weaken the Democratic Party's historical advantage in the south by painting it as the "Negro party" (Greenberg 1996, 107). Johnson's prophecy proved correct; that year, four of five white southerners voted for Nixon or for segregationist independent candidate George Wallace (108). A victorious Republican Party refined this racialized campaign strategy and, with the exception of Jimmy Carter's election in 1976, handily won the presidency through the 1980s.

In 1985, after Reagan's second victory, a group of predominantly southern conservative Democrats, including Bill Clinton and Al Gore, formed the Democratic Leadership Council (DLC) with two aims: first, to move the Democratic Party to the right by weakening its historical identification with FDR's New Deal and Johnson's Great Society programs; second, to counter the party's identification with black interests and the growing influence of African Americans in Democratic politics (Davis 2002; Hale 1995; Henwood 1997; Klinkner 1999; Reed 1999; Roediger 2002). Hoping to win back white Democrats who had voted for Reagan, the DLC took a page from the Republican playbook by capitalizing on racial divisions and anxieties. According to Kim, the DLC started from the assumption that because of Republicans' "indifference or outright hostility," black Americans had effectively been "captured" by the Democratic Party, which meant they were "unable to make a threat of defection and thus unable to exercise influence over the party's policies" (2002, 57, 60). With black loyalty to the party guaranteed, there was little risk in emulating the GOP's track record in using race as a "wedge issue to draw whites" (ibid.).

As the DLC's first presidential candidate, Bill Clinton "mimicked the Republican electoral strategy" of wooing white voters with "a symbolic distancing from and rejection of black interests and leaders" (ibid.) and by "forcefully disidentifying with black interests and concerns and aggressively courting white voters" (61). An architect of this strategy was Stanley Greenberg, Yale political scientist and Clinton pollster and adviser. Michigan's state Democratic Party recruited Greenberg in early 1985 to conduct focus group discussions with voters in Macomb County, a white suburb of Detroit once lauded as the most Democratic suburb in the U.S. that had become a Reagan stronghold (Greenberg 1996, 25). Greenberg found deep frustration among these "Reagan Democrats," who directed their wrath at African Americans:

> These white defectors from the Democratic Party expressed a profound distaste for black Americans, a sentiment that pervaded almost everything they thought about government and politics. Blacks constituted the explanation for their vulnerability and for almost everything that had gone wrong in their lives; not being black was what constituted being middle class; not living with blacks was what made a neighborhood a decent place to live (39).

The equation of "urban" and "black" (Davis 2002, 255) was also prominent:

> ... For these white suburban residents, the terms *blacks* and *Detroit* were interchangeable. ... These suburban voters felt nothing in common with Detroit and its people and rejected out of hand the social justice claims of black Americans. They denied that blacks suffer special disadvantages that would require special treatment by employers or the government. They had no historical memory of racism and no tolerance for present efforts to offset it. They felt no sense of personal or collective responsibility that would support government anti-discrimination and civil rights policies (39).

Clinton's 1992 campaign, with its praise for a virtuous middle class, emphasis on "personal responsibility," and interpretation of equality as "equality of opportunity, not of results" (Baer 2000, 265), was designed to appeal to such voters, including their sense of racial victimization.[1] The success of Clinton's campaign indicates the degree to

1   Clinton appeared in Macomb County on March 12, 1992—two days after Super Tuesday. To an audience of white "Reagan Democrats," Clinton

which Democrats had adopted underclass ideology, which provided a "way of talking about blacks (and, increasingly, Latinos) without talking about blacks" (Mills 1994, 859; see also Reed 1999b; Brown 1999; Abramovitz & Withorn 1999; Reeves & Campbell 1994; Roediger 2002). Ditto for Clinton's reluctance to address the economic crisis facing American cities after twelve years of disinvestment and neglect under Republican rule. Davis argues that the Reagan and Bush administrations' "de facto war against the cities"—which eroded traditional strongholds of Democratic support and shifted federal monies to the suburbs—has been "one of the strategic pillars of modern conservative politics" (2002, 245). In his zeal to appease "Reagan Democrats," Clinton cut a wide path around urban issues and race to "reassure white suburbanites at every opportunity that he was not soft on crime, friendly with the underclass, or tolerant of big city welfare expenditures" (257).

Claire Kim argues that Clinton and fellow New Democrats "adopted Republican positions on many race-related issues such as crime, welfare, and affirmative action in a considered effort to distance themselves from blacks and court white votes" (2002, 61). This was Clinton's "racial breach management strategy," which consisted in: "First, an initial electoral strategy of courting white support, in part through symbolic rejection of blacks; and second, an adjusted governing/reelection strategy of pleasing whites with substantive action on racial policy issues and placating blacks with largely symbolic gestures of support" (57).

Clinton's 1992 campaign promise to "end welfare as we know it" was a key element of that strategy. When Republicans in 1994 gained control of both houses of Congress for the first time in four decades, Clinton made welfare reform a centerpiece of his quest to win a second term in '96. Given that welfare is "one of the least popular components of the U.S. welfare state," and that "racial considerations are the single most important factor shaping whites' views of welfare," Clinton's

---

talked about "middle-class effort and middle-class values" (Greenberg, 1996, 219). In contrast, at a black church in Detroit the following day, his theme was "responsibility." Clinton "warned his listeners not to be 'misled by politicians who come here asking for hour votes and pretending that we can do something for you if you don't do things for yourselves,'" and said his promise was "a change to give you the opportunity to assume responsibility that every American should assume for his or her own life" (222).

campaign to "end welfare as we know it" was a key part of his racial breach management strategy to appeal to white voters (Gilens 1996, 594, 601).

Although welfare had always drawn criticism from certain quarters, vehement opposition issued primarily from the far right wing of the Republican Party until the 1980s, when the Reagan administration "intensified its assault on poor people and welfare programs for political and ideological gain" (Abramovitz & Withorn 1999, 154). This political assault, in combination with the social fallout from the continued upward redistribution of wealth, cuts in social spending, and bipartisan embrace of underclass ideology, set the stage for a shift in public attitudes, as reflected in opinion poll results from 1985 and 1995. When asked whether the U.S. public assistance system "works well," 56 percent of respondents in 1985 said no, whereas ten years later, 72 percent answered negatively. On the question of whether public assistance "discourages people from working," 55 percent agreed in 1985, compared to 73 percent in 1995 (Weaver, Shapiro, & Jacobs 1995, 611).

This change in public opinion has important racial implications. In his study of welfare and race, Martin Gilens argues that crime and welfare reform are "widely viewed as 'coded' issues that play upon race (or, more specifically, upon white Americans' negative views of blacks) without explicitly raising the 'race card'" (1996, 593). Gilens found that whites significantly overestimate the percentage of African Americans who are poor and on welfare, and that negative perceptions of blacks—in particular the view that blacks are "lazy"—was the strongest predictor of opposition to welfare among whites. In his words: "the white public's thinking about welfare is inordinately shaped by highly salient negative perceptions of blacks" (ibid). In Gilens' estimation, "race coded" issues, such as welfare, possess "symbolic value" because they afford politicians an opportunity to "exploit the power of racial suspicion and animosity while insulating themselves from charges of race-baiting" (602).

The media have played a substantial role in shaping public opinions about welfare and poverty through their habitual linkage of "homelessness, destitute urban neighborhoods, poverty, public housing, and welfare reform" with "deviance, dangers, and moral deficits of inner-city communities" (Macek 2006, 170; also Gray 1989; Reeves and Campbell 1994; Gans 1995; Rivers 1996; Gilens 1999; Gilliam 1999;

Entman and Rojecki 2000; Clawson & Rice 2000). In their study of television news coverage of the "war on drugs" under Reagan, Reeves and Campbell show how the "moral framing of economic distress" worked to connect increases in crime and domestic conflict and the growth of a drug-based economy in impoverished inner cities to cultural deficiencies, rather than to political-economic policies (1994, 103). Steve Macek's *Urban Nightmares* (2006) found that television's treatment of poverty, welfare, and the underclass escalated "during the national debate over so-called welfare reform that preoccupied Congress and the White House during much of the Clinton era" (175). Further, just as urban and black/Latino achieved "semantic identity" in popular discourse in the 1980s (Davis 2002, 255), poverty was similarly racialized as it was "disproportionately portrayed as a 'black' problem" in the media (Clawson & Trice 2000, 54; also Gans 1995, Gilens 1996 and Gilliam 1999). Winfrey's handling of welfare in the 1990s exhibits all of the above tendencies.

WINFREY TAKES ON THE "WELFARE MENTALITY": FAMILIES FOR A BETTER LIFE

Like Bill Clinton, Oprah Winfrey sought to navigate the black-white racial divide to maintain and maximize her market reach—a task that is particularly delicate when dealing with race and such racialized issues as welfare or affirmative action. To that end, she employed breach management strategies similar to Clinton's. Winfrey's legendary popularity with her majority white audience reflects a well-honed skill at affirming her black heritage while staying at arm's length from aspects of the black historical experience that might alienate her white fans. As Quentin Fottrell has observed, "while embracing the philosophies of Eleanor Roosevelt and Martin Luther King," Winfrey "subtly distances herself from feminist politics and the radicalism of the Civil Rights movement" (2000).

For Winfrey, as for Clinton, welfare provided an opportunity to curry support with white followers. From her first episode on welfare in 1986, Winfrey's handling of this and other poverty-related issues was consistent. From 1994 to '96, several episodes of *The Oprah Winfrey Show* focused on racially-coded topics (e.g., "I Kicked Welfare, You Can Too," "Violent Children: Detroit," "Is Affirmative Action Outdated?," "Should Welfare Pay for Her Kids?"), all of which were framed through the lens of underclass ideology. Success and failure were the consequence of individual attitudes and behavior. The poor were responsible for their fate and, with the exception of needy children, were not deserving of public assistance or compassion. Those receiving public aid were legitimate targets of resentment from taxpaying citizens. Political/structural explanations of poverty (and wealth) were minimal and the preferred solution to poverty was self-help and "personal responsibility" in most instances, or private charity in the case of the deserving few. In September 1994, as Winfrey sought to distance herself from mounting criticism of talk shows—which were proliferating and becoming increasingly outrageous—she launched one of her most publicized "empowerment" campaigns. To kick off the new season, Winfrey held a press conference to announce the creation of a program that she said would take 100 families off welfare within two years. "Families for a Better Life" (FBS) would target residents of Chicago Housing Authority developments and provide them with family and financial counseling, job training, health care, and educational opportunities. Winfrey committed up to $6 million to the project, which was to be administered by the Jane Adams Hull House Association. Families for a Better Life would seek out families "who are motivated to change," she said. Applicants would be carefully screened and subjected to drug testing, background checks, and home visits. In creating the program, Winfrey said, "It is my intention to take people out, to change their lives. But more importantly than changing their lives, I want to change the way they think about their lives. I want to destroy the welfare mentality" (McRoberts 1994).

Press coverage applauded Winfrey's commitment to help welfare recipients "get on the road to independence." A *Chicago Sun-Times* editorial praised Winfrey's stated intention to "destroy the welfare mentality, the belief in victimization." Families for a Better Life, the editorial said, was "bound to be the envy of state social service agencies whose fragmented approach to 'fixing' families rarely achieves long-term success" ("A Shining Star" 1994). Because Winfrey viewed being on welfare, living in public housing, and by extension, being poor, as psychologically based problems, Families for a Better Life was organized around the principles of positive thinking and self-help. By June 1995, Hull House administrators had identified seven suitable families to begin the eight-week "personal development" course. Participants attended a weekly three-hour class that began with an introductory video created by and featuring Winfrey, who also sat in on several sessions. Topics from making decisions to dealing with change were presented through a mix of self-help terminology and strategies from corporate human resources training (Kiernan 1996).

In September 1996, the point at which Winfrey had initially promised that 100 families would have broken "the cycle of poverty," Families for a Better Life was put "on hold" and Hull House officials said Winfrey's participation—and the future of the program itself—were in doubt. After an expenditure of $1.3 million ($843,000 came from Winfrey) five of the original seven families had completed the program. All were headed by single mothers—four African American and one Latina—with an average of two children each. When they started the program in 1995, all of the families were living in public housing and receiving AFDC benefits, with three parents working part-time or attending classes. By 1996, two parents worked fulltime, two part-time. One of the latter was attending nursing school and the fifth mother was enrolled in a computer-training program. Three of the families had left public housing, a fourth was in the process of moving out, and the fifth remained in a CHA project. The most "notable success" among the families was a mother who had gotten a $22,000-a-year job, but Hull House officials said they had seen changes in the attitudes of all of the parents, who had demonstrated "gains in the sense of control of over their lives" (ibid.).

Explanations for the discontinuation of Families for a Better Life pointed to the unanticipated length and high cost of the screening process. In truth, most of the money went to administration, but this fact was not publicized. Hull House organizers did note the challenges faced by participants who "lived so close to the edge" that "each crisis—whether transportation, illness, violence, or a family dispute—threatened to plunge them into a financial and emotional abyss." And, because all of the parents initially lacked high school educations or significant job experience, they had trouble finding and keeping work in the short time they were expected to develop "self-sufficiency" (ibid.). But these explanations were trumped by what became the official diagnosis of the program's failure: that it was almost impossible to "destroy the welfare mentality." A Hull House vice president expressed what would become the dominant theme in press coverage of the program's demise: "Even though we screened them, there was this mind frame of entitlement. We had to keep emphasizing that this is not about what you get. This is about what you do" (ibid.).

In news reports and editorials about the project's demise, "welfare mentality" and "mind frame of entitlement" were recurring phrases, coupled with praise for Winfrey's admirable intentions. By contrasting Winfrey's noble motives to the problematic attitudes of the program's participants, press accounts arrived at similar conclusions. As a *Chicago Tribune* reporter put it: "At its most basic, the lesson of Families for a Better Life may be that the lives of the poor are so chaotic and infused with a 'mind frame of entitlement' that they defy even programs specifically designed to overcome these obstacles" (ibid.). A *Tampa Tribune* editorial seconded this assessment: "Many in the project seemed determined to turn their lives around but were so accustomed to government safety nets that they failed to accept personal responsibility" ("Oprah's Difficult Welfare Lesson" 1996). In other words, poor people (i.e., the "underclass") were so disorganized and deficient that not even Oprah Winfrey could "empower" them.

Given this verdict, "welfare reform" was not only justified, but an altruistic necessity. As an editorial in the Tacoma *News Tribune* stated, the fate of the project "tends to buttress the argument for welfare reform with tough provisions for limiting the amount of time people can spend on welfare. … Too much can be made of this one experiment, of course. But it does suggest that ending the culture of dependency fostered by welfare requires tough love" ("Oprah's Welfare Idea" 1996). In contrast to the fanfare with which she announced the creation of Families for a Better Life, Winfrey held no press conference to mark its termination. When Hull House officials announced in September 1996 that the program had been put on hold, Winfrey declined all interviews.

The failure of Families for a Better Life became an indictment of welfare recipients' moral shortcomings. It was also an endorsement of the Personal Responsibility and Work Opportunity Act that Bill Clinton had signed into law a few weeks earlier. On August 22, 1996—months before his re-election—Clinton made good on his '92 campaign promise to "end welfare as we know it." The "welfare reform" act abolished AFDC, capped federal welfare spending, shifted all responsibility for public assistance to the states in the form of block grants, imposed a five-year lifetime limit regardless of circumstances, and allowed states to force recipients to work at sub-minimum wage to qualify for benefits (Lipman 1996; Pringle 1996; Ross 1996; Sherwood 1996). Casting welfare as a cause of dependency that destroys self-esteem and undermines personal responsibility allowed both Winfrey and Clinton to paint their support for welfare reform as an effort to empower people. It also figured in their strategy of courting white support, given that "the symbolic power of welfare as a political issue stems in large measure from its racial undertones" (Gilens 1996, 602).

CONCLUSION

That it was a Democratic president who signed the death warrant of a 60-year-old program to aid fatherless families, and that a black celebrity who built her empire on the idea of "empowering" women and children and whose mother had periodically relied on that program would endorse that fatality, attests to the political sea change that transpired over the last quarter of the twentieth century. That shift reflects the emerging consensus between New Liberals and conservatives around the notion of the "underclass" and the nature of the "race problem" in the U.S. The fusion of underclass theory and self-help ideology that began with Reagan and continued under Clinton provided a rationale for black poverty, an alibi for the continued contraction of the state, and a scapegoat for working- and middle-class whites also caught in the juggernaut of neoliberal restructuring.

This is the context of Oprah Winfrey's ascent to mainstream cultural icon, including her "transcendence of race." Widely portrayed as having overcome the obstacles of race, gender, and class solely through her indomitable spirit, Winfrey has won public acclaim by distancing herself from "the militant civil rights strata of black American life" (Mair 1994/1998, 180). From the early days of her career, she has quoted Jesse Jackson's statement that "excellence is the best deterrent to racism" (R.C. Smith 1986) and considers her own success as proof that "you can be poor and black and female and make it to the top" (Adler 1997, 278). By implication, other black poor people—if they were simply willing to take "personal responsibility"—could make it to the top too. If they do not, as Winfrey once stated, her life is a reminder that "they no longer have any excuse" (Mair 1994/1998, 183). This stance was entirely compatible with Clinton's New Liberal rhetoric of "personal responsibility," which represented a kinder, more palatable version of Reagan's blame-the victim agenda. An important consequence of the ideological convergence between America's two major political parties was a declining interest in the subject of poverty, black or otherwise.

This returns us to the question of what it means to say that a TV personality has transcended race. Like *The Cosby Show*, which supplied positive images of African Americans through the lovable Huxtable family and renounced anything that Cosby himself termed "downtrodden, negative, I-can't-do-I won't-do" (Miller 1988, 73), Winfrey's enterprise was designed to deliver what she called an upbeat "message of goodness" (King 1995, 368). The fact that these black stars attract a majority white audience has, in itself, been interpreted as a major advance in American race relations. But perhaps whites' embrace of black celebrities reveals more about the power of television than about the actual state of American race relations. Because the U.S. remains a highly race-segregated society, many whites' primary encounter with African Americans comes through television—a medium, Paul Street argues, that "presents a dangerously schizophrenic image of black America split between super-successful and largely admirable (not-all-that) black superstars (Oprah being the best of all) and dangerous (all-too) black perpetrators" (2005). According to Leonard Steinhorn and Barbara Diggs-Brown, television's pervasive, repetitive nature and intimate context of reception gives "white Americans the sensation of having meaningful, repeated contact with blacks without actually having it"—a phenomenon they term "virtual integration" (1999, 146). In their view, "Virtual integration enables whites to live in a world with blacks without having to do so in fact. It provides a form of safe intimacy without any of the risks. It offers a clean and easy way for whites to establish and nourish what they see as their bona fide commitment to fairness, tolerance, and color blindness" (157).

The relatively common presence of black faces in TV programs and ads, coupled with the fact that for most whites television may be the primary contact they have with blacks, helps fuel the "integration illusion"—an unjustified "belief that we are moving toward a color-blind society" (146). It also helps explain why Winfrey is so often described as a personal friend by her predominantly white followers, most of whom can probably claim no other black friendships. The fact that they feel so comfortable with her is a prominent part of her "transcendence of race," which is another way of saying white people like her. It allows fans to imagine that racism has been vanquished because they invite a black woman into their homes on a daily basis and "really love" her. Through virtual integration, "whites have made room in their lives for black celebrities" and take their affection for figures such as Winfrey and Cosby "as evidence of their own open-mindedness and as proof that the nation isn't so hard on blacks after all" (ibid.).

The irony of Winfrey's celebrated reputation for transcending race is the fragility of that accomplishment. When, in the 2008 presidential campaign, she endorsed Barack Obama—yet another figure hailed for transcending race—the message boards on Oprah.com lit up with criticism from white fans, who accused Winfrey of backing the candidate only because both of are black Americans, with some posters even labeling her endorsement a racist act. Nor is Winfrey unaware of the tenuous nature of "color-blindness." Facing the combination of public blowback from her support for Obama and declines in the ratings for her show and circulation of her magazine, she backed off from further involvement in the Obama campaign and resumed her less explicitly partisan philanthropic activities. Winfrey's career, seen as an exemplar of "virtual integration," represents both the power and the danger of the notion of "transcending race." It points to a genuine desire to break down the barriers that have historically divided us along racial grounds. At the same time, it obscures the actual history of political-economic conditions that have created the inequitable distribution of wealth and power on which divisions of race and class are based, and which helps legitimize and keep them in place.

REFERENCES

"A Shining Star Named Oprah." 1994. *Chicago Sun-Times*, September 15: 29.

Abramovitz, M., and A. Withorn. 1999. "Playing by the Rules: Welfare Reform and the New Authoritarian State." In *Without Justice for All*. Ed. A. Reed, 151–173. Boulder, CO: Westview Press.

Adelman, R. M. and J.C. Gocker. 2007. "Racial Residential Segregation in Urban

America." *Sociology Compass* 1 (1): 404-23.

Adler, B., ed. 1997. *The Uncommon Wisdom of Oprah Winfrey*. Secaucus, NJ: Birch Lane Press.

Auletta, K. 1982. *The Underclass*. New York: Random House.

Baer, K. S. 2000. *Reinventing Democrats*. Lawrence: Univ. Press of Kansas.

"Blacks Picket Winfrey Show in White County." 1987. *Chicago Tribune*, February 10: 4.

Brenner, R. 2006. *The Economics of Global Turbulence*. London: Verso.

"'Brotherhood March' Aftermarch." 1987. *Houston Chronicle*, February 12: 9.

Brown, E. 2002. *The Condemnation of Little B*. Boston: Beacon Press.

Clawson, R. and R. Trice. 2000. "Poverty as We Know It: Media Portrayals of the Poor." *Public Opinion Quarterly* 64: 53-64.

Cloud, D. 1996. "Hegemony or Concordance? The Rhetoric of Tokenism In Oprah Winfrey's Rags-to-Riches Biography." *Critical Studies in Mass Communication* 13: 115–137.

Davis, M. 1986. *Prisoners of the American Dream*. London: Verso.

———. 2002. *Dead Cities*. New York: New Press.

di Leonardo, M. 1999. "'Why Can't They Be Like Our Grandparents?' And Other Racial Fairy Tales." In *Without Justice for All*. Ed. A. Reed, 29–64. Boulder, CO: Westview Press.

Dillahunt, A., et al. 2010. "State of the Dream 2010: Drained." *United for a Fair Economy*, January 13. Accessed July 30, 2010. http://www.faireconomy.org/dream.

Drier, P. 2004. "Reagan's Legacy: Homelessness in America." *NHI Shelterforce Online Issue* #135 (May/June). Accessed November 19, 2010. http://www.nhi.org/online/issues/135/reagan.html.

Entman, R. M. and A. Rojecki. 2000. *The Black Image in the White Mind: Media and Race in America*. Chicago: Univ. of Chicago Press.

Firstman, R. 1989. "Oprah power." *Newsday*, November 1: Sec. II, 4.

"Forbes 400 richest Americans: Oprah Winfrey." 2010. *Forbes.com*. Retrieved December 15, 2010. http://www.forbes.com/profile/oprah-winfrey.

Ford, G. 2010. "Massive Race Divide: Blacks Will Never Gain Wealth Equality with Whites under the Current System." *Black Agenda Report*, May 21. Accessed July 30, 2010. http://blackagendareport.com/content/study-shows-blacks-will-never-gain-wealth-parity-whites-under-current-system.

Fottrell, Quentin. 2000. "The Cult of Oprah Inc." *The Irish Times*, weekend magazine, August 5. Retrieved March 2, 2001. http://web.lexis-nexis.com.

Gans, H. 1995. *The War against the Poor: The Underclass and Anti-Poverty Policy*. New York: Basic Books.

George, S. 2008. *Hijacking America: How the Secular and Religious Right Changed What Americans Think*. Cambridge: Polity Press.

Gilens, M. 1996. "'Race Coding' and White Opposition to Welfare." *American Political Science Review* 90 (3)(September): 593–604.

———. 1999. *Why Americans Hate Welfare: Race, Media, and the Politics of Antipoverty Policy*. Chicago: Univ. of Chicago Press.

Gilliam, F. D., Jr. 1999. "The 'Welfare Queen' Experiment: How Viewers React to Images of African-American Mothers on Welfare." *Nieman Reports* 53 (2) (Summer). Accessed November 19, 2010. http://escholarship.org/uc/item/17m7r1rq.

Gray, H. 1989. "Television, Black Americans, and the American Dream." *Critical Studies in Mass Communication* (6): 376-286.

Greenberg, S. B. 1996. "Private Heroism and Public Purpose." *American Prospect Online*. (September 1). Accessed July 5, 2004. http://www.prospect.org/web/printfriendly-view.ww?id=4891/.

Hale, J. F. 1995. "The Making of the New Democrats." *Political Science Quarterly* 110 (2)(Summer): 207–33.

Henwood, D. 1997. "Clinton's Liberalism: No Model for the Left." In *Socialist register 1997*, ed. L. Panitch, 159–175. London: Merlin Press.

Illouz, E. 2003. *Oprah Winfrey and the Glamour of Misery*. New York: Columbia Univ. Press.

Jameson, F. 1992. *Signatures of the Visible*. London: Routledge.

Jhally, S. and J. Lewis. 1992. *Enlightened Racism*. Boulder, CO: Westview Press.

Kiernan, L. 1996. "Oprah's Bold Plan to Confront Poverty Put on Hold." *Denver Post*, (September 8): 12A.

Kim, C. J. 2002. "Managing the Racial Breach: Clinton, Black-White Polarization, and the Race Initiative." *Political Science Quarterly* 117 (1): 55–79.

King, L. 1995. "Oprah Winfrey, January 4, 1995." In *The best of Larry King Live*, 366–378. Atlanta: Turner Publishing Inc.

Klinkner, Philip A. 1999. "Bill Clinton and the Politics of the New Liberalism." In *Without Justice For All*. Ed. A. Reed, Jr., 11-28. Boulder, CO: Westview Press.

Kozol, J. 2005. *The Shame of the Nation: The Restoration of Apartheid Schooling in America*. New York: Crown Publishers.

Lipman, L. 1996. "States to Distribute Public Assistance to the Poor." *Palm Beach Post*, August 23: 1A.

Macek, S. 2006. *Urban Nightmares: The Media, the Right, and the Moral Panic over the City*. Minneapolis: Univ. of Minnesota Press.

Mair, G. 1994/1998. *Oprah Winfrey: the Real Story.* Secaucus, NJ: Carol Publishing Group.

Massey, D. S. 1996. "The Age of Extremes: Concentrated Affluence and Poverty in the Twenty-First Century." *Demography* 33 (4) (November): 395-412.

———. and Fischer, M. J. 2000. "How segregation Concentrates Poverty." *Ethnic and Racial Studies* 23 (4): 670-91.

Max, D. T. 1999. The Oprah effect. *New York Times Magazine*, December 26: 37–41.

McRoberts, F. "Oprah Winfrey Commits $6 Million for CHA Families." *Chicago Tribune*, September 14: 3.

Mead, L. 1986. *Beyond Entitlement.* New York: Basic Books.

Mediamark Research Inc. 2003. *Oprah Winfrey Show* and *O: The Oprah Magazine.* (Fall).

Mills, C. W. 1994. "Under Class under Standings." *Ethics* 104 (July): 855–81.

———. 2000. *The Sociological Imagination.* 40th ed. Oxford: Oxford University Press.

Murray, C. A. 1984. *Losing Ground: American Social Policy, 1950–1980.* New York: Basic Books.

Novak, M. 1987. *New Consensus on Family and Welfare.* Washington, D.C.: American Enterprise Institute for Public Policy Research.

Oprah Winfrey Show. 1986. "Pros and Cons of Welfare," first broadcast November 17.

———. 1989. "Three Generations of Underclass," first broadcast March 22.

———. 1991. "Angry Taxpayers/Angry Tenants: The Public Housing Controversy," first broadcast June 18.

"Oprah's show on GA. March Bars Blacks; Protest Called." 1987. *Chicago Sun-Times*, February 9: 5.

"Oprah Winfrey's Biography." 2011. *Oprah.com.* Accessed February 1, 2011. http://www.oprah.com/pressroom/Oprah-Winfreys-Official-Biography

"Oprah Winfrey's Official Biography." 2006. *Oprah.com.* Accessed June 24, 2006. http://www.oprah.com/about/press/about_press_bio.jhtml/.

"Oprah's Difficult Welfare Lesson." 1996. *Tampa Tribune*, September 18: 8.

Paget, Karen. 1998. "Can Cities Escape Political Isolation?" *The American Prospect* 9, no. 36, January/February: 54-62.

Peck, J. 1993. *The Gods of Televangelism.* Cresskill, NJ: Hampton Press.

Perlstein, R., 2009. *Before the Storm: Barry Goldwater and the Unmaking of the American Consensus.* New York: Nation Books.

Pringle, Curt. 1996. "Welfare Reform." *(Los Angeles) Daily News*, August 25: p. V1.

Reed, A., Jr. 1999a. "Introduction: The New Liberal Orthodoxy on Race and Inequality." In *Without Justice for All.* Ed. A. Reed, Jr., 1–10. Boulder, CO: Westview Press.

———. 1999b. *Stirrings in the Jug: Black Politics in the Post-Segregation Era.* Minneapolis: Univ. of Minnesota Press.

Reeves, J., and R. Campbell. 1994. *Cracked Coverage.* Durham, NC: Duke Univ. Press.

Reich, R. 2010. *Aftershock.* New York: Alfred A. Knopf.

Richman, A. 1987. "Oprah." *People Weekly*, January 12: 52–55, 58.

Rivers, C. 1996. *Slick Spins and Fractured Facts.* New York: Columbia University Press.

Roberts, F. 1994. Oprah Winfrey Commits $6 Million for CHA Families. September 14: 3.

Roediger, David. 2002. *Colored White: Transcending the Racial Past.* Berkeley: University of California Press.

Ross, S. 1996. "Experts Disagree on the Impact of New Welfare Law." *St. Louis Post-Dispatch*, August 26: 12.

Sellers, P. 2002. "The Business of Being Oprah." *Fortune*, April 1: 50–54, 58, 60, 64.

Shapiro, T. M., T. Meschede, and f L. Sullivan. 2010, May. "The Racial Wealth Gap Increases Fourfold. Institute on Assets and Social Policy." Accessed September 20, 2010. http://iasp.brandeis.edu/pdfs/Racial-Wealth-Gap-Brief.pdf.

Smith, R. C. 1986. "She Once Trashed Her Apartment to Make a Point." *TV Guide*, August 30: 30–31.

Smith, J. 1997. "The Ideology of 'Family and Community': New Labour Abandons the Welfare State." In *Socialist register 1997.* Ed. L. Panitch, 176–196. London: Merlin Press.

Steinhorn, L., and B. Diggs-Brown. 1999. *By the Color of our Skin.* New York: Dutton.

Street, P. 2005. "The Full Blown 'Oprah Effect': Reflections on Color, Class, and New Age Racism." *Black Commentator*, February 24: 127. Accessed July 20, 2005. http://www.blackcommentator.com/.

"Television." 1991. *Ebony*, August: 50, 52.

Toner, R. 2004. "Southern Democrats Decline Is Eroding the Political Center." *New York Times*, November 15: A1, A14.

Weaver, R. K., R. Y. Shapiro, and L. R. Jacobs. 1995. "The Polls—Trends. Welfare." *Public Opinion Quarterly* (59): 606-27.

"'Welfare Queen' Becomes Issue in Reagan Campaign." 1976, February 15. *New York Times*: p. 51.

Williams, Raymond. 1977. *Marxism and Literature*. Oxford: Oxford Univ. Press.

Wilson, C. 2001. "O Sister, Where Art Thou? Buying "O" Winfrey's Touch Sparks Nearly Overnight Success for Magazine." *USA Today*, January 18: 10D.

Withorn, A. 1996. "'Why Do They Hate Me So Much?' A History of Welfare and Its Abandonment in the United States." *American Journal of Orthopsychiatry* 66 (4)(October): 496–509.

Wuthnow, R. and Liebman, R. C. 1983. *The New Christian Right*. Hawthorne, NY: Aldine Publishing.

CHAPTER 13

PUBLIC RADIO, *THIS AMERICAN LIFE,* AND THE NEOLIBERAL TURN

Jason Loviglio

INTRODUCTION

THIS CHAPTER IS ABOUT THE EVOLUTION OF PUBLIC RADIO from its liberal beginnings in the 1970s to a more conservative, or neoliberal, incarnation by the end of the twentieth century and the beginning of the twenty-first. National Public Radio (NPR) has been, over this more than forty-year period, an increasingly popular and important institution in the cultural landscape of the United States. One of NPR's most compelling contributions to the sound of American airwaves was a new approach to gender and voice. Female newscasters shared the microphone with their male counterparts, and men and women's voices explored a broader range of pitch and intonation than ever before. This change, an aural representation of the liberal politics characterized by the Women's Movement, persists on the public radio airwaves, on programs like *This American Life.* This chapter charts the journey of public radio from NPR's origins in liberalism to *This American Life*'s simultaneous embrace of liberal sound effects (the liberated voices of men and women broadcasters) and the turn away from the optimism of actual liberal politics.

In 1970, NPR hit the nation's airwaves. Funded by taxpayer money, dedicated to human uplift, NPR epitomized the faith in collective effort, spirit of progressive social relations, and optimistic experimentation that characterized several eras in twentieth-century American history: progressivism, The New Deal, and the Great Society. NPR's Founding Principles embraced a vision of utopian pluralism for the new radio service, one that would, "regard the individual differences among men with respect and joy, rather than derision and hate; ... celebrate the human experience as infinitely varied, rather than vacuous and banal; ... encourage a sense of active constructive participation, rather than apathetic helplessness" (Mitchell 2005, 55).

Twenty-five years later, in 1995, WBEZ, the NPR affiliate in Chicago, debuted a new sound for public radio. *Your Radio Playhouse*, soon to be called *This American Life*, began with host Ira Glass' meditation on the relentlessness of nostalgia, of the inevitability that anything, even his meditation on nostalgia, would one day be looked back upon with a sense of regret at the lost good old days. An episode later that same year, entitled "Quitting," and featuring an articulate young woman named Evan Harris who had made an art form out of giving up on jobs, relationships, and places to live, nicely captured the program's quirky spirit and ironic approach to the social and financial commitments that define entry into adulthood. Harris' preoccupation with perfecting the art of "the quit," echoes the loveable narcissism and misanthropy of the main characters on *Seinfeld*, the quintessential sitcom of the 1990s. The theme of quitting, like the preoccupation with nostalgia, captures a tell-tale turning away from the world, an ironic distancing from the present—the "now"—that seemed to be beckoning so insistently in the early broadcasts of *All Things Considered* 25 years earlier.

While not a complete refutation of NPR's founding principles, the new program, a one-hour mix of interviews and stories organized around a different theme each week, represented an almost radical transformation of the kinds of stories and people that would comprise the "celebration of human experience." And while *This American Life*'s producers proclaim the pursuit of "delight" as a worthy activity, the source of that joy lay in narrative surprise, in small cinematic stories of individual lives, interior landscapes, and private struggles. Rather than "encourage a sense of active participation," *This American Life* embodied the turn inward that has characterized the retreat from liberalism in the years that followed NPR's debut. The program's genius lies in its oscillating currents of empathy and interiority, emotional depth and disjunctive irony, journalistic precision and self-indulgent memoir. It epitomizes the changes to public radio and to many of the cultural institutions in the U.S. in the more than forty years since NPR first took to the air.

It has been widely acknowledged that NPR's origins are inextricably tied to Great Society liberalism, which had begun to collapse by the 1970s. (Mitchell 2005, 29; McCauley 2006, 18-22). The Public Broadcasting Act, which created the funding for NPR and PBS, passed into law in 1967 and *All Things Considered* debuted amidst the tear gas and tumult of the anti-war protests of 1971 (Douglas 1999, 321; McCauley, 28-29). The network's journalists, reporting live from protest marches, bore witness to the violence and rancor that challenged the optimism and faith in government embodied in the phrase "The Great Society." Even so, their reportage was marked by a profound curiosity and presence, even when it meant choking on tear gas and dodging billy clubs (Douglas, Ibid; Mitchel, 72-73; McCauley, Ibid.) In 1972, Susan Stamberg became the signature voice of *All Things Considered* and the first woman to anchor a national news broadcast in the U.S. Forged in a moment of danger, NPR saw collective human effort and human diversity as necessary and as equal to the challenges facing humankind.

NPR's reputation as a liberal bastion has been a durable one over the four decades that have elapsed since then. Recent historians of the network have praised it for attracting "highly educated, socially conscious, politically active" listeners (McCauley, 2). For conservatives, NPR fits nicely into a narrative of an out-of-touch media catering to an effete, liberal elite (Groseclose and Milyo, 2005).

At the same time, the network has grown into one of the biggest and most popular news outlets in the U.S. Starting in the late 1970s and picking up momentum in the early 1980s, NPR has enjoyed significant gains in the size of its audience, thanks in part to its embrace of technological modernization and ever-more commercialized standards of "underwriting" and audience research. The network pioneered the use of satellite uplinks as early as 1978. Around the same time, they hired audience-research guru David Giavannoni (Douglas, 289; McCauley, 73). A "drive to reduce the network's dependence on federal funds" was also central to the early 1980s restructuring of National Public Radio, which made it less public, less national, and more beholden to the financial support of "listener-members" (McCauley 2006, 8). Also in the 1980s, a self-conscious turn away from the network's origins in experimental and alternative programming and an embrace of "professionalism" transformed the network's approach to journalism to an "inside-the-beltway" media juggernaut. The network's reputation for liberalism, however, has remained largely unchanged (Dvorkin 2005; Anderson 2005; CPB 2003). As liberalism fell into disfavor in the corporate media, in think tanks, and in the common sense of the other cultural institutions of the nation, media outlets like NPR shifted perspectives rightward even as they found themselves increasingly on the defensive. NPR's liberalism lives on as a legacy, as a ghost haunting its present-day incarnation, even as it has moved away from the original commitments, perspectives, and alignments that embodied this liberalism. How can this be?

In a media landscape dominated by the likes of Rush Limbaugh on the radio and Fox News on television, and in a post- 9/11 climate in which other supposedly liberal media outlets like the *New York Times* and the *Washington Post* seem to have abandoned their gadfly roles with regard to government overreaching in foreign policy, torture, and civil liberties at home, perhaps NPR can seem liberal by virtue of having moved rightward more slowly than its peers (Dadge 2006). But it has been persuasively demonstrated that on many fronts, NPR's capitulation to the conservative status quo on major political issues has been significant (Rendall and Butterworth 2005; Rendall and Hart 2005; Naureckas 2008; Solomon 2008; DeMause 2010). For listeners and critics alike, NPR and the handful of public radio networks it has helped to create continue to *sound* liberal. Does liberalism have a sound signature? A particular voice?

This question serves as an apt introduction for two related observations about the cultural and political significance of the sound of NPR. The first observation is historical: to listen to NPR today—and really for most of its forty years—is to listen to the voices of women. Or, to put this more precisely, the voice of NPR has very often been a woman's voice. Since the 1971 inception of *All Things Considered*, NPR has more often featured female than male news anchors and hosts, with the result that NPR listeners have grown accustomed to hearing women narrate, announce, and author the news and cultural programming that comprise NPR's daily representation of America and the world. More recently, women have taken leadership positions off-mic as well.[1] This is in stark contrast to the rest of the electronic and print media.

---

1   In 2007, Ellen Weiss was named Senior Vice President for News. In 2008, Vivian Schiller became NPR's first woman president and Ellen McDonnell was named executive director of news programming. In early

The second observation is essentially aural in nature and its aurality is part of the explanation for why it has been so resistant to analysis: there is something unusual about the *sound* of the voices of the women and men of public radio that bears examination as we explore NPR and other public radio networks as cultural institutions constituted largely by sound. To put it in linguistic terms, it is a matter of prosody or paralanguage; that is, pitch, intonation, rhythm, loudness, stress, and tone. To put it in lay terms, it is "the music of speech" (Boutsen 2003; Karpf 2006, 33-47). The voices of women hosts, presenters, and correspondents on public radio's most widely heard programs, including Stamberg, are uncommonly low in pitch. Further, there is a pronounced lack of pitch variance in their voices, not so much a monotone as a kind of disciplined flat monotone delivery with few pitch shifts. The voices of NPR's men, on the other hand, are quite varied; some of the most distinctive and relatively new male reporters and hosts are distinctive precisely for their variance from common masculine vocal pitch (McConnell-Ginet 1983). Expressive and high-pitched men's voices and relatively low-pitched and monotone women's voices have become part of the signature sound of public radio, as much a part of its "branding" as its cultural work. As a student of mine put it succinctly, "the men sound like Truman Capote and the women sound like Bea Arthur."

Susan Douglas describes NPR's voice as the quintessential sound of the "Sensitive New Age Guy." She suggests that modern public radio's enlightened attitude about gender, and the "soft masculinity" that it produced, stands in stark contrast to that other development in radio programming with origins in the 1970s: AM talk radio. Mostly conservative in philosophy, AM talk radio has also been dominated by strident critics of liberalism and feminism (Douglas 1999, 317-319).

Liberal notions of gender roles have been one of the most compelling features of NPR since its inception in 1970. These unusual vocal performances signal some kind of social formation—a post-feminist generation and social class—eager for the sound effects of social change but not ambivalent about progressive social change itself (Loviglio 2008, 78). In the media landscape of the period beginning in the 1980s, when the backlash against feminism spread across journalism,

---

2011, Weiss and then Schilller resigned from their posts, under fire after two highly publicized incidents that shared, among other things, charges of liberal bias and provocations from conservative media outlets.

film, radio, and social science, NPR's feminist (and liberal) credentials may have been guaranteed by a relative lack of outright hostility to women's voices in the public sphere (Faludi 1991). NPR's flexible attitudes towards gender roles help to obscure the ways in which the once-liberal-leaning network has come to match the increasingly conservative spirit of the times.

Nowhere have the sound effects of this liberal social formation been more elegantly performed than on *This American Life*, whose origins and appeal lie in the broader shift of NPR from a liberal, alternative experiment to a mainstream neoliberal radio service. Straddling the twentieth and twenty-first centuries and the presidencies of Clinton, Bush, and Obama, *This American Life*'s tenure on the air is emblematic of the shift away from liberalism and the turn inward. The program exemplifies public radio's successful formula of high production values, virtuosic storytelling, and a laser-sharp focus on the demographic Barbara Ehrenreich called the "New Class" of highly educated professional and managerial workers (Ehrenreich 1989).

After more than fifteen years on the air, it is the most popular and critically acclaimed documentary-style radio program in the country, with 1.8 million weekly listeners on more than 500 stations, a half a million additional podcast subscribers, and an armful of prestigious awards (Lewin 2009). *This American Life* has done more than carve out its own piece of public radio airspace; it has changed the sound of public radio. Indeed, it is "in the vanguard of a journalistic revolution," "spawning imitators and attracting a generation of young producers to radio." (Fisher 1999; WBEZ 2005). Programs like *Radio Lab, Studio 360*—even NPR behemoths *All Things Considered* and *Morning Edition*—have taken up and extended some of *This American Life*'s most distinctive sound signatures: the musical accompaniment to storytelling, the seemingly artless conversational style of narration, and the dramatic arc of stories—even news stories—such that they conclude in "delight" or "surprise," two qualities that Ira Glass says *This American Life* strives for. Importantly, Ira Glass got his start as an editor, then reporter for NPR's *All Things Considered*, where he says he developed his approach to radio storytelling: "to document these real moments that surprise me and that amuse me, and that just gesture at some bigger truth" (Glass, 1998).

With its high-pitched, soft-spoken host Ira Glass, its mostly female staff of producers, and its stable of gay male commentators, *This*

American Life has mastered the sound signification of public radio liberalism. According to frequent *This American Life* contributor David Rakoff, Ira Glass is "a total fag but he's not homosexual." Glass offers this assessment: "I'm a Jewish guy who doesn't like sports and is into musicals" (Berquist 2002). Along with the aesthetics of the voice, the precision of the editing and the tinkling whimsy of the musical accompaniment to the stories (think "Close to Me" by The Cure)—in short, the elements of recorded sound—are also crucial features of this exemplary public radio program. As the producers of *This American Life* put it in their application to the Peabody Awards: "What makes the program different is partly a matter of tone. There's a friendly intimacy to the show" (WBEZ 2005).

The balm of human connection is a key to the appeal of electronic media in general and *This American Life* in particular. Regular listeners to the show's podcast tend to agree, emphasizing the power of intimacy and the comfort of universal themes. "It makes me feel connected to the world on a very human level," says one. "It's so relatable for anyone who is human," enthuses another. Still another confides that listening to the show "makes you feel connected and not so isolated in an often lonely cold world." The theme of finding universal human connection with strangers recurs with striking frequency. *This American Life* "helps re- affirm my faith in the universality of the human experience" (Johnson 2007, 36-37).

And the program's formal emphasis on personal narratives and interiority may well function as both an antidote to and a model of the anomie of contemporary neoliberal life. The narrative voices, while often amusingly quirky, are also frequently haunted by their singularity of perspective. Their loneliness makes listeners feel less alone in their own singularity, a response that comingles empathy and inwardness. "I find it to be very comforting in a way. It connects me to people that I've never met, but I feel like I now know in some special way," reports another podcast listener (Ibid. 37).

NEOLIBERALISM

I want to pause to address the meaning of neoliberalism, a term that has been discussed, historicized, and variously defined (Harvey 2005; Soros 2002; Peck 2008). In brief, neoliberalism refers to the passing of liberalism's faith in government in favor the more or less unfettered workings of the market. Neoliberalism represents a general agreement that radical or even progressive change in the ratio of haves to have-nots is unimaginable, unworkable, and undesirable and that "growing the pie," rather than dividing it differently, is the only viable solution to economic problems and the distribution of wealth. Neoliberalism also evokes a sense of having surpassed and outgrown the optimism of liberalism, its open-ended experimentation, and its concern for social progress.

Scholars like David Harvey have established the point that questions of political economy—i.e., the distribution of wealth—are rarely divorced from questions of social justice and the distribution of rights. "The neoliberal project is to disembed capital from ... a web of social and political constraints" (Harvey 2005, 11). The emergence of neoliberal consensus is part of a larger surrender of the social promises of the movements of liberation of the 1960s and 1970s, in particular, feminism, civil rights, and the war on poverty (Ibid., 39-63). Neoliberalism has a cultural dimension as well. "It has become incorporated into the common-sense way many of us interpret, live in, and understand the world" (Ibid., 3). The triumph of neoliberalism in the U.S. and beyond resulted from "a war of ideas," fought on many fronts (Ibid., 54). The economic and moral centrality of the individual—freed from social and political constraints—was a key feature in the framing stories that shaped a new common sense starting in the late 1970s.

It is useful to think about the rise of neoliberalism in the context of cultural institutions like public radio. A profound weariness of empathy, moral outrage, and the work of social change has taken hold of the cultural life of the professional middle class (Lasch 1978, 13-15; Ehrenreich). Along with the university and the print media, public radio was one of the central ideological apparatuses for the production and reproduction of professional and managerial workers in the 1970s and beyond. Barbara Ehrenreich has argued that this "New Class" of professional-managerial workers beat an ambivalent but steady retreat from public life, politics, and social justice in response to the social and political tumult of the 1960s. Drawn towards the comforts of upward mobility, and to the mixed blessings of privacy and inwardness, the New Class, born of liberalism, led the march toward a neoliberal future. The soundtrack for that journey? Public radio.

According to McCauley, NPR's appeal is mired in *nostalgia for* rather than *commitment to* liberal principles. He describes NPR's twenty-first century audience as "highly educated baby boomers whose idealistic dreams of community were shattered in the 1970s." The network represents a link to "the innocent days of their youth [and] the sense of idealism and community they felt while in college" (2). If the commitment to political engagement has weakened, the emphasis on the "highly educated" audience has not, and herein lies the link to the New Class of professionals and managers that Ehrenreich described. As these upwardly mobile listeners moved into positions of economic and cultural power, they sought a radio service "that focused on the societally conscious, not a service that was societally conscious."(Mitchell 2005, 184). McCauley makes a similar point: "NPR airs many stories *about* these [marginalized] groups, phrased in a manner that speaks to the sensibilities of its core listeners" (112).

The shift in the political culture of NPR has been gradual, but there have been several defining moments as well, when the very fate of a national public radio service hung in the balance. A financial crisis in 1983, when the network faced bankruptcy, became the occasion for a bold restructuring of the network's funding stream. Instead of receiving money directly from the Corporation for Public Broadcasting, NPR would henceforth sell programming to the local affiliates (member stations). It fell to these local stations to raise funds from listener members and secure "corporate underwriting" (a fancy name for low-key commercial sponsorship), in addition to the grants they would now receive directly from the CPB.

This new plan gave local stations more flexibility in purchasing network programming *a la carte*, and helped to spawn NPR's main competitors in the area of programming and distribution: Minnesota Public Radio, American Public Media, and Public Radio International. At the same time, these networks could shift their attention to other sources of revenue, like underwriting and marketing their "brands." The final piece of this emerging business model is the rise in importance of audience research, which took hold of the network in the mid-1980. The demographic profiles produced by this "cutting edge market segmentation" research, McCauley argues, "gave radio managers a better set of tools for mining [the] private funds of listeners" (79, 9). "Each station," according to McCauley, "could strengthen its long-term viability by reaching out to a particular set of listeners with a schedule of programs that spoke clearly to their values and needs" (9). For McCauley, these market-driven reforms of public radio are a "financial maturation"(5), and lie at the heart of its tremendous growth over the last two decades. Relying on voluntary listener support required a new approach to programming in order to attract a relatively homogenous, affluent audience tuning in more or less all day who felt compelled to donate generously.

By 1995, NPR was competing with Minnesota Public Radio, which was in the process of building its own production and distribution empire, combining regional and national music and news programs, *A Prarie Home Companion*, chief among them. In 1983, Minnesota Public Radio had helped to create Public Radio International, a network that sold programming, eventually including *This American Life*, to public radio affiliates across the country. American Public Media's *Marketplace* had been on the air since 1988, bringing the "public radio sound" to financial news and introducing a West Coast presence to the Eastern-oriented world of public radio. The audience for NPR, which had only been around 8 million in 1983, was 20 million by 1995 (Mitchell, Ibid., 135, 173). Others have credited the first Gulf War in 1990-1991, with the growth in listeners. When Americans who were glued to CNN's coverage of the war left their homes, they switched on NPR to continue following the conflict in their cars. Most of the listeners stuck around after the war ended, according to this theory, because they enjoyed hearing high-quality news reporting during their daily commutes (Fox 1991; Mitchell, Ibid. 142).

This American Life represented the 1990s as faithfully as NPR did the 1970s. In the context of a surging NPR, in the midst of a booming American economy, at the height of *Seinfeld's* reign on television, at the moment of Oprah's shift from tabloid sensationalism to a more "spiritual" and "positive" approach to talk television, and as Francis Fukuyama declared of the "End of History," Ira Glass took to the air with his quirky little show. As more local affiliates began to shed their locally-produced and locally-oriented programming in favor of "higher quality" programming produced by NPR, PRI, and American Public Media, programs like Glass's *Your Radio Playhouse* were met with great enthusiasm by station managers. By the end of the show's first year, it had a new name and a national syndication deal.

Several themes recur in *This American Life's* courtship of an audience of affluent, educated listeners for whom liberalism is a cultural touchstone and a set of sound effects, if not a coherent set of political commitments. The program's breadth of topics is impressive—stories touch on questions of gender identity, family mysteries, obscure financial instruments like credit-default swaps, and life aboard a U.S. aircraft carrier during the war in Afghanistan. The themes tend to reinforce ideas of the universal touchstones of human experience: home, family, love, and loss. And many of the stories across all these themes contain a paired set of contradictory impulses: nostalgia for human connection and a solipsistic turning in toward the self; an insouciant assumption that political battles of the 1960s and 1970s have been won and an embrace of the politics of neoliberal backlash; emotional depth and disjunctive irony.

What follows is an analysis of a particularly revealing example of the politics of neoliberalism as it plays itself out in the creation of a story for *This American Life*, right at the end of the twentieth century. The painstaking process of creating one of these stories—"little gems," as Ira Glass calls them—is described in detail by Glass and his production staff in Jessica Abel's graphic novel, *Radio: An Illustrated Guide*. The example they provide illustrates some of the contradictory impulses mentioned above. The first part of the book tells the story of the creation of an episode entitled "Do Gooders" which first aired in April 9, 1999. Producer Julie Snyder describes the process of how a show organized around the inevitable, sometimes tragic surprises that come from people attempting to do good in the world.

The inspiration came from a story pitched by an applicant for an internship about a successful labor action taken by black and white sharecroppers in 1930s, which resulted in higher wages for both. The story celebrates a moment of "active constructive participation" (to quote from NPR's Principles) and Snyder says it's "great" but " just not what we do": "The stories that we **do** do are really character-driven, … they follow the same structure, a literary structure that a fiction story might. The story needs one character, a character that you identify with, who interacts…with other characters in a very specific way and there's conflict, change, and resolution (and not always the resolution part) inherent to the story…and the characters change and grow and they learn something new and surprising, that's what we're always going for, something surprising" (3). The applicant follows up with a story pitch closer to Snyder's formula. It concerns an affluent white retired couple who return to their Missouri hometown to make improvements to the quality of life there. The producers jump at it and quickly build an entire show around the unintended consequences of do-gooders. The couple, Kenny and Jackie Whorton, fail spectacularly in their bid to help the small town, losing friends, an election for mayor, and ultimately, their vision of an improved community. This change in vision, Glass tells us, came courtesy of a bullet lodged in their bedroom wall, fired at their house by some unknown but disgruntled neighbor. The Whortons move away, retreating into the safety and quietism of affluent retirement.

The story is told with compassion for the Whortons and with some thoughtful background research on the economic problems facing the town, which has lost its railroad station and its agricultural base. Townsfolk complain about "Mexican immigrants" who take the few remaining agricultural jobs in the area. It is a well-reported, well-produced, slice-of-life kind of story about a community where people struggle over how best to live decently. It is typical of *This American Life* in its careful editing, its narrative pacing, and its journalistic professionalism.

If, as Glass insists, "radio is a very didactic medium," then what lessons are to be drawn from this episode and from its production backstory (Abel and Glass 1999, 6)? The shift away from a story about a successful alliance between black and white workers towards a story of the failure of a married couple to improve a town in decline, like the preference for stories that "surprise," represents a set of not only aesthetic but also political values. The story that was eventually aired is also typical in its preference for character-driven stories over those that look at a broader swath of social existence. The emphasis on the aspirations and disappointment of the Whortons sounds a typical theme: the impetus for social change resides in the character of specific people, not in the intolerable social conditions that many people confront. The research, reporting, and production process is typical in its rejection of a story featuring changes wrought by political activism in favor of a story with a decidedly neoliberal moral: community work, political work, any collaborative effort to effect positive social change is probably not worth it. Snyder and Glass puts it much better, of course: "In order to do good of any kind, you have to have a vision of the way you want things. There's a ruthlessness to changing anything, to imposing your will on what the world is. And the danger of having a vision is that your vision can cloud your eyes about what is already there" (17).

This message is dramatically underscored in the episode's next act, which examines the disastrous results of international aid in Rwanda, when international do-gooders supported the Hutus, who proceeded to slaughter the Tutsi by the tens of thousands. A brief piece on Paul Rusesabagina, the hotel manager who saved hundreds of Tutsis, and was the hero of the movie *Hotel Rwanda*, adds a much needed but flimsy counterweight to the program's main thrust.

It's also worth noting who *didn't* get to speak in this story about small-town America. The Mexican Americans, themselves likely also refugees from a lost world of economic stability, are here merely signs of decline, rather than victims of it. This narrative circling of the wagons around a particular kind of protagonist (white, affluent, English-speaking) is also a crucial feature of the neoliberal turn inward, not just into the self, but into the subjectivities that are most easily identifiable as "universal" or "human" by mainstream media outlets. In a 2010 fundraising appeal aired on NPR affiliates that carry his show, Glass has hailed listeners as, like him, "middle-class, with responsibilities." Michael Warner, among others, has pointed out the double-edge of this kind of "inclusive" cultural and political representation, describing it as both a moment of "utopian universality" (anyone can "belong") and a "major source of domination" (so long as they "fit in") (Warner 1993, 382). This critique, of the liberal model of the public sphere, as described by Jürgen Habermas, reveals that key features of neoliberalism have their origins in liberalism itself.

PLANET MONEY

Another compelling example of how *This American Life* has embraced the neoliberal perspective is its collaboration with NPR on the "Planet Money" series of reports on the economy. In exploring this collaboration, it is worthwhile to return for a moment to McCauley's line about NPR's increasing sophistication in "mining [the] private funds of listeners." Public radio's embrace of this strategy was key to its growing success in the last two decades of the twentieth century. "Each station," according to McCauley, "could strengthen its long-term viability by reaching out to a particular set of listeners with a schedule of programs that spoke clearly to their values and needs" (9). A crucial part of mining the private funds of listeners is attracting and keeping a set of listeners for whom the programming is meaningful. Public radio's new business model, based on voluntary listener support, requires a relatively homogenous, affluent audience tuning in all day and who feels compelled to donate.

This American Life's genius lies in its ability to mine the private funds of listeners in two distinct and complimentary ways. First, its popularity has been a boon to seasonal fundraising campaigns; indeed, the intensity of fans' love of the program combined with Ira Glass' creative fund-drive appeals has made it a rainmaker for the network affiliates across the country (Thomas 2009; Everhart 2010). Second, a key to the program's appeal has been the mining the private fund of *experiences* of the people whose stories it tells. "We have an abnormally high loyalty to the show because of the personal nature of the content," observes Seth Lind, the show's production manager (Everhart Ibid.). The intimacy of the voices on the program conveys a sense of being, in the double-edged magic of utopian universality, "just like you." "NPR news," according to McCauley, "is made by people like me for people like me" (114). Jack Mitchell, a former NPR producer, is also confident that "the listeners we attracted were pretty much like us" (145). The slippage between the audience, performers, and producers on *This American Life* represents a remarkably coherent and reflexive community. In this, it represents the epitome of public radio's promise of radio for "listeners... pretty much like us."

This American Life has become a "brand" rivaling that of NPR itself, the network that originally rejected the deal to distribute a show that has come to represent many of the network's own innovations and successes. It is significant and not at all surprising that the project that brought them together was *Planet Money*, a program dedicated to unraveling the knotty confusion of the nation's financial problems. The phrase "planet money" captures the essence of a neoliberal perspective on American life better than any I can think of. *Planet Money* has become a popular and influential podcast in its own right after having been incorporated into many of the episodes of *This American Life* in the months following the financial collapse of late 2008. Billed as a unique means of explaining complicated and esoteric financial instruments, products, and practices to an audience of non-specialists, the series was also an opportunity for *This American Life* to move beyond the familiar territory of personal narratives, gothic family dramas, and other explorations of interior landscapes of the human heart and take on journalistic assignments more connected to the broader world of economics, politics, and policy. The collapse of the housing market, the banking crisis, and the 2008 presidential election contributed to a sense of urgency about these matters. Perhaps the staff of *This*

American Life was stung by *The Onion's* mock headline, "This American Life Completes Survey of Liberal, Upper-Middle-Class Existence." Perhaps it also stung when a character on Fox's *The OC* referred to the program as "That show by those hipster know-it-alls who talk about how fascinating ordinary people are? Gawd!"

In any case, the 2008 economic collapse provided a tremendous amount of confusion, intrigue, conflict, and drama for the *Planet Money* team, comprised of Alex Blumberg from *This American Life* and David Koestenbaum, Chana Jaffe-Walt, and others from NPR, to sort out. The program, which describes itself as "a multimedia team covering the global economy," has been widely praised for the clarity with which it has explained complex and esoteric financial products and transactions at the heart of the collapse in the housing market.

The *Planet Money* collaboration represents an effort to engage in the larger world of politics, policy, and profound social dislocation—topics that had for many years been, if not anathema to *This American Life*, then at least most often "not what we do." However, these programs also represent an opportunity to extend its ambivalent perspective on other aspects of American life, combining empathy, irony, journalistic methods, and neoliberal assumptions about the problems with the economy. The *Planet Money* team tends to embrace, on the one hand, the democratic idea that complex financial issues should be made plain to the public. And on the other hand, the programs often embrace the neoliberal principles that flexibility, private enterprise, and efficiency are the best tools to build economic growth, fight poverty, etc. The short programs take on a single problem, often framed in terms that make clear the neoliberal agenda: why is business so slow in India? Too much bureaucracy ("In Search of the Red Tape Factory"). Why hasn't Haiti managed to thrive despite the outpouring of do-gooder efforts there for decades? Not enough entrepreneurship ("Island Time"). Such framing questions effectively remove from consideration any analysis that doesn't start and end in neoliberal models of success through growth, privatization, etc.

In a 2010 episode devoted entirely to General Motors' early experimentation with Japanese industrial methods in the 1980s, the poor quality, low morale, and contentious labor relations are laid, for the most part, at the feet of the United Auto Workers and their surly, corrupt, and even reckless approach to their work. The hidebound corporate culture of the company also comes in for a share of the criticism.

The solution promised by the Japanese and modeled in its Nummi auto plant in Texas, is an intense worker loyalty to and pride in the corporation and its brands ("Nummi"). While this may not, in itself, be an unhelpful insight, it is clearly one that privileges a corporate, profit-based perspective rather than one dedicated to the welfare of workers, consumers, or the environment, three concerns that were once more central to modern liberal politics. If disembedding capital from social and political constraints is the project of neoliberalism, then—in these episodes—*Planet Money* seems bent on identifying the cultural constraints that have reined in capitalism.

But the *Planet Money* episodes that have garnered the most critical acclaim (including a Peabody Award) are those that have dedicated themselves to explaining, with forensic detail, "what went wrong" in the 2008 subprime mortgage crisis and the cascading global credit crisis that followed. Taken together, the *Planet Money* episodes dealing most intensely with the causes of the crisis function as a primer in modern financial products like "credit default swaps" and "collateralized debt obligations." They also document, with the confident plotting of a police procedural, the steps in the expansion and implosion of the housing and credit bubble that characterized the crisis between 2000 and 2008.

There are elements in these stories of the liberal "muckraking" tradition that dates back to the Progressive era a century earlier, when the condition of the poor were juxtaposed to the outrageous fortunes amassed by industrialist to great effect. "The Giant Pool of Money," begins with two very brief vignettes. The first is set at an awards ceremony held at the Ritz-Carlton Hotel for mortgage brokers like Jim Finkel, honoring the creators of that year's best collateralized debt obligations (CDOs). CDOs are the instrument, reporter Alex Blumberg tells us, at the heart of the mortgage crisis that turned into a global credit crisis. The next scene is at a community college in Brooklyn, where a non-profit conference for people facing foreclosure is being held. There, Blumberg introduces us to Richard, a Marine and Iraq veteran, who breaks down as he describes the financial ruin he faces, the shame of raiding his son's college fund to make ballooned mortgage payments, and so forth.

But the rest of episode seems dedicated to providing a neoliberal interpretation of this almost Dickensian opening. "Now it's clear that these two groups are connected: Jim at his black-tie dinner and

Richard the Marine," Blumberg concedes cautiously. But in order to lay bare the entire process in detail, Blumberg turns to another homeowner in trouble, this one named Clarence Nathan, at risk of losing his home after borrowing half a million dollars, despite his lack of collateral and a patchwork of part-time and unreliable jobs. Nathan, whose desperate need for money is never explained, and who admits he may have had to do "something more drastic and dramatic" if he hadn't gotten a No Interest, No Asset (NINA) bank loan, and who also admits to what Blumberg calls "shadowy criminal contacts," represents what Blumberg called a "more nuanced" portrait of the mortgage crisis: "Stories like this have been in the news for months. They often feature an innocent homeowner who is duped by a lying greedy mortgage banker. Or if you're a more of a *Wall Street Journal* editorial page type, an innocent mortgage banker duped by a lying greedy homeowner. And no doubt, both kinds of people exist. But Clarence's case is more nuanced. And much more common." Blumberg's promise of nuance represents a neoliberal triangulation between, on the one hand, the *Wall Street Journal* editorial page's notorious arch-conservatism and, on the other hand, the equally dubious muckraking accounts that juxtapose partying mortgage brokers with weeping veterans fighting to save their homes. "The bank made an imprudent loan and I made an imprudent loan," Clarence confesses with equanimity.

To explain the problem at a macro level, Glass, Blumberg, and Davidson attempt to answer the pressing question of *why* banks would make such an imprudent loan. They do not, it should be noted, bother to ask why someone like Richard would take on such massive debt on confusing and even usurious terms. The *Planet Money* version of events suggests that the crisis was an aberration from the normal flow of global capitalism. Banks historically lent money prudently, "but then suddenly, the early 2000s, everything changed. Banking turned on its head. And went out looking for partnerships with *people like Clarence*. What happened?" (emphasis added). The *Planet Money* team bring their formidable resources to explaining what caused people to "throw out the old rules of banking," rules that, presumably, were basically sound. Such questions obscure a well-documented history of predatory lending, discriminatory lending, and bouts of wildcat speculation by U.S. financial institutions over the course of the last century(Lord 2004; Richardson 2005).

Blumberg and Adam Davidson explain that the surging global economy, thanks to the massive growth in China and other developing countries, created a "giant pool of money" that investors around the world were keen to invest. That, combined with U.S. monetary policy (a low federal funds rate), led investors to feverishly seek profitable returns from the U.S. mortgage industry. A speculative bubble fueled by a giant pool of money with an almost anthropomorphic drive to reproduce. The excesses of this frenzy are documented in the person of Glen LaRusso, a New York mortgage company sales manager who made and blew thousands on fancy Champagne and cars before the inevitable crash. A few modern-day Cassandras are interviewed as well, bankers whose intimations of doom went unheeded by peers. There is a quality of Greek tragedy to the story. The overweening greed of mortals, driven mad by an insatiable, immortal giant pool of money, led to a brief, heady rise followed by a predictable and pitiless fall.

No mention is made of the deregulation of the financial industry in the United States over the years since the 1999 Financial Services Modernization Act, which effectively repealed the 1933 Glass-Steagall Act, which was created as a remedy for the kinds of malfeasance that led to the Great Depression. No mention is made of the tremendous transfer of wealth from the poor to the rich that took place in the U.S. since the 1970s, setting the stage for the kind of speculative frenzy that leveraged the debts of poor Americans into massive profits for banks and global investors.

In the place where such context might have gone, however, we do get to hear Alex and Adam chatting amiably, stumbling over each other's job titles, and the pronunciation of the name of their International Monetary Fund source, Ceyla Pazarbasioglu. Blumberg, Davidson, and their colleague Chana Jaffe-Walt have taken this breezy conversational style to new heights. Juxtaposed to the arcana of modern financial products, the effect is to distance the listener from too-close an engagement with the experiences of others. The oscillation between empathy and ironic distance requires a mastery of tone, a virtuosic precision in delivery, an artful artlessness. If these episodes are meant to be didactic as well, then the lesson is clear: the giant pool of money requires no context, no historicizing, no political critique. Nor does the folly of men (and they really do interview men almost exclusively for this story). The centrality of money and human greed are simply givens, impervious to change.

CONCLUSION

The new sound of public radio, epitomized by Ira Glass' voice is, if nothing else, an effect signifying the insouciance of the hipster, whose sophistication casts into shadow all that is unworthy for consideration because it fails to "surprise." The world of politics, partisan battles, ideological divides, and policy questions are almost always shaded out of the central narrative of *This American Life* stories. Political anger, partisan enthusiasms, and sociological dilemmas are uninteresting because they make for predictable stories. Glass provides some helpful context in the introduction of a 2009 episode entitled, "This I Used to Believe": "I think I'm one of those people who—I had a lot of really strong beliefs about stuff when I was a kid. I had a religious phase and I had a very strong, like, atheist phase. And then I had a very political phase. And I was politically correct for years. The kind of politically correct where when I was in my 20s, I went to Nicaragua and I called it Nicaragua (Spanish accent). (laughs). And you know what I mean? I was horrible! (laughs)... I got older and I saw that things seemed more complicated than the way I believed them..."

This sensibility, based in a radical loss of faith in politics among other things, suffuses *This American Life's* exploration of human experience. It's a useful parable for the growth to "maturity" of National Public Radio, and the urgent political commitments that drove the journalists who got their start there in the 1970s. Importantly, it's not merely the content of his former beliefs that Glass repudiates in this episode, but their strength. The shibboleth, "it's complicated" (or "nuanced" or "surprising") acts to ward off politics, history, any system of ordering experience that isn't at heart, based on the universality of individual experience, the aesthetics of surprise, and the ambivalent emotional stew of empathy and disjunctive irony. The scandalous, bloody history of the U.S. in Nicaragua in the 1980s is a striking backdrop for an anecdote essentially justifying the exchange of political faith for a gauzy curiosity about human "complexity."[2]

There have been a handful of episodes over the years that have engaged a wider world of historical change, political conflict, and economic crisis. Episodes which are set in war zones and in the rest stops

---

2   Interviews were conducted via email with listeners who responded to a query at the May 7, 2009, (second) broadcast of *This American Life's* "C. Megan. (2009). Personal communication. June 4.

and shopping malls where the recession is felt most acutely. As I've said, the structure of feeling oscillates between empathy and inwardness—or, as Susan Douglas might put it, between a telescopic and microscopic perspective (Douglas 2006). "The mission of public broadcasting," Ira Glass has said, "is to tell us stories that help us empathize and help us feel less crazy and less separate" (Glass, 1998). Listeners respond enthusiastically to the partially telescopic impulse of these episodes as well: "It"s utterly pleasurable [sic] ... it feels like you're doing something good, staying in tune with the world, in the tiniest way possible and yet without being frivolous about it. It's unlike anything else out there" (Johnson, 37).

The aesthetics of voice are central to this pleasure, to being "in tune" with the world according public radio. It's an aesthetics of juxtaposed opposites—gravitas and whimsy, empathy and irony. The insouciant, conversational style of *Planet Money*'s correspondents conveys a chumminess without warmth. The "soft masculinity" of Glass and his metrosexual contributors provide for many listeners an antidote to the abrasive voice of mainstream news, while still making them feel connected to a wider world (Johnson 65-75). Carried on voices both intimate and cool, a neoliberal structure of feeling is conveyed at the place where "doing something good" and the "utterly pleasurable" meet.

This American Life grounds this celebration of individualism and hunger for human connection in the assumption that certain socially progressive values have trumped residual prejudices, leaving a landscape in which individual struggles for self-understanding, surprise, and joy take place beyond the hierarchies, exclusions, and struggles for power that may have characterized the past. In these ways, *This American Life* does more than echo neoliberal values. It represents a set of unusually sensitive and successful performances of, meditations on, and accommodations to the inwardness and historical amnesia of neoliberal subjectivity.

This American Life is a key site in the cultural field of neoliberalism. Central to this cultural field are stories that replace historical struggles with personal ones and the predictability of political context with the drama of surprise. *This American Life*'s impressive oeuvre of more than 400 episodes, its millions of listeners, and its myriad distinctive voices merit continued scholarly attention, for the impact they've had on public radio and beyond. The program serves as a fascinating soundtrack to an era in American life when "staying in touch with the world in the tiniest way possible," while pleasurable, may no longer be a sufficient level of engagement. *This American Life* has turned the space between "doing something good" and "being frivolous" into a format unto itself, an intensification of NPR's formula for balancing gravitas and whimsy. As this mode of storytelling comes to dominate the public radio landscape and individual identity replaces historical and social understanding as the quarry for engaged reporting and documentary work, we can look forward to hearing more voices bearing the sound signification of a liberal past and the moral perspective of a neoliberal future.

ACKNOWLEDGEMENTS

The author wishes to thank Janice Peck and Inger Stole for their invaluable help in re-conceptualizing the argument of this chapter.

REFERENCES

Abell, Jessica and Ira Glass. 1999. Radio: An Illustrated Guide. Chicago: WBEZ Alliance, Inc.

Anderson Brian C. 2005. *South Park Conservatives: The Revolt Against Liberal Media Bias.* Washington, D.C: Regnery Press.

Berquist, Kathryn. 2002. "The host with the most: with his hit public radio show, *This American Life*, Ira Glass puts gay and lesbian stories and storyteller front and center." *The Advocate.* Nov 26.

Boutsen, Frank. 2003. "Prosody: The Music of Language and Speech," *The ASHA Leader Online*, American Speech-Language-Hearing Association, January-March, 2003.

Corportion for Public Brodcasting. 2003. "Public Perceptions of Public Broadcasting. http:"www.cpb.org/aboutcpb/goals/objectivity/pollsummary.html Accessed on April 1, 2011.

Dadge, David. 2006. *The War in Iraq and Why the Media Failed Us.* New York: Praeger.

deMause, Neil. 2007. "Action Alert: NPR Gives Torture Credibility: Report treats torture-based confessions as news." Mediamatters.org. October 10.

Douglas, Susan J. 1999. *Listening In: Radio and the American Imagination.* New York: Crown Publishing.

———. 2006. "The Turn Within: The Irony of Technology in a Globalized World." *American Quarterly.* 58:3. 619-638.

Dvorkin, Jeffrey A. 2005. "NPR In 1988: 'News That Soothes.'" NPR.org

Ehrenreich, Barbara. 1989. *Fear of Falling: The Inner Life of the Middle Class.* New York: Pantheon.

Everhart, Karen. 2010. "Mobile giving a 'no-brainer' for *TAL* postcast audience." *Current.* April 19. Accessed on May 2, 2010.

Faludi, Susan. 1991. *Backlash: The Undeclared War Against American Women.* New York: Crown.

Fisher, Marc. 1999. "It's a Wonderful Life." *American Journalism Review.* July/August.

Glass, Ira. 1998. "Mo' Better Radio." Current.Org. http://www.current.org/people/p809i1.html. Accessed on February 2, 2010.

Groseclose, Tim and Jeffrey Milyo. 2005. "A Measure of Media Bias.*" *The Quarterly Journal of Economics.* November. 1191-1237.

Harvey, David. 2005. *A Brief History of Neoliberalism.* Oxford; New York: Oxford University Press.

Johnson, Kristine. 2007. "Imagine This: Radio Revisited Through Podcasting" MA Thesis, Texas Christian University, 36-37.

Karpf, Anne. 2006. *The Human Voice: How This Extraordinary Instrument Reveals Clues about Who We Are.* London: Bloomsbury, 33-47.

Lasch, Christopher. 1978. *The Culture of Narcissism: American Life in an Age of Diminishing Expectations.* New York: W.W. Norton.

Lewin, James. 2009. "Ira Glass: Podcast Increased *This American Life* Audience by Half a Million." PodcastingNews.Com. http://www.podcastingnews.com/2009/04/16/ira-glass-podcast-increased-this-american-life-audience-by-half-a-million/. Accessed on February 2, 2010.

Loviglio, Jason. 2005. "National Semiprivate Radio," *Radio Journal: International Studies in Broadcast and Audio Media*, 3:3: 199–204.

———. 2008. "Sound Effects: Gender, Voice and the Cultural Work of NPR," *Radio Journal: International Studies in Broadcast and Audio Media*, 5: 2: 67-81.

McCauley, Michael. 2005. *NPR: The Trials and Triumphs of National Public Radio.* New York: Columbia University Press.

McConnell-Ginet, Sally. 1983. *Intonation in a Man's World, Language, Gender, and Society.* Cambridge: Newbury House Publishers, 75.

McLuhan, Marshall. 1964. *Understanding Media.* New York: McGraw-Hill.

Mitchell, Jack W. 2005. *Listener Supported: The Culture and History of Public Radio.* Westport, Connecticut: Praeger.

"Mo Better Radio." 1998. *Current*. Current Publishing Committee, Takoma Park, Md. http://www.current.org/people/p809i1.html. Accessed on January 15, 2010.

Naureckas, Jim. 2008. "Extra!: NPR Disappears Iraqi Dead." *Extra!* New York: Fairness and Accuracy in Reporting. May/June.

Peck, Janice. 2008. *The Age of Oprah: Cultural Icon for the Neoliberal Era.* Boulder, CO: Paradigm.

Planet Money. 2010. "Hello From Sao Paolo."

———. "In Search of the Red Tape Factory."

———. "The Problem of Giving Free Food to Hungry People."

———. "These are the Guys Who Are Kicking Our Ass?"

Rendall, Steve and Daniel Butterworth. 2004. "How Public Is Public Radio? A Study of NPR's Guest List." *Extra!* New York: Fairness and Accuracy in Reporting. May/June.

Solomon, Norman. 2002. "NPR and the Fallow Triumph of Public Radio." Alternet.org. April 11. Accessed on February 2, 2010.

Soros, George. 2002. *George Soros on Globalization*. New York: Public Affairs.

This American Life. 2010. "Enemy Camp." #404.

———. 2010. "Island Time" #408.

———. 1998. "Notes on Camp." #109.

———. 2010. "Nummi." #403.

———. 2008. "Social Engineering." #358.

———. 2008. "The Giant Pool of Money." #XXX

———. 2009. "This I Used to Believe." #378.

"*This American Life* Completes Documentation Of Liberal, Upper-Middle-Class Existence." 2007. *The Onion*. April 20. 46: 26.

Thomas, June. 2009. "Let's Get Those Phones Ringing! The Cunning Genius of the Public Radio Fundraising Drive." *Slate*. March 2. Accessed on February 2, 2010.

Warner, Michael. 1993. "The Mass Public and The Mass Subject." In *The Phantom Public Sphere*. Minneapolis: University of Minnesota Press.

WBEZ. 2005. "This American Life Sampler," (Peabody Award nomination). Peabody Awards Collection. Call Number: 2005041. http://www.libs.uga.edu/media/collections/peabody/pbdatabase/index.html. Accessed on February 12, 2010.

"Where are the Women?" 2010. NPR Ombudsman. NPR.org. http://www.npr.org/blogs/ombudsman/2010/04/where_are_the_women.html Accessed on April 12, 2010.

CHAPTER 14

"STICKING IT TO THE MAN"

NEOLIBERALISM: CORPORATE MEDIA & STRATEGIES OF RESISTANCE IN THE 21ST CENTURY

Deepa Kumar

I N THE FALL OF 1997, THE GAME SHOW "WHEEL OF FORTUNE," ran a week of episodes starting on Labor Day titled "Wheel of Fortune Salute to America's Working Families." The producer of the show, Harry Friedman, stated that "Americans are working harder and smarter than ever before ... We think a salute to workers, their unions and the products and services they provide our society is a fitting tribute to offer" ("Union Label" 1997). All the contestants on the shows were either union members or their families, and the major prizes were union-made and identified as such, with prominent displays of union labels. The seal of the umbrella labor federation, the AFL-CIO, was seen in the center of the stage floor, and several thousand union members were present in the audience wearing their union T-shirts and carrying signs.

Such a ringing endorsement of the union movement on a popular game show in the mainstream media is rare and exceptional. It marked a significant moment in media history, in that, a normally pro-corporate and anti-labor environment was bent to accommodate a pro-labor stance. How and why did this happen? In a nutshell, a nationwide strike by 185,000 United Parcel Service (UPS) workers the previous month had successfully challenged the pro-corporate logic in the mainstream media and created an opening for the discussion of working class issues. They had succeeded in creating, for a short period of a time, a space in the corporate media to discuss the contradictions of neoliberalism and the inequalities produced by it. By showing that its grievances against UPS were similar to the conditions faced by working class people as a whole, the Teamsters union (which represents UPS workers) was able to win public support and put enough pressure on the corporate media so that for the first time in the era of neoliberalism there was a sustained conversation in the public sphere about the ravages of neoliberalism.

This chapter looks at the power of organized labor to resist the logic of neoliberalism, both in material and ideological terms. It begins by outlining the shift from the Keynesian economic system to neoliberalism and lays out the key contours of the neoliberal regime; it also outlines the price paid by labor. With a clear picture of what neoliberalism is and how it has impacted working class Americans (who are the majority, about 70-75 percent of the population), we then turn to the media to understand why this story has not been conveyed to the public. We start by examining how neoliberalism has shaped the media industry over the last three decades and how the giant media conglomerates of today have benefitted from these changes. This overview then helps to set the context for why there has been almost no criticism of the neoliberal model, and why the problems faced by working class people in the U.S., who have not benefited from the neoliberal turn, have largely been ignored in the media. The chapter then surveys the labor movement's responses to neoliberalism.

Finally, it looks at media coverage of the UPS strike to show how organized labor can successfully resist the neoliberal assault. This is a significant moment, and one worthy of study, as the same challenges faced by UPS workers in 1997 are those faced by the majority of Americans today.

FROM KEYNESIANISM TO NEOLIBERALISM

During the 1950s and 1960s, the "golden age" of the American economy, all measures of prosperity were high. The Gross Domestic Product (GDP) grew steadily and with it the wages of workers, particularly manufacturing workers, rose by a dramatic 84 percent (Smith 1992). This context allowed President Kennedy to talk about a "rising tide, raising all boats," although certainly not everyone benefited from the postwar boom—racism prevented the advancement of African Americans and other minorities and, even at that point, poverty was not eliminated. Nevertheless, the ideas of the British economist John Maynard Keynes held sway during this period. In a nutshell, Keynesianism is an economic theory that rests on deficit-based government stimulus spending and strong regulation of markets. The more popular version of Keynesianism is based on the idea that state intervention—including government social programs, infrastructural spending, and even in some cases, partial state ownership—is necessary to stave off the capitalist system's tendency toward deep economic crises, such as the Great Depression of the 1930s.

After 1965, profits began to decline and failed to recover their peak levels. As a result, the net investment in plants and equipment fell and productivity suffered (Ferguson and Rogers 1986). At the same time, American capital lost ground in the global economy. Burdened by high military spending and aging capital stock (e.g., tools, factories, etc.)—U.S. capital became less competitive on the world market against the freshly rebuilt and retooled economic powers in Europe and Japan. The relative decline of U.S. capital and global hegemony was further exacerbated when the Bretton Woods agreement collapsed in 1971.[1] Additionally, advanced capitalist countries around the world, from at least 1965, started to experience the problem of persistent inflation. All these conditions of low growth and high inflation produced an outcome known as "stagflation." The Keynesian economic model was unable to address this crisis and a space was created for a new economic theory that could address this situation and make the U.S. profitable again.

The theory that replaced Keynesianism, which is associated with a group of thinkers including Friedrich Von Hayek, Ludwig Von Mises, and Milton Friedman (and his protégées at the University of Chicago), came to be known as neoliberalism. In popular perception, neoliberalism has been seen as the rejection of state intervention into the economy, and thus as the opposite of Keynesianism. Yet, in reality, without the enthusiastic support of governments, neoliberalism

---

1   In 1944, 44 delegations from around the world met in Bretton Woods, New Hampshire, to take stock of the events of the previous 30 years and to restore and stabilize capitalism. The two participants who really had a say in drafting the original conference document were the British, represented by John Maynard Keynes, and the Americans, represented by Harry Dexter White. From this meeting, the International Monetary Fund (IMF) and the World Bank were set up as multilateral, international institutions that would deal with global financial problems. Under the new monetary system, all currencies would be tied to the dollar, which was valued at $35 per ounce of gold. When Bretton Woods collapsed, currencies were yanked from the dollar-gold standard and allowed to free float.

would not have been implemented. The neoliberal doctrine is more accurately understood as an all-out attack on the wages and lifestyle of the working-class, along with plans to cut government spending on social programs, increase tax breaks for corporations and the very rich, deregulate the economy and privatize publicly owned enterprises—a program carried out with the aid of cooperative governments. This corpus, known as "supply-side" economics, as opposed to the "demand"-oriented policies of Keynesianism, has been the dominant economic logic in the U.S. and globally since the 1970s.

One of the consequences of neoliberalism has been an alarming increase in class polarization. While a tiny minority of Americans at the top of society have become rich beyond imagination, the bottom 80 percent have seen their wages either stagnate or decline over the last few decades. Economist Paul Krugman (2002) shows that in the 1970s, the average real compensation of CEOs of the top 100 corporations was 39 times the pay of the average worker. In 2002, these CEOs earned 1,000 times the average worker's pay. In short, there has been a dramatic increase in class polarization during the neoliberal era. The next section lays out the key economic shifts precipitated by neoliberalism with a particular focus on aspects that have had a devastating impact on the working class.[2]

THE NEOLIBERAL TURN

The American version of neoliberal globalization, also known as the "American Model" and the "Washington Consensus," was crafted during the mid-1970s as a solution to the crisis that *Business Week* in 1974 summarized as follows:

> The U.S., like the world around it, is in sad shape today. Having borrowed too much in the expectation of perpetual plenty, Americans are desperate for answers to questions for which there are no pat answers ... Some people will obviously have to do with less, or with substitutes, so that the economy as a whole can get the most mileage out of available capital ... Yet it will be a hard pill for many Americans to swallow—the idea of doing with less so that big business can have more ... Nothing that this nation, or any other nation, has done in modern economic history compares in difficulty

---

2   It is beyond the scope of this essay to discuss all the dimensions of the neoliberal turn. Thus, I do not discuss neoliberal policies in relation to the financial sector, etc.

with the selling job that must now be done to make people accept the new reality (Carson-Parker 1974 121).

In short, the working class was being asked to pay the price for the mistakes and excesses of big business. To meet the challenge of selling this "new reality" and to craft a new economic agenda, business required a new strategy. This led to the growth of think tanks and Political Action Committees (PACs), the further expansion of the public relations industry, and the formation or revival of various business organizations (Herman and Chomsky 1988, Moody 1988). Additionally, the corporate media, which have benefitted from neoliberal globalization, have been at the forefront of selling this logic.

Corporate America's response to the structural crisis of capitalism consisted of two related strategies. The first focused on measures that the state could enact, such as deregulation, privatization, rolling back labor movement gains, cutting social spending, and increasing tax breaks to corporations (neoliberal policy). The second was a shift within corporations to what is called "lean" production (neoliberal corporate practice).

NEOLIBERAL POLICY

In the mid-1970s, as *Business Week* put it, workers were going to have to make do with less so that business could have more. Following this prescription, the government reduced spending on social programs and increased tax breaks for business. In 1978, Congress passed a tax reform bill that cut capital gains taxes by 40 percent, while substantially increasing social security, a regressive tax where everyone pays the same amount, and eliminating taxes on income over a certain amount (Bartlett and Steele 1992). The highest marginal income tax rate for the richest individuals, which in the 1950s was 95 percent and in 1980 was 70 percent, fell to 38.5 percent in the early part of the 21st century due to the Bush administration's tax reforms. Thus, while taxes on corporations and the wealthy decreased, those on the average person increased. During the same period that the corporate share of the tax burden was being lowered, welfare payments to the poorest Americans were also put on the chopping block. Reduced by the Carter administration and cut even more during the Reagan-Bush era, welfare payments were slashed under Clinton.

Privatization schemes have been less drastic in the United States than in other parts of the world, as its public sector is marginal. The little that is publicly owned—the airwaves, schools, public services such as welfare and healthcare—has already been or is in the process of being privatized. Deregulation began with the airline industry in 1978, followed by trucking in 1980, and telecommunications in the 1980s and 1990s. UPS lobbied hard for trucking deregulation (Hirshberg et. al 1995). Large corporations have been the prime beneficiaries of this process. They seized this opportunity to consolidate by either buying up, or merging with, smaller or equivalent corporations. Contrary to the claim that deregulation would spur competition in a "free" market and therefore reduce prices for consumers, precisely the opposite has occurred. For instance, deregulation depressed competition in the airline industry and ticket prices have gone up, particularly in cities where a single airline has a stronghold (Bartlett and Steele). The media industry has also benefited tremendously from privatization and deregulation, a point to which I will return to later in the chapter.

While large and multinational corporations have benefited from privatization and deregulation, the same cannot be said for workers. Stanley Wisniewski notes that in the telecommunication industry, privatization and deregulation have led to "massive lay-offs and dislocation, and there has been a serious erosion in worker morale associated with potential job insecurity. Similarly, fundamental restructuring in the transportation industries has produced major dislocation, wage cuts and job insecurity which has placed the burden of such 'privatization' squarely on the shoulders of employees" (1997, 42). While corporate profits grew, the employment conditions for workers deteriorated. The deregulation process has also created the conditions for overproduction, where more goods are produced than can be sold profitably.

These neoliberal policies have been enthusiastically supported by Democrats and Republicans alike, who have passed legislation favorable to business, marginalizing and even subverting the interests of labor in the process. For instance, the Carter administration targeted labor income as one of the causes of rising inflation, despite the fact that labor costs had, in fact, declined throughout the 1970s (Moody 1988). Under Reagan, collective bargaining received a further blow when striking air traffic controllers represented by PATCO (Professional Air Traffic Controllers Organization) were fired in 1981. This sent a clear signal that the Reagan administration would aid business by undermining labor.

In addition to these legislative changes, corporate America learned that it had to reorganize itself from within to better compete internationally and boost profitability. The restructuring process emphasized "flexibility" and adopted a mode of capitalist exploitation called "lean production." Ideologically, this shift put an end to some of the concessions granted to labor in the 1950s and 1960s. A telling indication of this shift was the success and proliferation of union-busting agencies. Union-busting firms were active in the 1950s, but they weren't very pervasive. In the 1970s, these firms grew and were sabotaging most union organizing drives. By 1979, more than 1,000 anti-labor consulting firms were earning an estimated half-billion dollars (Goldfield 1987). During the Keynesian era, when the economy was growing, labor could expect wage increases tied to productivity and state-subsidized home ownership and higher education programs, but not after the early 1970s (Coontz 1997).

NEOLIBERAL CORPORATE PRACTICE

In this section we examine one of the key aspects of corporate restructuring in the era of neoliberalism, i.e. the adoption of the lean production model. Lean production originated in Japan in the post-World War II era after militant trade unions had been successfully beaten down. The system's supporters claim that it is an efficient, decentralized method of organization that allows for maximum flexibility based on cooperation and mutual respect between workers and managers. Critics point out that while it has reduced costs and increased flexibility for corporations, it has increased class polarization and involuntary contingent employment. Furthermore, the Japanese model did not and could not come into existence until the militant trade unions had been defeated; that is, it is predicated on labor's acquiescence to management's goals. Much has been written about this new mode of capitalist organization and how corporations in Europe and the United States have selectively adapted it, both by advocates and critics.

Economist Bennet Harrison (1994) suggests that the restructuring that occurred after the 1970s developed a tiered system of production. Large firms entered into alliances and deals with governments, smaller firms, and one another, creating a network of suppliers and subcontractors. The result was a decentralized network that has been

314 A Moment of Danger

compared to a web with the core firm as its spider. Tasks once performed by the core firm are delegated, or outsourced (which is a method of busting unions), to other contractors, establishing several tiers, with work conditions deteriorating down the tiers. In such a tiered, decentralized network the core firm becomes more "flexible;" that is, it can adapt more easily to market changes. Note that decentralization does not loosen power hierarchies and decision-making abilities; rather, suppliers are under the direct control of the core firm without the core incurring their economic responsibilities.

The process of cutting down personnel, or downsizing, is central to the system's leanness. Thus, once the core has been determined, all the other jobs are delegated or contracted out. For instance, in 1980, Toyota had 168 first-tier subcontractors, 4,700 second-tier subcontractors, and 31,600 suppliers in the third-tier (Harrison 156). The footwear company Nike is headquartered in the United States but at the bottom-most level has suppliers who run sweatshops in Indonesia, China, and other developing nations. Nike's success has prompted other shoe companies, such as Vans and Adidas, to follow a similar path (Klein 1999). However, this method of production has not been applied uniformly. The tiered workforce at UPS, for instance, is grouped in a single location: permanent part-timers work alongside shrinking numbers of full-time workers. Additionally, key aspects of UPS's services, particularly parcel delivery, cannot be outsourced to workers in distant locations.

This tiered system relies on information technology that enables core firms to coordinate activities both within their firms and with suppliers. Contrary to the claims of technological determinists who argue that technology sets the pace of development, most of this technology did not exist when the lean production model was first developed. Rather, the growth in information technology was fueled by a system that moved beyond Japan and into the West and that created a demand for computer software, distance applications, and consistent platforms (Singer 1999). As we shall see in the next section, the media and information industries have been central to the coordination of multinational corporations.

One part of lean production is the shift to "team work," where management and unionists supposedly united to make the firm more efficient and profitable. In reality, however, such teams actually strip workers of control over the shop floor. As Mike Parker and Jane Slaughter

(1988) argue, "teams" are not really teams at all, but a way for management to elicit knowledge from workers without giving them control over the production process. They suggest that a more apt description of lean production is "management-by-stress," where every phase of the production process, including workers, is stretched to the breaking point. It uses as few materials as possible, and workers must work as fast as they can to make up for their inadequate numbers. Peer pressure is enormous, because if one worker slows or stops the production process, all the other workers are adversely affected.

At its core, lean production was about reorganizing the system of production materially and ideologically so that the balance of power would shift more decisively toward the employing class. This paradigm stands in contrast to the postwar Keynesian years, when the union leadership could expect a less hostile employer and unionized workers saw real wage increases. In the aftermath of the crisis of the 1970s, the rising tide would not again lift all boats. Yet, this story of increased class inequality and deteriorating work conditions for the majority has largely been ignored in the mainstream media. In the following section we examine why this is the case.

NEOLIBERALISM AND THE CORPORATE MEDIA

Today, the bulk of the media in the U.S. are owned by a handful of giant conglomerates. While neoliberal policy did not begin the process of media consolidation, since the early 1980s the trend toward concentration has accelerated, much like the mergers in other sections of the economy. The media industry has been at the forefront of this trend of consolidation, so that when the merger between Time-Warner and AOL was realized, it was not only the largest media merger but also the largest merger in the history of capitalism up to that point (Carroll 2001). Media scholar Ben Bagdikian has written about the concentration of media ownership since at least the early 1980s. When he published the first edition of *Media Monopoly* in 1983, about 50 corporations dominated the ownership of television stations, cable, films, recorded music, magazines, newspapers, books, and other media in the United States. In the 2004 edition, that same figure had decreased to five.

This level of media concentration and consolidation has been enabled by privatization and deregulation the world over. The United States, Great Britain, and Japan led the trend in the late 1970s. In the

United States, during the Reagan era, media lobbies actively pushed for an end to regulation, a policy consistent with the administration's agenda. The stated goal of deregulation was to create greater competition and enable the industry to "set professional standards," thus improving quality without "needless interference" by the state. The Reagan administration willingly obliged, reducing the standards required by government agencies like the Securities Exchange Commission (SEC) and the Federal Communications Commission (FCC) to mention a few (Gershon 1997).

The most enthusiastic supporter of deregulation was the FCC, under its former chairperson, Mark Fowler. As *Business Week* observed, the FCC in the 1980s had "become Washington's most advanced laboratory for the antiregulation theories of the Reagan administration" (Gershon 22). As a result, in the 1980s, cable television was deregulated, and control over programming and rates placed in the hands of cable providers; the number of TV and radio stations that could be owned by one corporation was increased; the standards for renewing broadcast licenses were reduced; and broadcasting rules about obscenity were weakened.

If the Reagan-Bush administrations began the process of media deregulation, the Clinton administration took it one step further through the passage of the Telecommunication Act of 1996. The core function of this bill was to remove restrictions on firms moving into other communication areas, such as telecommunication into cable, and to remove most, if not all, regulations on their behavior (McChesney 1999). Contrary to the industry's claims that the Telecommunication Act would spur "genuine market competition" and serve the public better, the outcome has been a consolidation beyond the expectations even of the lobbyists themselves (McChesney and Herman 1997).

Internationally, agencies like the International Monetary Fund (IMF) and the World Trade Organization (WTO) have aided in the consolidation of the media industry. As Robert McChesney and Edward Herman (1997) note, "The IMF is committed to encouraging the establishment of commercial media globally to better serve the needs of a market economy. The WTO's mission is to encourage a single global market for commercial media, and to oppose barriers to this, however noble in intent" (50). This mission has translated into policies where loans to economically underdeveloped nations are tied to demands that various state- owned sectors, including the media, be privatized and deregulated. The media corporations of the triad regions of North America, Europe, and Japan have consequently established a foothold around the world.

The benefits to media conglomeration are numerous. Apart from increased profitability, conglomeration and concentration has led to the creation of an oligopolistic market; that is, a market dominated by a handful of corporations, where the barriers to entry are extremely high. As capital outlays for media products tend to be high, only in markets with reduced or diminished competition are the returns on investment guaranteed. In addition, consolidation has allowed conglomerates to downsize their work force and outsource low-to-moderate skill labor, while coordinating their activities from national headquarters. In other words, lean production and the creation of a tiered work force are not unfamiliar to the media industry.

As Gerald Sussman and John Lent (1998) note, "the 'information society' is based on a new international division of labor of men and women sharing a production platform but dispersed into segmented zones of industrial, semi-industrial, and Third World societies" (1). From the production of computer and electronic components to data entry and information processing, aspects of the production process in media industries have been outsourced to regions with lower labor costs. For instance, John Lent (1998) shows how corporations from the triad regions, particularly Disney in the United States, have shipped out animation work to countries in Asia where, due to anti-union laws, workers are forced to work seven days a week. Additionally, Disney merchandise is produced in more than 3,000 factories worldwide, with a significant percentage concentrated in developing countries like Haiti, China, Vietnam, and India, where workers toil in sweat-shop conditions (Wasko 2001). Ewart Skinner (1998) demonstrates how the outsourcing of data entry to the Caribbean islands has reduced the data-processing budgets for U.S. companies by 50 percent, while creating low-wage, tedious, fast-paced, and unsafe conditions for the workers. The net result is super-profits for the media giants and a race to the bottom in terms of wages, work conditions, and union rights for media and information workers around the world.

Consequently, the media have an institutional interest in presenting the neoliberal global economy in a manner that favors their interests and those of other corporations. A vast body of literature argues that the news media overrepresent the interests of the elites.[3] Herman and McChesney, in their detailed study of the structure and functioning of the global media, make a strong argument that "the global media are the missionaries of our age, promoting the virtues of commercialism and the market loudly and incessantly through their profit-driven and advertising-supported enterprises and programming" (37).

The central premise of the procorporate ideology promoted by these "missionaries" is that the market is the most just means of allocating resources and that a free market, based on the absence of constraints on business, guarantees not only economic but political freedom. Another aspect of this ideology is that government intervention or regulation unduly burdens business and impedes economic growth. Government ownership or control over resources is seen as extremely inefficient. Thus, state-owned resources are best handed over to business, particularly if they are likely to generate profit. Furthermore, the ideal government does not govern, but supports and enhances the market's interests. It can do so by keeping inflation low to enable "sustainable economic growth;" that is, corporations would much rather have slow growth and high unemployment, if inflation is kept in check. Within this framework, economic growth is measured in terms of the Gross Domestic Product (GDP), which reflects the prosperity of business, while it hides income and wealth inequality (Herman and McChesney).

This neoliberal logic underpins much news media economic reporting. While occasional stories challenge the above assumptions, for the most part the interests of labor are subordinated to those of corporations. As George Lipsitz (1994) observes:

> For almost twenty years, working people and their interests have been absent from most public discussions about our national

3   Edward Herman, and Noam Chomsky, *Manufacturing Consent: The Political Economy of the Mass Media.* New York: Pantheon Books, 1988; Douglas Kellner, *Television and the Crisis of Democracy.* Boulder: Westview Press, 1990; Robert McChesney, *Corporate Media and the Threat to Democracy.* New York: Seven Stories Press, 1997; J. Eldridge, ed., *Glasgow Media Group Reader,* vol. 1, *News Content, Language and Visuals.* New York: Routledge, 1995; Robert Entman, *Democracy Without Citizens.* New York: Oxford University Press, 1989; James Winter, *Democracy's Oxygen: How Corporations Control the News* New York: Black Rose Books, 1997; Dennis Mazzocco, *Networks of Power: Corporate TV's Threat to Democracy.* Boston: South End Press, 1997.

political and cultural life. As deindustrialization and economic re-structuring have radically transformed U.S. society, the people and communities most immediately affected by these changes have been virtually erased. Business initiatives dominate the economic, political, and social agenda of the nation, while labor's perspectives and needs remain almost invisible within most of the country's mainstream media and economic institutions (1).

This trend is not new, but it has been accentuated over the past 50 years with the decline of the labor movement. In the 1930s and 1940s, a full-time labor editor or beat reporter was the norm among newspapers with medium-to-large circulations. The labor beat as such came into being in the context of the great labor struggles of that period and marked a recognition on the part of the elite that labor had to be taken seriously. Today, with the decline of the labor movement (discussed in the next section), most labor news is covered in the business pages. By 2002, there were fewer than five labor reporters left in the U.S. (McChesney 2002). Few reporters are assigned exclusively to cover labor issues. Additionally, while most daily newspapers have business sections, they lack a corresponding labor section. This shift to create a more business friendly environment took shape largely in the context of 1970s with the emergence of neoliberal policy.

The picture is not that different in broadcasting. National television, including PBS, offers dozens of business and investor programs but not one regular show on labor or consumer rights. Cable channels like CNBC are completely dedicated to the coverage of Wall Street; CNN, MSNBC, and other channels have slots in regular programming for business perspectives on the economy; similar labor slots or channels do not exist.

That corporate views therefore tend to dominate in the news is not surprising. For instance, a study of the coverage of the North American Free Trade Agreement (NAFTA) during a four-month period in 1993 in the *New York Times* and *Washington Post* found that the discussion was dominated by voices in support of the bill. Of the 201 sources quoted, supporters figured three times more often than critics, and not even one source represented a union. Six months prior to the vote, the *New York Times* ran a special advertising section on NAFTA but denied space to two unions opposed to it ("Happily Ever" 1993). The upshot is that coverage of the economy that emerges from a commercialized media system is highly limited in scope. Organized labor, however, has the ability to challenge this status quo as we noted above in reference to the 1930s and the origins of the labor beat. However, as we see in the following section, the official union movement has responded ineffectually to the neoliberal assault.

LABOR'S TAME RESPONSE

Organized labor's response to management's offensive has been less than adequate; instead of organizing to fight back, they have accepted the logic of labor-management cooperation. The union leadership's unwillingness to hold corporations accountable follows from the fact that they are not impacted by the terms of the contract they negotiate for their members. Unless pressed by rank and file workers, the labor bureaucracy would rather not rock the boat. This is the legacy of "business unionism," a form of unionism that is based on a business model where revenues are kept high, risks (such as strikes) are avoided, and the price of labor negotiated with capital under amicable conditions (Buhle 1999).

Through much of the 1980s and 90s, in the absence of rank and file pressure, the labor bureaucracy conceded to the employers' various demands from "partnership" to "teamwork" and the logic of lean production. Labor's timidity meant that by the late 1980s, almost 75 percent of all contracts covering 1,000 or more workers included concessions, and the figure was 90 percent for manufacturing workers (Smith 2006).

Nelson Lichtenstein (2002) argues that the current offensive on labor has its roots in the post-World War II era, when business leaders sought to overturn the gains made by the labor movement in the 1930s and erase from public consciousness any memory of that period.[4] It was in this context that the anti-union Taft Hartley Act was passed. Couched as way to rid labor of the "domination" of communists, Taft Hartley was actually a means by which the Wagner Law and the Norris-La Guardia Anti-Injunction Act (both labor victories of the 1930s), were overturned. The Taft-Hartley bill put into place a number of anti-union policies. For instance, it made it possible for employers to break strikes through injunctions against picketing, to refuse to bargain collectively, and even to shut down plants to postpone

4   See also Elizabeth Fones-Wolf, *Selling Free Enterprise: The Business Assualt on Labor and Liberalism 1945-60.* Urbana Champaign: University of Illinois Press, 1994.

negotiations. It also put a halt to the practice of sympathy strikes, where workers could strike in solidarity with other workers. Labor's failure to overturn Taft Hartley, and its willing cooperation with management's post-war agenda, laid the basis for a weakened labor movement that was unable to counter management's renewed offensive during the era of neoliberalism.

If the Chrysler bailout of 1978 indicated labor's willingness to acquiesce to capital, Reagan's firing of the air traffic controllers organized by PATCO in the 1980s showed that the elite would use any means necessary to achieve its goals. Labor was unprepared to meet the new challenge, clinging instead to the "social contract" ideology of the 1950s and 60s, when unions and management were supposedly involved in a mutually beneficial relationship.[5]

To make matters worse, as Sharon Smith (2006) argues, labor's political strategy of supporting the Democratic Party has been a dead end. After twelve years of Republican rule, when Bill Clinton was sworn into office in 1992, labor believed that it had an ally in the White House. However, the Clinton administration enthusiastically pursued neoliberal policies. Despite its many betrayals of promises made to labor, including the passage of NAFTA against labor's wishes, the labor movement continued to support the Democratic Party. While some in the union leadership have publicly acknowledged the weaknesses of this strategy, it has not reversed their general position.

The successes of the union movement have come from actions led by rank and file workers. In the 1930s, rank and file workers led by radicals—socialists, anarchists, and communists—were involved in strikes and other struggles which ultimately led to the formation of the CIO (the Congress of Industrial Organizations). In the era of neoliberalism, particularly during the late 1960s and early 1970s, groups of workers in various industries came together to challenge the corporate agenda. Black autoworkers fought against speed-ups and racial discrimination. They stood up not only to the big three automakers but also against racism within the UAW (Foner 1982). The Dodge

---

5 Yet, as Lichtenstein argues, the working class didn't really benefit from this "labor-management accord." While real wages did increase, strikes were ten times more prevalent during that time than after 1980. This is because the rise in wages during the post-war years didn't compensate for the increase in productivity. Instead, the vast profits generated by highly productive workers went into the coffers of the capitalist class.

Revolutionary Union Movement (DRUM) started in Detroit inspired rank and file black workers to form similar groups elsewhere and engage in unauthorized wildcat strikes (Georgakas and Surkin 1998). In almost all industries, wildcat strikes grew during the 1960s and reached a highpoint in 1970. Rank and file workers in several industries formed union reform groups.

However, by the end of the 1970s this rank and file upsurge, and labor militancy in general, would slow down considerably. For instance, in 1974 there were 424 strikes and lockouts (Sustar 2003). This trend continued, so that by 2003 the number of work stoppages dropped to 14 ("Work Stoppages" 2004). This decline in rank and file activity is a product of a number of factors, including the destruction of the labor left by McCarthyism in the 1950s, the hesitancy of the New Left of the 1960s to form links with labor, the lack of forces that could bring together the various rank and file efforts of the 1970s, the extirpation of labor traditions from the history and memory of the working class, and the part played by the corporate media in erasing labor history from public consciousness.

However, the 1980s and '90s did see some successes. The most significant among them was the UPS strike of 1997, not only because the Teamsters union won many of its demands, but also because the public supported the union over the company by a margin of two to one and identified with the issues raised by the workers. In the following section we examine how this strike brought to the fore the contradictions of neoliberalism and how the Teamsters were able to pressure the corporate media to accommodate a pro-labor stance.

THE UPS STRIKE AND MEDIA COVERAGE

On July 31, 1997, the contract deadline between United Parcel Service and the International Brotherhood of Teamsters expired. Agreement had not been reached between the two parties due to several unresolved issues. UPS's "last, best, and final" offer included the following proposals: withdraw from the union's multi-employer pension plan, provide a marginal increase in pay, create 1,000 new, full-time jobs, and secure a five-year contract. The union proposed staying with the multi-employer plan, increasing pay more substantially, creating 10,000 full-time jobs for part-timers, and obtaining a four-year contract.

The union's negotiating points were determined months prior to the strike, through a communications strategy known as the "contract campaign." The campaign revealed that the creation of full-time jobs was of utmost importance to a large number of workers (Kumar 2007). As part of the general trend in the era of neoliberalism towards creating a tiered work force, at UPS as well since 1993, 83 percent of the 46,000 jobs created were part-time, and base wages for part-timers had stayed stagnant since 1982. Since part-time jobs were first implemented at UPS in 1962, the composition of the work force changed to 60 percent part-time and 40 percent full-time. Since the 1993 contract, about 83% of new unionized jobs were part-time; that is, out a total of 46,000 new hires, only 8,000 were hired full-time (Kumar 2007). The gap between part-time wages (about $8-$10 per hour) and full-time wages (about $19.95 per hour) was significant. Hiring part-timers thus kept wages low, which helped UPS to realize $1 billion in profits in 1996. The union argued that the company did not need so many part-timers and could afford to create more full-time jobs. Instead of enriching management, the Teamsters argued that UPS's profits should be distributed to its employees. They further extended this argument to the U.S. working class as a whole who, in the era of neoliberal globalization, have only seen their wages stagnate or deteriorate.

UPS countered that part-time jobs made the company more "flexible" within the global market and able to compete with non-union transportation companies. It claimed that work flows in the company had "peak" and "slack" times and that hiring part-time workers to cover the "peak" periods was economically more efficient. The company stressed that the salient differences were pensions and withdrawal from the Teamsters' multi-union plan. It claimed that with its plan, UPS workers would receive as much as 50 percent more in pension benefits than if they stayed with the current plan (Kumar 2007).

While the company blamed the breakdown in negotiations on differences about pensions, the union sought to highlight the part-time issue, health and safety, subcontracting and wages, and to generalize from them to the condition of working-class Americans in the 1990s economy. After all, the increase in contingent employment, the creation of tiered work forces, the practice of subcontracting, etc., were not unique to UPS but had become standard corporate practices in the era of neoliberal globalization. By broadening the issues at UPS and encompassing all American workers, the Teamsters were, in effect, striking a blow at the logic of neoliberalism. In the absence of a settlement on August 4, a national strike ensued that was to last fifteen days.

Predictably, the mainstream media's initial coverage of the strike minimized its significance while focusing instead on the inconvenience to consumers. However, this would change in the second week of the strike when they were forced to think outside the box. Some sections of the corporate media, such as the *New York Times*, the *Washington Post* and the ABC television network, began to acknowledge inequality and to discuss the problems of the U.S. working class. This shift happened in a politicized context where individuals and groups were pressured to take sides. In the battle for hearts and minds, the Teamsters and their allies were able to win public support and thus bring into being pressures that normally don't exist on the media. In a sense, the Teamsters were able to break through the limitations of the anti-labor media framing mechanisms and reach out to the outside world. In turn, public support and the world outside would help shape and frame the way the story of the strike was told.

During week two of the strike, therefore, the central contradiction of the economic expansion of the 1990s and the real consequences of neoliberalism—i.e., the unequal distribution of profits—was exposed. An article by Jeff Madrick (1997), author of the book, *The End of Affluence*, appeared on the first page of the outlook section of the *Washington Post*. The article, titled "UPS Strikers Deliver a Message; Rosy Rhetoric Aside, the Boom's a Bust for Many," discusses how labor did not benefit from the profits generated by the 1990s boom. Madrick states: "Most troublesome in recent years is that labor has not even received its share of this slow-growing pie. The income that goes into the pockets of America's workers has fallen as a proportion of GDP in the past few years. By contrast, the proportion of GDP going into corporate profits has risen" (Madrick C01). He went on to argue that the reality for working people could not be more different from the "rosy rhetoric" about the economy. This theme was taken up again more generally by numerous media outlets after the conclusion of the strike.

In the *New York Times*, David Johnston (1997) wrote about the struggle for better pensions, showing how, over the previous twenty years, companies had downgraded retirement benefits and reduced spending on retirement plans. Stephen Greenhouse (1997), the *Times'* labor reporter, wrote about the burgeoning number of service-sector jobs, "especially low wage ones," and discussed the AFL-CIO's efforts to shift focus toward these workers. Speaking about the "contingent economy," he admitted, in contrast to previous articles, that "downsizing, the rise of part-time and temporary jobs, and the trend toward businesses offering fewer workers health insurance and pensions" had become problems. Louis Uchitelle (1997) characterized the strike as, in part, a protest against the "Age of Downsizing." This article argued that the profits of the 1990s had been generated not by increased productivity but rather at the expense of wages, justifying the strike. Taken together, these articles represented one of the most sustained criticisms of the policies of neoliberalism and the implications for workers.

In the immediate aftermath of the strike, the limited concession to labor problems in the national media was further generalized. When the Teamsters won the strike, media across-the-board, from the business press to news magazines, radio, and local newspapers, attempted to explain why this had happened, and perhaps more important, why the public sided two-to-one with the workers (Kumar 2007). What could explain the new pro-labor mood in American society and the concomitant failure of anti-union propaganda? In trying to address these questions, the corporate media had to admit, however grudgingly, that a rising tide had not lifted all boats; that is, the working classes had not shared in the promised fruits of neoliberal globalization.

Business Week would admit to the problem of rising inequality in an article titled "A Wake-up Call for Business: The Teamsters' win means that workers can no longer be taken for granted," where the magazine drew out the lessons for the employing class as follows: "More important than the union victory is the way the Teamsters' campaign captured what seems to be a new mood in America. For the first time in nearly two decades, the public sided with a union, even though its walkout caused major inconveniences. Polls showed the public supported the 185,000 striking workers by a 2-to-1 margin over management. The message: After a six year economic expansion that has created record corporate profits and vast wealth for investors, Americans are questioning why so many of their countrymen aren't getting a bigger piece of the pie" (28). Twenty three years after *Business Week's* article on the "selling job" that must be done to make workers in the U.S. make do "with less so that big business can have more," it had come full circle. U.S. workers were no long willing to accept this solution, and sided with the Teamsters who had dared to resist and to struggle for a better future. In so doing, the Teamsters won the best contract they had ever had with UPS, making the company go back on its "last, best and final" offer and concede on various points from creating more full time jobs to the pension issue.

However, this moment where labor was able to win both ideologically—in the media—and materially, through a good contract—was short lived. After the strike was over and its impact assessed, the space that was opened up for a critical discussion of corporate behavior was immediately closed off, and the media reverted to their standard modus operandi. When the pressures that forced the corporate media to discuss labor's concerns dissipated, so did any semblance of an "open marketplace of ideas." The labor movement, still weighed down by the legacy of business unionism, failed to push its advantage and the momentum shifted back again to the employing class. Indeed, UPS reneged on many aspects of the contract. Despite this turn of events, what the UPS strike showed is that collective struggle by workers does have the power not only to force the corporate media to treat labor issues sympathetically, but also to galvanize working class support and successfully resist neoliberal strategies.

CONCLUSION

This chapter outlined the impact of neoliberalism on the working class in the U.S. In addition to attacks on union workers' rights, neoliberalism has created harsh working conditions for labor and precipitated greater class polarization. Thus, in the new millennium while some enjoy $2,000 bottles of wine, many more Americans have to resort to food pantries as a way to meet their basic needs. The corporate media have been all but silent about this situation because they have a vested structural interest in the neoliberal regime. This state of affairs therefore keeps hidden the depth of inequality as well as class anger.

Still, the UPS strike showed that when working class issues are articulated in the media, the majority of workers act rationally in their interests and reject corporate power and dominance. This is an important lesson to remember in the context of the neoliberal crisis that has gripped the world in the second decade of the new millennium. Once again, governments around the world have decided to resolve the crisis through instituting austerity measures and spending cuts; in short, in the same manner they did three and half decades ago, i.e. on the backs of the working class. In this context, workers and students in various advanced capitalist countries have engaged in protests and strikes. The UPS strike shows that such actions are not only possible in the U.S, but that collective struggle is the only way to successfully resist the priorities of neoliberalism.

REFERENCES

Bagdikian, Ben. 2004. *The New Media Monopoly*. Boston: Beacon.

Bartlett, Donald L. and James B. Steele. 1992. *America: What Went Wrong?* Kansas City: Andrew and McMeel, a Universal Press Syndicate Company.

Carroll, Jill. 1997. "AOL-Time Warner Merger Clears FCC—Final Regulatory Approval $103.5 Billion Deal Is Won After Year Wait." *Wall Street Journal*, 12 January, A3.

Coontz, Stephanie. 1997. *The Way We Really Are: Coming to Terms with America's Changing Families*. New York: Basic Books.

Ferguson, Thomas and Joel Rogers. 1986. *Right Turn: The Decline of the Democrats and the Future of American Politics*. New York: Hill and Wang.

Foner, Phillip. 1982. *Organized Labor and the Black Worker 1619-1981*. New York: International Publishers.

Georgakas, Dan and Marvin Surkin. 1998. *Detriot I Do Mind Dying*. Boston: South End Press.

Gershon, Richard A. 1997. *The Transnational Media Corporation: Global Messages and Free Market Competition*. Mahwah, New Jersey: Lawrence Erlbaum Associates, Publishers.

Goldfield, Michael. 1987. *The Decline of Organized Labor in the United States*. Chicago: University of Chicago Press.

Greenhouse, Steven. 1997. "U.P.S. and Union Break off Negotiations." *New York Times*, August 10, A26.

Greenhouse, Steven. 1997. "Why Labor Feels It Can't Afford to Lose This Strike." *New York_Times*, August 17, D3.

"Happily Ever NAFTA?" October, 1993. *EXTRA!Update*.

Harrison, Bennet. 1994. *Lean and Mean: Why Large Corporations Will Continue to Dominate the Global Economy*. New York: The Guilford Press.

Herman, Edward and Noam Chomsky. 1988. *Manufacturing Consent: The Political Economy of the Mass Media*. New York: Pantheon Books.

Hirshberg, A., Ellison, D., Keaton, S., Johnson, K. and Anthony, P. 1995. *Best Practices in Strategic Management: Cases from the Front Lines of Competition.* Calverton, Maryland: Research Project 4853-01, Macro International, Inc.

Carson-Parker, John. 1974. "The Options Ahead for the Debt Economy." *Business Week*, October 12, 121.

Johnston, David Cay. 1997. "Pension Concerns Move to the Picket Line." *New York Times*, August 10, 11.

Moody, Kim. 1988. *An Injury to All: The Decline of American Unionism.* New York: Verso.

Klein, Naomi. 1999. *No Logo: Money, Marketing, and the Growing Anti-Corporate Movement.* New York: Picador.

Krugman, Paul. October 20, 2002. "For Richer." *The New York Times*, accessed February 16, 2011, http://www.nytimes.com/2002/10/20/magazine/for-richer.html.

Lent, John. 1998. "The Animation Industry and Its Offshore Factories." In *Global Productions: Labor in the Making of the 'Information Society.'* Eds. G. Sussman and J. Lent, 239-54. Cresskill, NJ: Hampton Press.

Lichtenstein, Nelson. 2002. *State of the Union: A Century of American Labor.* Princeton: Princeton University Press.

Lipsitz, George. 1994. *Rainbow at Midnight: Labor and Culture in the 1940s.* Urbana: University of Illinois Press.

Madrick, Jeff. August 10, 1997. *Washington Post*, C01.

Magnusson, Paul, Nicole, Harris, Linda Himelstein, Bill Vlasic, and Wendy Zellner. September 1, 1997. "A Wake-up Call for Business." *Business Week*, 28.

Mazzocco, Dennis. 1997. *Networks of Power: Corporate TV's Threat to Democracy.* Boston: South End Press.

McChesney, Robert W. January 18, 2002. "Why we Need *In These Times*," *In These Times.* Available on-line at http://www.inthesetimes.com/issue/26/06/feature1.shtml

McChesney, Robert W. and Edward Herman. 1997. *The Global Media: The New Missionaries of Corporate Capitalism.* Washington D.C.: Cassell.

McChesney, Robert W. 1999. *Rich Media, Poor Democracy: Communication Politics in Dubious Times.* Urbana: University of Illinois Press.

Parker, Mike and Jane Slaughter. 1998. *Choosing Sides: Unions and the Team Concept.* Boston: South End Press.

Schmidt, Diane E. 1993. "Public Opinion and Media Coverage of Labor Unions." *Journal of Labor Research*, 14, No. 2: 151-165.

Singer, Daniel. 1999. *Whose Millennium? Theirs or Ours?* New York: Monthly Review Press.

Skinner, Ewart. 1998. "The Caribbean Data Processors." In *Global Productions: Labor in the Making of the 'Information Society.'* Eds. G. Sussman and J. Lent, 57-90. Cresskill, NJ: Hampton Press.

Smith, Sharon. 1992. "Twilight of the American Dream." *International Socialism* 54: 3-43.

Smith, Sharon. 2006. *Subterranean Fire: A History of Working-class Radicalism in the United States.* Chicago: Haymarket Press.

Sussman, Gerald and John Lent, eds. 1998. *Global Productions: Labor in the Making of the 'Information Society.'* Cresskill, NJ: Hampton Press.

Sustar, Lee. 2003. "The New Employers' Offensive: Labor's War at Home." *International Socialist Review*, 28: 61-7.

Uchitelle, Louis. August 10, 1997. "What Goes Up Must Usually, Well, Stop Going Up." *New York Times*, D1.

"Union label week and the Wheel of Fortune." *BMWE Journal*, Vol 106, no. 10, November. Available on-line http://glo.bmwe.org/public/journal/1997/11nov/08.htm.

Wasko, Janet. 2001. "The Magical-Market World of Disney." *Monthly Review* 52, no. 11: 56-71.

Wisniewski, Stanley C. 1997. *Multinational Enterprises in the Courier Service Industry: Aspects of Employment and Working Conditions in Selected Enterprises.* Geneva: International Labour Organization.

"Work Stoppages Summary." released March 19, 2004. *Bureau of Labor Statistics.* Available on-line at http://www.bls.gov/news.release/wkstp.nr0.htm.

CHAPTER 15

CONTESTING DEMOCRATIC COMMUNICATIONS

THE CASE OF CURRENT TV

James F. Hamilton

LAIMS THAT MEDIA ORGANIZATIONS UNFAIRLY OR UN-
DEMOCRATICALLY CONTROL PROGRAMMING and, as a
result, unduly affect the quality and nature of public life
seem for many people to be out of touch with reality. If
the key to democratic communications is greater public
participation, some claim today that we are already there. As exemplified by projects of citizen journalism and nonprofit or noncommercial newsgathering organizations, the most optimistic of them assert
that commercial media companies are not standing in the way (as is
typically assumed), but are on the leading edge of such a change (Kim
and Hamilton 2004; Dahlgren 2009, 147; "Awards and Honors—
ProPublica" 2010). Such a trend is not limited to news, as so-called
reality television and user-created commercials attest (Deggans 2009;
Doritos Presents Snackstrong Productions"; Honda 2010; Mofilm
2010). Given these and other examples, it seems as though the citadel
of private media empires has clearly and forever been breeched, as has
the distinction between privately owned commercial organizations
that serve narrowly personal interests and publicly responsive media
in which regular users regularly participate. This seems to be the conclusion reached by *Time*, which at the start of 2007 voted as its Person
of the Year "you." As it claimed on its cover, "you control the Information Age. Welcome to your world" (*Time* 2007). Some scholars also
celebrate what they see as an increase in open platforms for expression free from corporate control, and that challenge the imperatives

of traditional commercial media companies (Jenkins 2006; Barlow 2008; Jenkins 2008; Dena 2008; Gordon 2007).

While it is clear that the nature and character of user participation in media companies has changed recently in some key ways, what needs to be challenged is its optimistic if not also utopian interpretation and assessment. It already has been by scholars such as Turner, who distinguishes between "democratic" and "demotic" participation. And, as Carpentier points out, even such seemingly wide-open shows as BBC's *Video Nation*, for which users send their own video related to a variety of themes proposed by the network, which then appears on the broadcast program, need to be reassessed (BBC 2010). Claims that it and similar such shows are participatory television programs based on textual evidence (that people who appear are not paid actors or media employees, and that user-provided footage is intentionally left "rough") and on immediate organizational structure (that "ordinary" people instead of studio executives decide whether their video contributions will air or not) downplays or ignores the determinations of the institutional, social, and cultural contexts that enable the project in the first place (Carpentier 2003). Power and authority emerges not so much from chains of command or personal commands, but from the deeply institutionalized conventions of the practice, themselves formed in, as well as contributing to, specific conditions. Ytreberg suggests as much by noting how participation in broadcasting means "mastering a set of performance roles that are given by the production context and by the requirements of the format," and that such mastery, as a condition of participation, means "conform[ing] to the [social and cultural] order of production" (Ytreberg 2004, 678).

What these and other critiques focus on is the peculiarity of the mode of control in these kinds of media participation. It is peculiar because outsider participation is not prevented so that private and professional authority and privilege is protected. Rather, outsider participation is invited and cultivated—the very thing that seemingly would cede control entirely. But, as already stated, participation per se is no guarantee of democratic process. As Oullette and Hay suggest, agency via participation may in some ways be opened up, but at the same time it is in other ways closed down (Ouellette and Hay 2008, 2).

Understanding the peculiar mode of control in user participation—and building an ability to clearly distinguish it as a mode of control—is now a key task in this era of ostensible digital revolution and user empowerment. The widespread view of control as democratic access and negative freedom constitutes, as Benjamin puts it, a "moment of crisis" that must be confronted through analysis, critique, and response (Benjamin 1969, 255). What is at stake is not only an understanding of this mode of control, but any sort of clear basis upon which democratic communication can be distinguished from the commercial cultivation of user participation for private gain. Such an aim requires a critical and historical approach. Paraphrasing Gamson's point about "wildly displaced enthusiasm over the political impact of a specific technological practice" such as the Internet, Dean notes the resulting deleterious tendency to "'bracket institutions and ownership, to research and theorize uses and users of new media outside those brackets, and to allow 'newness' to overshadow historical continuity'" (Gamson 2003; quoted in Dean 2009, 37).

This chapter seeks to contribute to such a task through an argument consisting of three interlocking points. First, to refute the claim that what we have today is an increase in user participation, I argue that participation is better seen historically in terms of the waxing and waning of different modes rather than an increase or decrease in amount. Second, to refute the understanding of control as only the restriction of outsider participation, I note key changes in capitalist manufacturing and marketing that have placed user desires at the center of strategic planning. This is not some surrender of control, but a more effective route toward it. Third, to substantiate the need to understand democratic communication in terms of different modes rather than an increase or decrease in amount, I use the case of Current TV to theorize the democratic potentials of participation through commercial media companies that rely upon user production.

PARTICIPATION THEN AND NOW

A basis for claiming that user participation today is greater than in the past depends on ignoring all the ways users and buyers have always participated. From the beginning of capitalist markets, a key need has been not to prevent, but to enable greater access and participation to earn higher profits and secure greater marketshares. Roles by which users have participated include as readers, listeners, and viewers; as buyers and subscribers; as contributors of letters, commentaries, and opinions; and as sources, subjects, and contestants. Indeed, Griffen-Foley points out that "media producers have been blurring the notion of the passive media consumer [a conception created in the midst of early twentieth-century functionalist fears about the fragmenting effects of mass media on society] for more than a century" (Griffen-Foley 2004, 545). Examples include mass-audience periodicals of the late nineteenth century, confessional magazines, mass-market women's magazines, and "talk-back" radio with its beginnings in the 1930s. To this list one could add the extensions of religious publishing, politically radical as well as popularized commercial newspapers, varieties of live entertainment including vaudeville, and even earlier traditions of publishing letters in newspapers. And, yet, claims that such participation is de-facto democratizing cannot be taken at face value. "There is, of course," as Griffen-Foley notes, "a significant contradiction between the [individual-empowerment] rhetoric of personalized journalism (for want of a broader term) and the structure of the modern, heavily capitalized mass media" (Griffen-Foley 2004, 545).

In a series of short essays about the rise of the commercial popular presses in nineteenth-century England, Williams makes clear this contradiction. To siphon readers from radical political publications, the emerging commercial press adopted long-standing popular forms of chapbooks, ballads, and pamphlets as well as selected "radical social and political attitudes." What enhanced the replacement of the radical-popular by the commercial-popular was the consolidation of the newspaper business into groups and chains and the securing of advertising revenue at a scale unimaginable only a short time previously, both of which gave the commercial-popular a productive capacity that moved it to a level entirely different from the radical-popular. As a result, "the control of popular journalism passed into the hands of successful large-scale entrepreneurs, who alone now could reach a majority of the public quickly and attractively and cheaply, on a national scale." Thus, for Williams, the contradiction between individual empowerment and media structure is the one between use and ownership. Large-scale entrepreneurs courted the popular, adopted a selection of popular attitudes, and included increasingly popular topics and stories, but "by their very ability to do this, by their control of resources, were separated from or opposed to the people whom this popular journalism served" (Williams 1970, 23).

The more general point needs to be made clearly. Then, as today, all user contributions do not automatically find a place in a publication, newscast, or entertainment program. To the degree that the organization requires user participation to achieve its goals, only those contributions—or portions of contributions—that best fit the publication appear in order to attempt to produce a seamless correspondence of readers' interests with the publication and its organization. Thus, recognizable forms of readers' experience are "re-presented" to those very same readers, but selectively so, yoked as the selection is to a corresponding effort to consolidate and secure a dependable market. But, again, this is nothing new. At the earliest stages of the emergence of a commercial popular culture, participation depended on a selective, intentional, unequal, but necessary collaboration between makers and users while at the same time redefining these relationships into the capitalist, abstract relationships of producers and consumers for private gain (Williams 1976, 69).

OUTSIDERS ON THE INSIDE

The claim that outsider participation in media companies is a de-facto democratizing development rests on similarly shaky evidence and similarly thin historical awareness. Over the course of capitalist development, companies have come to encourage and place at the center of their planning what users want. However, this is not a surrender of control, but a more effective means of gaining it, with user production only the most recent form of competitive advantage to secure.

It is well-known how the pressures of competition shape business strategies. But, since the 1970s and in the wake of an increasingly globalized economy, pressures of competition have intensified because capital has become ever more mobile (Harvey 1989, Harvey 2006). It restlessly searches not just for profits, but for greater and greater profits. These pressures intensified further in the United States due to the relaxation beginning in the 1980s of long-standing, already minimally obtrusive regulatory frameworks that applied to communications companies (Tunstall 1986). Pressures of competition have also intensified because transnational media networks and systems have created increasingly global markets. Thus, the range of competition for audiences is increasingly regional, national, and global. And competition is increasingly between indirect competitors in different industries as opposed to direct competitors within the same industry. These deep developments underlie the colossal debt loads and ever-more-spectacular collapses of media companies such as the Tribune Co., the Star Tribune, the Journal Register Co., Philadelphia Newspapers LLC,

Citadel Broadcasting, Pappas Telecasting Companies, and many others ("Next Stop" 2009, Spector and McBride 2009, Brickley 2008). Media companies by and large make plenty of money; they just don't make enough of it to prevent investors from pulling out and going elsewhere.

However, this intensification of competition and expanded range of competition for audiences is nothing new. For example, it had become clear as early as the 1940s, when a study at the time commented that "competition from other media of information, at the present time, is more serious for many newspapers than competition from other newspapers" (Kinter 1945, 46; Compaine and Gomery, 52–53). Such pressures and changes remade a number of media industries in the United States. For example, where television-industry growth came at the expense of radio, growth in cable-satellite networks came at the expense of broadcast television, and was aided by a gradual relaxation of ownership limits throughout the 1980s and 1990s and the beginning in 1975 of national satellite distribution (for a more detailed analysis, see Hamilton 2008, 207–8). By 2003, as part of its justification for relaxing cross-ownership rules, the Federal Communications Commission (F.C.C.) claimed that inter-media competition and the maturation of what it termed the "multimedia landscape" had reached the point where inter-media competition—and not government regulation—could serve as the primary means of ensuring localism and system diversity (F.C.C. 2003, 86–128).

This intensification of pressures of competition has changed what constitutes competitive advantages in the market. Traditionally, media companies have competed with each other on the basis of exclusive and unique content that is claimed to be more comprehensive, better written, more dependable, more relevant, and so on. What has called this competitive advantage into question is digitization and online content aggregation. Where digitized content is instantly and easily reproducible, content aggregation precludes the need to go to or pay for the source of information. Combined with other online services such as paid search, online content aggregation is now much more profitable than content creation. As just one example, profits of U.S. news organization Gannett (a content generator and the biggest news company in the U.S.) in the last three months of 2009 were $133.6 million, but profits for Google (paid search and content aggregator) over the same period of time—and even in the midst of the "Great

Recession"—were $2 billion, almost fifteen times that of Gannett (Doctor 2010).

As a result of these intensifying pressures, the problems commercial media companies face today derive from the loss of their traditional competitive advantage. Because exclusive content presents less and less a viable competitive advantage, the cutting edge of media marketing today in this time of savage competition is a search for a new competitive advantage which, in the age of social media, is innovative forms of user participation. And the most innovative forms of user participation are forms of user production—of users helping make the organization's products, with examples ranging from "modding" in the video-game industry to user-supplied stories and video footage, and user-composed video segments/packages for convention news organizations (Dyer-Witheford and de Peuter 2009). Indeed, users have become increasingly central to and necessary for the very survival of many media organizations. This is not an option for media organizations nor an altruistic move on behalf of a grand vision of aiding democracy, but a necessity for their very survival and a means of securing a key competitive advantage to consolidate marketshares.

Where the evolving political economy of media industries places users ever-more centrally in the production process, a second development places users at the center of business strategy and design. What has been called "consumer-led design" must also be understood historically, as it too casts doubt onto how revolutionary user participation is today.

Mass manufacturing in the U.S. early in the 20th Century followed what Whiteley calls "producer-led design," in which companies decided what products to make and what they should look like and do. Two different and in many ways opposing approaches at this time valued functionality over appearance and style, and they both placed the buyer/user at the end of the production process. Where the goal of the industrial-design approach of Modernism was to find the optimal "clear and logical form" based on the application of rational principles, a second, in some ways very different approach was Fordism, named for its namesake auto maker Henry Ford, in which the goal was to boost sales and profits. It did so by extending markets, and it extended markets by making products more affordable. And the key way of making them affordable was to keep them the same from year to year, and thus to emphasize function and downplay style, because any mechanical or styling alteration would increase costs (Whiteley 1993, 7–11).

However, by the 1930s, this emphasis on function and the restriction of users to simply buyers began to be rethought, at first due to the recognition of the economic value of style. This occurred in two ways. First, popularly appreciated styles were increasingly used for entirely nonfunctional reasons to boost sales, such as the use of streamlining (which connoted speed, power, and modernity, and that was functionally necessary for airplanes and trains to lessen wind resistance) to style static objects such as radios, clothes irons, jugs, cash registers, pencil sharpeners, furniture, and buildings. Second, in the form of "planned obsolescence," giving a product a fashionable appearance guaranteed it would soon become unfashionable, thus compelling people to buy a new product not because their old one wore out but because it just plain looked old (Whiteley 1993, 13–17).

By the 1960s and the maturation in the U.S. of a consumerist economy, buyers/users became central to a company's strategic decisions. This is captured well in a quotation at the time by American economist and Harvard professor Theodore Leavitt: "What a company offers for sale is determined not by the seller [the producer], but by the buyer [the consumer]" (quoted in Whiteley 1993, 20). This was not an abdication of ownership and control, but a more effective way to boost sales and profits. By the 1980s, "consumer-led design"— basing manufacturing decisions on market research instead of manufacturers' rational plans or short-term financial needs—came fully into its own. The task was to understand current needs and uses, to anticipate needs and desires, to create products that anticipated demand, then to encourage the demand once the product was released. Whiteley cites examples of Sony and of Swatch, which pioneered the use of social-trends research and lifestyle research in developing wildly popular consumer electronics (Whiteley 1993, 21–25).

The relevance of this Copernican remapping of the place of buyer/users in industrial design and manufacturing for understanding the emergence of user production in commercial media companies is that media companies are manufacturers of products, too. Like all manufacturers, they have also placed consumers at the center of their strategic decisions. Instead of defining content and programming based on an absolute or ideal, they like other manufacturers use lifestyle research, social-trend research, and readership studies of various kinds to understand current demand, anticipate product demand, create content that addresses this demand, and then to encourage its demand.

Thus, the changing political economy of media organizations and the emergence of consumer-led design helps account for how and why outsiders (buyers/users) have moved to the center of how commercial organizations operate. Like user production, users' participation via consumer-led design is not optional, but central and necessary for the organization's success. Contrary to many claims, it is not a popular storming of the corporate Bastille, nor did it emerge recently as a result of the Internet, but rather due to long-standing competitive pressures of capitalism and the structural changes they have wrought.

CURRENT TV AND THE CONTEST AS CONTROL

The final task of this chapter is to refute the deep equation of democratic communication with the amount of participation. The cutting edge of user production as a means to manage and control is represented well in the example of the cable and Internet venture Current TV and its use of what will be called here "republican communications."

Despite the correspondence of the terms "democratic" and "republican" with the labels of the major political parties in the United States, the terms as used here refer to long-standing social philosophies, not to today's party programs or identities. Granting their many complexities, what is of central importance here is their contrasting conceptions of how societies sustain themselves (Dahlberg and Siapera 2007). Where "democratic" carries with it a sense of shared effort and mutual aid, "republicanism" embraces competition of person against person as the means by which individuals improve and society becomes healthy.

The mode of participation with central importance to republicanism is the contest. In his exhaustive exploration of cultural currents in the U.S. and their traditions, Lasch places the social philosophy of republicanism in a complex line that can be traced from the Roman republic, its reappearance after the Middle Ages in the Florentine Renaissance, and its use in England and France in the early modern eras. Despite many differences, Lasch argues that its variations share two basic concerns. While the first is how to balance control and freedom in society, the second and crucial one for the argument of this chapter is a focus on the centrality of virtue as "the fullest development of human capacities and powers" (Lasch 1991, 172–173). In contrast to communitarian, democratic thinking in the U.S. and elsewhere, which was "designed to foster values [...] such as spirituality, cooperation, [and] economic equality," Lasch characterizes the republican ethic and the fostering of virtue as "nothing if not competitive," with the particular form of competition being the contest. "It was the ethic of the arena, the battlefield, and the forum—strenuous, combative, agonistic. In urging men [sic] to pit themselves against the most demanding standards of achievement, it also pitted them against each other. In politics, it set a higher value on eloquence, disputation, and verbal combat than on compromise and conciliation. Political life, for republicans, provided another outlet for ambition, another form of contest—not primarily a means of reconciling opposing interests or assuring an equitable distributions of goods" (Lasch 1991, 175).

Of course, the contest is no ancient fossil of bygone eras, but alive and well today in countless ways, from state-run lotteries to political races, sporting events, and marketplace rivalries. Added to this list should be countless media organizations that seek to incorporate user production. Contests are a primary way in which online contributions by users are sifted, prioritized, and valued—and thus managed and controlled. Where Current TV did not originate the use of contests to manage user participation, it pioneered a particularly effective variation that presents itself wholly undeservedly as the epitome of democratic communications.

The company that spawned Current TV is largely a vision of politician Al Gore and entrepreneur Joel Hyatt. As one of the principle founders as well as current company chairman, Gore served four terms in the U.S. House of Representatives and two in the U.S. Senate, as Vice President of the United States for two terms, and the Democratic Party candidate for President in the 2000 election (Current 2010o). He is also an Academy Award-winning filmmaker for the film *An Inconvenient Truth* about global warming, and a recipient of the Nobel Peace Prize. Hyatt, the second co-founder, is given credit for designing how the company engages users and user content. After leaving Stanford University's Graduate School of Business, where he taught courses in entrepreneurship, Hyatt founded Hyatt Legal Services, which provided low-cost services to low-income people. He also established Hyatt Legal Plans as a major provider of employer-sponsored group legal plans, before selling the company to insurance giant MetLife. In 2000, Hyatt also served as National Finance Chair for the Democratic Party, a position through which he met Gore (Current 2010o, Becker

2006). Other company officers include a range of experienced media and advertising executives, and technical managers (Current 2010o).

After a series of meetings following Gore's capitulation to George W. Bush in the 2000 presidential election, Gore and Hyatt formed the company that has become Current TV in September 2002, commencing to plan the business, recruit management, and raise capital. In May 2004, it purchased Newsworld International, a traditional cable and satellite network, from Vivendi Universal, which gave it access to independent distribution (Current TV 2008, pp. 5, 9). It continued to air Newsworld's programming until August 2005, when Current TV programming was launched and made available to 19 million households in the U.S. (Current TV 2008, p. 2). By May 2008, it reached 56 million households in the U.S., U.K., Italy, and Ireland (Current TV 2008, p. 2; Current TV 2010o).

In October 2007, it launched its Internet component Current.com. Unlike websites of most media companies, the purpose of Current. com was not to simply reproduce what was available on the cable channel, but to complement the cable channel in important ways (Current TV 2007; Current TV 2008, p. 16). It allows people not served by cable distribution to see selected Current TV programming. It enlarges Current TV's pool of viewer contributions of content by creating an easy way to send in these contributions. It also enlarges advertising revenue, although the advertising revenue of the company continues to be slight. By 2008, more than four-fifths of its revenue was from affiliate fees paid by systems that distributed Current TV, such as cable, satellite, and telecommunications operators, and it had yet to attract a sizable enough audience to be rated for viewership by Nielsen Media Services or any other rating service (Current TV 2008, p. 15).

Current TV exemplifies and brings to a new level the ideological sleight of hand practiced by "participatory" media organizations, whether commercial or noncommercial. On one hand, its self-portrayal as a "real television network" that is "created by you" draws on wording and imagery of democratic communications (Current TV 2010a). Current TV regards itself as part of a groundswell change in the "evolution of media," which makes possible an "active, collaborative community" (Current TV 2008, 82). For Gore (its public spokesperson), broadcast television is controlled by an "anti-democratic impulse" ("Al Gore" 2008). As Gore put it at the launch announcement for Current

TV in the U.K., his and Hyatt's vision was thus to "democratize the medium of television" (ITN Source 2007).

Gore expanded on the democratic claim at the 2008 launch of Current TV in Italy. Because "television production has been centralized, [...] individuals have been shut out of the conversation of democracy." As a result, stated Gore, "individuals were turned into consumers and viewers, an audience not able to effectively participate in the discussion," because broadcast television is "a passive medium in the experience of the consumer, who most often sits and watches television and consumes what is produced in a few studios." Gore claimed that "Current TV reverses the flow." The Internet lets Current TV "connect with millions of people, some of whom have their own ideas about what news should be, and they select the news stories they think are most important." Other users participate even more fully by making television "with the affordable digital video cameras and laptop editing software, and they send it to us over the Internet." A final way people participate in Current TV, argued Gore, is that "we ask our audience to help us select the most interesting, most compelling, most fascinating pieces, which we then put on television" (Al Gore, "Speech in Rome").

On the other hand, and despite such populist, democratic claims, the actual design and organization of Current TV puts into practice a competitive, individualizing form of participation that fits well Lasch's general characterization of republicanism, while also clearly benefiting the company. An analysis of the context, structure, and practice of Current TV suggests that participation is structured and managed to the benefit of Current TV in many ways.

User contributors must own or have access to digital video recording and editing equipment, as well as have access to a broadband Internet connection, none of which is universally available. They must learn and practice conventional forms of video composition, and follow Current TV's guidelines regarding length and content. They must agree to a legal arrangement, which allows Current TV to generate income through the contributions without taking on any liability. Structuring all these facets is the deep saturation of Current TV (and, variably, all similar commercial user-generated content projects) with the republican ethos of competition, which appears here and elsewhere in the form of contests in which viewers compete with each other. This produces a clear and compelling fit to neoliberalism as a way of managing public creativity and energy.

At a fundamental level, a user needs digital video recording equipment and access to a computer equipped with digital editing software. The suggested-equipment list from Current TV includes a "Budget" set of equipment (ranging in cost from roughly $1,000 to $3,000) and a "Not-So-Cheap Equipment List" of pricier equipment ranging in cost from roughly $8,500 to $40,000 and beyond (Current TV 2010c). Add to this a moderately equipped computer capable of efficiently editing video ($2,000), and the cost of just the fundamental level of participation ranges beyond the reach of all but the wealthiest or most-committed people. Users also need access to the Internet itself, which means that one must either be able to pay for the digital connection in one's home or have public access. However, presence of broadband in the home is skewed in favor of college-educated, non-rural whites, and against those least likely to have home access with less than a high-school education, making less than $20,000 per year, and living in rural areas (F.C.C. 2010, 23). Potential contributors must also live in a place that is served by a network broadband provider. While 95 percent of U.S. users live in areas that are wired for broadband, 14 million people (living mostly in rural areas) do not (F.C.C. 2010, 20).

Contributors must also have enough time to devote to conceiving, planning, and recording footage, and producing the story, which presumes a degree of flexibility and financial security not generally shared. While one estimate places the time for a person off-the-street to produce a seven-minute radio-news piece at a minimum of 8 to 10 hours, a segment requiring editing and syncing of video and audio adds significantly to this estimate (Fisher 2000, 47). In addition, demands of travel time and on-site organization for non-local videos plus funding to pay for all this restricts even further the potential pool of contributors.

Direct assistance by Current TV begins only for those potential contributors who can meet these fundamental requirements. Current TV does this through education and training, but in ways that reproduce conventional forms of commercially acceptable broadcast video instead of enabling more open experimentation. Guidelines exist for length as well as for form and content. While contributors can modify or ignore such guidelines, the chances of having one's video accepted lessen dramatically. Thus, at the same time as it enables participation, this assistance also channels and structures participation.

One way that Current TV manages participation is by categorizing possible contributions. Until recently, users could choose between three different kinds of contributions (but no others). The first kind, "pods," are "self-contained videos, usually under 7 minutes, that tell a story, profile a character and/or share an idea." The second kind, "VCAMs" (an acronym for "viewer-created ad messages"), are "DIY [do-it-yourself] commercials made by you," in which the "sponsors set the specs." In a 2007 speech to the Association of National Advertisers, Gore noted how VCAMs were distinctly better than "allowing anyone to post their own messages about brands in unregulated web environments." The advantage is that advertisers gain "control [over] the final product" (Naughton 2007). The third kind is any combination of "comments, viewpoints, reviews, rants, pod elements and one-shot stuff" that requires less editing and crafting, thus resembling YouTube home movies or mobile-phone shorts (Current TV 2010a). Specific topics for pod assignments include the most futuristic use of the Internet and the pros/cons of selling sports-stadium seating that comes with unlimited food, and for viewpoints/reviews, topics such as "What upcoming events are happening where you live?," "What can't sex sell?," and personal reviews on the latest movie, television, and music releases (Current TV 2010d; Current TV 2010e; Current TV 2010f).

Unlike the prior two kinds of contributions, VCAM assignments are offered by a company who wishes to advertise on Current TV. Far from offering a free hand, these assignments provide specific creative direction, such as in the example of a VCAM competition in 2007 on behalf of mobile-phone company T-Mobile, in which "would-be videographers were told to 'create a VCAM that illustrates how this brand keeps its users connected all the time,' given some suggested plotlines (the benefits and drawbacks of always-on, the perils of losing a Sidekick) and provided with the taglines T-Mobile wanted, such as 'How the super connected stay connected'. Current also supplied downloads of product photos, end-tag movie files and pre-approved music choices" (Quinton 2008).

The case of T-Mobile also illustrates the value of VCAMs for advertisers, particularly if the Current TV audience coincides with the advertiser's target market, as was the case with T-Mobile. During the seven-week contest, T-Mobile executives read all users' comments on the VCAMs submitted as well as viewed all submissions, thus gaining extensive insights into their target market. Current TV marketers claim that nine out of ten Current TV viewers regard VCAMs as more "authentic" than professionally produced spots, with the implication that they are more effective (Quinton 2008).

A second way assistance and guidelines structure participation is by listing more general compositional requirements for contributions, no matter which category they fall within. The same set of training and production resources is recommended for videos of all categories. Although the training-video host Laura Ling makes clear that there is no single, hard-and-fast formula for a VC2 ("viewer-content squared") video, simply offering these suggests then following them provides the best chance for having a video accepted. And clear guidelines exist. Current TV requests "short, documentary-style non-fiction films, usually 5–7 minutes in length," with other fare such as "fiction pieces, music videos, and trailers" not acceptable (Current TV 2010b). By implication, equipment and practices not listed here jeopardize chances of acceptance. The training program further directs the form of contributions. It begins with a "VC2 Producer Training Overview," and proceeds by addressing topics that deal with content and narrative ("Storytelling: What Makes a Good Pod," "Journalism: Case Studies to Learn From") or that deal with technical issues ("Broadband: Creating Video for the Web," "Gear: Essential Equipment," "Shooting: Getting it on Tape," "Editing: Putting it all Together") (Current TV 2010g). Those that deal with narrative present best practices that are derived from professional examples. For example, four approaches are offered for telling effective stories: "Your Story," "Someone Else's Story," "A Story About Something Else," and "Your Spin on 'Something Else'" (Current TV 2010h). Narratively speaking, these correspond to witnessing/testimony and objective-style documentary, both of which are lynchpins of traditional media programming (Hamilton 2008, 33–59).

A third way Current TV channels participation is through legal arrangements. Various legal agreements release the producer of the video from any claims of ownership by anyone associated with the video. Signed legal releases must be obtained from everyone who worked on or appeared in the video; a clearance release must be compiled that notes at which point in the video each person first appeared; and a location release needs to be obtained from the owner of any private property at which the shoot took place (Current TV 2010i; Current

TV 2010j; Current TV 2010k). Additionally, if music other than that in the public domain is used, music releases must also be obtained, in which ownership is retained by the composer while granting Current TV status as a legal licensee (Current TV 2010l).

Current TV profits from these legal arrangements in a way much different—and more beneficial—than outright purchase. The key innovation of Current TV compared to many other commercial projects that solicit and use user-generated content is its dual-medium nature as an Internet site and television station. Contributors of items retain ownership throughout, but Current TV benefits by exempting itself from all legal liability, thus sidestepping the possible legal problems of buying and thus being legally liable for contributions that do not abide by professional standards. With this agreement, all legal responsibility and potential liability (such as obscenity, fraud, indecency, defamation or harassment, or violation of copyright) remains with the contributor rather than with Current TV.

Yet, at the same time, the legal agreement that all contributors must abide by as a condition for acceptance allows Current TV very generous usage rights and ways to profit from content it received from users for free. This point emerges more easily when talking to advertisers and marketers. In a speech to the Association of National Advertisers in 2007, a member of the audience asked how Gore proposed to judge the return on investment for advertisers. He responded that "It's easy with us—production costs are zero!" (Naughton 2007). As a condition of acceptance, Current TV secures a "non-exclusive, royalty-free perpetual right" to distribute and show the contribution worldwide as often as desired. While a contributor can end the agreement, doing so means that the contribution is no longer seen on Current TV. At the same time and even if the agreement is ended, Current TV continues to be "free to use any ideas, concepts, know-how or techniques contained in any communication or Submitted Material you submit to us for any purpose, at any time, and without any remuneration or obligation to you." Submissions of user-generated commercials often have additional conditions that structure acceptance. Anyone who contributes material to Current TV is bound by this agreement as a condition of acceptance (Current TV 2010m).

Given the high economic and technical hurdles, and the complex guidelines and requirements, why would anyone contribute to Current TV?

Current TV addresses this by organizing as a contest. No one is barred from participating (provided they have the time, money, and expertise and they abide by the rules, guidelines, and agreements), but only a few people will have the ability, skill, and commitment to make a video, and only one can win by having the video judged as the best. Structuring the entire business as a contest is what "squares the circle" and makes it compelling to consider participating despite these limitations and restrictions. The logic is clear. Where those who cannot or choose not to participate are simply not up to the challenge, those who take up the challenge and commit themselves financially and personally push each other to see who can create the winning video. In this way, competition is enshrined as a shared, yet socially divisive principle consistent with republicanism. All aspects of the organization are geared to contests. Indeed, the Internet component Current.com was repurposed to better enable user competition. Prior to the relaunch of the website in 2007, it allowed largely unmonitored postings like, as a news report characterized it, a "talent outlet." After the relaunch, submissions became subject to review by freelance videographers and paid editors, who picked what goes on the front page (WPN Videos).

Voting is also configured at Current TV to maximize its public and competitive value. One does not simply vote with all votes tallied at the end to see which contribution received the most. Rather, voting moves a contribution higher or lower in a constantly displayed list of entrants, thus putting them in head-to-head real-tme competition with each other. As with the case in online participation generally, users need to register and log in to vote, with the resulting creation of a valuable demographic database of users that Current TV can use to enable their own audience research to help in advertising sales.

The incentive for winning the contest (and by implication giving Current TV what it wants) goes beyond satisfaction of having it voted the best. Put in baseball terms, Current TV's Internet site is the farm leagues, with the major league being the cable-television outlet. Voting selects from the user contributions available on the Internet which will appear on the cable-television outlet for Current TV. And it is only at this point that Current TV pays contributors. At the time of writing, it pays the contributors of winning sponsored user-generated commercials $2,500 per VCAM (a one-time payment, not per use). If the sponsor for whom the VCAM was produced wishes to use the VCAM in media other than Current TV, contributors are paid between $5,000 and $60,000 depending on the medium on which it is shown (Current TV 2010b).

The contest further emphasizes the importance of adhering to a narrow range of acceptable form and content. The "VCAM Hall of Fame" is a gallery of past award winners which serve as implicit guidelines to follow and emulate (Current TV 2010n). It also allows the commercial's sponsor to pass all of the development costs onto the shoulders of individual contributors as well as onto the entire Current TV community as voters, thus becoming a cheaper way of testing the effectiveness of different ads among this desirable target market (Current TV 2010b).

The social principle of the contest, which sets each member against the other, is institutionalized as well by ranking participation. The Current TV Community is striated in what Current TV calls "levels," which publicly rank members to encourage greater involvement. The initial level, "contributors," distinguishes people who make any contribution such as comments or unused videos. One step up from this is "commentators," a status earned by commenting or voting for favorites at least five times in a single day. And the step up from this is "producers," who upload a video that meets Current TV's requirements. Individual members' levels are visible to the rest of the community as "a level badge that comprises of three rows with four bars." One's progress is tracked via her or his online badge. "As you level up in a category, the bars on your badge will light up with the color that corresponds with that activity." Benefits in addition to distinguishing oneself within the community include what Current TV ambiguously refers to as "special abilities. And you never know, you might even get a surprise in your mailbox" (Current TV 2010b).

THE LIMITS TO USER PARTICIPATION

But there are limits even to this highly managed form of user production, and Current TV, in its quest to boost advertising revenue, soon reached them. Its in-house staff expenses skyrocketed to unsustainable levels due to the need to compensate for the dearth of user-contributed content of sufficient quality (Wallenstein 2010). In addition, as the trade press reported, "a TV schedule comprised of multi-minute clips is far less advertising-friendly than the half-hours that ensure viewer tune-in isn't so erratic," and short, unique pods cannot predictably attract large-enough audiences for the show to be included in

Nielsen ratings (Wallenstein 2010). As a cable-industry analyst put it in spring of 2010, "'They've got to become rated soon or advertisers will not go with them'" (quoted in Wallenstein 2010).

As a result, in early 2010 Current TV significantly revamped its practice and organization to lessen the focus on user content in favor of professionalized programming and traditional program scheduling, a change characterized in the trade press as the effort to "conform to the traditional network model in every way, shape and form" (Wallenstein 2010). After failing for two years to sell itself to other media organizations, Current TV replaced Hyatt at CEO in July 2009 with Mark Rosenthal, a board member of Current TV and formerly the chief operating officer of MTV Networks. Under his direction, and in addition to waves of layoffs, Current TV replaced its trademark short content pods from users with what a commentator calls more traditional "full-length series from the usual suspects in unscripted production" (Wallenstein 2010). Mainstays of its schedule include "Infomania" (a satirical half-hour news show), "Deadliest Journeys" (a reality travel show to dangerous locales), and "Stunts and Chaos" (described as "a dangerous blend of extreme sports, adventure, and goofiness") (Current TV 2010p). It is also exploring additional but less direct and thus more controllable modes of user participation, such as helping develop episodes of series—what Current TV calls "crowdsourced TV" (Wallenstein 2010; Koelsch 2010). Unlike programming, the main avenue for user participation remains user-created advertising. This is due at least in part to its comparatively small cost, much more flexible production schedule, and its research value to marketers whether or not a usable VCAM emerges.

The case of Current TV indicates the limits of user participation in a traditional broadcasting format, thus invalidating claims that the production requirements of traditional commercial broadcasting encourages open user production. Even the highly managed form of user participation developed at Current TV could not generate acceptably accelerating levels of revenue. In the ongoing case of Current TV, profitability requires even more remote, derivative, and controllable forms of user participation. This case suggests not only that hasty claims about user-contributed content to media companies as democratizing communications be roundly challenged. It also suggests that democratic communications require that existing systems be not simply adapted, but replaced.

REFERENCES

"Al Gore Speaks at Current TV." 2008. http://vimeo.com/1865919.

"Al Gore, Speech in Rome." 2008. 8 May, http://www.veoh.com/browse/ videos/category/news/watch/v9334027pDDzZY52.

"Awards and Honors—ProPublica." 2010. *ProPublica*, http://www.propublica.org/awards/.

Barlow, A. 2008. *Blogging America*. Westport: Praeger.

Becker, A. 2006. "The Other Man Behind Current TV; Legal Services Pioneer Hyatt Aims to Democratize Media and Empower Young Users." *Broadcasting and Cable*, 20 November, p. 18.

Benjamin, W. 1969. "Theses on the Philosophy of History." In *Illuminations*, Zohn, H., transl., pp. 253–264. New York: Schocken.

Brickley, P. 2008. "Pappas Telecasting Files for Bankruptcy, Blames CW Ratings." *Marketwatch*, 10 May. http://www.marketwatch.com/story/ pappas-telecasting-files-for-bankruptcy-blames-cw-ratings.

British Broadcasting Company. 2010. "BBC–Video Nation–Your Views and Experiences, on Camera and Online." http://www.bbc.co.uk/videonation/ contribute/.

Carpentier, N. "The BBC's Video Nation as a Participatory Media Practice: Signifying Everyday Life, Cultural Diversity and Participation in an Online Community." *International Journal of Cultural Studies* 6: 425–447.

Compaine, B. and Gomery, D. 2000. *Who Owns the Media? Competition and Concentration in the Mass Communications Industry*. 3rd edition. Mahwah: Lawrence Erlbaum.

Current TV. 2007. "Current Launches Fully Integrated Online and on TV Experience With Current.Com." News release. 15 October. http:// i2.crtcdn.net/pdf/CurrentcomReleaseFinalRev.pdf

Current TV. 2008. Amendment No. 4 to Form S-1; Registration Statement Under the Securities Act of 1933. United States Securities and Exchange Commission.

Current TV. 2010a. "Make TV: Learn How to Produce a Television Show or Pod on Current." http://current.com/make/.

Current TV. 2010b. "Frequently Asked Questions // Current." http://current.com/s/faq.htm.

Current TV. 2010c. "Equipment List." http://current.com/pdf/survival-guide/vc2gearguide.pdf.

Current TV. 2010d. "Make A Pod // Current." http://current.com/make/pod.htm.

Current TV. 2010e. "Make An Ad // Current." http://current.com/make/ad.htm.

Current TV. 2010f. "Make An Element // Current." http://current.com/make/element.htm.

Current TV. 2010g. "Producer Resources // Current." http://current.com/make/resources.htm.

Current TV. 2010h. "Producer Resources // Current: Storytelling." http://current.com/make/training/section/storytelling.htm

Current TV. 2010i. "Video Submission Release." http://i2.crtcdn.net/pdf/release.pdf

Current TV. 2010j. "Current Video Submission Clearance Report." http://i2.crtcdn.net/pdf/clearance_report.pdf

Current TV. 2010k. "Location Release." http://i2.crtcdn.net/pdf/location_release.pdf

Current TV. 2010l. "Master Use and Synchronization Use License." http://i2.crtcdn.net/pdf/music_master_use.pdf.

Current TV. 2010m. "Terms of Use // Current." http://current.com/s/terms.htm.

Current TV. 2010n. "VCAM Hall of Fame." http://current.com/participate/vcam/vcam-hall-of-fame/new/.

Current TV. 2010o. "Current/Management." http://current.com/s/management.htm.

Current TV. 2010p. "TV Shows // Current." http://current.com/shows/

Dahlgren, P. 2009. "The Troubling Evolution of Journalism." In *The Changing Faces of Journalism; Tabloidization, Technology and Truthiness*, ed. Zelizer, B., pp. 146-161.

Dahlberg, L. and Siapera, E, eds. 2007. *Radical Democracy and the Internet: Interrogating Theory and Practice*. New York: Palgrave Macmillan.

Dean, J. 2009. *Democracy and Other Neoliberal Fantasies; Communicative Capitalism & Left Politics*. Durham: Duke University Press.

Deggans, E. 2009. "Nielsen Reveals Most of Top Watched TV Programs in 2009 were Sports or Reality Shows." *The Feed*. http://blogs.tampabay.com/media/2009/12/nielsen-reveals-most-of-top-watched-tv-programs-in-2009-were-sports-or-reality-shows.html.

Dena, C. 2008. "Emerging Participatory Culture Practices." *Convergence: The International Journal of Research into New Media Technologies* 14: 41–57.

Doctor, K. 2010. "The Newsonomics of Profit: Google's and Newspapers." *Nieman Journalism Lab*, 25 February. http://www.niemanlab. org/2010/02/the-newsonomics-of-profit-googles-and-newspapers/

"Doritos Presents Snackstrong Productions." http://www.doritos.com/

Dyer-Witheford, N. de Peuter, G. 2009. *Games of Empire: Global Capitalism and Video Games*. Minneapolis: University of Minnesota Press.

Federal Communications Commission. 2003. *Report and Order and Notice of Proposed Rulemaking, In the Matter of 2002 Biennial Regulatory Review*. MB Docket 02-277, 01-235, 01-317, 00-244, and 03-130, 2 June.

Gamson, J. 2003. "Gay Media, Inc.: Media Structures, the New Gay Conglomerates, and Collective Sexual Identities." In *Cyberactivism: Online Activism in Theory and Practice*, McCaughey, M. and Ayers, M. eds., pp. 255–78. New York: Routledge.

Gordon, J. 2007. "The Mobile Phone and the Public Sphere: Mobile Phone Usage in Three Critical Situations." *Convergence: The International Journal of Research into New Media Technologies* 13: 307-319.

Griffen-Foley, B. 2004. "From Tit-Bits to Big Brother: A Century of Audience Participation in the Media." *Media, Culture and Society* 26: 533–48.

Harvey, D. 1989. *The Condition of Postmodernity; An Enquiry Into the Origins of Cultural Change*. Oxford: Basil Blackwell.

Harvey, D. 2006. *Spaces of Global Capitalism; Towards a Theory of Uneven Geographical Development*. New York: Verso.

Hill, A. 2005. *Reality TV; Audiences and Popular Factual Television*. London: Routledge.

Honda. 2010. Live Every Litre. http://www.liveeverylitre.com/.

ITN Source. 2007. "Al Gore in London for Launch of Current TV." 12 March. http://www.blinkx.com/watch-video/al-gore-in-london-for-launch-of-current-tv/8BSRG-5ZiGpfzd_UfgtlYg.

Jenkins, H. 2006. *Fans, Bloggers and Gamers: Media Consumers in a Digital Age*. New York: New York University Press.

Jenkins, H. 2008. *Convergence Culture*. New York: New York University Press.

Kavka, M. 2008. *Reality Television, Affect and Intimacy; Reality Matters*. New York: Palgrave Macmillan.

Kim, E.-G. and Hamilton, J.F. 2006. "Capitulation to Capital? *OhmyNews* as Alternative Media." *Media, Culture & Society* 28: 541–560.

King, G., ed. 2005. *The Spectacle of the Real; From Hollywood to 'Reality' TV and Beyond.* Portland: Intellect.

Kinter, C. 1945. "The Changing Pattern of the Newspaper Publishing Industry." *American Journal of Economics and Sociology* 5: 43–63.

Koelsch, D. 2010. "New TV Show Would Let Anyone Create an Episode." *Movieviral*, 31 March. http://www.movieviral.com/2010/03/31/new-tv-show-would-let-anyone-create-an-episode/

Lasch, C. 1991. *The True and Only Heaven; Progress and Its Critics.* New York: W.W. Norton.

Miller, T. and Zwerdling, D. 2010. "Brain Injuries Remain Undiagnosed in Thousands of Soldiers." *Pro Publica*, 7 June. http://www.propublica.org/feature/brain-injuries-remain-undiagnosed-in-thousands-of-soldiers.

Mofilm. 2010. MOFILM: The Biggest Brand Video Contests and Competitions. http://www.mofilm.com/

Murray, S. and Ouellette, L., eds. 2009. *Reality TV; Remaking Television Culture.* 2nd ed. New York: New York University Press.

"Next Stop For Newspaper Companies–Bankruptcy Court?" 2009. *Trading-Markets.com*, 23 February. http://www.tradingmarkets.com/.site/news/TOP%20STORY/2190334/.

Naughton, M. 2007. "Al Gore, Chairman and Founder, Current TV." ANA Marketing Maestros, Oct 13. http://ana.blogs.com/maestros/2007/10/al-gore-chairma.html

Ouellette, L. and Hay, J. 2008. *Better Living through Reality TV: Television and Post-Welfare Citizenship.* Malden: Blackwell.

Quinton, B. 2008. "From Backyard to Broadcast." *Promo Magazine.* 1 March. http://promomagazine.com/retail/current_tv_vcam_program_0301/

Spector, M. and McBride, S. 2009. "Citadel Files for Bankruptcy Amid Harsh Radio Climate." *WSJ.com*, 20 December. http://online.wsj.com/article/SB10001424052748704786204574608371640888490.html.

Time. 2007. 1 January.

Tunstall, J. 1986. *Communications Deregulation: The Unleashing of America's Communication.* New York: Basil Blackwell.

Turner, G. 2009. *Ordinary People and the Media: The Demotic Turn.* Thousand Oaks: Sage.

Wallenstein, A. 2010. "New Troubles at Al Gore's Current TV." *The Hollywood Reporter*, 24 June. http://www.hollywoodreporter.com/hr/content_display/news/e3ieb17ddd24af6bab6bb10df8ecbe598ed

Williams, R. 1970. "Radical and/or Respectable." In *The Press We Deserve*, ed. R. Boston, pp. 14–26. London: Routledge and Kegan Paul.

Williams, R. 1976. *Keywords: A Vocabulary of Culture and Society*. New York: Oxford University Press.

WPN Videos. 2007. "Current.com and Al Gore." 12 Oct. http://videos.webpronews.com/2007/10/12/currentcom-and-al-gore/.

Ytreberg, E. 2004. "Formatting Participation Within Broadcast Media Production." *Media, Culture and Society* 26: 677–692.

CHAPTER 16

CRITICAL MEDIA LITERACY

CRITIQUING CORPORATE MEDIA
WITH RADICAL PRODUCTION

Bettina Jabos

INTRODUCTION

IN EXAMINING THE ROLES THE MEDIA HAVE PLAYED in creating and maintaining a public sphere (a space in which the public can have democratic debate), cultural historian James Carey argued that the mass media, influenced by complex political and institutional forces, are an active site of conflict and struggle, and are thus swayed by a "political community organized as a discoursing public" (Rosen 1997, 192). There is considerable power that comes from the public—in not being silent spectators, but in being involved in the production and dissemination of ideas. To be active citizens, we must first understand how our U.S. media system works, so that we may be actively engaged in shaping its future as means to greater democracy.

As corporate interests control an increasing aspect of our shared social and cultural spheres, the act of countering that power and dominance has become an ongoing challenge. Take the following example: three students at the University of Northern Iowa created a mashup for a media culture class in which they juxtaposed YouTube clips of formal ballet performers to a medley of Alvin and the Chipmunks' songs (produced by Warner Music Group). The end product wasn't perfect, but its worthy point was to make the ballerinas look rather ludicrous while commenting on both the universality of the Chipmunks and the malleability of "high" culture. And yet, within hours of uploading the project, the students received a threatening take-down notice from Google/YouTube for copyright infringement of the Chipmunks soundtrack: "Attention: We have received copyright complaint(s) regarding material you posted…Please note: **Accounts determined to be repeat infringers will be terminated.** Please delete any videos for which you do not own the necessary rights, and refrain from uploading infringing videos."

With the rise in video and audio fingerprinting technology, takedown notices have become extremely common. Video and music identification companies like Audible Magic work with Google and other user-generated content sites to detect potential copyright violations and issue take-down alerts. As such, the students' efforts to create a non-commercial cultural critique were denied by the corporate stakeholders in their ongoing efforts to control online content and define the parameters for cultural expression.

An effort by the same three students to use traditional research methods, such as writing a research paper to discuss Alvin and the Chipmunks and their musical style, and juxtapose this discussion with a description of ballet dancers and the musical style that defines ballet culture, and then upload the paper to the Web, would quite likely have raised no complaint from the corporate copyright holders of Alvin and the Chipmunks' music. While a long-enduring fair use standard allows writers to quote from texts to make their points, this artistic protection appears moot once material from books, newspapers, magazines, music, movies, radio, and the like—moves to the Internet. Once digitized, "quotes" from a song or part of a video for an academic, noncommercial project seem to fall outside the realm of fair use as defined by our copyright laws.

The past ten to fifteen years have provided an increasing number of people with an opportunity to distribute creative work to a global audience via the Internet. At the same time, we are witnessing an era of digital rights management (DRM), in which copyright holders (usually large corporations) attempt to control the rights to the use of their creative work (known as "intellectual property"). The tension between the public (wanting to use available material) and digital copyright owners (wanting to control the way their content is experienced), are thus common occurrences, as citizens try to communicate in a world in which public discourse is no longer just spoken or written, but circulated in many forms in the converged environment of the World Wide Web. As this type of "illegal" production continues, citizens are constantly testing the boundaries of outdated copyright laws and the limits of discourse as corporations conversely assert the rights of their intellectual property and, in the process, challenge corporate dominance over cultural space.

This chapter first examines the history of media literacy in the United States, and looks at an important thread of it–critical media literacy–which educators have developed for the critical inquiry of the corporate media system. Second, this chapter discusses why now is an historic era for media production based on the ideas of critical media literacy. Using actual classroom examples, the chapter shows how inexpensive digital technology and access to the Internet–the most democratic mass medium invented–has spurred practitioners of "radical production" to employ fair use access to corporate media content and common media production tools to critique the corporate media system. Finally, this chapter gives examples of how students (and others) can engage in "radical production" with the end goal of becoming more literate about mass media.

MEDIA LITERACY:
FROM APPRECIATION TO CRITICAL PRACTICES

The idea of media literacy was developed in tandem with the rise of new technology in the classroom. Early media literacy efforts, for example, included "earmindedness" (listening skills for the Victrola) and film analysis/appreciation courses (Luke 1990; Spring 1992). The first formal textbook on media literacy, according to Luke (1990), was called *How to Appreciate Motion Pictures*, by E. Dale (1933, 38-41). Early media literacy practices meant preparing students before and after a record, film, radio/television broadcast, filmstrip or video. Advocates of each classroom technology praised each new medium for its ability to stimulate good "interactive" discussions or engaged participation (e.g., Berg and Freedman 1955; Levenson and Stasheff 1945). By exposing students to a variety of new experiences and then opening up these experiences to critical evaluation, new technologies were also thought to promote democratic values, "intergroup understanding," and world peace (e.g., Beuick 1927; Cartwright 1955; Darrow 1932; Du Wors and Weist 1955; Ickes 1936).

In some cases teachers used new media content to promote critical thinking and discrimination skills. This kind of critical literacy was evident during the educational radio era, a period that had teachers questioning the encroaching commercialization of the public airwaves. Students learned to critique commercial programs and the ads that supported them in their radio classes (Levenson and Stasheff 1945). Because radio was drastically more affordable as a production medium than records, film, or television, radio clubs evolved (spawned by the hugely popular educational radio movement) where students and teachers actively produced their own programs. Beyond radio, most media literacy efforts of this era focused on the analysis of content, not media production.

Throughout the 1960s and early 1970s, the beginning of a fledgling media analysis movement began to take shape, stimulated in part by the ideas of Marshall McLuhan and Fr. John Culkin. Establishing the Center for Understanding Media in 1969 (named after McLuhan's 1964 book), Culkin and other media educators began to integrate media analysis into public school curriculums and launch educational magazines such as *Media & Values* (est. 1977). At the same time, faith-based groups were reacting against sexual and violent mainstream media content and forming their own media literacy curricula for parents and children, while calling for media content reform. As equipment (television and video) was prohibitively expensive to allow students to create media, most media literacy efforts focused on content criticism. Meanwhile at the college level, media education classes developed along with the growing discipline of Communication Studies. Most programs focused on vocational skills in radio, television, and film courses; some courses supported media work through quantitative audience analyses; some supported media reform through content analyses of media violence or sexual depictions; others took a more critical approach to media culture, including the study of the political economy of the mass media.

By the late 1990s, a growing network of media literacy educators (both K-12 and college-level), health service providers, and community activists had organized across the U.S., and in 2001 formed the National Association for Media Literacy Education (NAMLE). NAMLE's established mission was to help "empower people to be both critical thinkers and creative producers of messages using image, language, and sound" and expand media education throughout the U.S. But by 2002, a dissatisfied group of educators had broken off from NAMLE to form a competing media literacy organization, the

Action Coalition for Media Education (ACME). Their reasons were based on ideological differences with NAMLE, which had forged alliances with members of the media industry (e.g., the National Cable Television Association; the Discovery Channel; the Newspaper Association of America), and had established a more apolitical, noncontroversial media literacy discourse that would have broader appeal to schools and the corporate media. Rather than question the economic structure of the mass media, including its fundamental profit-making enterprise, NAMLE "empowers" people at the content level, calling for content reform (e.g., less violent or sexual content; more diversity in program representation). In contrast, central to ACME members' media literacy critique were issues of media and educational reform, broadcast regulation, a political and economic understanding of commercialism (including classroom commercialism), media ownership and conglomeration, and issues of media and social justice. In short, their approach was towards radical democracy.

The history of media literacy in the U.S. has delivered three major strains of media literacy today, which consider our relationship to the media in significantly different ways:

+ Vocational media literacy focuses on the appreciation (aesthetics and narrative structure) of existing media content and on knowing the technical skills and conventions of mainstream media production. The ultimate goal of vocational media literacy is employment in the mass media industry.

+ Reformist media literacy (in line with the NAMLE educators) focuses on media content and aims to improve (reform) representations of class, gender, race, sexuality, and social views of media programming (including advertising) through semiotic and intertextual analysis. With a goal of redefining media content, reformist video productions often encourage personal narratives that challenge dominant representations and hegemonic master narratives, with a focus on original work.

+ Critical media literacy takes reformist production one step further by examining the commercial media system in which all media is created. In critical media literacy, an understanding of ideology, power relations, and domination are crucial components in understanding mainstream media content as a whole. This political approach to the media (the approach supported by organizations such as ACME and the media reform movement through groups like Free Press) acknowledges that the process of media production and all discourse is political.

Much of critical media literacy discourse has its roots in educational scholarship. Since the 1970s and 1980s educational reform scholars have commonly advanced that schooling is a political activity. With these notions came an expanded conception of literacy—critical literacy— that positions all discourse within a political, economic and social framework (Berlin 1993; Lankshear and McClaren 1993). Texts are understood as containing a political perspective and inhabiting a particular place on the political spectrum. Unlike traditional literacy practices, where an apolitical canon is advanced and students are expected to master and imitate these canonical texts, there is no canon in critical literacy. Students are not encouraged, as is common practice, to seek out the various "truths" within a canonical text. Instead, critical literacy students "attain perspective on perspectives" (Lankshear and McClaren 1993, 33). They are taught to understand the relationships between texts, the ideological underpinnings of texts, the struggle behind texts, and all information within a broader cultural context.

Critical literacy is allied, in many ways, with the project of critical pedagogy and the work of Brazilian educator Paulo Freire, who argued for the need to develop a critical consciousness and to act against oppression. Critical pedagogy educators are committed to expose, through the examination of race, gender, class and social identity, the relations of cultural domination and ideological hegemony in advanced capitalism (e.g., Giroux 1987, 1998; Kinchloe 2006; Livingstone 1987; Sehr 1997; Shannon 1992; Sullivan 1987). Through an analysis of educational institutions such as schools, mass media, and family, they aim to reveal and deconstruct power relations, help students achieve critical consciousness, and work towards empowering marginalized voices (Giroux 1998). Critical literacy educators, in working with texts and promoting a politically informed understanding of our world, likewise attempt to expose inequalities and advance democratic thought and practice.

In the field of education, critical *media* literacy, which applies critical literacy objectives to the mass media, has evolved relatively recently as a combination of media/cultural studies and critical literacy pedagogy (Kellner and Share 2007). Indeed, a long line of media scholars from

John Dewey to James Carey to Robert McChesney have been interested in exposing the ideology behind the mass media content and
understanding the political and economic context of the mass media
as a cultural institution. Because critical media literacy is often driven
by the desire to democratize the commercial media system, this schol-
arship/cultural critique and resulting pedagogy continue to operate
from the margins. It thus receives little support from the commercial
mass media, other corporations (which rely on the media system to
advertise their goods and services), and the incumbent political system
(which adeptly uses the mass media and advertising to win elections
and sustain power). In short, critical media literacy can be a threat to
the entire existing political economy.

AN OPPORTUNITY FOR RADICAL PRODUCTION

Critical media literacy productions are radical in that the work often
involves downloaded or recorded (copyrighted) mainstream media
content that is reedited to critique or challenge the status quo of corporate media. Downloaded content is thus turned against itself. *The
Daily Show* and *The Colbert Report* on Comedy Central often support
radical production; so do the Media Education Foundation, various
nonprofit documentary outlets, and people posting their work online.

We are now at an historic moment in our media culture, a moment
in which radical production makes sense to many people. Two factors are in play. First, we have all witnessed the rise of inexpensive
digital video and still cameras; digital audio recorders; digital media
players; multimedia mobile telephones; digital video recorders; non-
linear audio and video editing systems; software for animation, photo
alteration, and graphic design; computers with enormous hard drives;
social media services; user-generated media web sites (e.g., YouTube,
Vimeo, and Flickr); and perhaps, most significantly, high-speed broadband Internet connections, which link multimedia devices and enable
anyone to access and upload a plethora of media content. Large media
production systems which could have been found only in commercial
or university studio environments a dozen years ago have been consolidated into inexpensive, powerful desktop devices that now reside
in millions of teenagers' bedrooms.

Second, even if they're not fully cognizant of it, many people are
already immersed in radical media culture, as they question conventional media forms, dismiss typical news media channels, and push

for new media distribution systems. The production, distribution, and exhibition of films, television programs, popular music, political commentary, and other media content used to be the sole domain of massive media conglomerates (McChesney 1999). Today, hyperlinks are the new punctuation; gone is the sole authorship sprung out of multimedia corporations and the experts that are part of this system. Creating their own system of connections, users have built, bottom-up, a linked world of recommendations and navigations that has unlimited space and airtime and is often radically discordant to our hegemonic dominant mainstream culture. Even as this interlinked space is being vehemently pursued by the same (and other) media corporations, there has been a huge leveling of communication and collaboration. Moreover, some have observed that access to a huge array of often competing ideas has built a perspective in young people to think more critically (Shadbolt 2009). Indeed, today's Internet-connected users are fully conscious of their own ability to participate in a newly intertextual and interactive Internet culture, ably constructing meaning by subverting existing media power structures (from YouTube and Twitter to student-driven websites like IResist: http://www.iresist.org/index.html).

This emerging radical mindset first became clear to the rest of the world in 1999 with the rapid rise of Napster, which enabled millions of music fans (nearly all of them young) to trade music. Napster was radical in three ways: first, it was a distribution system created at the grassroots level by a young programmer (Shawn Fanning, then 19), and popularized by his peers around the world; second, it demonstrated the power of the Internet as an alternative media distribution system (an idea that took the music industry years to grasp); and third, it undermined traditional thinking about intellectual property and called attention to the issue of copyrights. (Napster as a free music trading site was ultimately shut down by the courts for copyright infringement in 2001.)

Napster was only the beginning of networked production and distribution; well beyond YouTube, Flickr, and Facebook (commercial networks) and the Internet Archive (one of the Internet's most significant non-profit digital archives); people are creating and joining niche networks and participating in a revitalized political discourse that, at least for now, mostly exists outside of commercial media control. Yale Law School professor Yochai Benkler (2006) interprets the advances of peer-to-peer networking and the organic growth of the web as an indication of a new kind of media, what he has dubbed the "networked public sphere." Thus, the argument goes, this Internet environment—an emerging creative commons—is collectively owned and *different* than all commercial media before it. This is a hopeful vision of the Internet, that the medium will prevail as a democratic tool for spreading ideas. Indeed, what Kellner (2000) advocated a decade ago—a critical media literacy that connects people to higher levels of civic engagement and goals for transforming culture towards democratic ends—has been happening, often with young people's avid participation. A new generation of youth can more easily question our dominant media system perhaps better than ever before, because alternatives to that system are their computing devices.

Beyond experiencing rich Internet content and engaging in social media sites, participation can mean creating critical production for a global audience. For example, CSPAN's StudentCam video contest encourages middle and high school students to remix CSPAN video content and create documentaries "to think seriously about issues that affect our communities and our nation." (http://www.studentcam.org/index.htm). Union organizations such as LabourStart in England and the Ontario Public Service Employees Union in Canada host video contests that they then publish on YouTube (for example, see *Just Another Cog in the Machine*: http://www.youtube.com/watch?v=LLGoKqPAhSk). BBC has released high resolution video footage featuring critical scholars and Internet industry players—shot for their broadcast documentary series, *Virtual Revolution*—with a challenge to global users to "make your own documentary" using the footage they provide (as well as other footage found or created). If the rock band OK Go (which became famous through viral videos on YouTube) can successfully go independent, ditch their media conglomerate parent company EMI, release their independently-produced videos on YouTube, and invigorate a growing movement of independent music production and distribution, so can eight-year olds, who are fully capable of recording songs in GarageBand, shooting footage, editing the video to their music, and uploading their creations to a global audience.

If the practices described above can be characterized as what Kellner calls "globalization from below" (Kellner 2000), because they contain the possibility of questioning and challenging corporate power, including corporate media power, it is important to remember that very powerful (because money does speak) commercial interests (Google, Microsoft, Amazon, Apple, Yahoo, and even Netflix at the content level; Verizon, Comcast, and AT&T at the distribution level), are rapidly moving towards the centralization and control of Internet content and delivery. The assertion here is that the Internet is *a continuation* of the existing commercial mass media. (McChesney 2008; Vaidhyanathan forthcoming). Thus, as it is more and more possible to create and distribute media content to a global audience, it is thus more and more necessary to create content that critiques this consolidation. By encouraging critical media literacy and radical productions as a major component of media literacy, educators join the evolved discourse of media criticism put forth by nonprofit media watchdog and education organizations such as the Free Press, the Electronic Frontier Foundation, the Media Education Foundation, The Center for Social Media, the Center for Media and Democracy, the Center for Science in the Public Interest, Commercial Alert, and the Edmond J. Safra Foundation Center for Ethics. Because video/multimedia is such a powerful medium for such ideas, using the media to critique the media is an effective way of becoming fully media literate.

Third, media activists have been hard at work challenging current copyright laws and assembling legal guidelines for the free and open remixing of media content. The inherent "problem" with many radical productions—that downloading, editing, and then uploading copyrighted footage is illegal—is overcome by keeping critical media literacy projects within the confines of Fair Use. In 1991, University of Massachusetts professor Sut Jhally edited together images of MTV videos and added new music and a voice over that critiqued the sexist representations in the videos. He also commented on the political economic environment in which MTV and its parent corporation Viacom marketed to an adolescent male audience; it made good business sense to use dehumanizing images of women in MTV videos. Jhally's "Dreamworlds: Desire/Sex/Power in Rock Video" was a radical production—so radical in its critique of MTV and the consumer ethos of music videos that MTV threatened Jhally and his university with legal action for copyright abuse. Jhally held his ground, arguing in 1991, "This sort of cultural commentary is what universities exist to do" (as reported by William Davis in the *Boston Globe*). MTV ultimately backed down. Since then, the Media Education Foundation has built a large body of critical/radical media work using copyrighted media content as the basis for their critiques.

Arguably, an important tool in doing this criticism is being able to "quote" examples of media content, as Jhally and the Media Education Foundation do in their videos, and as critical writers have done for centuries, citing other written documents in their own work (Lessig 2008; Mcleod 2007). Legally, nonprofit educational media producers are entitled to use portions of other media content under the doctrine of "fair comment and criticism" or "fair use":

> Fair use is the right, in some circumstances, to quote copyrighted material without asking permission or paying for it. It is a crucial feature of copyright law and what keeps copyright from being censorship. You can invoke fair use when the value to the public of what you are saying outweighs the cost to the private owner of the copyright (Center for Social Media 2006).

Thus, radical video producers and artists negotiate blurry legal horizons as they argue for the democratic value of their work in order to steer clear of copyright lawsuits. As video, music, and images become more central to our culture and as digital formats make this content more accessible, media corporations have wielded legal threats to protect their "intellectual property." In 2005, documentary producers mounted an initiative to stake out ground for their work. Through the Center for Social Media, a coalition of independent media producers and academics released a "Documentary Filmmakers' Statement of Best Practices in Fair Use" (2006), and asserted that a media producer should be able to use copyrighted material if it is used as the object of social, political, or cultural critique, if it is used to illustrate an argument or point, if it is captured in the background as part of a work on something else, or if it is used as part of an historical sequence. The doctrine even allows commercial works to invoke fair use if they are guided by the above principles. By 2010, the Center for Social Media had expanded its code of best practices to include "Fair Use in Media Literacy Education, Fair Use and Creative Practice, and Fair Use for Online Video Creators." More recently, the "transformative use" doctrine has become a dominant approach to determine fair use, and has been introduced legally (and successfully) in courts (Bunker, 2010). Although these doctrines in no way settle the battle between fair use and copyright (Lessig 2006), there exists today extraordinary flexibility to create critical and radical media productions that rein-terpret mainstream media content to assess our social, political, and cultural environment.

DOING RADICAL MEDIA PRODUCTION

I teach critical media theory classes at the University of Northern Iowa, and have been integrating production into these classes since 2006. I see students' radical production work as critical to their ed-ucation as media literate citizens, and part of a necessary discourse about the future of the Internet and the need for an articulate public discourse about media, power, and democracy. Based on my teaching (and feedback from students), I can easily say that a significant step in their understanding of the sometimes abstract concepts of media ownership and power relations comes from the act of re-cutting and remixing mainstream media content. I will describe below a number of projects that have encouraged students to recognize their own rela-tionship to the media.

PHOTOSHOP MANIPULATION

There are complex economic dynamics between the images and mes-sages controlled by the fast food, snack, and soda industries: constant-ly rising rates of obesity, and the ubiquitous pressure in our commer-cial mass media system for people to look excessively thin or ripped. As part of their analysis students look at print and television adver-tisements, news reports, public relation campaigns, lobbying websites, and Internet search results to build an understanding of how private enterprise advances an ideology of consumerism and individualism (which can basically be reduced to this message: if you're fat it's your fault). To help illustrate the dominant value of thinness (women) and steroid-induced bodies (men), and analyze how the ideology of thin/ ripped has reached new and impossible levels, we do an exercise in Photoshop—a now ubiquitous tool for (mis)representing the images of beauty we see every day. Although there are always exceptions, most students have minimal experience with Photoshop, so we spend a day in a computer lab learning the tools used by every photo retouch art-ist whose job is to tweak the images that appear in our mainstream media. Working with photographs I provide and images students take of themselves with their built-in computer cameras, we learn how to remove pimples, smooth out wrinkles, change the shape of our noses, elongate our necks, thin out our arms, and clone other body parts (from existing advertising images) onto our own. I ask students to perfect this (mis)representation of themselves outside of class. It's a small assignment with huge ramifications: students will never look at a magazine image the same way again, and they more deeply understand the economic conditions of advertising and marketing culture. Indeed, a powerful tool like Photoshop has had an enormous impact on the images that manipulate as much as they are manipulated. To make this assignment a radical production, students distribute their "before" and "after" images on the Web, and write captions about the beauty industry, the stampede towards plastic surgery operations that began with movie stars and now has filtered down to the middle classes, and impossible representations of thin. These images accompany an existing critical discourse about Photoshop and advertising practices that uphold dangerous beauty standards.

MEDIA RE-MIX

Twenty-first century copyright law, and the corporate media's drive to constantly extend copyright, is being interrogated by the counter-cultural remix movement, which advocates the downloading and remixing of copyrighted media content. After familiarizing students with the theories behind copyright law (the reasons it was put in place, the reasons why scholars are calling for sweeping revisions) and the tensions the Internet and user-generated content sites have brought to the content industry, I assign a mashup project asking them to challenge copyright law with the premise of Fair Use. They download copyrighted music, newscasts, movie footage, or television programming, and in mashing up elements of commercial media, their goal is to "cleverly" make something new through the juxtaposition of two or more parts. They download most of their footage via YouTube (we practice downloading during class), but they also rely upon recorded television programming, footage ripped from DVDs (this is increasingly difficult due to Digital Rights Management controls), downloaded footage from BitTorrent sites like Pirate Bay, or recorded footage from their own computer screens using screen capture software. Students have built mashups around political campaign advertising, popular cartoons (e.g., HeMan, Disney movies, *Dora the Explorer*), YouTube viral videos, movie trailers, State of the Union addresses,

TV shows (e.g., *Saved by the Bell, The Today Show,* John Madden on *NBC Sunday Night Football*), TV commercials (e.g., the "Be All You Can Be" U.S. Army campaign, Geico), and corporate training videos. The goal is to transform the content through juxtaposition, making new meaning that often critiques the original media content itself or certain resonating cultural values within the content. Students are required to upload their projects to YouTube, sending their work back into the system, where they often receive a surprising number of hits and commentary. As such, students learn that they can be contributors to the public media sphere, and are empowered by the act of creating a media project viewable by a global audience. "I am now completely absorbed by the idea of remixing and mashups, and really have a great respect for their place in the social media world," wrote one student after this assignment. For others who have never edited a video before, this process has an even further impact. "Before I took this class I just watched movies, now I can make them," one student noted. "That is just incredible to think about."

The most significant moment of learning, however, happens when students start receiving takedown notices about their posted videos from YouTube. This usually happens to about half the projects created for the class. Because media content is now embedded with digital fingerprinting, corporate copyright holders—on the prowl for misuses of their proprietary content—can more easily detect copyright violations now than ever before. This is where theory meets practice. As students have already learned (from reading Lawrence Lessig's work on remix culture), their creativity is constrained by copyright law, and no matter how "harmless" their message, it's still not acceptable in our current legal system. "We're building a legal system that completely suppresses the natural tendencies of today's digital kids," Lessig (2005) writes. "We're building a technology that takes the magic of Kodak, mixes moving images and sound, and adds a space for commentary and an opportunity to spread that creativity everywhere. But we're building the law to close down that technology" (47).

PUBLIC DOMAIN PROJECT

Another media project focuses on legality (rather than illegality) within our current media system, and thus works as a companion to the Media Re-Mix video project. Students first learn about the idea of "a commons"—a term that increasingly refers to the natural resources and public resources that are passed down to us, that we share, and that we need to protect for future generations. National parks and public libraries are two examples of commons, as are non-profit, shared on-line communities working towards the public interest. These sites are the opposite of the privatized web: public library digital archives that store vast numbers of public domain photographs, non-profit visual databases like the Internet Archive and Wikimedia Commons that allow anyone to upload and share valuable digital artifacts, and the Creative Commons movement (in which sites like Flickr and Vimeo are active players) that nurture a shared Internet culture. For this unit on copyright, the Public Domain Project requires students to pick a topic (preferably historical) to research both in terms of content and digital imagery. Sometimes I ask them to pick a professor on campus first, who gives them a topic related to that professor's own research interests (students confront topics they have never heard of, and thus connect more deeply to the mission of a liberal arts university). During the 2008 election year I assigned the topic of presidential campaigns between 1850 and 1920; each student got their own presidential race to research. Whether students pick their own topic or receive an as-signed one, their first goal is to become familiar with their research topic.

The second goal is to locate a set of 15 images related to a students' topic that are either in the public domain or are granted a Creative Commons or GNU copyleft license (allowing for non-commercial or share-alike uses). The process of digital archive searching invites them into the vast numbers of non-profit resources that are part of the "deep web," and that don't appear easily in search engine result lists. It can be revelatory to show students what exists outside their typically privatized experience of Facebook and Google. "Let me tell you," wrote one student in a post-assignment reflection, "I completely LOVED being exposed to the commons websites like archive.org and Wikime-dia Commons. I have already used media sources from these sites for many other non-class-related projects. Because video and multimedia creation is something that I take particular interest in, this will defi-nitely help me in the greater scheme of my career."

The third goal is documentation. Students are required to create a table document that catalogs each image: its pixel quality, its detailed description, its URL linking to its permanent location, and a record of email contact and communication with librarians or individual copyright holders about each image's availability for educational purposes. In other words, I require students to be *accountable*, as any photo researcher would have to be in the legal world of copyright protection, and provide good evidence that the images they find are in the public domain, and/or require attribution, and/or can be freely used for noncommercial projects.

Finally, the fourth goal of the project is for students to get creative and build an interactive slideshow using the images they located. They use Soundslides, a photographic storytelling software tool to build a narrative around their images using their own captions and sometimes an audio narration and/or original music. This final goal yields a project that students present to each other in class and sometimes upload to the Web.

The finished production itself is not radical. However, the pre-production process invites students to fully grasp the "radical" alternatives to the privatized web (non-profit digital archives) and also navigate a tricky copyright terrain. It turns out that this process, even though it can be difficult, sticks with students. "I learned that the public domain is a great place to look for stuff, and I've also learned how I can put my own pictures in the public domain," recalled a student. By interacting with the commons for a particular project, they come to understand that this part of the web *belongs to them*, and they can participate in its functions. The commons is therefore not an abstract concept, but suddenly worth protecting, and in the long run worth fighting for. Another student observed this about the project: "I think the most important aspect of this [project] was the hands-on approach of actually creating media projects with the copyright issues in mind. The photo slideshow project was a fantastic challenge in this regard. Not only did we read scholarly articles on copyright and engage in class discussions, but we learned how to specifically *apply* Fair Use Policy and copyright limitations by making a project that involved extensive research and attribution."

This project works best when juxtaposed with the "Media Re-Mix" video project (described above), which blatantly disregards copyright law. I think that being able to create something without worrying about copyrights and then having to turn around and be totally aware of them was the best way to do those assignments," another student noted. "Because the first one was practically a free-for-all, we didn't have to pay that close attention [to copyright], but when we started the second one it made me more aware of what's copyright protected and why." A third student added: "I know some things to do so I don't run into problems with THE MAN. I want to make sure I credit everyone that I use; I want to make sure I'm transforming the pieces I have into new works." In the end, students are aware of becoming visual contributors to our public discourse, and are able to better recognize the grassroots efforts within our democracy to disseminate digital sounds and images in light of extreme, corporate-friendly copyright laws. And maybe, perhaps, they'll get informed enough to do something about them.

RADICAL MEDIA DOCUMENTARY

In many media classes dealing with issues of democracy, the public sphere, the state of journalism, and hypercapitalism, instructors may require a final paper, perhaps, or an exam. In my classes the final project more often than not is a radical media documentary. I usually introduce the project during the second week of class, and throughout the first half of the semester students are asked to be mindful of class topics that energize them. Depending on the course, topics may revolve around any aspect of the media industry (e.g., TV news, media ownership, advertising, public relations); lately students have been making radical media documentaries on the political economy of new media—a frequent course focus of mine. Based on past experience, I advocate that students use one existing, well-researched, well-argued journal article or book chapter as the foundation for their piece. One could provide students with any chapter from this book, for example, or articles read and discussed earlier in the semester, and challenge them to visualize—using existing downloaded media—these scholarly arguments. In a recent class, students used as their "scholarly foundation" the high quality, HD interview excerpts from the BBC documentary *Virtual Revolution*. Using this impressively captured public domain footage, students covered a range of topics, including sexting, Facebook, copyright, and the Y Generation, and supplemented the BBC footage with a range of other visuals, mostly downloaded from YouTube.

Work on the actual documentary production begins mid-way through the course as students develop ideas, do outside research, work out scripts, find supporting footage (using media to critique the media), and begin the process of building their narrative. For anyone intimidated by working with digital media technology, know that students can figure it out. There will be obvious setbacks, especially when they are new to downloading and video editing (this is increasingly rare), but no problem has ever been insurmountable. Indeed, students seem to embrace the chance to create and comment on media culture as an exciting challenge, and they find it especially empowering to send their work out into the networked public sphere and receive feedback (and in some cases, gain notoriety and win awards). "I think knowing that someone other than the class will see this is scary in a way that makes us have to be on top of our game," one student wrote about this assignment. "We don't want the rest of society to see our last minute slopped together project, we want to impress!" Another student noted, "The responsibility, I believe, is to actually contribute and be an active member of this digital world. If we are not participating we are going to be left behind and I feel it is important to create content whatever it may be and share it with the masses." Some student projects are collected on the Website www.uni.edu/fabos/criticalmedia. They are also located in the Fair Use category of the Center for Social Media (http://www.centerforsocialmedia.org/).

BECOMING MEDIA LITERATE

Critical media documentaries, like the ones I have described above, are deeply worthwhile on multiple levels. First, the finished videos are uploaded to YouTube or another accessible site, and producers become immediately aware that they will be contributing to an important discourse, that they are spreading ideas about the significant role the media plays in our lives, and that they will have a global audience. Indeed, this global audience is real: one student's project was highlighted on the popular blog BoingBoing; others have had thousands upon thousands of hits; others have won media activism awards. In the production process, people (such as students) can become unusually committed to creating something they hope is impressive; they often spend many hours on the research itself, and then even more time sifting through clips for the right soundbite, visual example, or shot juxtaposition.

Second, the process of building a media critique using visual examples *from the media* gets producers to experience their arguments at a deeper level, and thus grow as media scholars. The notion that one can become more critically astute about the media when working very closely with the sources of one's critique is significant. Of all the topics students recently touched upon as they reflected on the process of making their critical media documentaries, nearly every one mentioned in some way that they deeply connected with their research topic and their arguments due to the process of making a video critique. In some cases, the experience affected them profoundly in terms of their own sense of media activism. For example, a student doing a critical media project on WiFi became committed to bringing WiFi to an underserved trailer park community in Ohio.

Finally, these are critical times. Despite the occasional takedown notices and lawsuits for illegal downloading practices (courtesy of business groups like the Recording Industry Association of America), we are still experiencing intense freedom with regard to online activities. And yet, our current decade in Internet history can easily be compared to the period in radio history (from the mid-1920s to the mid-1930s) when the public played such a large role in producing radio content, establishing educational networks, and finding noncommercial outlets that empowered marginalized groups (McChesney 1994). What happened to radio is a cautionary tale for what could happen to the Internet. Despite the huge potential of radio to be a significant public platform, the commercial forces won the struggle for control of the medium: educational radio production had ceased by World War II; nonprofit voices were silenced, and a handful of media conglomerates began to control the medium—an ownership structure that endures today. The public airwaves became public no more, and radio's potential as a public sphere became (and still is) negligible.

As users and producers of Internet content, we need to be intensely aware that the rules of the Internet are not set. Our current practices—of accessing "free" information, uploading and downloading media content; creating media mashups; archiving valuable documents in nonprofit library and public archives—are not the way the Internet will necessarily play out in the next decade as commercial forces (especially broadband providers AT&T, Comcast, and Verizon, and enormously powerful content providers like Google and Apple) work steadfastly toward a privatized, more heavily controlled Internet. Takedown notices—like the one issued to UNI students for a "misuse" of Alvin and the Chipmunks content—are the beginning of a much larger battle, and it is for these reasons that we have to recognize the need to work toward an understanding of the political and economic nature of corporate media systems. As such, we need to continually encourage critical media literacy productions that reveal the democratic limitations of our media system, especially the Internet. And more significantly, we need to immerse ourselves in a fight for more liberal copyright laws and a public online commons. In doing so, we can allow future generations to continue on as a discoursing public.

REFERENCES

Benkler, Yochai. 2006. *The Wealth of Networks: How Social Production Transforms Markets and Freedom.* New Haven: Yale University Press.

Berg, Esther L., and Florence B. Freedman. 1955. *The Recording as a Teaching Tool: A Bulletin for Parents and Teachers.* New York: Folkways Records and Service Corp.

Berlin, James A. 1993. Literacy, Pedagogy, and English Studies: Postmodern Connections. In *Critical Literacy, Politics, Praxis, and the Postmodern*, ed. Colin Lankshear and Peter McClaren, 247-270. Albany: State University of New York Press.

Beuick, M.D. 1927. The Limited Social Effect of Radio Broadcasting, *American Journal of Sociology* 32: 615-622.

Bunker, Matthew. 2010. The Song Remains the Same: Transformative Purpose Analysis in Fair Use Law. *Journalism & Mass Communication Quarterly* 87(1): 170-183.

Cartwright, Marguerite. 1955. The Use of Records in Intercultural Education. In *The Recording as a Teaching Tool: A Bulletin for Parents and Teachers*, ed. Esther L. Berg and Florence B Freedman, 3. New York: Folkways Records and Service Corp.

Center for Social Media. 2006. *Copyright and Fair use.* School of Communication, American University, http://www.centerforsocialmedia.org/resources/fair_use/.

Darrow, Ben H. 1932. *Radio: The Assistant Teacher.* Columbus, OH: R.G. Adams & Company.

Du Wors, Richard E. and William B. Weist. 1955. Records in Sociology. In *The Recording as a Teaching Tool: A Bulletin for Parents and Teachers*, edited by Esther L. Berg and Florence B. Freedman, 3. New York: Folkways Records and Service Corp.,

Giroux, Henry A. 1987. Critical Literacy and Student Experience: Donald Graves' Approach to Literacy. *Language Arts* 64 (February): 175-81.

————. 1998. Education in Unsettling Times: Public Intellectuals and the Promise of Cultural Studies. In *Power/Knowledge/Pedagogy: The Meaning of Democratic Education in Unsettling Times*, ed. Dennis Carlson, and Michael W. Apple, 41-60. Boulder, CO: Westview Press.

Ickes, Harold. 1936. In *Educational Broadcasting 1936: Proceedings of the First National Conference on Educational Broadcasting*, held in Washington, D.C., on December 10, 11, and 12: 7-14. Chicago: The University of Chicago Press.

Kellner, Douglas. 1995. Preface. In *Rethinking media literacy: A Critical Pedagogy of Representation*, ed. Peter McLaren, Rhonda Hammer, David Sholle and Susan Smith Reilly: xiii-xvii. New York: Peter Lang.

————. 2000. Globalization and New Social Movements: Lessons for Critical Theory and Pedagogy. In *Globalization and Education*, ed. Nicholas Burbules and Carlos Torres, 299-322. London and New York: Routledge.

———— and Jeff Share. 2007. Critical Media Literacy is Not an Option, *Learning Inquiry* 1(1): 59-69.

Kinchloe, Joe. 2006. Forward to the Expanded Edition. In *Literacies of Power: What Americans are Not Allowed to Know*, Donaldo Macedo, xi-xvi. Boulder, CO: Westview Press.

Livingstone, David W. 1987. *Critical Pedagogy and Cultural Power*. New York: Bergin & Garvey Publishers.

Lankshear, Colin and Peter McClaren. 1993. *Critical Literacy: Politics, Praxis, and the Postmodern*. Albany: State University of New York Press.

Lessig, Lawrence. 2006. Keynote Address. Presented at the Association for the Education of Journalism and Mass Communication, August 1, in San Francisco, CA.

————. 2005. *Free Culture. The Nature and Future of Creativity*. New York: Penguin.

————. 2008. *Remix: Making Art and Commerce Thrive in the Hybrid Economy*. New York: Penguin Press

Levenson, William B. and Edward Stasheff. 1952, revised from 1945. *Teaching Through Radio and Television*. New York: Rinehart & Company, Inc.

Luke, Carmen. 1990. *Constructing the Child Viewer: A History of the American Discourse on Television, and Children, 1950-1980*. New York: Praeger.

Mcleod, Kembrew. 2007. *Freedom of Expression: Resistance and Repression in the Age of Intellectual Property*. Minneapolis: University of Minnesota Press.

McChesney, Robert. 1994. *Telecommunications, Mass Media, & Democracy: The Battle for the Control of U.S. Broadcasting, 1928-1935*. London: Oxford University Press.

————. 1999. *Rich Media, Poor Democracy*. Urbana: University of Illinois Press.

————. 2008. *The Political Economy of Media: Enduring Issues, Emerging Dilemmas*. New York, NY: Monthly Review Press.

Rosen, Jay. 1997. Introduction/"We'll Have That Conversation": Journalism and Democracy in the Thought of James Carey. In *James Carey: A Critical Reader*, ed. Eve Stryker Munson and Catherine A. Warren, 191-206. Minneapolis: University of Minnesota Press.

Sehr, David T. 1997. *Education for Public Democracy*. Albany: State University of New York Press.

Shadbolt, Nigel. *Virtual Revolution: Rushes Sequences - Nigel Shadbolt Interview*, Video, directed by Russell Barnes (2010; London: BBC/Video). http://www.bbc.co.uk/blogs/digitalrevolution/2009/10/rushes-nigel-shadbolt-london-v.shtml.

Shannon, Patrick. 1992. *Becoming Political: Readings and Writings in the Politics of Literacy Education*. Portsmouth, NH: Heinemann.

Spring, Joel. 1992. *Images of American Life: A History of Ideological Management in Schools, Movies, Radio, and Television*. New York: State University of New York Press.

Sullivan, Edmund V. 1987. Critical Pedagogy and Television. In *Critical Pedagogy and Cultural Power*, ed. D. Livingstone, 57-75. New York: Bergin & Garvey Publishers.

Vaidhyanathan, Siva (forthcoming). *The Googleization of Everything: How One Company is Disrupting Culture, Commerce, and Community...and Why We Should Worry*. See: http://www.googlizationofeverything.com/

ABOUT THE AUTHORS

Edward Alwood received a Ph.D. from the University of North Carolina. He worked for fourteen years as a news reporter at several television outlets, including CNN. His research concentrates on newsgathering and First Amendment freedom of the press. Alwood is the author of *Dark Days in the Newsroom: McCarthyism Aimed at the Press* (Temple UP, 2007), which won the 2008 Tankard Award from the Association for Education in Journalism and Mass Communication, and *Straight News: Gays, Lesbians, and the News Media* (Columbia UP, 1998). He is Professor of Journalism at Quinnipiac University in Hamden, Connecticut.

Bonnie Brennen is Nieman Professor of Journalism in the Diederich College of Communication at Marquette University. Her scholarly work focuses on journalism history and cultural studies of the relationship between media and society. She is the author of *For the Record: An Oral History of Rochester New York Newsworkers* (Fordham, 2001), and co-editor, with Hanno Hardt, of *The American Journalism History Reader* (Routledge, 2010), *Picturing the Past: Media, History & Photography* (Illinois, 1999) and *Newsworkers: Toward a History of the Rank and File* (Minnesota, 1995). She has published research in a variety of peer-reviewed journals, including the *Journal of American History*, *Critical Studies in Media Communication*, *Journalism: Theory, Practice and Criticism*, and *Journalism Studies*.

Bettina Fabos is Associate Professor of Visual Communication at the University of Northern Iowa. With a background in journalism, media production, and media literacy pedagogy, she has written extensively about the role of the U.S. media in democracy. She is the author of *Wrong Turn on the Information Superhighway: Education and the Commercialization of the Internet* (Teachers College Press, 2004), and the co-author of a leading college textbook, *Media and Culture* (Bedford/St. Martins), which is used in mass communication survey classes across the country. She received a Ph.D. from the University of

Iowa. She teaches courses in digital studies, media literacy, and multimedia production.

Nathan Godfried is the Adelaide & Alan Bird Professor of History at the University of Maine. His scholarly work focuses on twentieth-century American history, especially labor, mass media, foreign relations, and political history. He is the author of *WCFL, Chicago's Voice of Labor, 1926-1978* (University of Illinois Press, 1997) and *Bridging the Gap Between Rich and Poor: American Economic Development Policy Toward the Arab East, 1942-1949* (Greenwood Press, 1987). His work on labor and political radicals and radio, television, and film has appeared in *Labor History, The Democratic Communique*, and *The Historical Journal of Film, Radio and Television*. Currently he is working on a collective biography of leftist radio news commentators during the 1940s and 1950s.

James F. Hamilton is Associate Professor in the Grady College of Journalism and Mass Communication at the University of Georgia. He holds a Ph.D. in Mass Communications from the University of Iowa. In addition to many articles in leading academic journals, he is most recently author of *Democratic Communications: Formations, Projects, Possibilities* (Lexington Press, 2008) and, with Chris Atton, *Alternative Journalism* (Sage). He teaches courses in critical, cultural, and historical approaches to communications.

Deepa Kumar is Associate Professor in the Department of Journalism and Media Studies at Rutgers University. A critical media studies scholar whose areas of research include media, war, and imperialism; media, globalization, and class; media and gender; and Islam, the Middle East and U.S. foreign policy, she has also been active in various social movements for peace and justice and was awarded the Young Scholar Leader Award for 2007 by the National Communication Association's Critical Cultural Studies Division. The author of *Outside the Box: Corporate Media, Globalization and the UPS Strike* (2008), she is currently working on her second book, on the U.S. media, political Islam and the Middle East.

Jason Loviglio is Director of Media and Communication Studies and Associate Professor of American Studies at the University of

Maryland Baltimore County. He received a Ph.D. in American Studies from the University of Minnesota. He is author of *Radio's Intimate Public: Network Broadcasting and Mass-Mediated Democracy* (University of Minnesota Press, 2005) and co-editor, with Michele Hilmes, of *Radio Reader: Essays in the Cultural History of Radio* (Routledge, 2001). He teaches courses in cultural history, media history, and US cultural diversity.

Steve Macek is Associate Professor of Speech Communication at North Central College in Naperville, Illinois, where he teaches courses on media studies, urban studies, persuasion and gender and women's studies. He writes frequently about the media, politics and media policy for various newspapers and magazines, and is the author of the award-winning book *Urban Nightmares: The Media, the Right and the Moral Panic over the City* (University of Minnesota Press, 2006). He is currently writing a critical history of Chicago journalism in the 20th century.

Laurie Ouellette is Associate Professor in the Department of Communication Studies at the University of Minnesota working in the area of critical media and cultural studies. She is co-author, with James Hay, of *Better Living Through Reality TV: Television and Post-Welfare Citizenship* (Wiley-Blackwell, 2008), co-editor, with Susan Murray, of *Reality TV: Remaking Television Culture* (NYU, 2008) and author of *Viewers Like You? How Public TV Failed the People* (Columbia, 2002). Her work has also appeared in *Cultural Studies, Media, Culture & Society, Television and New Media, Continuum: Journal of Media and Cultural Studies, The Communication Review, The Velvet Light Trap,* and *Afterimage*

Janice Peck is Associate Professor of media studies at the University of Colorado at Boulder, where her research and teaching focus on U.S. media, politics, culture and history. She has published articles and chapters on media theory, television and the family, cultural studies, TV talk shows, advertising, and representations of race in media *Communication Theory, Journal of Communication Inquiry, Communication Review,* and *American Studies.* Peck is author of *The Gods of Televangelism: Religious Television and the Historical Crisis of Meaning* (Hampden, 1993) and *The Age of Oprah: Cultural Icon for the Neoliberal Era*

(Paradigm, 2008), a political history of Winfrey's media empire. Her current research is on the political significance of celebrity philanthropy, with a particular focus on the issue of education reform.

Victor Pickard is an Assistant Professor in the Annenberg School for Communication at the University of Pennsylvania. He received his Ph.D. from the Institute of Communications Research at the University of Illinois, Urbana-Champaign. His research focuses on the politics and history of media policy, and has been published in over two dozen book chapters and scholarly articles. Currently he is finishing a book on the history and future of news media.

Carol A. Stabile is the Director of the Center for the Study of Women in Society at the University of Oregon, where she teaches in the School of Journalism and Communication and the Department of English. Her interdisciplinary research interests lie in the intersections of gender, race, class, and sexual orientation in media and popular culture. She is the author of *Feminism and the Technological Fix* (Manchester, 1994), editor of *Turning the Century: Essays in Media and Cultural Studies* (Westview, 2000), co-editor, with Mark Harrison, of *Prime Time Animation: Television Animation and American Culture* (Routledge, 2003), and author of *White Victims, Black Villains: Gender, Race, and Crime News in U.S. Culture* (Routledge, 2006). Her articles have appeared in *Camera Obscura, Cultural Studies, Critical Studies in Media Communication,* and *Journalism.* For the past five years, she has been doing archival research on women writers who were blacklisted during the 1950s and is presently completing that book.

Inger L. Stole is Associate Professor in the Department of Communication at the University of Illinois at Urbana-Champaign. Her first book, *Advertising on Trial: Consumer Activism and Corporate Public Relations in the 1930s,* was published by the University of Illinois Press in 2006. Her work has been published in *International Journal of Communication, The Journal of American Culture, Consumption, Markets and Culture, Advertising and Society Review,* and *The Communication Review.* Her present research explores the political and economic role of advertising during the Second World War and beyond.

James F. Tracy is Associate Professor of Media Studies at Florida Atlantic University. His research interests include the political economy of communication and the historical relationship between labor, management, and technology in American media institutions. Tracy's work has appeared in numerous scholarly venues, including *Journalism & Communication Monographs*, *Journalism Studies*, *American Journalism*, *Canadian Journal of Communication*, *Mass Communication and Society*, and *European Journal of Communication*.

Dinah Zeiger is Assistant Professor at the University of Idaho, where she teaches mass communication law. She received an MA in Art History and a Ph.D. in Mass Communications from the University of Colorado at Boulder and has 20 years experience as a business-economics-financial journalist working for *Wall Street Journal-Europe*, *Investor's Business Daily* and the *Denver Post*. Her primary areas of research relate to the interface between mass media and public protest and the new tactics of control deployed by law enforcement to silence citizens and discourage public participation in social and political protest. She has published articles and chapters on media representations of Islamic women, portrayals of war and women soldiers, arts funding and New Mexican art history.

INDEX

A

ABC. *See* American Broadcasting Company

Abel, Jessica, 293

ACLU. *See* American Civil Liberties Union

Action Coalition for Media Education (ACME), 359, 360

Adventures of Robin Hood, The (ATV), 121

Advertising, 27, 42, 44, 60, 71, 73, 211, 238n2, 371; classified, 70; criticism of, 13, 14, 17, 23, 29, 47-48; defense production and, 16; display, 60, 216-217; economic conditions of, 21, 367; institutional, 20, 160-167; losses of, 70; monopolies, 52; morale and, 27; outdoor, 49; politics and, 15; product, 24; production and, 16; profits from, 59, 60, 348; public and, 15, 24-25; radio, 47, 52; regulating, 25; role of, 13-14, 21; sale of, 180; soap operas and, 45; television, 188, 212; theory, 46; useful/patriotic sides of, 16, 17, 20; user-created, 349; war and, 14, 15-17, 18, 21, 22, 24, 25, 27

Advertising Age, 17

Advertising & Selling, 15

Advertising Council, 15, 17-18, 24; public debate and, 25; public relations and, 28; Washington officials and, 19, 20. *See also* (War) Advertising Council

Advertising industry, 4, 23, 28, 49; economic situation and, 14, 17; government and, 20-21; as pillar

of society, 29; public relations organization for, 14; taxation and, 15-16; war and, 18, 20, 25

AFDC, 264, 272, 274

AFL. *See* American Federation of Labor

AFL-CIO, 158, 162, 165, 166, 172, 210, 213, 307, 325; AIFLD and, 170; liberal ideology of, 169, 170, 173, 174; Los Angeles Newspaper Guild and, 212; public relations program by, 164; television and, 167, 173

Agnew, Jean-Christophe, 1

AIFLD. *See* American Institute for Free Labor Development

Air traffic controllers, strike by, 312, 321

A.J. Liebling Counter-Convention, 249, 251

Aldrich Family, The, 111

All Things Considered, 284, 286, 288

Allen, Fred, 44

Almanac Singers, 170

Alvin and the Chipmunks, 355, 356, 373

AM, 42, 287

American Broadcasting Company (ABC), 37, 41, 161, 165, 181, 188, 324; serials and, 46n4

American Business Consultants, 87, 120

American Civil Liberties Union (ACLU), 136, 137

American Council for Better Broadcasts, 189

American Economic Foundation, 26